SOCIALIST REGISTER 2010

THE SOCIALIST REGISTER
Founded in 1964

To get online access to all Register volumes visit our website

http://www.socialistregister.com

CONTENTS

CONTRIBUTORS

Robert Albritton is professor emeritus in the Department of Political Science at York University, Toronto.

Kalman Applbaum teaches medical anthropology at the University of Wisconsin, Milwaukee.

Hugh Armstrong is a professor in the School of Social Work and the School of Public Policy and Administration at Carleton University, Ottawa.

Pat Armstrong is professor of sociology and the CHSRF/CIHR Chair in Health Services and Nursing Research at York University, Toronto.

Sanjay Basu is a physician in the Department of Medicine at the University of California, San Francisco and the San Francisco General Hospital.

David Coburn is a professor in the School of Public Health at the University of Toronto.

Hans–Ulrich Deppe is professor of medical sociology and social medicine at the J.W. Goethe-University of Frankfurt.

Julie Feinsilver is a visiting researcher at the Center for Latin American Studies at Georgetown University in Washington and an independent consultant.

Marie Gottschalk is a professor of political science at the University of Pennsylvania, Philadelphia.

Julian Tudor Hart is a retired family doctor and a research fellow at the Medical School of Swansea University, Wales.

Lesley Henderson is senior lecturer in Sociology and Communications and deputy director of the Centre for Media, Globalisation and Risk at Brunel University, West London.

Christoph Hermann is a researcher at the Working Life Research Centre (FORBA) in Vienna.

Meri Koivusalo is a senior researcher in the Finnish National Research and Development Centre for Welfare and Health (STAKES) programme on Globalism and Social Policy, Helsinki.

Rodney Loeppky is an associate professor of political science at York University, Toronto.

Maureen Mackintosh is professor of economics at the Open University in London.

Mohan Rao is a medical doctor and chair of the Centre of Social Medicine and Community Health in Jawaharlal Nehru University, New Delhi.

Paula Tibandebage is an independent researcher and senior research associate with the Economic and Social Research Foundation based in Dar es Salaam, Tanzania.

Shaoguang Wang is a chair professor in the Department of Government and Public Administration at the Chinese University of Hong Kong.

PREFACE

Neoliberal globalisation, a predominant theme of the Socialist Register over the past 15 years, is brought into focus in this volume in relation to its impact on the most important area of human life: health. All the elements of public health, from a balanced diet to decent housing, job security and job satisfaction are crucial in determining how well and how long people live. This is partly a matter of giving the human body what it needs to reach its full physical potential, but also a matter of preventing disease and, to a lesser extent, a matter of curing illnesses. The turn that capitalism has taken in recent decades has, in both these respects, been replete with morbid symptoms – the title of this volume, the Register's 46th, on health under capitalism.

A vast amount has been written about health, but very little from a systematically critical standpoint. The path-breaking work in the political economy of health begun in the 1970s by pioneers such as Lesley Doyal, Vicente Navarro and Julian Tudor Hart has been too little followed up by others, at least in the English-speaking world. This is all the more remarkable, given the size and scope of the global health industry and its growing centrality as arena of capital accumulation. Our goal in preparing this volume was to help develop the historical materialist analysis of health under capitalism, focusing on the economic, social and political determinants of health in the neoliberal era; and on health *care* as an object of struggle, between commercial forces that seek to make it into a commodity and popular forces trying to make (or keep) it a public service and to reduce the current gross inequalities of access. It is crucial for the Left today to address, in particular, the marketisation of public health services, and the way the pharmaceutical, insurance, medical technology and healthcare corporations push to make health care everywhere into a field of capital accumulation and expand the consumption of medical commodities – services as well as goods. Many of the morbid symptoms flow directly from this, including the corporate control of medical research and training, the misuse of scientific data for commercial gain, the generation and mistreatment of an epidemic of mental illness, and the newest frontier of capitalist accumulation – the turning of genes into commodities.

In most societies today health and health care are rarely out of the news: the spectre of new epidemics, or the return of old ones; the food industry's production of both obesity and hunger; the emergence of 'superbugs'; lapses in hospital care; breakthroughs in medical research or surgical techniques; new 'wonder drugs'; and, of course, ever-present hand-wringing about 'runaway' healthcare costs. It is in the rich capitalist countries that resources exist for increasingly sophisticated and costly biomedical research and medical technology; and as the range of medical knowledge increases, so does the range of possible medical interventions, and with this, the demand for still more resources for research and treatment. Most of these countries also have healthcare systems funded by general taxes or social insurance which at least in principle treat everyone alike, without reference to ability to pay. This involves a transfer of income from rich to poor (who have worse health) and makes public hospitals and clinics some of the few places in these class-based societies where there is relatively little class distinction – no separate 'business' and 'economy' cabins. But this also helps explain why there is capitalist and state support in these countries for the drive by the global private healthcare industry to get access to the rich pools of public revenue out of which public health systems are funded. They energetically promote the call for costs to be contained, and for the services to be handed over to private providers who will cut costs through the efficiencies allegedly produced by competition. No analysis of the relationship between health care and capitalism can avoid a heavy focus on the affluent 'north', where the interplay of these forces has so far been heavily concentrated, but the dynamics of this are played out world-wide, with profound effects, as many of the essays in this volume clearly demonstrate.

The current global economic crisis brings into sharp relief the morbid symptoms associated with health and health care under capitalism today. The crisis was born in the USA, and it is not coincidental that the issue of healthcare reform has moved to the top of the political agenda there, alongside the American state's attempts to cope with the crisis. It was in the US that a market-based healthcare system persisted throughout the post-war era, while other states – reflecting a different balance of class forces – moved away from it. What has always been at stake here is a profound class issue. The UAW's Walter Reuther once explained why General Motors refused to support the campaign for a national health insurance scheme which would have lifted the burden of healthcare costs from the company: 'There's something more important to them than their own self-interest'. That 'something' was collective capitalist class discipline; it reflected the common interests of employers in keeping workers dependent on them for health care through company-based insurance, and the larger project American capitalists shared in spreading market relations to every facet of life, if possible in every part of the world. With the increasing achievement of this in the neoliberal era we have seen the effective Americanisation of other healthcare systems, not only through the relentless penetration of public health care by corporate capital, but also through state-led marketisation. In the poorer capitalist countries of the world, with the most notable exception of Cuba, this has combined with the exacerbation of global inequality to ensure that the 'Health for All' goal adopted in the UN's 1978 Alma Ata Declaration soon became a dead letter.

Any serious political economy of health under capitalism must be centred on the fundamental contradiction involved: health and health care are use values *par excellence*, of limited interest to capital unless it can convert them into exchange values; where publicly-funded health services were secured, the productivity of a healthy workforce was always a key element in capital's acquiescence. Where publicly-funded health care becomes seen as a problem for accumulation, the use values of health and health care must be obscured and distorted. Much public discussion of and official policy towards health and health care today has this aim. The basic requirement for a valid political economy of health and health care is to subject all such discourse and policy to critical scrutiny. But that is by no means enough. What is essential, especially for building effective forces of opposition capable of organising on this terrain, is to make the fundamental contradiction of health under capitalism the pivotal issue of a revitalised socialist strategy.

One of the most rewarding aspects of editing this volume was the range of new contacts we made with experts in the field, and their enthusiasm for what they, like us, saw as an important project. We are especially grateful to Roddy Loeppky for his help in planning the volume. We are also grateful to all the other contributors; though we must add, as always, that neither they nor we necessarily agree with everything in the volume. Again as usual, we are indebted to Alan Zuege and Adrian Howe for their editorial work, to Louis McKay for his arresting cover design, and to our publisher Tony Zurbrugg for his encouragement and support.

With this volume, two important transitions occur in the editing and publishing of the Register. After 12 years as co-editor, Colin Leys is stepping down to join Alfredo Saad Filho as an associate editor; Greg Albo and Vivek Chibber are joining Leo Panitch as co-editors. This represents a first step in handing on the direction of the Register, as it approaches its 50th year of publication, to a younger generation. The commitment to the future of the Register extends beyond the change in editors to some turnover within the editorial collective. With are deeply grateful to Huw Beynon, Varda Burstyn, David Coates, Terry Eagleton, Steve Jefferys and Ellen Meiksins Wood for the many invaluable contributions they have made to the Register over the years, and are confident that the Register will continue to be able to rely on their help when needed, including, we hope, as authors of future essays. We are delighted that Bashir Abu-Manneh, Johanna Brenner, David Harvey, Christoph Hermann, Nancy Holmstrom, Martijn Konings and Charles Post have agreed to join the editorial collective, and look forward to productive collaboration with them.

The second transition, also reflecting a generational shift, is that this volume is the first to be published on-line simultaneously with the print edition, while at the same time all 45 previous volumes will be made similarly available on our new website, www.socialistregister.com. This has involved a major commitment of time and resources on the part of many people. We are especially indebted for this to Rea Davakos, Gabriela Mircea and Colin Prince at the Scholarly Communication Unit, University of Toronto Libraries, as well as to our own 'e-team' of Alan Zuege, Frederick Peters, Lana Goldberg, James Parisot and Jason Sykes at the Department of Political Science, York University. The groundwork has been laid; the next step is to ensure that all Register readers subscribe, and persuade their libraries and friends to subscribe.

When we assumed the editorship of the Register we were also taking over from a previous generation, and it is with a special sense of the remarkable socialist commitment of that earlier generation that we must sadly note here the death of John Saville, who founded the Register with Ralph Miliband in 1964. One of things that spurred us on in our co-editorship was how we could possibly face John if the *Register* were to go under on our watch. The 1989 volume of the *Register* was the last John was directly involved in editing. It was entitled 'Revolution Today: Aspirations and Realities', and its Preface's articulation of the concern to raise 'a host of issues' regarding the 'problems and dilemmas' which the quest for 'a cooperative, egalitarian, democratic and classless society' had encountered in the 20th century and how they might be overcome in the future, effectively expressed what the Register had been about since its inception. When John decided, after the completion of that volume, to step down after 25 years as co-editor, this was noted in the Preface to the 1990 volume as 'a real wrench' since 'his steadiness, lucidity and good sense have been of immense value through the years'.

The theme of the 1990 *Register* was 'The Retreat of the Intellectuals', but John was not retreating. On the contrary, the 1990 volume included his trenchant critique of *Marxism Today* for its role in the retreat of the intellectuals from class politics to what would become known as the Third Way. For the 1991 *Register*, John wrote a personal appraisal of the 20th century Communist experience, including of his own decision to join the Party in 1934, which he put in terms that ought to have considerable resonance today: 'For young intellectuals with any generosity of spirit there were additional factors beyond the poverty of so many of their own people, and the brutalities of fascism. Bourgeois society was under increasing criticism for its callousness, greed and cultural emptiness'. And for the 1994 *Register*, John produced an essay, occasioned by Edward Thompson's death the previous year, on the stand the two of them took in 1956, including by founding the *New Reasoner*, the forerunner of the *Socialist Register*. The statement that John and Edward issued in response to their suspension from the Communist Party in November 1956 was an appendix to that essay. What they wrote there also speaks to the contemporary condition of the Left: 'The times call above all for a new movement of ideas, reaching out beyond party barriers and bringing socialists together on the basis of principle rather than of opportunism'.

We will always be very grateful for the extremely helpful role John played during the transition years to our co-editorship of the *Register* after Ralph Miliband's death. We especially recall sitting with John in brilliant sunshine overlooking the pond at Hampstead Heath in the summer of 1997, and expressing our by no means false modesty about our capacity to come near matching what Ralph and John had accomplished with the *Register*. We can still hear John saying, with his unique ability to combine comradely sternness with personal warmth: 'Just get on with it, mates'.

We also have to note the passing of Victor Kiernan, who with John Saville, E.P. Thompson and Eric Hobsbawm was a member of the famous British Communist Party's Historians' Group. Having lived in India, and written extensively about Indian history and culture and the struggle for Independence, he strongly identified with the anti-imperialist cause. He contributed frequently to the Register during its first decade on the theme of imperialism, and these essays formed the basis of his important book, *Marxism and Imperialism*.

We are very sad to note here as well the deaths in 2009 of Giovanni Arrighi and Peter Gowan, brilliant representatives of a younger generation of socialist intellectuals. One of Arrighi's first publications was his 1969 Register essay with John Saul on 'Nationalism and Revolution in Sub-Saharan Africa'. His extremely wide-ranging contributions to political economy and historical sociology over the subsequent decades included his most famous book, *The Long Twentieth Century*. His interest in the evolution of the world proletariat was a constant in his work, and we were especially pleased to be able to commission his essay with Beverly Silver on 'Workers North and South' as one of the centerpieces of the 2001 Register on *Working Classes: Global Realities*.

The Left has also suffered a major loss with the death at 63 of Peter Gowan. Through the 1970s and early 1980s he played a key role as an activist-intellectual by editing (under the pseudonym of Oliver Macdonald) *Labour Focus on Eastern Europe*, the best source by far for evidence of strikes and other forms of protests in the authoritarian Communist regimes. He not only went on to analyze (including in his 1998 Register essay) the continuing class struggles in Eastern Europe amidst 'shock therapy' after the fall of Communism, but was one of the first to see clearly that globalisation was not an inexorable process taking place behind the backs of states, but rather was the product of a determined state strategy. This was the central theme of his celebrated book, *The Global Gamble: Washington's Faustian Bid for World Dominance*, and it was developed further in his Register essays in the 2000 and 2003 volumes. With his engagingly provocative style of speaking, he was much sought after for conference appearances wherever the Left gathered to take intellectual stock, and he became a mainstay at the annual Left Forums in New York each spring and at the Historical Materialism conferences in London each autumn.

In taking leave of these comrades, we found comfort in two lines from a poem by the Urdu poet Faiz Ahmed Faiz, translated into English by Victor Kiernan:

> Last night your faded memory filled my heart…
> Like peace somehow coming to one in sickness.

LP
CL
July 2009

HEALTH, HEALTH CARE AND CAPITALISM

COLIN LEYS

There is a widespread belief that capitalism is responsible for the huge improvements in health that have occurred over the last century and a quarter. Capitalism is seen as the supreme engine of growth, and growth is seen as the crucial condition for health improvement. But it is not. Poor countries can and sometimes do have better health than rich ones. The US is held up as a 'world leader' in medicine when it is really a world leader in healthcare market failure, spending almost a fifth of its huge national income to produce overall health outcomes little better, and in some respects worse, than those of neighbouring Cuba, with a per capita income barely a twentieth as large. 'Breakthroughs' in health science and technology – in nuclear medicine, genetic medicine, or nanotechnology – are treated as triumphs of capitalist investment in research. But most innovative medical research is actually done in state-funded medical schools and research laboratories.

The origins of the idea that capitalism is good for your health lie in the 'mortality revolution' that began in England in the late nineteenth century. Throughout all prior recorded history the physical health of most people, as measured by life expectancy, remained very poor. Infectious diseases were prevalent, many of them originally transmitted from domestic animals following the development of settled agriculture. People ate contaminated food and drank water from rivers that also served as sewers, as hundreds of millions in the global 'south' are still forced to do today. When industrialisation moved masses of people into towns from the countryside the effects became even worse. In Liverpool in 1840 the average life expectation of children born into working-class families was just 15 years, and in upper-class families, only 35.[1] Moreover with very few exceptions (such as vaccination against smallpox, adopted widely from 1800 onwards) most treatments for infectious diseases were useless or, like the practice of bleeding, worse than useless: as late as the 1850s patients were still being bled to death when they might have recovered if left alone, and women were safer giving birth at home than in hospitals, where in some cases more than a quarter died of puerperal fever.[2]

Then, starting effectively in England in the 1870s, population health began to improve dramatically. In 1850 average life expectancy in England and Wales as a whole was about 40 years. By 1950 it had risen to about 70, an increase unequalled at any previous time in human history. Since then the rate of improvement has slowed, but average life expectancy has continued to increase by about two and a half years every decade. This general pattern has been repeated, with variations, in western Europe and North America and, with a further delay, by often very different routes, and with big differences between social classes, throughout much of the rest of the world.[3] The change involved is often also called the 'epidemiological transition', from the era when infectious diseases were the main causes of death to one in which non-infectious chronic diseases, mostly developing in older people, are the chief causes. And it did occur first in England, the epicentre of industrial capitalism. But to the extent that capitalist industrialisation aggravated the threat from infectious diseases, and that English capitalists often resisted the measures that eventually overcame them, it occurred in spite of capitalism, as much as because of it. Capitalist employers in western Europe also opposed the protection given to workers by the social insurance systems that began to be put in place from the 1880s onwards, to head off the growing political challenge from organised labour. At first social insurance was chiefly significant for providing financial support for workers while they were ill or recovering from accidents, but in the 1930s medical science finally advanced from understanding the causes of diseases, and so making it possible to prevent people getting them, to finding cures for them – the so-called therapeutic revolution that occurred just before, during and after the Second World War. Now a growing range of life-threatening illnesses could be successfully treated; health *care* suddenly became really valuable, and the labour movement was strong enough to ensure that workers – and their families – were the chief beneficiaries of it. Various forms of socially-provided health care for all were eventually established in most western and communist countries after 1945.

The fact that the therapeutic revolution coincided with the creation of social-democratic and communist welfare states throughout much of the world was thus of historic significance. But at the same time an increasingly powerful capitalist health industry also developed, especially in the US but also in some west European countries, focused not on what would bring the greatest benefit to the greatest number of people but on what was most profitable. The private health industry has successfully resisted all efforts to introduce a universal healthcare system in the US, and since the 1980s it has been engaged in a drive to convert the universal-access healthcare systems built up elsewhere after 1945 back into healthcare markets, in which equal access will disappear. It has also increasingly subordinated health research and training to its interests. And the era of neoliberalism has demonstrated once again how capitalism still fosters, or at least perpetuates, ill-health in today's new medical environment, above all by increasing inequality, both between and within nations. Even in some of the richest countries the life expectation of poor people can be ten or even twenty years less than that of the rich).[4]

In spite of the abundant evidence on all these points, the myth that 'capitalism promotes health' is consciously or unconsciously accepted by, probably, most people in the world. Disposing of it is the necessary starting-point of any rational analysis.

CAPITALISM AND THE MORTALITY REVOLUTION

What was the relation between capitalism and the dramatic decline in the death rate that occurred in England between 1850 and 1950? The decline could not have been due to the market-based health care available at the time, since it had hardly any effective treatments for diseases. Until recently the prevailing view was that improved nutrition, resulting from rising real incomes, was chiefly responsible, but further historical research has shown this to be at best a partial explanation.[5] During the first two-thirds of the nineteenth century death rates in the cities, where incomes and nutrition levels were rising, did not fall; death rates were lower in rural areas, where incomes remained low. A significant fall in urban mortality began only when the effects of the 'sanitation movement' began to be felt from the 1870s onwards, providing sewers and clean water supplies, improved housing and uncontaminated food. The sanitation drive was often resisted by capitalists – for example by employers who did not want to pay higher taxes for sewage or spend money on replacing unfit workers' housing, and by private suppliers of water and purveyors of unclean food. But the sanitation movement gradually prevailed, thanks to the fear of epidemics, to which the middle and upper classes were not immune; to the determination of leaders in the local government reform movement of the period; and, towards the end of the nineteenth century, to the impact on educated public opinion of the advances that were beginning to be made in understanding the causes of illness.

The sanitation movement was initially based on mistaken ideas about what caused diseases (especially the idea that they were caused by foul air, or 'miasmas'). The discovery in the 1870s that infections were caused by germs showed that good sanitation was indeed a key part of the solution; but the new knowledge also led to an extension of the scope of public health activity and to health education for schools and households – in hygiene, baby and child care, and so on. The source of one infectious disease after another was identified, and new preventive measures were adopted, including immunisations. The overall result was dramatic. Between 1871 and 1940 the share of infectious diseases in total annual deaths in England and Wales fell from 31 per cent to 10 per cent. By 1951 infectious illnesses accounted for only 6 per cent of deaths, while the overall annual death rate had fallen from 22.4 to 6.1 per thousand people.[6] It is important to stress, once again, that almost all this decline was due to prevention. For most of this time there were still no effective cures for most infectious diseases (sulphanilamide drugs only began to be available in 1935, penicillin in 1941, and broad-spectrum antibiotics from 1947 onwards).

Richard Easterlin has summed up the historical verdict on the relation between the capitalist market and health as follows.[7] First, life expectancy remained stagnant, or at best mildly improved, throughout most of the nineteenth century in the areas of the world that were undergoing rapid economic growth. Life expectancy (and physical stature) improved dramatically only when disease prevention became effective; increased nutrition due to rising workers' incomes did not on its own produce this effect. Second, most of the preventive measures involved in bringing about the mortality revolution – clean water supplies for all, sewage, etc – are public goods, requiring collective action, and benefiting everyone whether or not they contribute to their cost. Capitalist markets will not deliver such goods, and did not. The same applies to vaccination and immunisation – they only work reliably if they are applied as universally as possible. Since a majority will be unlikely to pay for it, the state must do it. Similarly with household hygiene: 'because the new knowledge was not proprietary, the market could not be relied on to disseminate it'. Third, the cost of the dramatic improvements in health that were achieved by medical science and preventive measures was modest. They did not depend on the major increases in national income that capitalism produced, and indeed dramatic advances in longevity have been achieved in recent times in even very poor countries, from China in the 1950s to Cuba in the 1960s and Kerala in the 1970s.[8] Finally, the cost of the research which led to these advances in health was itself quite small, and did not depend on capitalist-driven growth. 'When one considers the rudimentary laboratories of scientists like Pasteur, Koch and Fleming,' Easterlin comments, 'it is hard to believe they involved requirements that much exceeded those of their predecessors two centuries earlier.' As late as 1929 the total cost of research and development, public and private, in all fields of science in the USA was just 0.2 per cent of GDP, and biomedical research was a small fraction of that.[9] Today the costs of medical research have hugely increased, but the social benefit derived from it is another matter, as we will see.

The sanitation movement that sparked the mortality revolution in England was, then, hardly an achievement, in the sense of an intended effect, of capitalism, any more than the Russian revolution was an achievement of Czarist autocracy, or Indian independence an achievement of the British Raj. The sanitation movement that produced the mortality revolution was a reaction against the social costs of capitalism, not a benefit that the capitalist class sought to confer; while on the other hand non-capitalist countries have matched and sometimes even surpassed the achievement of many capitalist countries in raising life expectancy. Nonetheless the mortality revolution was undoubtedly associated with the rise of industrial capitalism. There were eventually more profits to be made from building water mains for the state than selling water to a limited number of private customers. The driving forces of the revolution in the death rate were multiple, and often contradictory.

What was certainly important was science itself. The physical sciences – especially physics and chemistry – had prospered because they had amply proved their worth for capital accumulation. Advances in the biological sciences came later, and showed their full profit potential later still. But support among the capitalist class for science in general, resulting from the economic benefits derived from the physical sciences, was an important factor in enabling the crucial advances in both sanitation technology and medical science to be made, and this in turn was a consequence of the intellectual freedoms secured by the preceding bourgeois revolution. So while the mortality revolution was not a willed achievement of capitalists, the rise of the bourgeoisie did provide, though often in indirect and complex ways, the context in which the scientific basis for it could be developed.

It is worth noting, though, that at the height of the mortality revolution in the late 19th century medical research was still relatively disinterested and critical. It had not yet begun to lose its integrity, as Marx pointed out was the case with mainstream economics:'[The class struggle] sounded the knell of scientific bourgeois economics. It was thenceforth no longer a question of whether this or that theorem was true, but whether it was useful to capital or harmful... In place of disinterested enquirers there stepped hired prizefighters; in place of genuine research, the bad conscience and evil intent of apologetics'.[10] A hundred years ago the age of hired prizefighters in biomedical research – doctors being paid large sums to put their names to articles in medical journals written by and for pharmaceutical companies, health policy researchers blatantly distorting evidence in the interests of insurance companies – had not yet arrived.[11]

AFTER THE MORTALITY REVOLUTION

So much for capitalism's contradictory role in the mortality revolution. What about its role once the mortality revolution was substantially completed? Since the middle of the 20th century life expectancy has continued to rise, especially in the advanced capitalist countries, where in 2000 it averaged about 80 years.[12] Some of capitalism's intellectual prizefighters have argued that this shows that economic growth does after all raise life expectancy, regardless of how the additional resources are used, and so should be a prime goal of health policy-makers (a thesis summarised by Larry Summers in 1996, when he was Deputy Secretary to the US Treasury in the Clinton administration, in a much-cited article entitled 'Wealthier is Healthier').[13]

Given the much greater understanding of the causes of illness that now exists compared with 150 years ago, an improvement in the living standards of the poorest citizens even in very poor countries can in favourable circumstances lead to health improvements through changes in individual behaviour alone (via improved diet and personal hygiene, the use of mosquito nets, and so on). But in general the evidence does not support the 'wealthier is healthier' thesis. Most of the continuing gain in life expectancy in the advanced capitalist world has come from a continued deepening of the preventive practices that produced the initial revolution in mortality. Relatively little is due to improved nutrition or other elements of individual consumption, and only some 10–15 per cent is thought to be attributable to health care.[14] Moreover the gain over time has been greatest where incomes are most equally distributed, not where they are highest. Among the richest countries it is not their ranking in terms of GDP but the degree of equality among their citizens that determines average life expectancy.[15]

Yet the one thing capitalism tends to do without fail is to produce and reproduce inequality: first, through the normal operation of the market for labour power and the appropriation of the surplus by the owners of capital, in the form of dividends and rents; and second, through the influence of capital on public policy – on the tax system, social services (education, health, long-term care and social security), and social infrastructure (housing, transportation, public space, libraries, etc).[16] The thrust of capitalism is consistently to widen inequality on all these dimensions, and the more unconstrained it is, the wider the inequality becomes. In the neoliberal era, beginning in the late 1970s, inequality widened almost everywhere, especially in countries like the US and the UK where neoliberal policies were pursued most consistently, but also between rich and poor countries.[17] In many former Communist countries the effects of a sudden transition to capitalism were even worse, producing a shocking increase in mortality, particularly for men.

The ways in which inequality produces ill-health are complex, and much debated.[18] Poor material conditions, to which poor people are more exposed, directly cause physical risks (infections, malnutrition, chronic disease, and injuries); developmental problems (delayed or impaired cognitive and social development); and social problems (socialisation, preparation for work and family life); and all of these can interact and have cumulative effects, leading to different kinds of illness at different ages.[19] Evidence for Richard Wilkinson's much-cited theory that low economic or social status in itself generates pathogenic physiological responses, seems weak, but there is little doubt that, as Wilkinson also argues, the positive influence and reciprocities of active and close human relations do support good health in various ways, and inequality does also tend to militate against these things.[20] This is particularly relevant to mental illnesses, including depression, which now occur on an epidemic scale – affecting between a fifth and a quarter of all adults – in the most unequal countries.

This complexity has to be tackled by studying the various determinants of ill-health over the life-course of individuals in different historical cohorts and in specific social settings. For example, some later-life diseases like stomach cancer, TB, and strokes have causes linked to events in early childhood that are more often experienced in poor families. Others are caused by events or behaviour in young adulthood, such as accidents and workplace injuries, which also occur more often in unskilled manual jobs; and still others by factors that only arise in old age. The effects of inequality at earlier stages can combine to cumulatively increase the likelihood of being exposed to further causes of ill-health at subsequent stages.

The causes of ill-health can also include, at any stage, getting insufficient medical attention, which tends to be least accessible to those who are least well off, or are disadvantaged by gender, ethnicity, disability, and so on. Even in the UK, with a health service almost entirely paid for out of tax revenue and effectively free to everyone, Julian Tudor Hart's famous 'inverse care law' tends to hold – the amount of health care given is inversely related to the need for it. The rule applies to whole geographic communities, and to individuals and groups within communities: for instance the poorest patients

with schizophrenia get treatment on average eight years later than the most
affluent; and across the population the poorest get much less treatment for
serious heart disease than the affluent.[21] In many if not most developing
countries the publicly-funded and provided healthcare systems set up after
1945 have atrophied, giving way to private, unregulated and dangerous
services, so that in some areas the health gains of earlier years have been
reversed.[22] The WHO reported in 2008 that 'originally limited to an urban
phenomenon, small-scale unregulated fee-for-service health care offered by
a multitude of different independent providers now dominates the healthcare
landscape from sub-Saharan Africa to the transitional economies in Asia or
Europe'.[23] A somewhat similar regression took place in the countries of the
former Soviet Union, especially those which were subjected to rapid mass
privatisation after 1990. In the five most affected countries unemployment
jumped to 23 per cent and led to an appalling 42.3 per cent rise in adult male
mortality.[24]

The determinants of average longevity for any given society are thus
historically determined and complex. In rich countries (where almost all such
detailed research on the links between social conditions and health has been
conducted) we find a combination of contrary tendencies: declining average
mortality rates, but also a *widening spread* of life expectancies related to social
and economic inequality. George Davey Smith sums it up perceptively:

> it is… possible to identify social processes which lead to
> unfavourable exposures being concentrated on those in less
> privileged social circumstances, from birth to death… The socially
> patterned nutritional, health and environmental experiences of the
> parents and of the individuals concerned influence birthweight,
> height, weight and lung function, for example, which are in turn
> important indicators of future health prospects. These biological
> aspects of bodies (and the histories of bodies) should be viewed as
> *frozen social relations*…[25]

PUBLIC HEALTH[26]

Social relations are, then, key determinants of the health of populations, yet
since the 1980s changing the social relations of contemporary capitalism has
not been on the political agenda of any major state; depressingly little of
the evidence we now have on the social causes of ill-health is reflected in
public policy anywhere today. Government policy in relation to the social
determinants of health has been essentially to ignore them. Even such modest
measures as making taxation less acutely regressive, reducing class sizes in

schools, or reducing the precariousness of work – all such state-dependent measures which could improve the health of the least healthy sectors of the population have had low priority, whatever the political rhetoric, while inequality has inexorably grown. Health policy has instead been focused, first of all, on individuals and their supposedly voluntary behaviour – on 'taking responsibility for one's own health'; and second, on the provision of 'high-tech' medicine to deal with individual cases of disease, a significant proportion of which need never have arisen had social conditions been different.

This represents a dramatic retreat from the ambitions of the profession of public health as it emerged from the successes of the mortality revolution, with its focus on the health of the population rather than individuals, and on prevention rather than cure. As social issues came to the fore, with the rise of the labour movement in the first half of the twentieth century,

> Medicine began to fix its gaze on a morass of deep-seated and widespread dysfunctions hitherto hardly appreciated: sickly infants, backward children, anaemic mothers, office workers with ulcers, sufferers from arthritis, back pain, strokes, inherited conditions, depression and other neuroses and all the maladies of old age... The health threats facing modern society had more to do with physiological and psychological abnormalities, broad and perhaps congenital tendencies to sickness surfacing among populations rendered dysfunctional and unproductive by poverty, ignorance, inequality, poor diet and housing, unemployment or overwork. To combat all this waste, hardship and suffering, medicine had to become a positive and systematic enterprise, undertaking planned surveillance of apparently healthy, normal people as well as the sick, tracing groups from infancy to old age, logging the incidence of chronic, inherited and constitutional conditions, correlating ill health against variables like income, education, class, diet and housing.[27]

By the end of the 1980s, however, such ideals (with their inherently statist character and, perhaps, faintly authoritarian undertones) had been decisively rejected, and not just in the leading neoliberal countries. Public health doctors pointed out that the need for social and economic policy to be based on the lessons of public health was greater than ever. All areas of public policy, they insisted, ought to be seen as elements of health policy, and both the physical environment (pollution, global warming, energy, soil degradation, etc) and the social environment (unemployment, housing, transport, food production) should be tackled as public health issues. Public health and healthcare services should be complementary. But in practice the opposite was often the case, as a British doctor noted at the time:

> The failure to comprehend this complementarity is starkly demonstrated each time a minister ignores greatly increased poverty, involuntary unemployment, homelessness and other health hazards over the last decade and brags that the National Health Service is 'treating more patients than ever', clearly believing that this is some kind of *health* achievement![28]

When even the social-democratic parties in Europe had abandoned the original ideals of public health, the once prestigious practitioners of public health lost much of their influence. Their former advocacy role in linking social and economic policy (full employment, for example) to health policy, typically through their close links with social-democratic policy-makers, and their central role in planning health care provision based on the study of population needs, were both replaced by the new reliance on 'market signals'.[29] The role of public health was reduced to planning responses to threatened global pandemics and seeking to influence the 'lifestyle choices' of individuals through public education. Money is spent on media campaigns to reduce smoking and alcohol abuse, and to induce people to take more exercise and eat better food, while the basic conditions, linked to inequality, that lead people to smoke, drink excessively, and eat poor food (because good food costs more, and costs even more in poor areas than in affluent ones), cannot be talked about, let alone changed. Writing in 1997 two leading public health doctors in Britain concluded:

> Inequalities in health in the UK are substantial and of increasing magnitude. The main way to address such health differentials is clearly through broader social and political changes leading to a more equitable society. Public health practitioners are failing in achieving their major objective – an improvement in population health status – if they do not become advocates for such changes.[30]

But it is one thing to advocate such changes in professional journals, and another to do it vigorously in public debate when all the main parties have decided that they can't or don't even wish to make them. Public advocacy of that kind risks foregoing research funding and promotion and even government-inspired attacks on your professional reputation.[31] Matters have not been significantly different in any country where neoliberalism secured hegemony.

HEALTH CARE SINCE THE THERAPEUTIC REVOLUTION

The twentieth-century revolution in medical science and technology made it possible for the first time to cure many lethal illnesses and to prolong life, alleviate pain, and enhance the quality of life. Once this was understood, access to health *care* became the focus of people's most intense fears and hopes. Health care was even defined as a human right in article 25 of the 1948 Universal Declaration of Human Rights.[32] Aneurin Bevan, the architect of Britain's National Health Service, introduced in 1948, appropriately described it as offering 'freedom from fear', and by the end of the 1950s the government of almost every country with a strong labour movement had found the demand for universal access irresistible. More or less comprehensive public systems, funded through social insurance or general taxation, and covering women and children as well as workers, replaced private healthcare markets and second-rate, class-ridden services, and opened up a huge new field of skilled public-service employment.[33] In 1965 even the US introduced free public provision (at the point of use) for the very poor (Medicaid), and for everyone over 65 (Medicare). In the Communist countries state-provided health care for all became standard. In the 'third world' state provision struggled with a lack of resources and huge demands, but the principle of universal access, secured by state action, was widely accepted.

As with the measures that brought about the mortality revolution, capitalist interests – and all too often doctors too – initially resisted the introduction of comprehensive health care. Its huge popularity, however, overcame resistance by the medical profession, which sought and generally got excellent terms of employment in return for agreeing to make the new systems work. In some west European countries a large private sector was allowed to remain alongside social insurance-based public systems. In most of the new public healthcare systems doctors were allowed to continue to be paid on a fee-for-service basis, with its inherent incentive to over-treat and drive costs up. The resulting weaknesses would be exploited by the enemies of public and universal healthcare systems when the post-war compromise came to an end in the 1970s. But the basic principle of free health care for all became deeply embedded in most OECD countries.

The therapeutic revolution, however, also gave rise to the dramatic growth of a science-based pharmaceutical industry, to be joined later by the closely related biotechnology industry. These forms of capital exercise massive economic and political power, and are closely linked politically with the also powerful private health insurance and healthcare provider industries, especially in the US.

In 2008 world sales of pharmaceuticals were estimated at more than $600 billion, two-thirds of which came from the twenty largest companies, most of them American or west European. Biotechnology companies had estimated revenues of $51 billion in 2005, but were expected eventually to overtake pharmaceuticals in value; and there were in addition fast-expanding medical technology industries at the centre of advances in drug delivery, imaging and computerised surgery, with annual sales of the order of $200 billion. The pharmaceutical industry now accounts for up to 10 per cent of health spending in OECD countries.

Before 1900 the limited number of effective drugs then in use, such as aspirin, were increasingly provided by Bayer and other spin-offs of the German chemical industry. The research that initiated the therapeutic revolution was mainly done in state-funded university laboratories or charity-funded research institutes. But as the potential of the powerful new drugs became clear in the 1930s many of the household names of today's pharmaceutical industry – Hoffman La Roche, Merck, Eli Lilly, the component companies combined into GlaxoSmithKline, and so on – expanded dramatically, taking on research staff and investing in drug testing and marketing.

By the 1980s, however, the era of discovery of new drugs offering major improvements for patients with important medical conditions, let alone cures for them, seemed to be over, and the rate of innovation has declined further since: the number of new drugs being registered has dwindled from fifty a year in the 1990s to about twenty today.[34] In spite of constant promises of breakthroughs to come, the sombre judgment of Oxford's Regius Professor of Medicine in the 1990s still seems broadly correct: 'We seem to have reached an impasse in our understanding of the major killers of Western society...although we have learned more and more about the minutiae of how these diseases make people sick, we have made little headway in determining why they arise in the first place'.[35]

One response of the drug companies has been to patent 'me too' drugs – near-copies of existing drugs that have the potential to add at best very small improvements over the benefits given by a drug belonging to another company, but just different enough to be patented. Up to half of all new drugs are now of this kind.[36] They have also used their enormous advertising resources to promote the idea of other conditions which they claim their existing drugs are able to relieve. Sometimes these are comic inventions, like 'restless leg syndrome', but more often they are common, essentially normal conditions that are given new names, like 'erectile dysfunction' (impotence) and 'social anxiety disorder' (shyness). Huge fortunes are made in this way. Marcia Angell, a former editor of the New England Journal of Medicine, says: 'The strategy of the drug marketers – and it has been remarkably successful – is to convince Americans that there are only two kinds of people: those with medical conditions that require drug treatment, and those who don't know it yet'.[37] Angell cites Pfizer's drug Neurontin, originally approved for the treatment of epilepsy when other drugs failed:

> By paying academic experts to put their names on articles extolling Neurontin for other uses – bipolar disease, post-traumatic stress disorder, insomnia, restless leg syndrome, hot flushes, migraines, tension headaches, and more – and by funding conferences at which these uses were promoted, the manufacturer was able to parlay the drug into a blockbuster, with sales of $2.7 billion in 2003.[38]

The complicity of some doctors – again, chiefly in the US – in this process has already been mentioned, but paying doctors very large sums of money (half a million dollars is not uncommon) to sign articles written by drug company staff is only part of the story of the pharmaceutical industry's corruption of medical science. Equally contemptible is its record of suppressing trial evidence, thanks to lax regulation (for which it always lobbies hard), leading to the approval of drugs that later prove dangerous or even lethal (for instance the US Federal Drug Agency's ignoring of evidence that Merck's analgesic drug Vioxx increased the risk of strokes and heart attacks in some people). The industry's attitude to scientific evidence is sometimes not so different from that of the $40 billion 'alternative' medicine industry, whose hallmark is to ignore scientific evidence as irrelevant.[39]

In countries with universal public healthcare systems the drug industry applies enormous pressure on governments to buy drugs that offer at best a small prolongation of life for people suffering from what are mainly late-life diseases. They also press for the highest possible prices, arguing that the costs of research and development must be recouped from the sales of the relatively few drugs that prove effective, even though their spending on promotion far exceeds their spending on research and development (estimates vary from twice to three times as much, or even more). And where they can they don't hesitate to threaten to relocate their operations abroad if their demands are not met.[40] So far, there is no indication that any state where the main drug companies are located is willing to act effectively to rein in their abuses. At the same time the pharmaceutical industry does not like to invest shareholders' funds in research on treatments for the diseases of people in poor countries, who have no money to pay for them. The Global Forum for Health Research estimates that 90 per cent of the $70 billion spent annually on medical research worldwide is devoted to diseases that are responsible for only 10 per cent of the global burden of disease.[41]

The pharmaceutical industry's heavy spending on drug promotion also has an ideological impact, reinforcing the preoccupation with therapy rather than with the determinants of ill-health. The media collaborate, highlighting stories about miracle cures to be expected from advances in stem-cell research which will regenerate 'the eyes of the elderly, the spinal cords of the paralysed, and the insulin-producing cells of the diabetic',[42] or research in genetic medicine and nano-technology ('molecule-sized robots may be able to repair individual cells and even strands of DNA, with the result that people will be able to live two hundred years without showing any signs of aging').[43] By contrast conditions like mental illness and alcohol addiction, which account for a much higher share of the burden of illness in the rich countries than any of these conditions, get less attention. Tackling them would require doing something about their socio-economic causes.

The therapeutic revolution, then, has under capitalism produced contradictory results for global health. Fundamental medical research, mainly conducted in tax-funded university and other non-profit laboratories, has produced cures for infectious diseases that used to be killers and continues to produce marvellous benefits for individuals rich enough to pay for them, or fortunate enough to live in countries that still have adequately funded equal-access healthcare systems. The achievements of immunology and of advanced medical technology and surgery are undeniably brilliant. Yet while there have been significant trickle-down benefits for poor countries from these advances, most of it is directed at problems that are not a priority in most of the world. There is also a growing anxiety that even university-based medical research is increasingly driven by the interests of pharmaceutical and medical technology companies: how far are the problems researched chosen because corporate funding is available for them?[44] The story of how commercial interests have been able to thwart, suppress, or denigrate and dismiss research into the environmental causes of cancer, and confine progress to individual treatments while their products continue to produce the disease, does not encourage confidence in the beneficence of medical science in practice.[45] And capitalism sometimes even destroys what medical science has achieved, for example by promoting the excessive and often unregulated use of antibiotics, leading to the emergence of new drug-resistant strains of bacteria.[46]

HEALTH CARE AND LEGITIMATION: IDEOLOGY

Critical analysts have always recognised the legitimising role of health care, while also emphasising that a sophisticated modern economy needs workers to be fit for the work they are hired to do.[47] But how many need to be fit, and how fit they need to be, is a different matter. The fact that inequality and the resulting health costs have been allowed to grow, and the fact that work has been steadily relocated from rich countries to countries whose workforces have much poorer health and lower life expectancies, suggest that this is not a strong constraint. It may have become widely accepted in the twentieth century, as Porter says, 'that the smooth and efficient functioning of intricate producer and consumer economies required a population no less healthy than literate, skilled and law-abiding',[48] but state policy in the era of neoliberalism suggests that only the last of these is a strongly-felt requirement.[49]

This became clear after 1990, when neoliberal policy-makers embarked on the re-commodification of publicly-funded health care – opening it up as a field of private capital accumulation. What this revealed was how far health care is an ideological construct, almost as much as a material reality. It is not the quality of health care, or even its accessibility, but the way it is articulated with other elements in the dominant ideology, that is crucial to legitimation. In public discourse publicly-provided health care is not articulated with 'poverty', 'housing', 'industrial pollution', or 'inner-city deprivation', but with 'cost', 'taxation', 'bureaucracy', 'welfare', 'self-reliance', and with 'state' itself (with negative prefixes like 'nanny' state, 'centralised' or 'Stalinoid' state, etc.). Successfully embedded in neoliberal ideology – i.e. articulated with 'productivity', 'efficiency', and 'choice' – health care can be represented as a commodity like any other. The US private healthcare industry has spent massively to oppose the introduction of publicly-financed health care for all, but by itself this would not have been sufficient: the wider ideological context has been crucial. The belief that private enterprise delivers health care more efficiently, that providing it out of tax revenues would weaken the self-reliance for which Americans are famous, and the charge that it is 'socialist', have so far regularly trumped the desire for more equal access.

As for Europe, two themes in particular run through the rhetoric of the drive to re-commodify universal-access health care: cost-containment, and efficiency. Cost-containment is presented as an unquestionable necessity because costs are said to be rising inexorably; and this, it is insisted, is because the demand for health care is infinite, driven by constantly increasing public expectations, ageing populations, and the constant development of expensive new treatments – whereas public spending is not only finite, but already, it is alleged, at the limits of 'affordability'. This makes efficiency – the second key trope in the privatisation rhetoric – all-important; and efficiency, it is claimed, can only be achieved by private provision, driven by competition. Neither of these arguments withstands critical scrutiny.

In a 1998 paper that should be required reading for every health policy-maker and health journalist, Penelope Mullen demonstrates conclusively that demand is not infinite – people are finite and have finite needs, and in most cases finite wishes, for medical attention. The abstract argument from economic theory, that there is an infinite demand for anything with a zero price to the 'consumer', may commend itself to neoliberal think-tank staffers, but not to common sense, least of all when it comes to health care.[50] Moreover such empirical evidence as exists shows that the need for specific kinds of treatment could be met with quite reasonable outlays on provision. It is also false to assert that new medical technologies always imply rising costs. Much so-called keyhole surgery, for example, has reduced costs through shortening or even eliminating stays in hospital, as have many drugs; and the cost of new technologies, which often contains a large element of monopoly rent, tends to fall rapidly once they become widely adopted. The rise in costs due to ageing populations is also frequently exaggerated, since people also stay healthy longer. About half of all healthcare expenditure is still concentrated in the last few months of life, however old we are when we die.

Mullen also points out that while spending on health care is indeed also finite, its actual level is a political question – what is 'affordable' is a matter of collective choice: the argument that when spending on health care reaches 8 or 10 or 15 per cent of GDP the time has come to make what are always called 'hard choices' about rationing is nothing but a (typically right-wing) political opinion. What is really at issue is not the percentage of national income spent on health care, but the amount of it paid for out of taxes; people with money prefer to spend it on themselves. The US currently spends 18 per cent of its GDP on health care, much the highest proportion in the world, rising by nearly a percentage point a year in recent years; in 2007 the Congressional Budget Office forecast that by 2082 the share would have risen to 49 per cent of GDP.[51] This extrapolation from recent trends was intended to highlight the high costs of healthcare in the US, but was taken by many readers as indicating the 'infinite' nature of the demand for care and the need for cuts in the half of total US healthcare spending that is funded out of taxation (nine per cent of GDP in 2007). The real problem, namely that the costs of US health care are high because of its market character, was not pointed out in the report.[52]

There is in any case no necessary limit to the share of GDP that might be spent on health care so long as GDP is rising. As William Baumol pointed out long ago, in that context a rising proportion of GDP can be spent on health care (or any other irreducibly labour-intensive service) while still leaving more to be spent on the products of sectors in which labour costs steadily decline. [53] And a country that spent half of its national income on making people healthy by all possible means (including a rationally-organised system of universal health care) would in fact not be a bad place to live. The progressive potential of the German medical scientist Rudolf Virchow's much-quoted remark, that 'politics is nothing else but medicine on a large scale', would be realised there.[54]

As for the argument that for-profit health care is more efficient than public or non-profit provision, its common acceptance owes nothing to evidence. The best empirical evidence comes from the US itself, where large enough samples permit comparisons to be made between Health Maintenance Organisations (HMOs) that are run on a non-profit basis and those run for profit (so-called 'investor-owned' facilities). The conclusions of the leading US researchers on this subject, in a 1999 study covering 56 per cent of total HMO enrolment in the US, were categorical on one central point: 'Compared with not-for-profit HMOs, investor-owned plans had lower rates for all 14 quality-of-care indicators. ... investor ownership was consistently associated with lower quality...'.[55] This finding should not have been surprising: in a service sector that depends to such an extent on skilled labour, the main way profits can be extracted is to shift to an industrial model of provision – fewer staff, lower skill-mix, shorter consultation times, and so on – at the expense of the quality of care. Unless, that is, competition leads to greater efficiency in the use of resources. But such evidence as we have on this aspect also indicates the opposite. A review of 132 studies comparing for-profit and non-profit hospitals, nursing homes, HMOs, home care organisations and dialysis centres in the US between 1980 and 2000 showed that non-profits were more often found to be superior to for-profits in terms of cost-efficiency, as well as in terms of quality.[56]

And these comparisons only tell half the story, since in the US all providers operate in a market. The costs of operating a market – the costs of promoting and advertising insurance plans and providers' facilities, of making contracts between insurers and providers, of accounting and invoicing for every individual treatment, of recording payments and chasing non-payments, of auditing and litigation – are huge.[57] It is often reckoned as a rule of thumb that a third of every dollar spent on health care in the US is spent on administration. In contrast, the administrative costs of the British National Health Service in the mid-1970s, before it began to be converted into a market, were estimated at between 5 and 6 per cent of the total.[58]

The claim (or more often the assumption) that healthcare provision by for-profit companies is more efficient or cost-effective than public provision even contradicts the economic theory on which the advocates of markets always pretend to rely. In an interesting episode, when the British Treasury attempted in 2003 to set out a rationale for judging the productivity of public services it found itself concluding, on basic public-choice theory grounds, that for the provision of universal-access health care, markets were not efficient. 'Information asymmetry' between patients and doctors, inherent local monopoly power on the part of providers, the difficulty and cost of making and monitoring enforceable contracts, the impossibility of transferring risk to private providers ('it is difficult to let failing hospitals go bust', as the paper candidly put it), the perverse incentives involved in private medical insurance[59] – all the factors which make private provision of universal care less efficient and cost-effective than public provision were faithfully set out (evidently by a civil servant of the old school, not yet ready to supply the kind of 'policy-based evidence' ministers want to receive, as opposed to the 'evidence-based policy' they always say they are committed to).[60] But the government completely ignored the paper's conclusions. By 2009 the NHS in England (Scotland and Wales used their devolved powers to resist) was well on the way to being fragmented into a healthcare market in which private companies were playing a steadily expanding role.[61]

THE RE-COMMODIFICATION OF HEALTH CARE

As early as 1976 Vicente Navarro presciently described what would prove to be the dominant theme of health under capitalism for the next three decades:

> ... it is the tendency of contemporary capitalism to convert public services into commodities to be bought and sold on the private market. Reflecting that tendency is the push by both conservatives in the UK and conservatives and large numbers of liberals in the US to shift the delivery of health services back to the private sector (supposedly to enable them to be run more efficiently and more profitably) and to keep them there. And in this scheme, the payment for services is public, while the appropriation of profit is private.[62]

This was a key component of the neoliberal counter-revolution of the 1970s. Previously capital had been content to build hospitals and sell equipment and other supplies to publicly-provided health services. Now it moved to take over the services themselves. Given the importance of health care in people's lives, and the popularity of the public systems established in so much of the world after 1945, the speed with which the capitalist assault has so often succeeded needs explaining. In the case of countries in the global 'south', with most of their revenues mortgaged to servicing their debt, and obliged by IMF-imposed structural adjustment policies to abandon much of their state-provided services, there is no mystery. The same is true of the former Soviet bloc countries, bankrupted by the 'shock doctrine', their populations briefly infatuated with the rhetoric of Reagan and Thatcher, and with American health companies advising governments and selling private insurance policies to everybody who could afford one.

But in western Europe and other industrialised countries, where public health services were deeply entrenched and popular, the fact that so many governments have been able to push ahead with the conversion of public systems of health care back into fields of capital accumulation is at first sight more puzzling. Differences between national healthcare systems and many other historical, cultural and political factors ensured that the explanations would vary from place to place. What led to the privatisation of significant parts of the German hospital sector is a different story from what led to the privatisation of primary care in Sweden, or the adoption of 'public-private partnerships' for the building and servicing of hospitals in Australia and Canada. In each case, however, some common elements recur.

First, the public healthcare systems have always had various weaknesses, which the capitalist media have relentlessly exploited. Subject to state budgetary restraints, they have often been forced to ration access through delays. Large bureaucracies, with their normal shortcomings, are required to operate and administer them. Politicians were apt to interfere on behalf of special interests. Initial compromises with vested interests (such as parts of the medical profession, or private hospital owners) gave rise to organisational irrationalities, such as the perpetuation of fee-for-service systems of payment which have high transaction costs and reward over-treatment, or a lack of integration between primary and secondary care, and so on. The fact that for-profit provision suffers from the same problems as well as many others goes unmentioned in the media, as does the desire of middle-class patients to be treated separately from working-class patients (a significant undercurrent of much private health-industry advertising). Above all what is hardly ever discussed is how to develop a democratic approach to making public healthcare bureaucracies accountable and responsive to the public.

Second, a private healthcare sector is nearly always active alongside the public system, providing parallel provision for those who can pay, cherry-picking profitable services, offering 'hotel' style hospital accommodation, short waiting times for treatment – i.e. in general offering a model of a commodified service that looks attractive precisely because it is expensive. In England the existence of a small, high-cost, private health sector providing secondary care has served as such a model. Catering to the well-paid business and professional classes (and wealthy patients from abroad), it functioned until recently entirely on the basis of treatments provided by National Health Service (NHS) doctors, working in their spare time, and for extremely high fees. When the private healthcare companies were given an opportunity to take over a growing share of normal NHS work, at closer to NHS costs, they developed a completely different business model for NHS-paid patients, based on high turnover and no frills.[63] A telling contrary example to the power of the private healthcare sector is Canada, where the Canada Health Act in effect prevents the development of a parallel private healthcare sector. Everywhere else the private healthcare sector has functioned as a base from which new inroads into the public sector can be made.

Third, exploiting this base, capital has worked hard to penetrate the relevant elements in the state and its adjacent structures, including the medical profession. The most extreme example is probably England, where the private health sector achieved a text-book case of 'state capture'. In mid-2006 the 32-strong leadership team in the Department of Health contained only one career civil servant. Six came from the private sector, and eighteen from clinical or management jobs in the NHS. Only five had been in post more than five years – in other words, their collective memory of the original structure and philosophy of the NHS was heavily outweighed by their collective involvement in marketising it.[64] In 2007 the Commercial Directorate of the Department, which was the dominant driver of the marketisation process, had a staff of 190, of whom 182 were recruited on short-term contracts from the private sector.[65]

But the most important common factor in the success of capital's drive to convert state-funded health care into a profit-making commodity has undoubtedly been the wider hegemony of neoliberalism, both as a system of social practices and as a system of ideas. Britain, again, is a leading case, but one that is symptomatic of what has happened in many other western countries. Hegemony resulted from the neutering of the trade union movement and the conversion of the Labour Party into an organ of professional politicians, reliant on rich donors rather than a mass membership. By the beginning of the new century the great majority of voters no longer felt connected to or responsible for public policy, which allowed the marketisation of the NHS to be carried out with minimal public debate. Moreover since the main opposition parties and most of the press were in favour of marketisation, informed critics had nowhere to turn for support. In some countries resistance has been stronger, due to historic differences in political alignments and culture, while in others – such as the Netherlands – the drive to a full healthcare market has gone further than in England.

The success of the privatisers also reflects the extent to which the notion that everything should be, and ultimately is, a commodity, had became 'common sense'. People's everyday experience as patients leads them to value universal, equal-access health care, and many have protested when local facilities have been closed as 'uneconomic', or handed over to private companies. But in the abstract people also see health care as something consumed, and themselves as ultimately paying the bill for it, even though treatment remains free to the patient receiving it. The idea that demand is infinite and resources are limited, and that rationing is needed to contain costs, is largely accepted as true. Even the industrial model of health care, with factory-style processing of patients in 'walk-in centres' and 'super-surgeries' (large-scale clinics), currently being promoted in England, has been favourably received, insofar as it is presented as offering the same convenience as a supermarket.

In England this combination of factors allowed the marketisation of NHS clinical care to proceed in a series of more or less well-calculated steps, beginning with the introduction of private companies to provide some routine NHS surgery, and ending with a large number of private hospitals and clinics doing increasing volumes of NHS-paid work, while plans have also been announced to transfer up to 64 per cent of all NHS hospital outpatient work to new health centres built and operated by private firms, or by joint ventures between the NHS and private firms.[66] Finally, primary care services (family medicine and other community health services) have begun to be handed over to private health providers. This process could eventually lead to a large, consolidated private-provider sector living off the NHS budget, alongside an increasingly residual sector of publicly-owned providers, and the re-emergence of charges for better quality treatment. Or the sheer weight and scale of the public system could prove to offer too few pickings for the private sector. It is too early to say.

What is already clear, however, is that in all the countries where the marketisation process has been pushed ahead, it is steadily reorienting publicly-provided health care itself on commercial lines. Profitability becomes a declared objective, and staffing levels and terms of service are driven down, with a corresponding decline in the quality of care. An industrial concept of efficiency, corresponding to the concept of health care as a commodity, is substituted for the goal of meeting health needs – to be followed, inexorably, by the introduction of charges ('co-payments') for a growing range of treatments.[67]

CONCLUSION

How might the global economic crisis precipitated by financial capital affect the ongoing erosion of equal-access comprehensive health care, and the abandonment of redistributive social and economic policies? The situation has all the makings of Gramsci's definition of an 'organic' crisis, a 'real crisis of the ruling class's hegemony'. The ruling class has indisputably failed in a 'great political undertaking for which it… requested, or forcibly extracted, the consent of the broad masses' – the dream of creating a global economy on neoliberal principles (not to mention the imperialist dream of a 'new American century'). The ruling class has responded in precisely the way Gramsci described, working hard to restore order with a bare minimum of change: modestly increased financial regulation, modestly reduced scope for tax avoidance by the super-rich, slightly smaller bonuses for billionaire financiers, plus the – temporary, of course – reintroduction of fiscal deficits.[68]

Whether this will work in the longer run remains to be seen. The effects of the global economic crisis will not be short-lived, and will converge with the impact of the accelerating ecological crisis. Millions of people will remain unemployed for years (many older workers will never work again), while governments cut social services in order to repay the enormous debts they have incurred to rescue the banking system and reflate their economies. In this context, the anti-egalitarian character of neoliberal health policy seems likely to become more and more apparent. The rhetoric of consumer 'choice' will have a much narrower appeal. It will no longer be possible to ignore or gloss over the gross inequality of incomes and taxation inherited from the neoliberal era, with their critical impact on the health of the least well-off; the declining quality of publicly-provided health care; the flow of tax revenues to corporate healthcare providers; above all, perhaps, the contraction of free health services to a 'basic' package, and the increasing reservation of other treatments for those able to afford fees. All this could in due course lead to the emergence of a new common sense in which the link between health and equality is once again seen to be fundamental.

NOTES

I am very grateful to Nancy Leys Stepan for invaluable help with sources, and to her and David Rowland for trenchant criticisms and suggestions.

1   Friedrich Engels, *The Condition of the Working Class in England in 1844* (1845), in K. Marx, *Karl Marx and Frederick Engels on Britain*, Moscow: Foreign Languages Publishing House, 1953, p. 140, citing the *Report on the Sanitary Condition of the Working Class*. So long as infectious diseases remained prevalent average life expectancy was pulled down by the high level of infant mortality. People who survived childhood generally lived long enough to reproduce.

2   Roy Porter, *The Greatest Benefit of Mankind: A medical history of humanity from antiquity to the present*, London: Fontana Press, 1999, pp. 369-70.

3   Japan, for example, raised its average life expectancy from around 37 years in the late nineteenth century to the highest in the world today, even though as late as the 1930s very few Japanese houses had running water or water-borne sewage. See James C. Riley, *Rising Life Expectations: A Global History*, Cambridge: Cambridge University Press 2001, pp. 19ff.

4   In the US the gap can be over 20 years when factors such as ethnicity and gender are taken into account. See Christopher Murray et al., 'Eight Americas: investigating mortality disparities across races, counties, and race-counties in the United States', *Public Library of Science Medicine (PLoS Medicine)*, 3(9), 2006, available from http://www.plosmedicine.org.

5   The view that it was improved nutrition that was responsible for rising longevity rested on detailed statistical research by Thomas McKeown. For the critique of it see especially Simon Szreter, *Health and Wealth: Studies in History and Policy*, Rochester: University of Rochester Press, 2005.

6   Richard Easterlin, *The Reluctant Economist*, Cambridge: Cambridge University Press, 2004, p. 108.

7   Ibid., chapter 7, 'How Beneficent Is the Market? A Look at the Modern History of Mortality'.

8   'The low cost of life expectancy improvement is illustrated dramatically by the experience of China, which raised life expectancy from, around 40 years in the early 1950s to 60 years by the late 1960s. At the end of this period, China's income level was about three-fourths of the 1820 level in Western Europe, where life expectancy averaged under 40 years... China was allocating an estimated 2 percent of GDP to health spending during this period' (ibid., p. 132). See also J.C. Caldwell, 'Routes to low mortality in poor countries', *Population and Development Review*, 12(2), 1986, 170-220.

9   Easterlin, *The Reluctant Economist*, p. 134.

10   Karl Marx, 'Postface to the Second Edition of Capital' (London 1873), in Marx, *Capital*, Volume 1, London: Penguin Books, 1976, p. 97.

11   The prostitution of doctors' reputations by the drug companies has been widely reported. For a recent commentary see Marcia Angell, 'Drug companies and doctors: a story of corruption', *The New York Review of Books*, 56(1), 15 January 2009, pp. 8-12. For a gross example of the misuse of data in the interests of the

health insurance industry, see the account of Richard Feachem et al., 'Getting more for their dollar: A comparison of the NHS with California's Kaiser Permanente', *BMJ (British Medical Journal)*, 324(7330), 2002, which purported to show that Kaiser Permanente offered better value for money than the NHS, in Allyson Pollock, *NHS plc*, Second Edition, London: Verso, 2005, pp. 217-19.

12   See John Bongaarts, 'A decomposition of life expectancy levels and trends', Population Council, New York, 15 February 2006, Table 1.

13   Lant Pritchett and Lawrence H. Summers, 'Wealthier is healthier', *Journal of Human Resources,* 31(4), 1996, pp. 841-68. The authors argue that since not all the recorded increase in longevity can be explained by public policy, it makes sense for governments to make income growth *per se* a health policy goal.

14   See Richard Wilkinson, *The Impact of Inequality: How To Make Sick Societies Healthier*, New York: The New Press, 2005, p. 59. The fundamental reason is quantitative: the life-prolonging effects of new medical treatments are 'dwarfed' by the scale of the medical conditions for which the treatments are given.

15   Ibid, chapter 4, esp. pp. 119-23.

16   These processes are analysed in my book, *Market-Driven Politics: Neoliberal Democracy and the Public Interest*, London: Verso, 2001; see also Leys, 'The cynical state', in *Socialist Register 2006*, pp. 1-27.

17   George Davey Smith, Daniel Dorling, David Gordon and Mary Shaw, 'The widening health gap. What are the solutions?', in George Davey Smith, ed., *Health Inequalities: Lifecourse approaches*, Bristol: The Policy Press, 2003, pp. 459-65.

18   See especially Davey Smith, *Health Inequalities*, pp. xxxv-xxxvii and 440.

19   Dennis Raphael, 'Social determinants of health: present status, unanswered questions, and future directions', *International Journal of Health Services*, 36(4), 2006, pp. 651-77.

20   Richard Wilkinson, *The Impact of Inequality: How to make sick societies healthier,* New York: The New Press, 2005; and with Kate Pickett, *The Spirit Level: Why more equal societies almost always do better*, London: Allen Lane, 2009, pp. 66-7.

21   Julian Tudor Hart, *The Political Economy of Health Care: A clinical perspective,* Bristol: Policy Press 2006, pp. 67 and 145 n.58; Davey Smith, *Health Inequalities*, p. 494.

22   In Sub-Saharan Africa average life expectancy fell from 50 in 1990 to 46 in 2002. In other areas the health costs of structural adjustment are liable to be revealed in the statistics later.

23   *World Health Report 2008*, Geneva: WHO, 2008, pp. 13-14. The report points out the dangerous nature of unregulated health care: 'In the Democratic Republic of the Congo, for example, "la chirugie safari" (safari surgery) refers to a common practice of health workers moonlighting by performing appendectomies or other surgical interventions at the patients' homes, often for crippling fees'.

24   David Shukler, Lawrence King and Martin McKee, 'Mass privatisation and the post-communist mortality crisis: a cross-national analysis', *Lancet*, 373(9661), 31 January 2009, pp. 399-407.

25 Davey Smith, *Health Inequalities*, p. xlvii (italics added).
26 Definitions of 'public health' vary considerably, but most refer at their core to activities focused on improving the health of the whole population, with a strong emphasis on prevention, and the public institutions that undertake them.
27 Porter, *The Greatest Benefit*, pp. 633-4.
28 Peter Draper, 'A public health approach', in Draper, ed., *Health Through Public Policy: The greening of public health*, London: Greenprint, 1991, p. 20.
29 In 2007 the share of public health in total health spending in the OECD countries averaged 3.1 per cent. OECD, *Health at a Glance 2007: OECD Indicators*, Paris: OECD, 2007, p. 91.
30 George Davey Smith and Yoav Ben-Shlomo, 'Inequalities in health: what is happening and what can be done?', in Davey Smith, *Health Inequalities*, p. 496.
31 For an example of the abuse of government power to try to discredit an active public health critic see Pollock, *NHS plc*, pp. 219-23.
32 For other texts purporting to commit states to health care as a right see Center for Economic and Social Rights, *The Right to Health in the United States of America: What Does It Mean?*, Brooklyn: Center for Economic and Social Rights, 2004, available http://www.cesr.org.
33 For a sobering account of the way general practice in England was riddled by class distinctions see Porter, *The Greatest Benefit*, p. 644.
34 Ben Goldacre, *Bad Science*, London: Fourth Estate, 2008, p. 185.
35 Porter, *The Greatest Benefit*, pp. 595-96.
36 Goldacre, *Bad Science*, p. 185.
37 Marcia Angell, 'Drug companies and doctors', p. 12, citing Melody Petersen, *Our Daily Meds: How the Pharmaceutical Companies Transformed Themselves into Slick Marketing Machines and Hooked the Nation on Prescription Drugs*, New York: Sarah Crighton/Farrar, Strauss and Giroux, 2008.
38 Ibid. The article contains a useful list of references to the fast-growing literature on the industry's abuse of science.
39 See Simon Singh and Edzard Ernst, *Trick or Treatment? Alternative Medicine on Trial*, London: Bantam Press, 2008; and Goldacre, *Bad Science*. Singh and Ernst estimate the UK spending on alternative medicine at £5 billion, of which £500 million is spent – on acupuncture, homeopathy, etc. – by the National Health Service, under relentless pressure from the media, the Prince of Wales, gullible patients and some doctors (p. 240). In a notable example of the use of market power to protect health industry interests, in May 2009 the British Chiropractic Association successfully sued Simon Singh for libel, over a newspaper article in which he 'criticised the BCA for claiming that its members could use spinal manipulation to treat children with colic, ear infections, asthma, sleeping and feeding conditions, and prolonged crying. Singh described the treatments as "bogus" and based on insufficient evidence, and criticised the BCA for "happily promoting" them'. Chris French, '"Witch hunt" forces chiropractors to take down their websites', *Guardian,* 20 June 2009. A group of eminent scientists issued a statement condemning the judgment.

40   The UK pharmaceutical giant GlaxoSmithKline has twice threatened to move its UK operations abroad: once in 1999 when its anti-flu drug Relenza was judged not cost-effective enough for the NHS to buy, and again in 2008 over a tax dispute with the UK government. By spreading its legal locations around the world, GSK paid only £450 m. tax in the UK, though its worldwide profits were £7.4 bn. AstraZeneca has also threatened to move its UK operations to Ireland, to escape the constraints of UK tax law. In 2004 its tax avoidance arrangements enabled it to pay only £103 m. in tax on profits of £2.6 bn. UK corporation tax is 30 per cent of profits.

41   Global Forum for Health Research (GFHR), *The 10/90 Report on Health Research 2000*, Geneva: GFHR, 2000. Patrick Bond has calculated that 89 per cent of all global health spending is spent on 16 per cent of the world's population. 'Globalisation, pharmaceutical pricing and South African health policy', *International Journal of Health Services*, 29(4), 1999, pp. 765-92.

42   Sarah Boseley, 'Medical marvels', *Guardian*, 20 January 2009, citing among others Dr Thomas B. Okarma, the CEO of a NASDAQ-listed biotech company, Geron.

43   Luke Mitchell, 'Sick in the head', *Harper's Magazine*, February 2009, p. 39, reporting the predictions of John Hammergren, the chairman, president and CEO of McKesson, the largest healthcare corporation in the US.

44   See George Monbiot, *Captive State: The corporate takeover of Britain*, London: Macmillan, 2000, chapter 9, 'The Corporate Takeover of the Universities'. Confidence in the beneficence of hospital-based research on drug therapies has not been helped by recent moves to make NHS hospitals into official collaborators of the pharmaceutical industry.

45   Devra Davis, *The Secret History of the War on Cancer*, New York: Basic Books, 2007.

46   Examples include the indiscriminate sale of drugs to the public in countries like India and Brazil, and the excessive use of antibiotics in the intensive livestock industries of Europe and North America. The risk that this will happen to the latest – and in some places only – effective anti-malaria drug, Artemisinin, is a serious concern among doctors.

47   See for example the pathbreaking account by Lesley Doyall (with Imogen Pennell), *The Political Economy of Health,* London: Pluto Press, 1979, pp. 37-39.

48   Porter, *The Greatest Benefit*, p. 631.

49   Vicente Navarro, *Medicine Under Capitalism*, New York: Prodist, 1976, pp.160-61. Furthermore, if a healthy workforce was the only or chief function served by universal health care it would not make sense to extend it to the retired, who are its main users.

50   Penelope M. Mullen, 'Is it Necessary to Ration Health Care?', *Public Money and Management*, 18(1), January-March 1998, pp. 53-58. See also George Davey Smith, Stephen Frankel and Shah Ebrahim, 'Rationing for health equity: is it necessary?', in Davey Smith, *Health Inequalities*, pp. 513-21. The authors point out that calculating the apparent cost of anything needs to be done critically. Drug costs, for example, are often treated as given, yet a particular statin which

cost £500 for a year's treatment in the UK could be bought for only £67 per year in India.

51 *The Long-Term Outlook for Health Care Spending*, US Congressional Budget Office, November 2007, available from http://www.cbo.gov.

52 'CBO's projections assume that to avoid a reduction in real consumption of items besides health care, employers, households, and insurance firms will change their behavior in a variety of ways (potentially including higher cost sharing, increased utilization management, reduced insurance coverage by employers, and greater scrutiny of new technologies based on evidence of their comparative effectiveness) to slow the rate of growth of spending in the nonfederal part of the health system. The projections also assume that, even in the absence of changes in federal law, some of the measures adopted to slow growth in the rest of the health care system will moderate spending growth in Medicare and Medicaid and that regulatory changes at the federal level and policy changes at the state level will help to slow cost growth in those programs' (ibid., pp. 1–2).

53 William J. Baumol and William G. Bowen, *The Performing Arts: The Economic Dilemma*, New York: Twentieth Century Fund, 1966, and papers by Baumol and his wife Hilda Baumol, collected in Ruth Towse, ed., *Baumol's Cost Disease: The Arts and Other Victims*, London: Edward Elgar, 1997.

54 Cited in Porter, *The Greatest Benefit*, p. 643. Virchow supported the 1848 revolution and was banished from Berlin for eight years following its failure, but eventually became a dominant figure in German public health as well as in scientific research.

55 David U. Himmelstein, Steffie Woolhandler, Ida Hellander and Sidney M. Wolfe, 'Quality of care in investor-owned vs not-for-profit HMOs', *Journal of the American Medical Association*, 282(2), 1999, at p. 159.

56 P. Vaillancourt Rosenau and Stephen H. Linder, 'Two decades of research comparing for-profit and nonprofit health provider performance in the United States', *Social Science Quarterly*, 84(2), 2003, pp. 219-241; see also Vaillancourt Rosenau and Linder, 'Comparison of the performance of for-profit and nonprofit US psychiatric inpatient care providers', *Psychiatric Services*, 54(2), Feb 2003, pp. 183-187.

57 In 1994 the administrative costs of US public hospitals accounted for 22.9 per cent of total costs; in private non-profit hospitals they accounted for 24.5 per cent; in for-profit hospitals they accounted for 34 per cent. Steffie Woolhandler and David Himmelstein, 'Costs of care and administration at for-profit and other hospitals in the United States', *New England Journal of Medicine*, 336(11), 1997, pp. 769-74.

58 Charles Webster, *The NHS: A Political History*, Second Edition, Oxford: Oxford University Press, 2002, p. 203. 'After [the introduction of the so-called internal market in the NHS] administrative costs soared; in 1997 they stand at about 12 per cent; managers talk of 17 per cent as an eventual target'. That was before the establishment of a full market in hospital care, including 'payment by results' (i.e. billing for every individual hospital treatment). By 2009 NHS

administrative costs must have been not far behind those of US non-profit hospitals.

59   The perverse incentives included refusing to insure high-risk patients, 'cream-skimming' profitable treatments, over-treatment thanks to fee-for-service payments, and many others.

60   HM Treasury, *Public services: meeting the productivity challenge. A discussion document*, London: HMT, 2003. When a newspaper reported that the newly-appointed government adviser on drugs policy had earlier written an article in a medical journal arguing that taking Ecstasy was less dangerous than horse riding, the Home Secretary (the cabinet minister responsible) told him this was not the kind of scientific advice she wanted – it 'went beyond the scientific advice that I expect of him'. Press Association, 'Jacqui Smith slaps down drugs adviser for comparing ecstasy to horse riding', *Guardian*, 9 February 2009.

61   The story is outlined in Pollock, *NHS plc* and John Lister, *The NHS after 60: For patients or profits?*, London: Middlesex University Press, 2008. For the first step in privatizing NHS clinical care see also Stewart Player and Colin Leys, *Confuse and Conceal: The NHS and Independent Sector Treatment Centres*, Monmouth: The Merlin Press, 2008.

62   Navarro, *Medicine Under Capitalism*, p. 216.

63   The CEO of BMI, the largest for-profit healthcare company in Britain, said that for private patients the aim was to 'raise clinical quality and offer unparalleled excellence in care and service'; for NHS patients there would be 'a tailored service based on a low-cost operating model'. Nigel Hawkes, 'The giant of private care will bid for NHS work', *The Times*, 10 January 2005.

64   Scott L. Greer and Holly Jarman, *The Department of Health and the Civil Service: From Whitehall to department of delivery to where?*, London: The Nuffield Trust, 2007, p. 20 tables 1 and 2.

65   Nicholas Timmins, 'Private sector role in pioneering healthcare scheme to be slashed', *Financial Times*, 15 November 2007.

66   Lord Darzi, the minister responsible, speaking to a health conference in December 2008. See *Public Private Finance* at http://www.pppbulletin.com/Document.aspx%20?ppf=true&ID=1459959.

67   On the industrialisation of primary care in Britain see Steve Iliffe, *From General Practice to Primary Care: The industrialisation of family medicine*, Oxford: Oxford University Press, 2008.

68   Antonio Gramsci, *Selections from the Prison Notebooks*, New York: International Publishers, 1971, pp. 210 and 178.

THE NATURE OF HEALTH CARE: COMMODIFICATION VERSUS SOLIDARITY

HANS-ULRICH DEPPE

Health and sickness are deeply rooted in the conditions of life, the conditions of work and the social relations of society. Health care is similarly socially embedded. And just as health or sickness are never purely individual matters, nor is health care. Dealing with the origins of sickness and caring for the sick are tasks for society. There is a collective and public dimension, which goes by the label of 'health policy'. There are political issues which are more important, but in recent years, when almost all countries have been confronted by the processes of globalisation, deregulation and privatisation, health care has been high on the political agenda

The leading sector in the process of deregulation and privatisation was financial capital, which dictated how other sectors of the society were to be structured and what governments had to do, using loan conditionality as its main instrument.[1] The conditions often included the privatisation of public property, on the basis that social relations should be governed more by markets and competition than in the past. Business management thinking penetrated all social niches. The social question was marginalised, irresponsibly neglected.[2] One result was a worldwide rise of instability, uncertainty and social polarisation – not only between the rich and the developing countries but also inside the rich countries. Poverty, violence and migration increased in many parts of the world. And when global accumulation, driven by the ambitions of financial capital, resulted in a financial crisis, predictably enough the apologists of the market and competition called for help from the state. Like the head of the Deutsche Bank, Josef Ackermann, they suddenly doubted the self-regulating capacity of markets and called on the state to regulate them again, and to provide financial compensation to the capitalists who had lost their capital.[3] When it affects healthcare systems, this process raises fundamental questions about the development and renewal of the relationship between health, medicine and society.

HEALTH CARE HAS STRONG ROOTS IN THE NATIONAL STATE

In contrast to the increasing globalisation of capital, healthcare systems are strongly linked to national states. A healthcare system mirrors a society. It reflects its development and its character. Whenever I am visiting a foreign country and want to understand more about its healthcare system than I can learn from statistical data, I ask to visit a psychiatric clinic, where some of a society's most vulnerable patients are treated. After that I understand more. This means that the transformation of a healthcare system implies more than mere technical changes. Structural change in a healthcare system is in fact always the result of social and political struggles: a given system of health care has always been fought for. In many parts of the world healthcare systems have undergone structural change after revolutions and wars – for instance after the defeat of fascist and military dictatorships, or after the collapse of socialist regimes. They have changed when the social system was threatened. In most countries of the 'north' healthcare systems are typically the result of the post-war compromise between capital and labour. But the struggle for a given healthcare system is never finished in a single battle. It is a permanent struggle.

At present, the healthcare systems of most countries are hard-pressed for resources. It is extraordinary. This is mainly a question of distribution, and we have to recognise – even in medical science – that this is a question of social choice and political power. Almost all health systems are said to be 'too expensive'. The myth of a 'cost explosion' has been energetically promoted and the costs are seen solely as a burden on economic development – an issue affecting where, in global economic competition, capital will locate. This implies a radical change in the concept of health care, from the traditional idea of collectively dealing with a social risk, to health care as a support for private capital accumulation. Solidarity in health care is displaced by individual and private interests, in a process of re-individualisation and commercialisation.

Meanwhile, we know that the health of the population in countries which are most advanced in the neo-liberal transformation of their healthcare systems is far from being the best. The US, where the neoliberal model was chiefly developed, is the prime example. The US spends more on health than any other country in the world, both as a share of GDP and per capita, and medical technology is very advanced. But this is not reflected in the country's health indicators. The administrative costs involved are extremely high. Moreover, the spread of poverty in the US increases the inequality of healthcare provision. About 47 million people have no health coverage,[4] more are underinsured, and the number of uninsured and underinsured is increasing.[5] We have to learn from this concrete experience – above all from its mistakes.

HEALTH AND SICKNESS ARE NOT COMMODITIES

These considerations lead us to think hard about the basic principles on which we deal collectively with sickness and health. Health and sickness cannot acquire the character of commodities, goods and services which are produced for sale. There is no healthcare system in the world which is organised solely on market principles. Even the US has Medicaid and Medicare, both publicly-financed programmes. This is due, among other things, to the following peculiarities. First, health is an existential good: it is a use value, which in most western societies is seen as a collective and public good – like air, drinking water, education or traffic safety and the rule of law. Second, one cannot choose not to be sick, as one can choose to consume, or not to consume, a commodity in the market; people don't know when or why they will become sick, or what illness they will suffer from in the future. Nor can they determine the appropriate extent, timing, or type of treatment. It is a general life risk. And such a risk often cannot be regulated by the individual alone. Third, a patient's demand for medical help is initially non-specific. It must first be defined and specified by the competence of an expert, and this gives medical professionals a large power of discretion in diagnosis, and in determining what treatment is undertaken. We will see in a moment what it means when physicians become entrepreneurs, or work like entrepreneurs, as happens with the commercialisation of health care. Fourth, the patient is in a vulnerable position of uncertainty, weakness, dependency and need, often combined with fear and shame. And last but not least: those patients who have the greatest need of care, most of whom come from the lower social classes, have the least financial resources.[6] Moreover the increasing pressure of economic competition aggravates the situation. Competition always produces winners and losers. The losers are the weakest – in medical terms, the chronically ill and seriously ill. It is precisely the social group which needs medical care and social support most, and most urgently.

What all this shows is that public protection is necessary: the delivery of health care for all cannot be reconciled with the mechanisms of supply and demand. The distributive function of the market does not do this.[7] The market is a blind power without any social orientation; it cannot solve social problems. The state, the at least potentially democratic instrument of society, must decide how health care is to be delivered and distributed.

The principle of competition makes sense on the football pitch or the stock exchange, but not in a hospital.

BUSINESS RATIONALITY AND MEDICAL DECISIONS

Many different medical responses to the same or similar medical condition cannot be explained purely as a result of the knowledge of medical science. For example, comparing two societies of similar economic and cultural status, in 1993 doctors in the US performed hysterectomies two and a half times as often as doctors in Sweden, and caesarean sections twice as often. And doctors in the US performed 4.4 times more coronary bypasses than doctors in Canada.[8] Another revealing comparison can be made between certain professions and everyone else. The American Medical Association conducted a study of medical intervention in cases of stage II prostate hypertrophy. They asked urologists what they would do if it were their own case. Just 40.5 per cent of the urologists asked said they would opt to have a transurethral prostate resection, yet for the population as a whole the rate of transurethral resections actually carried out in cases of stage II prostate hypertrophy was 80 per cent.

We find similar behaviour elsewhere. In Switzerland in 1993 tonsillectomies, hysterectomies, cholecystectomies and haemorrhoidectomies were performed much less often on physicians and lawyers than on the general population.[9] The rate of interventions for the general population was between 19 and 84 per cent higher. In Germany, internists who possess their own X-ray equipment carry out 3 to 4 times more X-rays than those who don´t. Even the German Radiologists Association says that more than a third of all X-ray interventions in Germany are unnecessary,[10] and a study of arthroscopies of the knee joint in the Netherlands found that 78 per cent of these interventions were unnecessary. A similar finding applies to the rate of micro-invasive procedures in the abdominal and pelvis cavity.[11]

These empirical findings are from rich countries which have similar social norms and values, and moreover where medical students learn from more or less the same medical textbooks. What they reveal is that the field of health care is person-oriented, uncertain, sensitive and complex. It is susceptible to external impacts. Money, competition, legal insecurity, professional career ambitions (or deep-rooted anxiety about losing one's place in the work-force) can all easily influence clinical decisions, consciously or unconsciously.

In these countries today many physicians and health workers see a fundamental contradiction between market pressures and individual patients' needs. Few accept utilitarian cost-benefit thinking about health care. But gradual changes are taking place quietly. External influences are penetrating medical decisions and choices. For instance, under German law public health insurance, which covers almost 90 per cent of the population, pays for all treatments which are 'medically necessary', and the power to define what 'medically necessary' means is assigned to the medical profession. Already in 1998 a study found that in the background of clinical decisions more and more indicators like age, privately or publicly insured, the profession, education and social status of a patient become a criterion. But in the words of one physician interviewed, 'Nobody would say this publicly. None of these criteria is legitimised by a moral code, by law or by medical norms'.[12] A more recent study, from 2005, found that 86 per cent of German hospital physicians refuse to ration treatment on financial grounds.[13] But they have to refuse every single day. In the literature this contradiction is called 'moral dissonance'.

The discretionary power of the medical profession, its space of decision, and what we call 'medical necessity', constitute the core of the debate about unnecessary operations, unnecessary cardiac catheterisation and angioplasty, the prescription of ineffective drugs or avoidable stays in hospitals. Increasingly the problem is understood and responded to in the industrial mode drawn from business: 'evidence-based medicine' in the form of guidelines to be followed by everyone replace the practical experience of highly-trained doctors.

Health care for the majority of the population in all European countries except Switzerland and the Netherlands is still largely financed not by private insurance but by non-profit institutions, state-controlled social health insurance organisations based on the principle of solidarity, or directly by the state out of tax revenues (as in the British National Health Service). But there is a strong tendency towards privatisation and commercialisation. The statutory health insurance organisations are starting to operate like private business. They increasingly take on features of the private insurance policies (co-payments, a choice of premiums and levels of coverage, reimbursing patients rather than paying doctors directly, etc.).[14] In addition to economic pressures, pressure also comes from the juridical and political institutions of the EU. The European Court of Justice has decided that healthcare systems must as far as possible conform to the principles of the European Single Market (the free movement of persons and free trade in commodities, services and capital). As statutory or social health insurance systems begin to adopt elements of private insurance practice, and abandon the principle of solidarity, through legislative changes at the national level, the possibility increases that they acquire the juridical character of private enterprises.[15] Since the EU's Lisbon summit of 2000 an 'open method of coordination', an instrument of integration, has been established. It started with guidelines, then established indicators, and finally supervised the adoption of the guidelines in the policies of Member States. The idea is to foster political commonalities between the Member States, not by transferring powers of control to the EU but rather by advancing a process of coordination and learning that leaves the formal authority and autonomy of the Member States intact – so-called 'soft regulation'.[16] This instrument is being used to adapt the EU's different healthcare systems on common, pro-market lines.

CONFIDENCE OR CONTRACT

Thanks to the 'soft' character of medical science and practice, medical institutions have been particularly challenged by the hard implications of the neo-liberal economic model. The expansion of the market, competition and profit in health care threatens to change the patient–physician-relationship fundamentally. A relationship which is currently still based on confidence is under pressure to change to a commercial relationship based on contract, and a contract is not an expression of confidence, but of mistrust.

Confidence implies a close relationship which makes it possible for a patient to provide the physician with intimate personal information which is essential for his or her medical care, and which is therefore protected by medical confidentiality. The patient–physician relationship is asymmetric. The expert is expected to care for and cure a patient to the best of their knowledge and belief. The patient can count on the expert's competence, rely on their good intentions, and believe their statements. Confidence assumes responsible behaviour. Treatments which are offered on the basis of confidence are intended to fulfil a credible promise, based on reliability and good faith. It is not possible to buy confidence.

Contracts, on the other hand, are part of the system of laws. Contracts confirm common intentions with fixed mutual obligations between persons more or less unknown to each other. In the market proprietors exchange their commodities for a negotiated price. Both buyers and sellers are interested in their own personal advantage. A contract is there to ensure that someone else can enforce the agreement if the parties' conflicting interests lead to disagreement or breakdown.

The growing commercialisation of the patient–physician relationship increasingly demands that the physician provides a particular measurable service for a fixed price. This service acquires more and more the character of a commodity, which will be produced and distributed under the conditions of economic competition. The patient is increasingly pushed into the role of a customer or purchaser, from whom the seller of the commodity will earn money. And the best customer is normally one from whom the most money can be made. Under such conditions patients will perhaps get the good service due to a customer, but not always the care due to a sick human being. And insofar as economic competition increases, so will the demand for good patient purchasing–power. This generates a true market incentive: more treatments will be given that patients want, rather than those they need. In this situation patients increasingly define what is meant by medical quality. In some cases this can make sense – one thinks of chronic illnesses and long-term care (e.g. Bekhterev´s disease, Parkinsonism or rheumatism). But in most cases it reduces the question of medical quality to one of short-term satisfaction. Satisfaction may not produce good health but it is what makes for loyal customers.

ETHICS

With the increasing commercialisation of health care even well–informed patients will find themselves in a difficult and confused situation. What is the real meaning of routine medical recommendations and information given to them in this situation? For example, 'This is not medically necessary'; or 'The risk of this intervention is in your case too high'; or 'This therapeutic intervention is not effective in your case'. Does this mean 'it is not compatible with medical knowledge and experience', or does it just mean, 'it is too expensive'? How can the patient know why the doctor makes this recommendation? Is it indeed the best therapy? Will alternative treatments not be mentioned? Do such recommendations or prescriptions really reflect the career or work–place interests of the physician, or perhaps the credit-worthiness of a private hospital, which determines its share price and dividend? Best regards from 'shareholder value'! In this case business rationality may be profitable, but it profoundly contradicts the social norms of our civilisation.[17]

This is a problem not only of practical health care, but also of 'theoretical' medicine, its research and experiments with humans. Many researchers are losing the necessary care and responsibility in their research. Patients´ rights are not sufficiently protected, due to the advanced commercialisation of medical research. Research results must be achieved quickly, and giving precise and fair information to the people or patients involved as research subjects takes time. On top of this many medical scientists take a commercial interest in the products of their clinical research. A German pharmacologist states: 'The quality of health care is threatened by the increasingly uncritical submissiveness of researchers to the interests of industrial sponsors. This is the consequence of the retreat of the state from the promotion of clinical research.'[18] One recent example among too many was the fraud committed by the stem-cell researcher Woo Suk Hwang in South Korea, in his publications on the possibility of cloning stem cells.[19] Or this headline in the journal of the German Medical Association: 'Research fraud: Every third researcher is dishonest. For the first time a US study presents numbers about the manipulation of data and inappropriate scientific behaviour. On their own admission every third researcher (33%) had committed a punishable crime in their own research during the last three years – mostly manipulations of the design, the methodology or the results of empirical studies, due to pressure of the financial sponsors.'[20]

SOLIDARITY

All these considerations lead to the conclusion that a society must have protected social sectors which are oriented to the common welfare and which cannot be entrusted to the blind power of the market, and the deregulating force of competition. We must recognise that if physicians have to work like entrepreneurs and medical institutions have to be primarily interested in profits, then the direction and orientation of health policy is wrong,. We must have specified spaces in our societies which may not be privatised or commercialised, because that will destroy the humane and social values on which our societies rest. We have to respect and sustain areas in which communication and co-operation is not commercialised, where services do not have the character of commodities. Such protected sectors extend from the way vulnerable groups are dealt with (children, the elderly, psychiatric patients, etc.), to social goals such as solidarity and equity, and vulnerable communication structures – especially those which are based on confidence, like the health worker-patient relationship. Indeed, these protected social sectors form the basis of a humane social model. We must struggle for an efficient public non-profit structure to implement this principle. Of course that is not easy. We are constantly told – even by academics – that the commercialisation process is too far advanced, that the point of no return has already been passed, that these things are subject to objective necessities which we cannot resist. But economic models are man-made constructs, not conditions of nature. And human constructs can be changed by the materialisation of new ideas.

The general characteristics of universal care are now very well known. The whole population has free access to health care and medical benefits are equal for all, regardless of ability to pay. Patients are accepted as social subjects; their individual health conditions are a social product. Health care is oriented solely to medical need and not to commercial interests. It is financed from taxes or social insurance on the basis of solidarity, and if it is funded primarily by taxes then national tax policy must be equitable. And health promotion is expanded without neglecting the cure of disease.

Elements of a universal healthcare system already exist in many countries, in developing countries as well as in the rich welfare states. The elements are not identical, because they have different histories. They confront different difficulties. They vary in what services are covered completely, covered partially, or not covered at all. But they all are based on different forms of solidarity. And it is from that – from the meaning of solidarity – that we have to see the future of health care. Solidarity was and is the alternative to neo-liberal commercialisation. Human health care is not possible without solidarity.

The concept of solidarity has a long history, which is strongly related to the history of the labour movement, to social groups which have been politically and economically oppressed. It is based on what we have in common, and not on egoistic individuals acting in the market. It means common values and common experiences: it means collective consciousness. The ability to solve problems with solidarity is a collective one. Every member of the community makes a contribution which is determined by his or her personal capabilities, on the basis of fairness. Solidarity requires a consciousness of a common interest in coping with big problems like unemployment, poverty, lack of rights, and last but not least, health care. The most powerful kind of solidarity is its organized form, with strong participation from below.

When we analyse health and sickness we come very quickly to central social, economic, political and cultural problems. In fact, the right to health is a human right. This was the implication of the UN's 'health for all' proclamation at Alma Ata in 1978. Human rights are not to be commercialised. They can't be marketised without destroying their meaning. And that means, for health in general, a political and also basic scientific principle: health is not a commodity!

NOTES

1   For example on May 11, 2005 the IMF promised the Turkish government a credit of $10 billion on condition that it reformed the social insurance system: *Frankfurter Allgemeine Zeitung*, 23 January 2006; J. G. Gottschlich, Angst vor der Privatisierung, *Dr. med Mabuse*, 154(March/April), 2005, pp. 42–44.

2   Robert Castel, *Die Metamorphosen der sozialen Frage*, Konstanz: Universitätsverlag, 2000.

3   See Josef Ackermann in *Frankfurt Allgemeine Zeitung*, 19 March 2008.

4   One of the first laws Barack Obama signed as President was one to insure 4

million more children than before against sickness. 'Obama weitet staatliche Krankenversicherung aus', *Frankfurter Allgemeine Zeitung*, 6 February 2009.

5   David Himmelstein, Steffie Woolhandler, Ida Hellander, *Bleeding the patient, The consequences of corporate health care*, Monroe: Common Courage Press, 2001.

6   Hans-Ulrich Deppe, *Zur sozialen Anatomie des Gesundheitssystems*, Frankfurt/Main:VAS-Verlag, 3rd edition, 2005, pp. 176-8.

7   Francis M. Bator, 'The anatomy of market failure', *Quarterly, Journal of Economics*, 72, 1958, pp. 351-79; see also World Bank, *Weltentwicklungsbericht 1993, Investitionen in die Gesundheit*, Washington 1993, p. 5ff.

8   OECD Health Data 1997.

9   Sachverstaendigenrat in der Konzertierten Aktion, *Special Report* 1996, Issue 246.

10   Gianfranco Domenighetti, 'Revisiting the most informed consumers of surgical services', *International Journal of Technology Association. in Health Care*, 4, 1993, p. 505-13; Norbert Schmacke, *Aerzte oder Wunderheiler?*, Opladen: Westdeutscher Verlag, 1997, p. 150.

11   Hans-Ulrich Deppe, 'Solidarität statt Komerzialisierung', in Moritz Gerhardt, Stephan Kolb et al., eds., *Medizin und Gewissen*, Frankfurt/Main: Mabuse, 2008, p. 137f.

12   Ellen Kuhlmann, '"...zwischen den Mahlsteinen". Ergebnisse einer empirischen Studie zur Verteilung knapper medizinischer Ressourcen in ausgewählten klinischen Settings', in G. Feuerstein, E. Kuhlmann, eds., *Rationierung im Gesundheitswesen*, Wiesbaden: Ullstein Medical, 1998, p. 72.

13   Hagen Kühn, 'Patient-Sein und Wirtschaftlichkeit', in *Jahrbuch für Kritische Medizin*, Hamburg: Argument, 42, 2005, pp. 8-25.

14   Rolf Schmucker, 'Gesundheit als "Dienstleistung von allgemeinem Interesse"', in Gine Elsner, Thomas Gerlinger and Klaus Stegmüller, eds., *Markt versus Solidarität*, Hamburg: VSA, 2004, pp. 181-93.

15   Thomas Gerlinger, 'European integration; the open method of coordination and the future of European health policy', in Alexis Benos, Hans-Ulrich Deppe and John Lister, eds., *Health Policy in Europe, Contemporary dilemmas and challenges*, London: Lightning Source, 2007, pp. 50-61.

16   Gerlinger, 'European Integration', p. 54.

17   Norbert Elias, *Über den Prozess der Zivilisation*, 2 Volumes, Frankfurt/Main: Suhrkamp, 1978.

18   Peter Schönhöfer, 'Missbrauch, Betrug und Verschwendung', in Hans-Ulrich Deppe and Wolfram Burkhardt, eds., *Solidarische Gesundheitspolitik*, Hamburg: VSA, 2002, p. 119.

19   'Koreanischer Klonforscher der Fälschung überführt', *Frankfurter Allgemeine Zeitung*, 24 December 2005, p. 1; 'Klonversuche komplett gefälscht', *Frankfurter Allgemeine Zeitung*, 30 December 2005, p. 1.

20   *Deutsches Ärzteblatt*, 26, 2005, p. 1475.

INEQUALITY AND HEALTH

DAVID COBURN

Social Injustice is killing people on a grand scale.
WHO[1]

In 1820 average world life expectancy was about 26 years. By 1890 it had risen to thirty years. There was rapid improvement in the 20th century – by the year 2000 global life expectancy had increased from 33 years in 1910 to nearly double that figure.[2] In 2004 average world longevity was over 65 years, about the same as life expectancy in Europe alone in 1950.[3] Much of the early improvement in life expectancy was due to declines in infant and child mortality, rather than to a general lengthening of the lifespan. Even in the years since 1960 the world's under-five mortality rate has been more than cut in half, from 198 per 1,000 live births to 83 by the year 2000.[4]

Yet general improvements have been accompanied by persistent inequalities in health which have recently increased. In every country the rich and more powerful live longer, healthier lives than do the poor. White men in the ten healthiest counties in the United States live over 15 years longer than black men in the least healthy counties.[5] In Britain in 1930-32 the mortality rate of unskilled male workers was 1.2 times higher than for professional men, and by 1991-93 the gap had widened to 2.9 times higher. The life expectancy difference between males in unskilled versus professional occupations increased from 5.4 years in 1972-76 to 7.3 years in 2002-2005.[6] The WHO Commission on the Social Determinants of Health reports that the male life expectancy in a socially deprived area of Glasgow (Calton) is 54, much less than the male life expectancy in India (62) and 28 years less than in an affluent area in Glasgow (Lenzie), only 13 kilometres away. Among the 30 OECD nations within-country inequality far outweighs between-country inequality. There are similar or even greater inequalities within non-OECD countries. The situation in Peru resembles that in other less developed nations: over 40 per cent of all child deaths in that country occur among the poorest 20 per cent of Peruvians, eight times the rate among the richest 20 per cent.[7]

Internationally, poorer nations generally, but not always, have much worse health than the wealthy nations. Japan and Sweden have the highest expected years of healthy life (Health Adjusted Life Expectancy) at about 73 years; Angola has 29 years. A child born in Swaziland is 30 times more likely to die before the age of five than a child born in Sweden; a child in Cambodia 17 times more likely to die before five than a child in Canada. A 15 year-old Canadian male has five times as much chance of reaching 60 as a male in the Russian Federation.[8] While there are general, if recently slowing, world-wide improvements in health, some regions or nations – notably sub-Saharan Africa, countries of the former Soviet Union, Iraq and North Korea – have been declining in life expectancy.[9]

In the first decade of the 21st century we are confronted with a world of seeming paradoxes in health. There are simultaneous 'epidemics' – in the richest countries epidemics of obesity, in the poorest nations, epidemics of undernutrition, disease and death. The healthiest nations, such as Sweden and Japan, enjoy increasing life expectancy and extremely low infant mortality, while the US stands near the bottom of the thirty OECD nations in infant mortality in 2004, just better than Turkey and Mexico but worse than Poland and the Slovak Republic.[10] In Russia life expectancy has actually been in decline, particularly since 1989. The life expectancy of Russian men and women was lower in 2004 than in 1965.[11]

The relationship between wealth and health, nationally and internationally, is not the only one where inequalities are important. Sex and race/ethnicity are important too. Women generally live longer than men, although experiencing greater illness, while aboriginal or native populations in colonised nations show very poor health compared to their non-aboriginal counterparts. But it is with the relation between general socio-economic status and health that this essay is primarily concerned.

The massive health problems of the poor or developing nations, alluded to above, are not due to a lack of world capacity with which to correct these. We are not living in a world of scarcity but in a world in which resources are radically maldistributed relative to need. A very minor part of the amount spent on armaments, a tiny percentage of the GNP of the richer nations, or even only a part of the wealth of the worlds 1,000 billionaires would suffice. We have the ability to do something about world poverty, disease and premature death, but we don't. When a comparatively small amount of money would help save lives yet is not spent one has to conclude that such a situation is both unjust and morally puzzling. Why isn't more done? One of the answers to that question in today's world is that until the economic crisis that was precipitated in 2007/8 the dominant political philosophy of neoliberalism has justified doing nothing, or at least doing nothing much collectively.

CAPITALISM AND NEOLIBERALISM

Contemporary health inequalities have developed within a world capitalist system with a long history. But capitalism is not unitary. It has developed through particular phases, the latest of these being global neoliberal capitalism. Contemporary capitalism also displays specific types, in the advanced nations these usually are viewed in terms of different kinds of welfare states. Despite its recent dominance, neoliberalism, based on the doctrine that economic growth solves all problems and that free markets and free trade are the best way to produce economic growth, has lost its credibility. Even before the current crisis, the 'trickle-down' theory of the benefits of capitalist growth had been decisively disproven, although powerful business interests have managed to keep it alive.

We are now in the midst of a global economic crisis and the future of capitalism itself is unclear. We may be faced with more of the same, a newly-regulated capitalism, or more radical changes. But whatever the long-term outcome, the hegemonic status of neoliberalism, the ideology and practice of the dominance of markets over society, has been seriously undermined. This particularly implies a challenge to the 'surplus' inequality produced by the pursuit of neoliberalism over and above the inevitable inequalities associated with any form of capitalism. Paradoxically, the dominance of neoliberalism and the vast inequalities it has created has led to increasing attention being paid to health and health inequalities as measures of human well-being, and a questioning of the economistic view which equates increases in GNP/capita with human betterment.

This change in the balance of class forces lies behind both national differences in health status, and the inequality in health within nations. Class mobilisation and politics are critical for health and health inequalities, because progressive social and class movements and parties are the dynamic forces pushing for improvements in the human condition, rather than simply more of everything for the rich. Improvements in human life require social struggle. Many if not most of the material benefits 'brought by capitalism' in the world today were only won after immense struggles against the powerful forces of capital seeking to prevent them.

Ironically, in view of the prominence in the literature on the social determinants of health of the idea that 'social capital', social cohesion and trust are key contributors to health, neoliberals attacked all forms of collective or state action. In their view we have to face markets only as individuals or families. But the lack of non-contractual connections amongst citizens, which follows from the reduction of all social relations to market relations, implies a generalised increase in scepticism or distrust towards others. It is thus utterly perverse that so much is now being made of the notion of 'social cohesion' and 'social capital' as means to improved health status and more inclusionary societies within the OECD and the EU, where neoliberal policies have been almost entirely anti-collectivist.

The Anglo-American nations, and particularly the United States, have been instrumental in implementing neoliberal policies directly as well as through their influence on international organisations. Yet there is change. The IMF and the World Bank have been shaken in their fundamentalist beliefs through public opposition and the failure of many of the reforms they initiated. There are glimpses of recognition of the social embeddedness of economic life. The World Bank now focuses on poverty, social capital, social infrastructures such as health and education and not simply on free-market panaceas.[12] Previous rhetoric about economies simply being engines to human improvement are now passé; economies, states and civil societies are viewed as parts of the same social formations, inextricably intertwined. Well-functioning and governed societies are as much a determinant of economic growth as economic growth is in producing improvements in human well-being. The conclusions of the WHO Commission on Macroeconomics and Health illustrate the reciprocal influence of economic growth and health.[13]

While all countries were affected by neoliberal economic globalisation the social structures of some of the more social-democratic ones were more resistant to privatisation, commoditisation and attacks on welfare than were the Anglo-American nations. A major explanation for differences in welfare regimes or between nations with differing welfare profiles is a class or class coalitional perspective. Greater working-class strength and/or upper-class weakness, and various combinations of class coalitions and degrees of class cohesion and organisation, produce stronger welfare regimes – or at least help preserve them in the face of attack.[14]

THE SOCIAL DETERMINANTS OF HEALTH

Any really serious analysis of health today starts out from the premise that health is more a product of the way we live than it is of health care. This approach began with Virchow, Engels and Chadwick who, in the 19th century, wrote about the stunting and early deaths of the working classes as produced by their horrendous living and working conditions. And, as McKeown showed, most health problems were indeed declining long before any medically efficacious remedies had been introduced.[15] The social determinants of health approach has been supported in recent years by reports of the WHO Commission on the Social Determinants of Health.

Yet one must be careful not to push the social determinants of health thesis too far. Health care is more important at some times than others, and in some nations or regions more than in others. While material social conditions may have predominated as causes of mortality until about the 1970s, after that time health care was of increasing importance in the developed nations. This is partly because the richer nations had developed a pattern of mortality in which most deaths occurred at older ages from chronic diseases. For example, medical care has probably played a significant role in the recent decline of deaths due to cardiovascular disease.[16] Nutrition, sanitary and social conditions are more crucial in poor nations. But the provision of simple primary health care such as oral rehydration therapy for infants, and immunisation, could also radically improve the health of the least healthy nations of the world. Underlying the increasing emphasis on the social determinants of health is the traditional public health conceptualisation of disease in terms of host, pathogen, environment interaction. Hence the importance of adequate nutrition and water supplies which enhance human robustness and individual resistance to disease. Health is produced by both social factors and by healthcare systems.

Not only is the incidence of disease socially conditioned, healthcare systems themselves are socially and politically determined. Even in countries where there are few if any financial barriers to getting health care the poor tend to receive less, or at least not as effective or as high quality, care than the rich. The 'inverse care' law first noted by Tudor Hart,[17] that health care is provided in inverse proportion to its need, is still the rule, although more so in nations with market-oriented systems.

Measuring health and health inequalities is not always straightforward. Many studies rely on rates of infant mortality (IM) or of life expectancy (LE). Infant mortality is assumed to more directly reflect current social conditions (conditions that for example influence the health of mothers) than does longevity. Life expectancy, especially in the developed nations characterised by a high incidence of chronic diseases, is a product of long-time exposure to various risk factors. Childhood deprivations play a substantial role in influencing later health and development, which means that a life-course perspective is important: past social conditions influence current patterns of health. Both absolute and relative health inequalities are significant. A decline in the Swedish infant mortality rate of 33 per cent would mean that one more infant per thousand would survive to one year of age. In Angola, on the other hand, the same percentage decline would refer to an absolute change from 154 infant deaths per 1,000 to 103. Two nations could have similar relative inequality in mortality between manual and non-manual workers although one nation might show twice the absolute manual mortality rate of the other.

In leaving this issue something should be added about 'socio-economic status' or SES, which is used throughout the literature as an index of the factors which make up the social determinants of health. People with high SES do indeed live longer than those with less. SES, however, is a mere ranking of people according to income, educational attainment or occupational position. It reflects standards of living generally, and because these standards are related to many different types of disease, it is a good correlate of health status.[18] But SES is itself a result of class forces. The nature of the capitalist class structure, and the outcome of class struggles, determine the extent and type of socio-economic inequalities in a given society, and socio-economic inequalities in turn shape the pattern of health – and of health care.[19] But while many theorists of the social determinants of health proclaim an interest in the basic determinants of health and health inequalities, much of their literature omits any consideration whatsoever of the political and class causes of SES and the SES-health relationship. While they speak of analysing the 'causes of the causes' of disease, they seldom go far enough up the causal chain to confront the class forces and class struggles that are ultimately determinant.

EXPLANATIONS OF HEALTH INEQUALITIES WITHIN AND BETWEEN NATIONS

A seemingly obvious explanatory factor for health improvements is economic growth, because economic growth and improvements in health show parallel trends. The per capita incomes of nations (economic level) is highly correlated with their average health status although improvements in infant mortality flatten out at higher levels of GNP per capita.[20] However, the relationship between economic growth and health is much less consistent and historically variable. The real difficulty with the economic growth argument historically, however, is that many factors co-vary with economic growth, particularly advancements in health-relevant knowledge, from understanding about water and milk contamination to more recent knowledge about the health effects of smoking and nutrition, as well as factors like administrative competence versus inefficiency, patronage or corruption. But crucial to all of these are the class struggles and social movements which help translate economic growth into improvements in human well-being.

Despite the high correlation of infant mortality and other measures of health with national income, for the most advanced nations the notion that 'national wealth is related to national health' does not hold. Taking the thirty OECD nations, the richest in the world, higher GNP per capita is unrelated to average national health indicators, although for the non–OECD countries there is a close correlation between GNP and health status. This fact, in conjunction with the universal finding that, within nations, the higher the wealth or income the higher the health, has led to a variety of hypotheses seeking to link these two diverse findings.

Explanations of health inequalities amongst the rich and amongst the poor nations may differ because the rich nations show quite different disease and mortality profiles from poor countries. In the former, infant mortality rates are low and most people die after the age of 70 from various forms of chronic disease. In the poorest nations, infant mortality is high and the mortality pattern is characterised by the effects of infectious disease at early ages, though non–communicable diseases are also important in later life. These characteristics have led to the richer nations being viewed separately from the developing nations.

The most prominent, but still contentious, contemporary hypothesis regarding health status and health differences focuses on income inequality.[21] Wilkinson has argued that the major determinant of the health of the developed nations (hence, of between nation inequalities) is not GNP/capita but rather the degree of income inequality itself. On this view hierarchy (i.e. a wide spread of socio-economic status) is related, through bio-psychosocial mechanisms, to lowered self-esteem. The influence of socio-economic hierarchy is shown, for example, by the fact that high level bureaucrats in the British Civil Service have better health than somewhat lower level managers, although the second group have ample access to adequate material conditions for good health.[22] A further social consequence of inequality from the Wilkinson perspective is lowered social capital/cohesion or trust, which itself contributes to poorer health. Wilkinson's explanation views income inequality as explaining both within-nation health inequalities (seen as an effect of the socio-economic status 'gradient') as well as the between-nation inequalities among OECD nations (seen as effects of their respective degrees of income inequality).

However, the income inequality hypothesis, while having many adherents, has been criticised on a variety of grounds. It is argued that the relationships found by Wilkinson are artifactual – if, in fact, the relationship between income and health within nations is curvilinear – any decrease in a country's income inequality would 'automatically' bring increases in average levels of health because it would improve the health of the poor more than it would decrease the health of the rich.[23] My own approach and that of Navarro, Muntaner and colleagues is that income inequality is really a proxy for many forms of social inequality which all influence health and which reflect differences in the degree to which different regions or nations provide for the well-being of their populations.[24] A broader conception of the causal sequence produces a picture of class-related structural factors which produce both elongated SES hierarchies (and many other kinds of social inequality), and worse average levels of health. Income inequality per se is important but it does not have the singular causal significance given it by Wilkinson and colleagues.

A third hypothesis, not very well explicated, implies that national differences in health and health differences within nations are due to the differential speed and spread of health-relevant knowledge, technologies and capabilities.[25] Within nations those higher in status and education are quicker and more able to adopt healthy ways of living, and have access to more health promoting resources, than those with lower status and education. This would explain, for example, not only why the obesity epidemic in the richer nations mentioned earlier is worse in some than in others, but also why within the rich nations at least it is the poorer strata, those lower in SES, who now tend to be more obese. Similarly there are historical changes in cross-national and within-nation differences in tobacco use; in the past upper classes and wealthier nations had higher smoking rates, while the opposite is now generally true. There certainly is some evidence to support the view that economic growth and health innovations, for example, will, or can be, taken advantage of more quickly by the more educated and those with greater resources, than by the poorer and less educated.

What can reconcile these perspectives is a move away from the notion of particular 'variables' or separate factors producing health and health inequalities. Instead the three hypotheses mentioned could all be accommodated within a perspective which focuses on asking what particular types of society are associated with enhanced human well-being. We are talking about different kinds of society, rather than simply those with low or high income inequality or other single 'variable' explanations.

OECD HEALTH AND HEALTH INEQUALITIES

The Thatcher and Reagan regimes in the UK and the United States, followed by similar regimes in other Anglo-American nations introduced a new fundamentalist and dogmatic brand of liberalism. These regimes and their neoliberal policies are closely tied to rapidly increasing social inequalities. Prior to the 1970s income inequality was declining in the US and the UK. However, beginning about 1968 in the US and 1977/78 in the UK, income inequality began a steep and rapid rise and both nations reached inequality levels that had not been experienced in decades.[26] There was a massive enhancement of the wealth of the rich. The increases in inequality under Thatcher in the UK were mostly halted, although not reversed, under subsequent Labour governments. A similar but even more dramatic increase in income inequality was sustained in the United States during and after the Reagan regime. In the US the lowest 60 per cent of households actually experienced a *decrease* in after-tax income between 1977 and 1999. Dooley and Prause reveal that 'American males in the 25th percentile earned less in real terms in 1997 (a year of supposedly 'good' economic times) than their 25th percentile peers did in 1967'.[27] During the same period, the incomes of the top 5 per cent of households grew by 56 per cent and those of the top 1 per cent mushroomed by 93 per cent.[28] Income inequality also increased in many, though not all, OECD nations.

However, not all countries were as neoliberal as the English-speaking nations. OECD data indicate that welfare regimes actually did what they were supposed to do, lessen poverty and inequality. Comparing nations, not only the US and the UK but also Canada and Australia show much higher income inequality than Switzerland, Germany and the Netherlands which, in turn, show higher inequality than the Scandinavian countries. [29] After the turn of the century the neoliberal nations showed higher inequality than the still significantly social-democratic nations with Gini indices ranging from .32 to .38 as compared to the social-democratic nations range of .23 to .28 (the higher the Gini the greater the inequality). The incomes ratio of the top 10 per cent to the bottom 10 per cent of the population was even more extreme, averaging about 2.9 in the social-democratic nations and 4.66 in the neoliberal countries.[30]

Not surprisingly, despite economic expansion in the 1970s and 1980s, health inequalities increased. A study showed all-cause inequalities in mortality between low and high SES areas to have risen amongst adults in the US by 50 per cent for males and 58 per cent for females from 1969 to 1998,[31] while in Britain health inequalities between occupational classes and between deprived and rich social/geographical areas at the end of the century were higher than they had been for decades.[32]

If we then examine national levels of health by directly comparing more neoliberal with the more social-democratic regimes amongst the more developed nations, we find that the neoliberal nations had poorer average levels of infant mortality for all decades from the 1960s through to the year 2005. Moreover, between 1960 and 2005 the US, the UK, Ireland and

Canada all ranked increasingly poorly relative to all the other OECD nations in respect to infant mortality. Using measures of 'de-commodification' as an indication of the degree of a country's welfare orientation, rather than welfare state type, decommodification is much more highly related to national levels of infant mortality than is GDP/capita.[33] Navarro and others have also shown that welfare measures, and health, are positively related to basic class/political institutions such as higher union membership or years of left political party power.[34]

The more Social Democratic nations thus show greater equality, less poverty and better overall health status. It does seem that there can be a 'virtuous circle' in which economic growth is actually translated, through social policy, into lowered inequalities of many kinds, and (perhaps partially because of lowered inequalities), higher average levels of health and lessened health inequalities. Even within the category of neoliberal nations the degree of market-orientation makes a difference. Studies comparing the United States and Canada, the latter with a more developed social welfare system than the former (including a public health insurance system), find that Canadians have better health status than Americans, as well as less income inequality and a weaker relationship between income inequality and health.[35]

THE NON-OECD WORLD

For studying differences in health indicators between poorer countries there are as yet no fully developed equivalents to the typology of different kinds of welfare states used in the previous section although Gough, Wood and colleagues, Moore, and Labonte and collaborators have made steps in that direction.[36] It is obvious, however, that class relations in the developing nations are different from those within OECD nations. The developing nations are much more diverse than the richer countries and show quite different political economies – many are either still mainly agrarian peasant-based economies, or are in transition from peasant to industrial societies, while others are highly industrialised. Moreover they are 'developing' in a world dominated by already developed states though market theories assume an approximately 'level playing field'. Tommy Douglas, the father of medicare in Canada, had a saying for such a situation: 'Everyone for themselves said the elephant dancing amongst the chickens'.

We mentioned earlier the huge differences in child mortality that exist between the developing and the developed world. Some of these differences are increasing, particularly in sub-Saharan Africa. In 1980 child death rates in sub-Saharan Africa were 13 times higher than in rich countries; 25 years later they were 29 times higher.[37] While some countries seem to have been successful in translating wealth into improvements across society, others have been less so. For example, despite India's significantly improved per capita GDP in recent years, some Indian states have amongst the highest child and maternal mortality rates in the world.

Categorising nations according to under-five mortality levels, Ruger and Kim found three distinct groups: 117 low under-five mortality countries, 45 with mid-level mortality and 23 with high mortality.[38] Twenty-two of the 23 countries with the highest under-five mortality were in sub-Saharan Africa (the twenty-third was Afghanistan). A similar pattern was found in adult mortality (ages 15–60). Both these patterns of inequality in mortality persisted from 1960/70 to 1990/2000. This was especially true for adult mortality, in which gaps have actually become wider, primarily because of rising mortality in sub-Saharan Africa.

Average national health levels do not reveal within-country inequalities. Out of a group of 22 low- or middle-income nations studied over a three to six-year period in the late 1990s, 14 had increased inequality by income for under-five survival rates, while eight had less.[39] Moreover, this study showed no relationship between overall national levels of improvement in health and health inequalities, suggesting that policies to reduce inequalities need to be aimed specifically at the poor.

There are similar inequalities in almost every nation. Within India the death rates for children under five in Kerala was 19 per thousand as opposed to 123 in Uttar Pradesh. Kerala also showed other positive health data, such as 80 per cent of children receiving vaccination compared to 11 per cent in Bihar.[40] It is relevant that Kerala for many years had a communist led coalition government; literacy is amongst the highest in India at 91 per cent, the state has been ranked as the least corrupt, and political participation is high. China has achieved rapidly increasing economic growth in the past two decades, yet has witnessed a slowing of improvement in average health and rapidly increasing income and health inequalities. The under-five death rate is 8 per 1000 in Shanghai and Beijing compared to 60 in Guizhou, the poorest province. The situation is similar in other world regions – ten times as many children of the poorest 20 per cent of people in Bolivia are severely under height for their age as those of the richest 20 per cent.[41]

The Structural Adjustment Policies of the IMF and similar programmes aimed at market liberalisation between and within nations created many more economic, social and health problems than they solved.[42] Extremely poor nations, dependent on the IMF for loans, had little choice but to submit to lengthy lists of IMF prescriptions for smaller government, less subsidies, including for food or basic commodities, and moves towards markets in health and health care. They often had to pay more to repay loans than on health and education combined. In some nations there was a net capital drain when debt repayments are taken into account.

It is true that most of the unhealthiest nations are also the poorest. However, there are wide disparities in health for nations at similar levels of GNP/capita. Vietnam has better infant mortality levels than Malaysia, which has over three times Vietnam's average income. Sri Lanka has better infant and adult mortality levels than both Thailand and Indonesia, which have twice Sri Lanka's income per head. Ecuador has just as good health data as the twice as rich Brazil. Costa Rica and Cuba are respectively middle income and very poor countries yet both have better adult death rates than the United States, one of the richest nations in the world. There are sometimes startling comparisons, even between the developed and the less developed world. The infant mortality rate among white people in the US is worse than Malaysia's.

What differentiates poor nations with good health from less healthy poor nations? The evidence suggests that those which retain some control over their role in the world economy are both able to profit from processes of globalisation in terms of economic growth, and better able to translate that growth into improved health. One study compared the policies and policy outcomes of Indonesia, Thailand and Malaysia during the economic crises of the late 1990s. The former two nations followed World Bank prescriptions for adjustment, including cutbacks in government spending, and had negative health outcomes. Malaysia, on the other hand, pursued its own independent policy, and the crisis had little impact on it's health status. The author of this study noted the 'importance of social safety nets and the maintenance of government expenditures in minimizing the impact of economic shocks on health'.[43] Analysis of health and health inequalities amongst non-OECD nations leads to the following conclusions: 1) even among the developing nations high GNP/capita is not a necessary condition for good average national levels of health; 2) some types of economic growth, of 'development', are better than others. Some forms of development bring general improvements in health and fewer health inequalities, while others exacerbate inequalities. All of this is not to downplay the importance of economic growth for the very poorest countries. It is to recognise that to get out of economic poverty-health traps means focusing on how higher 'human capital' can improve national income and how national wealth can actually be translated into higher human well-being and not only on economic growth.

HEALTHCARE SYSTEMS

Much of what we have noted regarding the social determinants of health also applies to health care. Neoliberal policies undermined the positive social determinants of health and also weakened those social institutions which might have buffered the negative influence on health of weakened social structures. Health care can be classed in the 'buffering category'. Whether or not nations had national health systems, as in Britain, or national health insurance schemes, as in Canada, or mixtures of public and private systems (in fact no system is entirely public, or entirely private), as in the United States and perhaps Australia, all must be considered, as Navarro has argued, as products of the differential balance of class power in these various nations.[44] Higher working-class power and weaker right-wing power means more equitable healthcare systems. Many of the poorest nations in the world, however, do not have the funds to provide even the most primitive forms of primary care without external help. In many African countries the lack of infrastructure means that even the care that does exist is difficult for the poor to access. Other countries have quite mixed healthcare systems with good health care for some and very poor for others. Even in some OECD countries out-of-pocket payments, sometimes including bribes for healthcare workers, are common and a major barrier to access for the poor.

Healthcare systems are at the confluence of powerful forces – the healthcare industry, dominant providers such as the medical professions, states, and business interests. Navarro's comments on class, referred to above, were intended as a corrective to the then prevalent idea that medicine determined everything within health care. He pointed out that medical power was contingent on the broader class structure of interests. Today, paradoxically, even within such countries as the United States, the collective financing of health care is as much in the interests of major sections of big capital as it is against it, though it contradicts key elements of neoliberal doctrines. Yet, internationally big capital, together with neoliberal international organisations, has pushed hard for the marketisation of health care in the developing world – even though the experience in the developed world shows that public systems, and perhaps single-payer systems in general, are more efficient and more effective than private systems.[45]

A prime example here is Canada's health system, contrasted with the complex mixture of mostly private 'non-systems' in the neighbouring US. US health care is more expensive, spends more money on administration, and covers only part of the population for a smaller number of procedures than does the Canadian system. But in policy-making for the developing countries these lessons were ignored. In the current crisis, a somewhat chastened IMF and World Bank are departing from their previously ideologically rigid doctrines. The very poorest nations would in any case benefit more from improved nutrition, water and hygiene than from formal health care per se.

No matter what the form of financing and organisation, however, Tudor Hart's 'inverse care law' is still in effect in both rich and poor nations. Studies in Britain and the more industrialised nations demonstrate that wealthier areas still tend to get greater funding than poor areas. Britain is in advance of most countries in policies aimed at bringing the poorest health regions closer to the national average. At the same time Britain and other nations are still being pressured to introduce 'competition' between the public and growing private systems which tend to cream the easiest and most lucrative cases from public systems. In Canada only the fervent support of the public has prevented governments from succumbing to the continual pressure from private health interests to commodify parts of the national health insurance system. Such pressure is inevitable within a capitalist system. De-commodified services, from health to education, are always in a continuous struggle to resist private takeover.

In the poorest nations, despite efforts to aim programmes at the most underprivileged, the rich continue to benefit more. In one study of 21 countries or areas within countries in 2003, the top 20 per cent of the population in income gained on average over 26 per cent of total financial subsidies provided through government health expenditures, while the lowest income quintile received less than 16 per cent.[46] There are also, predictably enough, much greater inequalities in private than in government services, with income differences in service twice as great as in the public sector. In a study of fifty developing countries the distribution of six maternal and child services such as full immunisation and medically attended delivery were all regressive, favouring the more well-off, particularly regarding attendance at childbirth. In 41 developing countries full immunisation coverage was 66 per cent in the richest quintile compared to 38 per cent in the poorest quintile.[47] For seven African nations, those most in need, the percentage of benefits of services gained by the top 20 per cent in income was five to twenty times higher than those gained by the poorest 20 per cent.[48] One researcher concluded: 'In brief, health systems are consistently inequitable, providing more and higher quality services to the well-off who need them less than the poor who are unable to obtain them'.[49] In both China and India healthcare systems were increasingly privatised after the 1980s, although both nations are now trying to remedy the resulting inequalities and lack of services. India has one of the most privatised systems in the world producing untold human suffering from disease and from the costs of health. The lack of public systems in many nations means that illness is a major cause, and not only the result, of poverty. In the meantime healthcare workers, trained at great public expense, are drawn off to work in Europe or North America. For example, 900 doctors and 2,200 nurses trained in Ghana are working in high income countries despite the fact that Ghana has only 0.92 nurses per 1,000 people while Britain, for example, has 13 times as many.[50]

CONCLUSION

We are in the midst of yet another capitalist crisis. What is to come is unknown. Capitalism means market inequality. Neoliberal capitalism means extreme and far-reaching inequalities not seen since before the Second World War. Capitalism has brought unimaginable wealth for the few but that wealth coexists with the most profound poverty, illness, disease and personal stunting for billions of the world's population.

How can there be health equality in fundamentally unequal societies? The wealth and resources are there, the equitable distribution is not. The very system which produces goods and services militates against their equitable use. But there is today a legitimation crisis touching on the core of capitalist beliefs and certainly the core of neoliberal ideology. The old certainties about economic growth leading to all good things are vanishing. When Jeffrey Sachs, one of the authors of Russia's capitalist shock therapy, writes about *The End of Poverty* and lauds the social democratic nations in *Common Wealth*, something has changed. Even the central policy discipline and the main academic legitimator of free-market capitalism, economics, cannot evade re-examining its own premises, now clearly inadequate as documented even by its most prominent international practitioners.[51]

The economic crisis from 2007 to the present had its roots in the rise of an unalloyed corporate dominance established in the 1970s and 1980s. The overwhelming predominance of business power exacerbated the tendencies within capitalism towards a huge imbalance between the immense profits and wealth of capital and the ability of the vast majority of workers to buy the goods and services produced. The 'resolution' of the crisis to date involves sacrificing the financial and social well-being of populations to save capitalism from the consequences of the dominance of capital itself.

Health reformers have been central critics of pure market capitalism and this is as true in the 21st century as it was in the 19th century, although recent critiques tend to avoid direct mention of class politics. A focus on health does lead to assessing societies, not simply by their GNP/capita but more by the degree that they improve the welfare of their citizens. And, it is in improving the human condition throughout the world that neoliberalism has proved a dreadful failure.

No one now has legitimacy in an era of widespread and profound cynicism. However, it is clearer today than previously that there are alternatives. It is in such a field of contestation that a multitude of organisations, institutions, reformers, NGOs and individuals, some affiliated with traditional class organisations, others not, focus on some facet of human health and well-being and in so doing, challenge the limitations of a system based on the exploitation of the many by the few.

NOTES

1   WHO Commission on Social Determinants of Health, *Closing the Gap in a Generation: Health Equity through Action on the Social Determinants of Health. Final Report of the Commission on Social Determinants of Health,* Geneva: World Health Organization, 2008.

2   James C. Riley, *Rising life expectancy: a global history,* New York: Cambridge University Press, 2001; R. McNamara, 'Mortality Trends', in J.A. Ross, ed., International Encylopedia of Population, Volume 2. New York: Free Press, 1982, pp. 459-61.

3   Jeroen Smits and Christiaan Manden, 'Length of life inequality around the globe', *Social Science and Medicine,* 68(6), 2009: 1114-23.

4   WHO, *The World Health Report 2006: Working Together for Health,* Geneva: WHO, 2006.

5   Michael Marmot, 'Inequalities in health', *New England Journal of Medicine,* 345(2), 12 July 2001.

6   UK Department of Health, *Tackling health inequalities: a programme for action,* London: UK Department of Health Publications, 2003, p. 7; UK Office for National Statistics, *Trends in life expectancy by social class 1972-2005,* London: UK Office for National Statistics, 2007.

7   WHO, *World Health Report 2006*; World Bank, *World Development Report 2006,* Washington: World Bank, 2006.

8   World Bank, *World Development Report 2006.*

9   Keith Moser, Vladimir Shkalnikov and David A. Leon, 'World mortality 1950-2000: divergence replaces convergence from the late 1980s', *Bulletin of the World Health Organization,* 83(3), 2005, pp. 202-9.

10   OECD, *OECD Health Data 2007,* Paris: OECD, 2007.

11   Denny Vagero, 'Health inequalities across the globe demand new global policies', *Scandinavian Journal of Public Health,* 35, 2007, pp. 113-14.

12   World Bank, *World Development Report 2006.*

13   Commission on Macroeconomics and Health, *Macroeconomics and Health: Investing in Health for Economic Development,* Geneva: WHO, 2001.

14   A. Hicks, *Social democracy and welfare capitalism,* Ithaca and London: Cornell University Press, 1999; J.S. O'Connor & G.M. Olsen, eds., *Power resources theory and the welfare state: A critical approach,* Toronto: University of Toronto

Press, 1998; D. Brady and K. Leicht, 'Party to inequality: right party power and income inequality in affluent western democracies', Luxembourg Income Studies Working Paper No. 460, 2007, available from http://www.lisproject. org.

15   T. McKeown, *Dream, mirage or nemesis*, London: Nuffield Provincial Hospitals Trust, 1976; S. Szreter, 'Rethinking McKeown: the relationship between public health and social change', *American Journal of Public Health*, 92, 5, 2002, pp. 722-25.

16   Angus Deaton, 'The great escape: a review of Robert Fogel's *The escape from hunger and premature death 1700-2100*', *Journal of Economic Literature*, XLIV, March, 2006, pp. 106-14.

17   J. Tudor Hart, 'The Inverse Care Law', *Lancet*, 97(7696), 1971, 405-12.

18   J.C. Phelan, B.G. Lin, A. Dioez-Roux, I. Kawachi and B. Levin '"Fundamental Causes" of social inequalities in mortality: a test of the theory', *Journal of Health and Social Behavior*, 45(3), 2004, pp. 265-85.

19   D. Coburn, 'Beyond the income inequality hypothesis: globalization, neoliberalism and health inequalities', *Social Science and Medicine*, 58(1), 2004, pp. 41-56; D. Coburn, 'Income inequality, social cohesion and the health status of populations: The role of neoliberalism', *Social Science and Medicine*, 51(1), 2000, 135-46.

20   Correlation of 0.87, Spearman's rank order correlation – my calculation from WHO data, 2005; S.H. Preston, 'The changing relation between mortality and level of economic development', *Population Studies*, 29(2), 1975, pp. 231-48; A. Deaton, 'Global patterns of income and health: facts, interpretations and policies', WIDER Annual Lecture. UN University World Institute for Development Economic Research, Helsinki, 2007.

21   I. Kawachi, B. Kennedy, & R.G. Wilkinson, eds., *The society and population health reader: Income inequality and health*, New York: The New Press, 1999; R.G. Wilkinson, *Unhealthy Societies: The Afflictions of Inequality*, London: Routledge, 1996.

22   Michael Marmot, 'Social determinants of health inequalities', *Lancet*, 372(9650), 2005, pp. 1099-1104.

23   G.T.H. Ellison, 'Letting the Gini out of the bottle? Challenges facing the relative income hypothesis', *Social Science and Medicine*, 54(4), 2002, pp. 561-76; H. Gravelle, 'How much of the relation between population mortality and unequal distribution of income is a statistical artifact?', *British Medical Journal (BMJ)*, 316, 23 May 1998, pp. 382-85.

24   Coburn 'Income inequality' and 'Beyond the income inequality hypothesis'.

25   D. Cutler, D.A. Deaton, A., and A. Lleras-Muney, 'The determinants of mortality', *National Bureau of Economic Research*, Working Paper no. 11963, 2006, available from http://www.nber.org; A. Deaton, 'Health, inequality and economic development', *Journal of Economic Literature*, 41(1), 2003, pp. 113-58.

26   A.B. Atkinson, 'Top incomes in the UK over the 20th century', *Journal of the Royal Statistical Society*, 168, Part 2, 2005, 325-43; Coburn 'Beyond the income inequality hypothesis'.

27   D. Dooley and J. Prause, *The social costs of underemployment: inadequate employment as disguised unemployment*, Cambridge: Cambridge University Press, 2004, p. 3.

28   J. Bernstein, L. Mishel, and C. Brocht, 'Anyway you cut it: Income inequality on the rise regardless of how it's measured', Economic Policy Institute. Briefing Paper No. 99, 2000, available from http://www.epinet.org.

29   P. Gottschalk and T.M. Smeeding, 'Empirical evidence of income inequality in industrialized countries', in A.B. Atkinson and F. Bourguignon, eds., *The handbook of income distribution, Volume 1*, Amsterdam: Elsevier, 2000; L. Kenworthy, 'Do social-welfare policies reduce poverty? A cross-national assessment', *Social Forces,* 77(3), 1999, pp. 1119-39.

30   Ginis, my calculations from OECD, *Growing Unequal? Income Distribution and Poverty in OECD Countries,* Paris: OECD, 2008.

31   G.K. Singh, and M. Siahpush, 'Increasing inequalities in all-cause and cardiovascular mortality among US adults aged 25–64 years by area socioeconomic status, 1969–1998', *International Journal of Epidemiology*, 31(3), 2002, pp. 600-13.

32   UK Department of Health, *Tackling health inequalities*.

33   Coburn, 'Beyond the income inequality hypothesis'; C. Bambra, 'Health status and the worlds of welfare', *Social Policy and Society*, 5(1), 2005, pp. 53-62.

34   H. Chung and C. Muntaner, 'Political and welfare state determinants of infant and child health indicators: an analysis of wealthy countries', *Social Science and Medicine,* 63(3), 2006, pp. 829-42; V. Navarro et al., 'The importance of the political and the social in explaining mortality differentials among the countries of the OECD, 1950-1998', *International Journal of Health Services*, 33(3), 2003, pp. 419-94; V. Navarro, and L. Shi, 'The political context of social inequalities and health', *Social Science and Medicine*, 52, 2001, pp. 481-91.

35   Nancy A. Ross and John Lynch, 'Commentary: the contingencies of income inequality and health: reflections on the Canadian experience', *International Journal of Epidemiology,* 33, 2004, pp. 318-19; N.A. Ross, et al., 'Relations between income inequality and mortality in Canada and in the United States', *BMJ*, 320(1), 2000, pp. 898-902; A. Siddiqi and C. Hertzman, 'Towards an epidemiological understanding of the effects of long-term institutional changes on population health: a case study of Canada versus the USA', *Social Science and Medicine*, 64(3), 2007, pp. 589-603.

36   G. Wood and I. Gough, 'A comparative welfare regime approach to global social policy', *World Development*, 34(10), 2006, pp. 696-712; S. Moore, 'Peripherality, income inequality, and life expectancy: revisiting the income inequality hypothesis', *International Journal of Epidemiology,* 35(3), 2006, pp. 623-32; R. Labonte and R. Torgerson, 'Interrogating globalization, health and development: towards a comprehensive framework for research, policy and political action', *Critical Public Health*, 15(2), 2005, pp. 157-79; R. Labonte, T. Schrecker, and A.Sen Gupta, *Health for Some: Death Disease and Disparity in a Globalizing World,* Toronto: Centre for Social Justice, 2005.

37   United Nations, *International cooperation at a crossroads: aid, trade and security in an unequal world,* New York: U.N. Human Development Report, 2005, p.28; M.

Garcia, G. Virati, E. Dunkelberg, 'The state of young children in sub-Saharan Africa', in M. Garcia, A. Pence and J.L. Evans, eds., *Africa's future, Africa's challenge*, Washington: World Bank, 2008.

38   J.P. Ruger and H-J. Kim, 'Global health inequalities: an international comparison', *Journal of Epidemiology and Community Health*, 60, 2006, pp. 928-36.

39   K.A. Moser, D.A. Leon and D.R. Gwatkin, 'How does progress towards the child mortality millennium development goals effect inequalities between the poorest and least poor?', *BMJ*, 331(7526), 2000, pp. 1180-82, Table 1.

40   UNDP, *UN Human Development Report 2005*, New York: UNDP, 2005, Chapter 1, page 30; R. Jeffrey, *Politics, women and well-being: how Kerala became a model*, Second Edition, New Delhi, Oxford University Press, 2001.

41   UNDP, *UN Development Report 2005*; World Bank, *World Bank Development Report 2006*.

42   Joseph Stiglitz, *Globalization and its discontents*, New York: W.W. Norton, 2006; R. Labonte, et al., *Health for Some*.

43   S. Hopkins, 'Economic stability and health status: evidence from East Asia before and after the 1990s economic crisis', *Health Policy*, 75(3), 2006, pp. 347-57.

44   V. Navarro, 'Why some countries have national health insurance, others have national health services, and the US has neither', *Social Science and Medicine*, 28(9), 1989, pp. 887-98.

45   D. Drache and T. Sullivan, eds., *Health Reform: Public Success, Private Failure*, London: Routledge, 1999; S. Woolhandler, T.Campbell, and Himmelstein, 'Costs of health care administration in the United States and Canada', *The New England Journal of Medicine*, 349(8), 21 August 2003, pp. 768-75.

46   D.R. Gwatkin, Abbas Bhulya, and Cesar G. Victora, 'Making health systems more equitable', *Lancet*, 364, 3 October 2004, pp. 1273-80; Owen O'Donnell, 'Access to health care in developing countries: breaking down demand side barriers', *Cadernos de Saude Publica*, 23(12), 2007.

47   D.R. Gwatkin, et al., 'Socio-economic differences in health, nutrition and population within developing countries: an overview', Washington: World Bank, 2007; D.R. Gwatkin, 'Health inequalities and the health of the poor: what do we know? what can we do?', *Bulletin of the World Health Organization*, 78(1), 2001; A. Wagstaff, 'Inequalities in health in developing countries: swimming against the tide', World Bank Policy Research Paper No. 2795, World Bank, Washington, 2002; D.R. Gwatkin, 'Reducing health inequalities in developing countries', in R. Detels, J. McEwan, R. Beagelhole, H. Tanaka, eds., *Oxford Textbook of Pubic Health*, Fourth Edition, London: Royal Institute of Public Health, 2004.

48   D.R. Gwatkin, 'The need for equity oriented health sector reform', *International Journal of Epidemiology*, 30, 2001, pp. 720-23.

49   O'Donnell 'Access to health care', p. 1279.

50   WHO CSDH, *Closing the Gap in a Generation*; WHO, *World Health Report 2006*.

51 Jeffrey Sachs, *The end of poverty: economic possibilities for out time,* New York: Penguin, 2005; J. Sachs, *Common-wealth: economics for a crowded planet,* New York: Penguin, 2008; J. Stiglitz, *Globalization and its discontents,* New York: N.W. Norton and Company, 2002; J. Stiglitz, *Making globalization work,* New York: N.W. Norton and Company, 2006; Peter H. Lindert, *Growing public: Social spending and economic growth since the eighteenth century,* 2 Volumes, New York: Cambridge University Press, 2004.

CERTAIN WEALTH:
ACCUMULATION IN THE HEALTH INDUSTRY

RODNEY LOEPPKY

There is growing disquiet over market incursions into the arena of health delivery and the transformation of health care into a commodity. The global health industry at the centre of this has become increasingly visible, raising critical questions about the structural integrity and survival of health systems everywhere.[1]

Despite these palpable concerns, capturing an image of the private health industry as a whole is as overwhelming as it is complicated. It is difficult to determine which social processes should or should not be included, and the blurred lines between public activity and private accumulation make strict identifications of the industry near impossible. By way of example, private social insurance funds can be non-profit, with a clear public interest, but can also be amenable to being converted into internal markets and, ultimately, entering into for-profit competition. Still, it is important not only to try to map the most important elements of this industry, but also to consider its politico–economic strategies in relation to existing public–private health system configurations. This essay contends that the health industry, while undoubtedly encouraging a uniform trend toward private accumulation of 'wealth in health', settles for pragmatic strategies of institutional adaptation that optimise its returns within existing political conditions. To the degree that expanding accumulation meets with blockages, commercial health 'providers', in particular, seek ways of harnessing prevailing political and institutional arrangements towards their most profitable ends.

COMPELLING ACCUMULATION

The health industry can be understood as a chain of accumulation processes, from health research through to service delivery, but it proves no easy task to capture these processes conceptually. The task is further complicated by the fact that 'diversity' across regions undermines homogeneous accounts of the capitalist world, meaning that any useful conceptual representation of this industry must incorporate the lessons of comparative political economy. It must, in other words, struggle with the reality that '... capitalist development is driven by encompassing competitive imperatives to adapt to the world market and the laws of accumulation, but it is also always differentiated by particular strategies of social actors, mediating institutions, and political conflicts'.[2] While it would be virtually impossible to enumerate in concrete detail the many specificities of the health industry, establishing its general tendencies is not beyond our grasp.

In this vein, the Hayekian accumulation regime that accompanied the rise of Thatcher and Reagan included a far wider conception of what counts as justifiable terrain for private profit-taking. As Richard Peet has pointed out, the onslaught of neoliberalism signalled more than just the re-adoption of unbridled liberalism – it also connoted an outright disdain for all things associated with the Keynesian state;[3] and the provision of health care *via* public channels was included among the domains targeted for dismantling, dismemberment or transformation. David Harvey's conception of 'accumulation by dispossession' captures this phenomenon as one in which hitherto existing forms association, organisation, identity and creativity are forcibly channelled into the private domain, so that value can be either siphoned off or extracted anew. In fact, in relation to health, Harvey goes so far as to say that 'the reversion of common property rights won through years of hard class struggle (the right to state pension, to welfare, to national health care) to the private domain has been one of the most egregious of all policies of dispossession pursued in the name of neo-liberal orthodoxy'.[4] There is a strong sense in which Harvey's formulation successfully captures the objectives and accomplishments of the health industry. Robust, commercially-driven research agendas; ongoing spectacular profit levels in health-related corporations; and a worldwide drive to open health delivery to private channels; all imply a forceful sweeping-up of common achievements during (especially) the post-Second-World-War period.

We can, to be sure, emphasise a feature of all parts of the health industry – the drive to accumulate. In keeping with the neoliberal turn, the industry exhibits an almost unquenchable thirst for better than average and, often, extraordinary profits. While always seeking political shelter from the vicissitudes of capitalist competition, the industry's various segments nevertheless evince a compulsion to maximise returns within a widespread shareholder culture that has come to 'bet on' health as a lead sector in the (falsely advertised) 'new economy'. Health represents a domain in which the maximisation of returns appears limitless. There is neither a ceiling for how healthy societies should be, nor a shortage of medical conditions

– real or contrived – that require diagnosis and (preferably prolonged) treatment. Health, moreover, surely must be seen as a basic human need, and is often even portrayed as a right. As such, what I have elsewhere called the production–provision–profit dynamic of the health industry occurs in a sectoral environment that is politically unique.[5] The various components of the health industry enjoy the luxury of self-identifying as social actors who are first and foremost in the business of meeting human needs, obscuring the reality of their enormous returns on investment and being able to represent these, when they are noticed, as being of secondary importance. Who, after all, can be against the pursuit of health?

There is, however, also a sense in which 'accumulation by dispossession' does not capture the subtle actions of the health industry. In its various guises, it is never the case that the industry necessarily seeks out systemic *transformation* along privatised lines. Precisely because health constitutes a terrain that is politically unique, it is also a sensitive one for which different societies exhibit varying degrees of entitlement and protectiveness with regard to publicly-arranged social programmes. While the extension and growth of the productive and service elements of the health industry has undoubtedly gone far, the degree to which this involves dispossession varies across time and geography. Processes of privatisation and corporatisation can meet bitter resistance in relation to health, and, as a result, the health industry manoeuvres very carefully when trying to assure or extend its avenues of accumulation. This side of the sector is better captured by the idea of accumulation by institutional adaptation, wherein the industry seeks to optimise its operating environment, given current and probable future circumstances. Here, institutional specificities cannot be sidestepped. As Greg Albo has put it:

> [T]he agencies of capitalist social relations act through, are constrained by, and transform institutions. Institutions are, in a very real sense, the crystallization of power relations and class struggles of specific social formations; but institutional social forms are not reducible to class relations as their very materiality in terms of rules, norms and resources are quite distinct from class actors themselves. This conception carries two important implications. The social structures and economic imperatives that constrain and condition social agents are the unintended results of these same social agents acting through institutions ... And although social agents are embedded in institutional contexts, their conflicting strategies for reproduction continually transform and reorder these institutions.[6]

Such institutional 'crystallisations' cannot be over-emphasised in relation to the health industry, because state and quasi-public organisations play sizeable intermediary roles in many aspects of the sector.

Adaptation means enabling an environment in which agents of the health industry can gain the most from existing institutional parameters, as they change over time. In instances where market competition – or some reasonable facsimile – is the objective, dismemberment or dissolution of (particularly state) institutional control over specific health spheres becomes the order of the day. However, it need not always imply erosion or dissolution of institutional formations. In fact, it can very well mean the maintenance or even expansion of these formations, particularly if the prevailing political environment ensures that the industry's best strategy is to harness existing arrangements to their advantage. This is not to say that the health industry remains passive in the face of institutional rigidities or political caprice. On the contrary, struggles are engaged in regularly on its behalf (whether by companies or, more likely, trade associations) which seek to defend or enhance private accumulation. But this remains a rather meticulous and vigilant game of 'thrust and parry', wherein agents of the industry realise that consolidating routes to accumulation can take counter-intuitive pathways. Ostensibly non-commodified mechanisms can be encouraged, because they offer the most plausible means to foster the best returns to the industry.

This pragmatism requires an attentive and ever-ready industry, prepared and able to intervene in every crevice of the institutional environment. As the industry relies heavily on the stability afforded by this environment, very little is left to political chance. Corporations, trade associations, societies for the treatment of myriad medical conditions (such as the Heart and Stroke Foundation or the American Cancer Society), and public institutions receiving substantial private funding (such as Tufts University or Scripps Medical Centre) all stand ready to advocate the interests of various parts of the industry, in order either to prevent damage to accumulation streams or strategically redesign them. To the greatest degree possible, the industry fights to firewall itself from the debilitating effects of market competition. This is not altogether surprising in any industrial sector, but the remarkable success of pragmatic institutional strategies within health place it atop the list of dynamic sectors in contemporary capitalism.

THE INDUSTRIAL CORE OF HEALTH

At the heart of accumulation by institutional adaptation stands a multifaceted health industry that remains, even through recessionary periods, highly profitable. However, while health may appear unique in its potential for unbounded commodification, there is nothing inevitable about the exploding growth witnessed in this sector over the last three decades. While the industry is subject to much evaluation on a national scale, with some cross-country comparisons in health care or the pharmaceutical industry, on a global scale data simply do not exist. That said, we can rest assured that the industry is gargantuan in scale and growing. In the United States alone, health spending – both private and public – is projected by 2014 to be in the range of $3.5 trillion, constituting 18.7 per cent of US GDP. This represents a spectacular climb from $888 billion, or 13.4 per cent of GDP, in 1993.[7] And although the United States is the most vigorous market for health spending, it is followed by other growing markets, predominantly in the OECD.[8] While worldwide health spending reached $4.5 trillion in 2006, $2 trillion was accounted for by the United States, while another $2.2 trillion came from other OECD countries.[9] This upward spending dynamic now regularly gets chalked up to (i.e. blamed on) ageing populations in the advanced industrial states, but the slow and steady growth of the latter cannot plausibly account for explosive growth in accumulation.

Rather than seeing this industry's fortunes as a mere response to populations' 'natural' demands, it is the health industry's self-expanding accumulation strategies that must be examined as candidates for the prime movers of growth. This rightfully begins with mention of research-related industrial activity, a phenomenon fostered by competitive growth strategies on the part of many states. At the centre of this frenzy has been the pharmaceutical industry, with its encompassing drive to extract value (real or imagined) from every possible source. As pharmaceutical profits took off in the early 1980s, much of it occurred in the guise of an innovation-led 'biotechnology revolution' – a 'revolution' which has, in turn, laid the basis for new industry claims to be enhancing health outcomes. The fact that biotechnology's rise was closely linked to pharmaceutical funding and business development finds virtually no recognition among industrial or academic commentators. But the reality is something different, as Koyin Chang has rightly pointed out:

> Most NBFs [new biotechnology firms] have relied on other established firms for investments. The role of established enterprises as investors in NBFs is suggested by the fact that between 1976 and 1985, they provided 56 percent of the total funds invested in NBFs. [The] dependence of NBFs on corporate partners is further illustrated by considering the role of contract R&D for two of the oldest and largest NBFs: *Genentech* and *Cetus*. Revenues from development contracts funded 70 percent of Genentech's total

R&D between 1976 and 1980. Contract R&D under-taken by Cetus accounted for 65 percent of its total R&D expenditures in 1981 ... Although not the intention of the NBF founders, the biotechnology industry, in its early years, took on the characteristics of a specialised R&D supply sector. Indeed, it could be argued that the biotechnology industry emerged as a market for R&D, with NBFs on the supply side and established chemical and pharmaceutical enterprises on the demand side.[10]

This is not to say that there was never 'entrepreneurship' chasing venture capital, but this cannot be characterised – then or now – as biotechnology's prime mover. Instead, leading pharmaceutical firms, facing a severe drought of patent-protected products, ensured the launch of myriad research-driven small firms (and continue to bolster them today) in order to fill a void in upcoming commodities that could be promoted as innovative.

Naturally, such a depiction of events runs counter to the claims of the newly minted 'biopharmaceutical' sector, where bountiful discoveries are said to be key to tomorrow's health. Indeed, the Pharmaceutical and Research Manufacturers of America (PhRMA) claims that research and development (R&D) in 'life-saving' medicines reached an astounding $65.2 billion in 2008, despite the downward economic pressures.[11] Used to justify extraordinary mark-ups in drug pricing, such R&D claims (along with a host of other claims) have been severely taken to task by critics.[12] It is very unlikely, for instance, that the costs of developing successful drugs are anywhere near the numbers declared by industry, which are mostly accepted at face value in governmental, academic and popular circles. Probably more insidious is the fact, in tune with the FDA's own regulatory reporting standards, that only a small fraction of biopharmaceutical products can be characterised as anything akin to innovative.[13] It is, however, precisely along these lines that the industry makes its most emphatic pleas for societal legitimacy and industrial support.

In the context of this investment hype, industrial advocates pursue a politically sophisticated strategy for institutional adaptation in ways that glorify their putative market objectives, all the while pursuing relative shelter from the market. The entire endeavour to save lives is subjected to a bottom line by biopharmaceutical spokespeople, holding for ransom the perceived future well-being of populations. Billy Tauzin, the CEO of PhRMA, consistently reiterates an oft-heard call from the biomedical industry: '[in] order to foster these much-needed medical breakthroughs, we must continue to pursue public policies that provide...[an] opportunity to recoup and secure the benefits of their significant investments'.[14] The Biotechnology Industry Organization (BIO) echoes this by asserting that '[b] iotechnology product development is also fraught with high risk, and the vast majority of experimental biotech products fail to ever reach the marketplace. Investors will invest in capital-intensive, long-term, and high-risk research and development endeavours only if they believe there will be a return on their investment'.[15] Importantly, this rationalisation of extraordinary market returns rarely brings with it an environment of extreme investment risk, with which biopharmaceutical protagonists always fend off critics. The extent to which these same firms seek a 'free market' remains strictly limited; accompanying the quest for remarkable profits is an equally strong imperative to control structures and procedures which affect the industry's unique context. This means, first and foremost, ensuring that public budgets are heavily tapped to provide the infrastructures needed for biomedical development. Infrastructural outlay is the first condition for an increasingly expanding biomedical sphere, dependent on a vast array of information-based (as distinct from innovative) production. In this case, accumulation by institutional adaptation manifests itself in the constant incorporation of publicly-financed spheres of R&D as a way both to force open access to mental labour and to defray corporate investment costs.

The biopharmaceutical sector forms the archetype, where the rush to capitalise on decades of research stemming from biotech firms, university laboratories and public research could not be more evident – witness the flurry of public-private contracts with the National Institutes of Health (NIH); gargantuan funding agreements between pharmaceutical and biotech firms; and waves of takeovers, buyouts, alliances and mergers. Within the US, the desire to keep feeding research with funding to back this public-private configuration continues to grow: NIH-backed research exceeded a remarkable $29 billion in 2008.[16] Even the otherwise distracted Bush Administration encouraged and endorsed a doubling of the funding for the NIH.[17] Previous to this, of course, Congress and several administrations went out of their way to validate and underwrite the execution of the Human Genome Project, an infrastructural endeavour to provide genetic cartography for the highly expectant biotechnology and pharmaceutical industries.[18] The next round of support has long since started with the progressive exploration of proteomics, an attempt to map out the vastly complex terrain of the human protein complement.

This is hardly confined to the United States, as competitive strategies on the part of industrial states abound in the arena of biopharmaceutical development. The newest and fastest growing competitor in the European context, Germany, recognised (albeit somewhat late) the potential returns to a refurbished health industry. In relation to biotechnology, the government's air of desperation suggests that the industry is, '... a decisive touchstone as to whether Germany will capture a leading international position, pushing forward in innovative fields of the future, which open new employment opportunities'.[19] The degree to which the future of economies like Germany's is seen as dependent on the expansion of health industrial possibilities could not be more marked. Germany's creation of the 'BioRegio' contest (a publicly-financed attempt to create four regional biomedical clusters) helped to usher in a new era of governmental assistance for biopharmaceutical research and development.[20] This story, of course, can be repeated for a large array of OECD and non-OECD competitors, including (but not limited to) Canada, the United Kingdom, France and India. Each programme depends on a specific and carefully balanced configuration of accumulation imperatives and socially distributed risk. In the end, biopharmaceutical capital relies on an *optimal* evasion of market principles to acquire the mental commodities that it either fails to generate or cannot afford on its own.

Just as the pursuit of 'wealth in health' cannot be confined geographically (even if its epicentre is the United States), it should also not be seen as solely attributable to biopharmaceutical actors. Other sectors seek to intensify the need for health products, not the least of which is biomedical instrumentation, including diagnostics. This industrial sector, represented most forcefully by the Advanced Medical Technology Association (AdvaMed), seeks both industrial protection (via patents) and systems of health care delivery that endorse leading-edge medical procedures and the burgeoning use of diagnostic tests. [21] The industry's revenues for 2007 were hardly trifling, at $180 billion, a 6.4 per cent increase over the previous year.[22] Moreover, the sector echoes the growing refrain of the wider health industry – that intense research and development constitutes its most important driver of success. The push for constantly enhanced biomedical instrumentation, and – more ominously – diagnostics, represents a strong contribution to the push for a rate of industrial growth that probably far exceeds any reasonable measure of patient 'need'.

AdvaMed, in fact, takes an aggressive stance vis-à-vis the opportunities to expand the utilisation of medical technologies through US trade mechanisms. Like PhRMA, it interacts with the US Trade Representative and Congress (USTR) to save more lives abroad:

> AdvaMed believes the USTR, Department of Commerce and Congress should monitor regulatory, technology assessment and

reimbursement policies in foreign health care systems and push for the creation or maintenance of transparent assessment processes and the opportunity for industry participation in decision making. We look to the Administration and Congress to actively oppose excessive regulation, government price controls, foreign reference pricing schemes, and arbitrary, across-the-board reimbursement cuts imposed on foreign medical devices and diagnostics.[23]

The industry zeros in on a range of OECD and non-OECD markets, with an eye to ridding its potential sales markets of 'unnecessary' regulation and reimbursement regimes. It decries cost control measures in Brazil, India and China, insisting in the case of the last of these that health care be included in the Strategic Economic Dialogue. Opening up such markets is certainly in the interest of AdvaMed member firms, but the real targets are still the OECD's healthcare systems, where the 'barrier' is constituted by efforts to control lucrative public spending. The industry urges the USTR to pursue EU countries (particularly Germany and France) on the issue of reimbursement and health technology assessment, insisting that each should match practice in the United States. The industry makes the claim that '[b]reakthrough products available in the United States to a majority of patients are still available to only a small fraction of eligible patients in the major European markets'.[24] More likely than unavailable, such technologies are, from the perspective of industry, simply under-purchased. Indeed, AdvaMed reveals its deeper anxieties concerning under-spending in the case of Japan, protesting the fact that the second largest healthcare market after the United States also has the lowest percentage of GDP spent on health. Here is the essence of the health industry's strategy of institutional adaptation: to the degree that exceptional spending levels within health economies can be encouraged, provider industries seek to enhance their exposure to this spending through whatever mechanism is both lucrative and politically expedient.

This brings us to the pressure point of the entire health industry: healthcare delivery. Configurations of healthcare delivery vary enormously and in response to this fact the health industry consistently makes a virtue out of necessity, operating in a shifting terrain of private and public venues, where spending is, to the greatest degree possible, always 'optimised' in capital's favour. But this optimisation of spending is deeply intertwined with political realities, including a widespread extra-economic attachment by local populations to the institutions that provide health care. This is why the specific forms these institutions take constitute the industry's most serious strategic concern. As investment in biomedical and biopharmaceutical research, design and development intensifies, and an increasing number of saleable health commodities (in both products and procedures), meet with the different manifestations of rationing, reimbursement and economisation that are inherent in healthcare delivery. Because of this, choices about how many private channels are to be involved in health care matter less in relation to 'efficiency' (as reform advocates insist) and far more in terms expandable accumulation opportunities.

The epicentre of private health care is, again, the United States, with a highly developed – and exceptionally complicated – market in healthcare financing and provision. While a substantial portion of the American population receive either Medicare or Medicaid benefits, the vast majority have their health care arranged through some form of managed care organisation or health maintenance organisation (HMO). The dynamic strength of US private health delivery should not be underestimated, and the manner in which Medicare and Medicaid consistently endure, albeit on the edge of systemic survivability, is a very strong indication of this fact. As Jacob Hacker has pointed out:

> By taking the most costly and difficult-to-insure populations out of the private insurance system, Medicare and Medicaid at once strengthened private insurance and removed much of the remaining political pressure for reform. This was not the only reason that proposals for universal health insurance failed in the 1970s and 1990s, but it did contribute to these political defeats and, more subtly, to a continuing transformation of the goals of reformers.[25]

US per capita health spending is now over $6,000, roughly double that of most other OECD countries.[26] That so much is spent on health might make it surprising that over 47 million Americans have no health insurance, if it were not for the fact that private actors underwrite the majority of coverage.[27] US health insurers have clearly opted to exclude the most vulnerable portions of the population and keep their prices high, rather than expand their market and have to set premium-reducing precedents for low-income patients. Related to this, in a market where purchasers of services and products are parcelled out, and a competitive marketplace in health is celebrated, any serious possibility of system-wide cost leverage held by financers/purchasers over providers is largely relinquished. Purchasers may be able to get costs lowered on a firm-to-firm basis, either through securing discounts on procedures or products purchased in sufficient volume or through policing individual benefits. However this has very little to do with *system-wide forms of cost-containment*, as there is no agent with enough leverage either to lower dramatically the costs of provision or to impose universal decisions about which treatments and/or products are medically *necessary*.[28] Add to this the fact that purchasers must compete for segments of the population for whom refusal to cover the 'innovative' care is not good advertising. Market competition leads to a progressively more open-ended set of transaction possibilities, in a political context in which there is no universal regulation of allowable treatments, prescriptions, price or reimbursement. As a result the politically-constituted prices of biomedical and biopharmaceutical industries are protected. A divided health care system is able to control costs only on an individual basis, patient by patient – or, more appropriately, consumer by consumer.

The particular blend of public and private healthcare provision in the United States has been in keeping with an ensemble of state policies and structures typically subordinated to market-oriented civil society. Considerable amounts of public revenue devoted to health structures are carefully routed through for-profit channels. Given the runaway costs, it would seem a logical move for policy-makers to grasp at control by turning to a publicly-oriented reorganisation of health. However, certain matters are taboo in US health politics, chief among them the issue of 'price'. In relation to the biopharmaceutical sector and health care, Sherrod Brown has appealed to congressional colleagues to reconsider their overly favourable attitude to the industry:

> [We] jump when the drug industry says jump, and whether its pediatric exclusivity, whether its PDUFA [see below], whether it's a whole host of issues. It rushes to pass legislation when the drug industry wants us to pass legislation ... This industry knows that 70 million Americans, many of them seniors, have no coverage for drugs. The uninsured have the distinction of paying the highest prices in the world with no insurance for their medicine.[29]

In this political environment moments of reform, and even expansion, of public delivery are regularly transformed into new accumulation opportunities. Despite the overwhelming popular support for universal care in the United States, the Medicare + Choice Act of 1997 and the Medicare Modernization Act of 2003 are good examples of how 'reform' is configured. The former Act tried aggressively to funnel public funds through HMOs, by contracting with them to cover Medicare for seniors. The latter Act supplies a very spotty prescription drug coverage for seniors (roughly 22 per cent of costs will be covered, according to the Congressional Budget Office), while creating incentives to process this coverage through for-profit channels, explicitly prohibiting the purchase of cheaper drugs from Canada, and disallowing any use of federal bargaining leverage to reduce drug prices.[30] Presidential and Congressional administrations of both Democratic and Republican stripes pay close attention to industrial advocates, harnessing public demand for the optimal – i.e. least offensive – financing and provision scenarios. The fanfare of the Obama Administration is very unlikely to change this, although it may occasion a rolling back of some of the previous administration's more egregious corporate hand-outs (particularly the Medicare Advantage program, in which private insurers received an extra 14 per cent on regular government reimbursement rates simply for taking on Medicare recipients).[31] Private insurers are positioning themselves to take on the remaining population who currently lack health coverage, but with a strictly controlled number of benefits. This will likely be the political trade-off for the Administration – extension of coverage to the full population, but only with 1) the preservation of market-led, segmented health financing, and 2) reduced expectations on the part of enrolees. With a firmly entrenched financing and provision configuration that privileges private over public transactions, market advocates have time on their side. To create meaningful solidarity systems requires an all-or-nothing approach, whereas accumulation by institutional adaptation involves only incremental change.[32]

There is no doubt that, in a broader international context, all service industries have generally sought to carve out greater opportunities for accumulation. The Global Services Coalition, for instance, recently told the leaders of the G-20 countries that '[r]enewed and reinforced commitments by leaders to maintain open markets and to provide enhanced opportunities for growth through further liberalisation are needed urgently'.[33] In relation to health the desire of American and European service providers to expand operations is particularly clear, and given the comparable size of the health markets in OECD states the possibilities of increased private accumulation in health delivery are substantial. The Coalition of Services Industries (CSI), representing US service firms, regrets the fact that '... health care services in many foreign countries have largely been the responsibility of the public sector. This public ownership of health care has made it difficult for U.S. private-sector health care providers to market in foreign countries'.[34] As such, it aims at '[o]btaining market access, national treatment commitments, and the right to fully own healthcare facilities in foreign markets'.[35] American style managed care has long been the US's principal health–oriented export to many countries in South America.[36] Such precedent–setting incursions into middle–income markets may form the basis for enhanced access within OECD systems in the future.

Certainly, the ongoing attempts to expand and foster bilateral and multilateral trade agreements in the areas of intellectual property (IP) and services lays the basis for altering public/private configurations in a number of countries. Elsewhere, I have referred to a TRIPs/GATS nexus within the WTO process – but applicable to a host of other trade arrangements as well – that forms the basis for expanding the accumulation potential of private US health providers in foreign markets.[37] While such agreements suggest the strong potential for incursions into the domain of health, the behaviour of the United States Trade Representative (USTR) in recent rounds of the 'Special 301' process is even more telling.[38] With trade sanctions and the threat of withdrawal from the Generalised System of Preferences to back them up, the 'Special 301' trade mechanism furnishes successive US executives – both governmental and corporate – with powerful leverage above and beyond the multilateral negotiating process. Corporations regularly consult with the USTR to use 'Special 301' on issues of intellectual property (IP) infringement, as a way to protect current and future accumulation strategies which they deem threatened by the public policies of non–US territories.[39] Utilising this leverage, PhRMA and the USTR have recently catalysed a dramatic shift in trade policy, specifically with regard to healthcare regulation and delivery.

PhRMA, like the CSI, has long protested over the public delivery of health care across the OECD world. In relation to Germany, the PhRMA decried the fact that 'physicians operate under strict budgetary controls' and that these 'create a bias away from innovative therapies that may be the most appropriate for patients. The end result is that U.S. companies are disproportionately impacted because U.S. industry is the global leader in bringing new drugs to market'.[40] Until recently, this kind of protest appeared as background noise, but the biopharmaceutical industry has now thrown its full support behind a reformulation of trade policy in this area. PhRMA's 'Special 301' submissions to the USTR now go well beyond intellectual property concerns, directly into areas associated with public delivery. PhRMA's submission requests that both Canada and Germany be listed as 'Priority Foreign Countries', the most severe of 'watch categories' under the 301 Report. These countries' ostensible IP offence has been the maintenance of 'price control' and healthcare regulation, now understood as trade barriers for innovation-based industries. [41] For example, Germany's attempts to get healthcare spending under control are said to 'distort the marketplace, limit market access for US research-based pharmaceutical companies, and deny patients the most effective medicines'.[42] The USTR's Special 301 Report reproduces this industry language, indicating a dramatic shift in government policy. The report, mandated to deal specifically with IP issues, now focuses attention on

> regulatory barriers that impede [industry's] ability to sustain the cycle of innovation and may inhibit the availability of new, ground-breaking products. These types of regulatory barriers include, for example, non-transparent administrative regimes; decision-making that lacks a scientific basis; and cumbersome and lengthy drug listing and other administrative processes.[43]

The document goes so far as to list, in detail, the regulatory barriers which Canada and Germany are said to maintain through their healthcare cost control policies. Such deliberate attempts to extend the use of a unilateral trade mechanisms are indicative of a trend set by providers to expand the basis for enhanced private accumulation outside the already swollen US market.

The degree to which stronger incursions into health markets can be successful remains an open question. The United States may represent a kind of paradigmatic private health market, but since accumulation by institutional adaptation necessarily reflects national circumstances, this means that replication of the US model is in no way guaranteed. It is hard to evaluate the extent that public/private configurations have been altered, because much depends on whether you view the question quantitatively or qualitatively. In the case of the former, Chris Holden argues that, to date, there has been a slow but steady advance of private provision in health care, most dramatically in countries in the global 'south'.[44] Here, the influence of international organisations, primarily the World Bank and International Monetary Fund, is extensive in promoting privatised care. Advances in OECD countries are, according to the data, more limited, but 'the political climate suggests that a more fundamental trend may be underway'.[45] This largely fits with advocates' expectations that managed care 'opportunities' will be greatest in southern countries where, after the United States, out-of-pocket spending and private health insurance are most prevalent. In European-style systems, by contrast, such enthusiasts argue that managed care's greatest prospects lie only in complementary forms of health coverage and provision.[46] The numbers suggest a convoluted mix of public and private provision in the OECD countries that is not apparently swinging rapidly in favour of the latter. However, a qualitative look at the kinds of restructuring that have taken place suggests at least the strong potential for more pronounced change. After all, accumulation by institutional adaptation does not require wholesale transformation – incremental 'tinkering' can, over time, maximise private actors' opportunities, even within public or quasi-public venues.

Considered more closely, one finds varying attempts within OECD countries to redesign health systems that parcel out greater autonomy to public healthcare 'trusts' or regional and local authorities. Across Europe, delivery systems are being reconfigured to maximize performance, with very little public admission that such reconfigurations may form precursors to enhanced privatisation. Much is made in health literature of the 'purchaser-provider split', and it is, no doubt, a significant warning sign that public provision is changing shape. The objective, putatively, is to create 'efficiencies' by devolving authority, and autonomy, to regional or sub-national agencies that are, in turn, responsible for leveraging better conditions from providers. The similarity to – and often direct borrowing from – managed care arrangements in the US is unmistakable. In the case of the UK's National Health System, this has been precisely the approach, both in terms of regional health financing and hospital provision.[47] Stewart Player and Colin Leys have outlined how such autonomy, combined with a strategic national orientation to involve more private provision, can be used to fragment a single-payer health system, so that private accumulation is both enhanced *and guaranteed*.[48] Far from efficiency, the result is 'a change in focus: a switch from a national to a local programme of procurement of an extended range of services from the private sector, but with the overall scale of funding unchanged, if not expanded'.[49] This trajectory is in no way limited to 'solidarity' systems (such as those of Sweden, the UK and Canada), as the case of Holland's social insurance reform makes abundantly clear. Although reform of Dutch healthcare financing and delivery has involved devolution of authority that still ostensibly protects solidarity, it is not a very radical step from decentralisation or *autonomisation* to subsequent forms of privatisation.[50] In the Dutch case,

> ... the new health insurance legislation will have a profound impact upon health care, in particular upon the concrete meaning of the concepts of solidarity and equal access, going far beyond what many expect from it. The tensions between the public function and private structure will work as a driving factor. The tension will

be resolved by a redefinition of what the public function of health insurance legislation should be.[51]

It is important to note that divisions between healthcare purchasers, whether in public, private or hybrid form, foster or ensure diminishing cost leverage and population-wide planning. This is the optimisation effect of the industry's pragmatism, wherein private providers can accumulate capital flow within the system, and those responsible for planning and purchasing retain less-than-optimal influence over either pricing or which substantive procedures and/or products are authorised for reimbursement.

The industrial core of health needs, then, to be properly seen in its entirety. The alteration of health care systems cannot be seen as a coincidental restructuring stemming merely from either a fiscal crisis of the state or an ideological rejection of welfare structures. Instead, the total purchase-provision-profit cycle must be understood as a tactical pressure-point in an industrial strategy for new and expanded avenues of accumulation. This is why, for instance, biopharmaceutical corporations invest their energies across the board, from searching out and purchasing patentable research, to ensuring the viability of products among clinical practitioners, to prying open or adapting elements of healthcare delivery for their advantage. In order for corporate and state strategies to obtain the future returns touted by industrial advocates, all elements of the industry will be expected to work in sync, minimising the effects of expenditure control and maximising the domain of health production in our lives.

REGULATORY OUTCOMES AND CERTAINTY

In the context of large societal investments in health-related research, production and delivery, the regulatory conditions surrounding health have become the subject of considerable scrutiny. As states supply infrastructural capacities to foster expanding accumulation in health, they also come under pressure to ensure that the mandate to protect citizens translates into mechanisms that '...do not constitute unnecessary barriers to trade in services', and are '...not more burdensome than necessary to ensure the quality of the service'.[52] Here, virtually all players – corporate, state and institutional-academic – are invested in a similar outcome: regulatory regimes that facilitate the production-provision-profit cycle. This gets projected as a harmony between market and civic objectives, but it is more likely that regulatory conditions are being increasingly drawn into a process whereby government oversight is harnessed (but never fully captured) to achieve increased *certainty* within an uncertain capitalist market.

While there is no space here to cover the myriad regulatory structures that relate to health across states, the US example again presents a valuable reference point. The Food and Drug Administration (FDA) promotes itself as the world's 'gold standard' for human health product review, and it is fair to say that many if not most other national agencies follow its lead.[53] Embedded in the most market-oriented system of health production and delivery in the world, the FDA nonetheless represents a curious mix of governmental mandate and corporate loyalty. While biopharmaceutical firms, along with segments of Congress, like to characterise it as a slow-moving governmental behemoth, the FDA has in fact become a finely tuned instrument of industrial legitimisation and protection that these same actors would hardly relinquish. As such, exploring the contemporary state of the FDA reveals something about the two-sided nature of accumulation by institutional adaptation, and shows how building a market can go hand-in-hand with avoiding competition.

The FDA has garnered broad appeal as a regulatory institution of public trust, particularly in relation to human health. It carries the responsibility for regulatory review of all biomedical commodities in production or circulation within the United States and should operate with a priority for public health and safety. As with all regulatory agencies, it must tackle issues of potential conflict of interest: how closely can advocates of a particular social objective (enhanced biomedical production and its profitable realisation in the market) be linked to the regulation of that same objective? In view of the heavy civic burden it bears, it would accord with common sense to find a critical distance between FDA regulators and industrial and/or state advocates. At a foundational level, however, this proves largely untrue. The Congressional oversight bodies that give life to the FDA's mandate are the same ones that have supported and bolstered the health industry in its three-decade long expansion within and beyond the American market. One result of this is a contradictory plea from policymakers and regulators alike: maintain rigorous standards for regulation while facilitating robust industrial development. Even the staunchest Congressional criticism of lax pharmaceutical regulation always stops short of challenging the 'legitimate incentives and rewards for innovative drugs and biologics'.[54]

In fact, the FDA forms one of the central arenas in which the 'fuzzy' boundary between state regulation and industrial advocacy is most evident. Increasingly, the very power source that afforded the FDA relative autonomy from the industry it regulates – its governmental funding source – is being eroded. In 1992, under enormous pressure from biopharmaceutical corporations (as well as patient advocacy groups) to step up approval times,

Congress passed the Prescription Drug User Fees Act (PDUFA). Under this legislation – subject to review every five years – corporations pay a user fee for their drugs and biologics approval applications. The legislation ensures that the funds are used only for this purpose and that certain benchmarks (set out by Congress) are met. PDUFA continues to meet with overwhelming support in Congress, heralded as the source of patient well-being, regulatory streamlining and a boon to US competitive practice. Throughout periods in which the act has been reviewed, policymakers state incessantly how obvious it is that Congress must 'ensure quick, clean, reauthorisation', and that such actions will 'guarantee patients' continued access to innovative drugs, and meet our country's gold standards of safety and efficacy'.[55] More than just a 'pet project' of Congressional members, however, the results of the PDUFA are touted by FDA officials as emblems of American competitive success. Indeed, the FDA's key criterion for evaluation of this programme is *how quickly* the agency is able to accelerate processing times. In testimony, FDA Deputy Commissioner, Lester Crawford, boasts of the link between PDUFA and industrial competition:

> We now have 8 years of data on our efforts to achieve PDUFA goals. During this period the FDA faced a total of 73 performance goals. We met or exceeded 71 of those goals. If you add procedural goals to that total, the Agency met or exceeded 86 out of 92 PDUFA goals. The result has been a dramatic reduction in product approval times. Drugs are now reviewed in the U.S. as fast or faster than anywhere in the world, without compromising the very stringent standards that Americans have come to expect. With the enactment of PDUFA, U.S. companies have overtaken their European counterparts, and now have a commanding lead in world markets. A July 2001 report found that the European share of the world pharmaceutical market fell by 10 percent over the past decade, while the U.S. market share rose by more than 10 percent.[56]

This unabashed support for accelerated approval times has met with serious criticism. While there are no existing systematic studies, strong anecdotal evidence suggests that the FDA has grown far too close to the industries that it ostensibly regulates. This has fostered an atmosphere in which safety precautions are downloaded onto physicians; extraordinary pressure is placed on drug reviewers (even the Director of the Center for Drug Evaluation and Review admitted publicly to a 'sweatshop' environment), resulting in a 'revolving door' turnover pattern; and there is a prevailing 'basic message to approve'.[57]

The results of such a 'cooperative' relationship between state and industry can be said to go well beyond the acceleration of approval times. It reaches, instead, into a range of industry-friendly policies designed to maintain or improve upon conditions for accumulation – from slow administrative reaction to failing drugs, such as Vioxx, Redux and Prozac, to lax standards on direct-to consumer advertising and post-marketing surveillance of drugs, ongoing agency-related loopholes on patent and exclusivity extensions.[58] Recently, the FDA went so far as to block the re-importation of US-produced prescription drugs from Canada. Although they had been cleared by the FDA, their brief time in Canada was used as pretence to label them 'unsafe'. This transparent move was aimed at protecting US pharmaceutical firms from their own products, which are far less expensive (often due to price regulation) outside the US market.[59] Accumulation by institutional adaptation operates here in a manner that goes beyond 'regulatory capture', a situation in which state agencies come to identify too closely with the groups they regulate. Instead, there is an interlocking dynamic of policymakers, regulatory officials, corporate players and extremely sophisticated industrial lobby groups.[60] At most, this merits occasional concern among politicians: to quote Representative Sherrod Brown again, 'when the drug industry wants us to move quickly to ensure that the FDA doesn't hold their products up from getting to the market, we move with lightning speed to do their bidding'.[61] Since the FDA is engaged in a public-private partnership to facilitate the competitive position of the US health industry, its objectives are to foster certainty and fend off destabilising threats. When it appears to industry advocates that these objectives are compromised, the reaction is swift and telling. For example, when the FDA considered invoking its authority in limited cases to require manufacturers to switch drugs from prescription to over-the-counter status, opponents argued that 'to allow such a practice would create uncertainty and unnecessarily complicate the already highly risky business of drug development. New research and development would be chilled as a result'.[62] This threat summarises the endgame in most regulatory debates related to health: any conditions that make accumulation less than optimal are said to be inherently obstructive to *innovation* and, therefore, detrimental to *quality of care* for citizens. In the end, regulatory institutions are a terrain of struggle for industrial advocates, who use threats of diminishing quality to enforce the further integration of the state and the health industry and ensure that the pursuit of generous profits in the health sector remains a worthwhile endeavour.

CONCLUSION

The corporate presence in biomedical research, treatment options and healthcare delivery assumes new forms each day, particularly in the wake of greatly augmented trade and market possibilities, actualised globally in the WTO and regional trade agreements. Human agency within such a commodified field is, of course, complicated – we are, after all, eager patients of our own volition. A profoundly difficult question emerges out of the health industry's accumulation strategy: how much health is enough? Efforts to massage increased corporate access into even tightly regulated systems means decreasing influence of structures that might otherwise have limited surges in medicalisation. In middle-income and 'northern' economies, where corporate objectives are especially intensive, populations are all too well disposed to 'acquiring health'. As the late biochemist Erwin Chargaff bluntly put it, 'we've turned into such outrageous whiners. Just as humans are not born to be rich, they're not born to be healthy. Health is nice, but it's not an argument. People live longer now, but how do they live longer? And why?'[63] For all their faults, publicly-oriented life science and health delivery systems make choices about human need that derive in some way from social consensus rather than accumulation potential, and it remains a critical social brake on our increasing desire to both medicalise and 'performance enhance'.[64]

The difficulty is that the politically pragmatic strategies of the health sector have worked ingeniously to blur the lines between private and public objectives. There is no health system, no existent combination of purchase and provision, which avoids the scenario wherein private actors make the most of public objectives. As this essay has tried to show, those who provide for health – whether through product or service – ensure that profit streams are maximised. In more solidaristic societies, we find attempts by the industry to undermine, to the extent that it is politically feasible, the mechanisms which seriously restrain growth in health spending; not necessarily aiming for system transformation, but seeking to harness existing institutions for maximised returns. In less than solidaristic systems, especially the United States, we find a vigilant effort to ensure that 'dangerous' policy precedents (such as those that would lead to general price control) are placed in check, watered down, or morphed into something more palatable. Despite all the claims about efficiencies, whether public or private, those who purchase health care are experiencing less cost leverage as a result of autonomisation, regionalisation or localisation. Meanwhile, regulatory bodies still play prominent roles, but with their objectives subtly altered, through changes in policy-making environments and/or their sources of funding. In this milieu, the push to expand health spending – to realise profit on the full array of corporate, state and institutional health-related investments – can only intensify. The fact that OECD countries, in particular, have bet on health as the growth sector of the future will mean no shortage of protagonists at all levels of this process. This is why projects of universal health care remain highly significant: as a check on medicalisation (now largely a function of commodification) and as a barrier to the health industry's strategies for maximising its accumulation potential. To the degree that universal planning – whether through highly regulated but localised systems or through single-payer systems – can be defended, the expansive imperative of the health industry can also be held at bay, for the good of citizens and patients alike.

NOTES

1   Philippe Cullet, 'Patents and medicine: the relationship between TRIPS and the human right to health', *International Affairs,* 79(1), 2003, 139-60; Sanjay Basu, 'AIDS, empire and public health behaviouralism', *International Journal of Health Services* 34, no.1 (2004), 155-67; Stine Jessen Haakonsson and Lisa Ann Richey, 'TRIPs and public health: the Doha Declaration and Africa', *Development Policy Review* 25, no.1 (2007): 71-90. Allyson Pollock, *NHS, plc: The Privatization of our Health Care,* London: Verso, 2004; Allyson Pollock and David Price, 'Rewriting the regulations: how the World Trade Organisation could accelerate privatisation in health care systems', *Lancet* 356(2000), pp. 1995-2000; Sarah Sexton, 'Trading health care away? GATS, public services and privatisation', The Cornerhouse Briefing, 23, 2001; Meri Koivusalo, 'World Trade Organisation and trade-creep in health and social policies', Occasional Paper, Globalism and Social Policy Programme, Helsinki, 1999.

2   Greg Albo, 'Contesting the "new capitalism"', in David Coates, ed., *Varieties of Capitalism, Varieties of Approaches,* Basingstoke: Palgrave Macmillan, 2005, p. 68.

3   Richard Peet, *Unholy Trinity: The IMF, World Bank and WTO,* London: Zed Books, 2003, p. 8.

4   David Harvey, *The New Imperialism,* New York: Oxford University Press, 2003, p.148

5   Rodney Loeppky, 'International restructuring, health and the advanced industrial state', *New Political Economy,* 9, no. 4 (2004): 493-514.

6   Albo, 'Contesting the "new capitalism"', p. 79.

7   Stephen Heffler et al., 'US health spending projections for 2004-14', *Health Affairs,* 23 February 2005, W5-75.

8   Sule Calikoglu, 'Trends in the distribution of health care financing across developed countries: the role of political economy of states', *International Journal of Health Services* 39, no.1, 2009: 59-83.

9   'Medical industry overview', *TheMedica* online, available from http://www.themedica.com.

10   Koyin Chang, 'The organization of the R&D intensive firm: an application to the biotechnology industry', Ph.D. dissertation, University of Kentucky, 1998, p. 17.

11   PhRMA, 'R&D spending by U.S. biopharmaceutical companies reaches record levels in 2008 despite economic challenges', Press Release, 10 March 2009, available from http://www.phrma.org.

12   See: Marcia Angell, *The Truth About Drug Companies: How They Deceive Us and What To Do About It*, New York: Random House, 2004; Merrill Goozner, *The $800 Million Pill: The Truth Behind the Cost of New Drugs*, Los Angeles: University of California Press, 2004.

13   For a recent critique on this count, see Marc-André Gagnon, 'The nature of capital in the knowledge-based economy: the case of the global pharmaceutical industry,' PhD dissertation, York University, Toronto, May, 2009; Arnold S. Relman and Marcia Angell, 'America's other drug problem: how the drug industry distorts medicine and politics', *The New Republic,* 16 December 2002, p. 30.

14   US Senate, 'Paying off generics to prevent competition with brand name drugs', Testimony of Billy Tauzin, Committee on the Judiciary, 17 January 2007.

15   US Senate, 'Patent reform: the future of American innovation', Testimony of Katherine Biberstein (on behalf of BIO), Committee on the Judiciary, 6 June 2007.

16   National Institutes of Health, *Summary of the FY 2010 President's Budget*, 7 May, 2009, available from http://officeofbudget.od.nih.gov.

17   US House, 'NIH: moving research from the bench to bedside', Committee on Energy and Health, Subcommittee on Health, 10 June 2003.

18   Rodney Loeppky, *Encoding Capital: the Political Economy of the Human Genome Project*, New York: Routledge, 2005.

19   Bundesministerium für Bildung und Forschung (BMBF), *Bundesbericht Forschung 1996*, Bonn, 1996, p. 42.

20   Dirk Dohse, 'Technology policy and the regions – the case of the BioRegio contest,' *Research Policy,* 29, 2000, p. 1113.

21   AdvaMed speaks on behalf of more than 1300 of the world's leading medical technology corporations and manufacturers of medical devices, diagnostic products and medical information systems.

22   Ernst & Young, *Pulse of the Industry: US Medical Technology Report 2008*, p. 7, available from http://www.ey.com.

23   US House, Testimony submitted for the record by the Advanced Medical Technology Association, Hearing on Trade and Globalization, Ways and Means Committee, 30 January, 2007, p. 3.

24   US House, Testimony submitted for the record by the Advanced Medical Technology Association, p. 6.

25   Jacob Hacker, *The Divided Welfare State: The Battle over Public and Private Social Benefits in the United States*, Cambridge: Cambridge University Press, 2002, p. 290.

26   Organization of Economic and Co-operation and Development, Health Data 2007, Frequently Requested Data, available from http://www.oecd.org.

27   Ida Hellander, 'The deepening crisis in US health care: a review of data, Spring 1998', *International Journal of Health Services* 38, no.4 (2008): 607.

28   Uwe E. Reinhardt, 'The predictable managed care *kvetch* on the rocky road from adolescence to adulthood', *Journal of Health Politics, Policy and Law*, Vol.24, No.5, 1999, p. 904.

29   US House, 'Reauthorization of the Prescription Drug User Fee Act', Statement of Sherrod Brown, Committee on Energy and Commerce, Subcommittee on Health, 6 March 2002.

30   See John P. Geyman, 'Privatization of Medicare: toward disentitlement and betrayal of a social contract', *International Journal of Health Servcies* 34, no.4 (2004): 573-94.

31   Reed Abelson, 'Insurers, poised for round 2', *New York Times*, 1 March 2009, section BU, p. 1.

32   Hacker, *The Divided Welfare State*, pp. 45-6.

33   Global Services Coalition, Open letter, 19 March 2009, available from http://www.uscsi.org.

34   Coalition of Service Industries (CSI), 'Response to Federal Register Notice of March 28, 2000 [FR Doc.00-7516]', p. 65, available from http://www.uscsi.org.

35   CSI, 'Response', p. 66.

36   Howard Waitzkin and Celia Iriat, 'How the US exports managed care to third-world countries', *Monthly Review* 52, no.2 (2000).

37   Rodney Loeppky, 'International restructuring, health and the advanced industrial state'.

38   'Special 301' is the name given to an annual process whereby the US government identifies countries that in its estimation deny adequate and effective protection of intellectual property rights or fair market access to American industries that rely on such protection. See Lisa Peets, Mark Young and Marney Cheek, 'Special 301', available from http://www.cov.com.

39   John Braithwaite and Peter Drahos, *Information Feudalism: Who Owns the Knowledge Economy?*, New York: New Press, 2003.

40   PhRMA, 'Germany', Submission for the National Trade Estimate Report on Foreign Trade Barriers (NTE): 2002, 17 December 2001, p. 102; similar concerns arrive in relation to France. See: PhRMA, 'France', Submission for the National Trade Estimate Report on Foreign Trade Barriers (NTE): 2002, 17 December 2001, p. 99.

41   PhRMA, 'Special 301 Submission', Appendix C, available from http://www.phrma.org.

42   PhRMA, 'Special 301 Submission', p. 16.

43   United States Trade Representative (USTR), *Special 301 Report*, p. 10, available from http://www.ustr.gov.

44   Chris Holden, 'Privatization and trade in health services: a review of the evidence,' *International Journal of Health Services* 35, no.4 (2005): 675-89.

45   Ibid., p. 685.

46   Johnathan P. Weiner, Joanna Case Famadas, Hugh R. Waters, and Dkorde Gikic, 'Managed care and private health insurance in a global context', *Journal of Health Politics, Policy and Law* 33, no.6 (2008): 107-31.
47   Allyson Pollock, *NHS, plc.*
48   Stewart Player and Colin Leys, *Confuse and Conceal: The NHS and Independent Sector Treatment Centres*, Monmouth: Merlin, 2008.
49   Ibid., pp. 109-10.
50   Hans Maarse, 'The privatization of health care in Europe: an eight-country analysis', *Journal of Health Politics, Policy and Law* 31, no.5 (2006), p. 988.
51   Hans Maarse and Yvette Bartholomée, 'A public-private analysis of the new Dutch health insurance system', *European Journal of Health Economics* 8 (2007), p. 81.
52   World Trade Organization, General Agreement on Trade in Services, article VI.4 and VI.4 (b).
53   For one such example, see Joel Lexchin, 'Drug safety and Health Canada: going, going...gone?', Canadian Centre for Policy Alternatives, April 2009.
54   US House, 'Recent developments which may impact consumer access to, and demand for pharmaceuticals', Comments of Sherrod Brown, Committee on Energy and Commerce, Subcommittee on Health, 13 June 2001.
55   US House, 'Reauthorization of the Prescription Drug User Fee Act', Statement by Chairman Michael Bilirakis, Committee on Energy and Commerce, Subcommittee on Health, 4 March 2002.
56   US House, 'Reauthorization of the Prescription Drug User Fee Act', Statement by Lester Crawford, Committee on Energy and Commerce, Subcommittee on Health, 6 March 2002.
57   See David Willman, 'How a new policy led to seven deadly drugs', *Los Angeles Times*, 20 December 2000. See also Gardiner Harris, 'At FDA, strong drug ties and Less monitoring', *New York Times*, 6 December 2004; 'Study condemns FDA's handling of safety', *New York Times*, 23 September 2006.
58   See testimony of Janet Woodcock (Director, Center for Drug Evaluation and Research) before US House, 'Recent developments which may impact consumer access to, and demand for pharmaceuticals', Committee on Energy and Commerce, Subcommittee on Health, 13 June 2001; see also John Swasy Aikin and Amie Braman, *Patient and Physician Attitudes and Behaviours Associated With DTC Promotion of Prescription Drugs*, Report for US Department of Health and Human Services, FDA and Center for Drug Evaluation and Research, November 2004.
59   Ceci Connolly, 'FDA steps up enforcement on drug imports', *The Washington Post*, 30 September 2003, p. A2.
60   This extends to the medical instrumentation industry, with a Medical Device User Fee Act (MDUFA), also highly coveted by relevant industrial actors. See: Ernst & Young, *Pulse of the Industry*, p. 23.
61   US House, 'Reauthorization of the Prescription Drug User Fee Act', Statement of Sherrod Brown.

62   US House, 'Recent developments which may impact consumer access to, and demand for pharmaceuticals', Statement of Richard Kingham, Committee on Energy and Commerce, Subcommittee on Health, 13 June 2001.

63   Jordan Mejias, 'Research always runs the risk of getting out of control', Interview with Erwin Chargaff, *Frankfurter Allgemeine Zeitung*, 4 June 2000.

64   David Amsden, 'Life: the disorder', *Salon.com*, 25 November 2005, available from http://www.salon.com.

MARKETING GLOBAL HEALTH CARE: THE PRACTICES OF BIG PHARMA

KALMAN APPLBAUM

Medicines and health care represent an ultimate arena for the application of marketing because our needs in that province of experience are deep and subject to the sort of manipulation at which marketing excels. In the United States, marketing has created an 'Overdo$ed', 'Overtreated' 'Rx Generation' (the titles of just three recent bestsellers).[1] Meanwhile, in most of the rest of the world people suffer from diseases whose incidence would be dramatically reduced if they had ready access to the medicines already in use in the west fifty years ago. The overconsumption of pharmaceuticals in affluent countries, and the degradation of health services for poor people in most other countries, are related. Critics such as Paul Farmer point out that the principal culprit in causing growing health inequality is the relinquishment of formerly public administrative responsibilities to market forces; market forces are a form of 'structural violence' that brings together opportunistic profit-taking and inept or uncaring state planners to produce a dangerous combination of international exploitation and indifference.[2] We can greatly advance our understanding of market forces by studying the powerful, organised design of 'big pharma', the world's wealthiest industry, as it confronts the world's healthcare infrastructure in an attempt to standardise and control its sources of profit.

Nineteen of the twenty top earners in the pharmaceutical industry are American or western European firms. The industry is moreover globalising and concentrating through mergers, leading to a replication and amplification of the managerial practices common to these firms. At the nucleus of these practices and the aspiration to global dominance is marketing, the conceptual tool with which expansion is conceived and enacted.

A marketing-driven focus is to be contrasted with a needs-oriented one. A needs-oriented outlook, which is what marketers claim actually organises their work, would be characterised by a firm's careful reading of the needs of consumers and the opportunities and obstacles entailed in meeting those needs. A marketing-driven outlook, by contrast, begins with an inward focus. The goal is to satisfy company requirements, the most important of which is growth at all costs. The distinction is subtle but quite real. In the case of pharmaceuticals, a needs-oriented approach would be one in which firms listen to experts – physicians, epidemiologists, pharmacologists and public health workers, as well as patients – en route to developing cures. The marketing-driven firm searches for 'unmet needs' that conform to company-defined values and which do not necessarily overlap with needs as the medical community defines them.[3]

Since the early 1990s, pharmaceutical sales have grown considerably, both in absolute volume and as a percentage of world healthcare expenditures. Estimated 2008 worldwide revenues reached US $775 billion, representing a compound annual growth rate of roughly 10 per cent per year from 1999 onwards. The steep rise in pharmaceutical spending contributes to the escalating costs of health care. Pharmaceuticals account for 18 per cent of healthcare expenditures worldwide, a percentage that has grown in double digits in recent years and which appears to conform to a general rise in the dependence of biomedicine on pharmacological interventions at least since the Second World War.[4] While just a handful of wealthy countries account for the bulk of pharmaceutical expenditures at present, emerging market regions are increasing their pharmaceutical spending rapidly.[5]

This expansion can be explained as a result of two related processes. The first is medicalisation, a term that medical anthropologists use to describe what happens when previously non-medical phenomena come to be classified in terms of illnesses, disorders or potential disorders, and thereby come under the purview of medical treatment. Strategic medicalisation, or what some writers call disease-mongering, is:

> ... the effort by pharmaceutical companies (or others with similar financial interests) to enlarge the market for a treatment by convincing people that they are sick and need medical intervention... The market for treatment gets enlarged in two ways: by narrowing the definition of health so normal experiences get labelled as pathologic, and by expanding the definition of disease to include earlier, milder, and presymptomatic forms (e.g., regarding a risk factor such as high cholesterol as a disease in itself).[6]

The second process is what João Biehl and others refer to as 'pharmaceuticalisation', the adoption by individuals and healthcare administrators of so-called 'magic bullet' solutions – meaning the use of pharmaceuticals – to treat most ailments. Strategic pharmaceuticalisation begins with drug companies seeing their products not as complementary to other forms of therapy, but in competition with them. Success is defined relative to the industry's ability to instil overconfidence in drugs, resulting in a reduction in other forms of therapy. If we see strategic medicalisation and pharmaceuticalisation as key elements in the commodification of health, we begin to perceive the managerial intentions and practices that exert the greatest force over health care today.

GLOBAL HEALTH CARE
THROUGH THE LENS OF MARKETING

As pharmaceutical expansion is global in scope, in what follows I will discuss three processes that correspond to conventional analyses of the broadening and deepening of capitalism, but with particular application to the contemporary pharmaceutical industry: (1) Seeking to expand the market for one's products by exporting to new markets, and by deepening consumption in existing ones. (2) Muscling into local healthcare policy and administration to guarantee country environments well adapted to pharmaceutical market growth. (3) Seeking to lower costs through foreign sourcing of raw materials – in this case clinical trial subjects.

Pharmaceuticalisation I: stimulating demand

Most industries have moved toward the realisation that the most profitable resource to be extracted even from poor countries is not raw materials or labour, but the readiness to consume. To capitalise on this potential, firms take two allied approaches. First, they seek to influence exchange environments (distribution channels, treatment guidelines, reimbursement policies) to enhance the flow and profitability of their drugs. Second, they invest in doctor and consumer awareness campaigns, referred to as 'education', to stimulate demand directly. Here I will point out a few features of demand stimulation in pharmaceuticals.

Medicines were traditionally thought to be inelastic goods, meaning that promotion (or lowering prices) would not lead to an appreciable expansion of consumption. No one who does not have high blood pressure, for instance, will start taking antihypertensive medicine because of a billboard advertisement, nor will people who already take it increase their dosage. Doctors prescribe these drugs to patients who require it, and we assume that doctors are informed by scientific studies, not advertisements.

This is often not true. Each link on the entire medical information chain – from research funding, scientific journal publications, FDA approval, public health therapy guidelines, product labelling, the scientific programming at medical conferences, to medical education in medical schools and clinics – is the focus of concerted persuasion campaigns. The money spent to hire prominent academic doctors ('key opinion leaders') to publicise the results of corporate-ghostwritten research at medical schools and in sponsored 'satellite symposia' at professional conferences may constitute the largest single component of marketing costs, at 20 per cent of the total. By comparison, 14 per cent is spent on advertising.[7] Some areas of medicine, such as psychiatry, have proven more vulnerable to marketing encroachment than others, but all of medicine has been deeply affected.

What this all means is that physicians rather than laypeople are the principal targets of pharmaceutical propaganda. The average physician has neither the training nor the time to evaluate the merits or veracity of scientific research reports or the claims of key opinion leaders. The industry exploits this ignorance to our collective detriment. In the meantime, the practice persists partly because most doctors discount the possibility that they are not masters of their own field of knowledge and practice. Without necessarily understanding all the ways in which private interests (including those of HMOs and insurance companies) affect medicine in the US, the public has reportedly lost much of its past trust in doctors. Ironically, this presents an opportunity for the drug industry to develop a direct relationship with consumers, who increasingly turn to sources other than their doctors for information about their health.

In other parts of the world, dismantling public health services in favour of a dependency on pharmaceutical solutions achieves the same result: a shift in the information source away from experts and into the waiting arms of pharmaceutical sales agents. Drug companies devote large resources to shaping the information we see when we search for symptoms or the name of a medical condition on the internet. Wikipedia, for example, is a prime site of pharmaceutical company manipulation.[8] The result is that many patients visit their physicians with a request for specific medicines and diagnostic tests already on their lips. At risk of estranging these patients, who in a privatised medical world are valued customers, even reluctant physicians acquiesce.

Aiding the trend towards self-diagnosis and medication is the prevalence of drugs developed to treat invisible disorders (i.e., those for which we have no symptoms) such as hypercholesterolemia or pre-diabetes, producing what Jeremy Greene describes in his book, *Prescribing by Numbers*, as 'the modern predicament of the subjectively healthy but highly medicated individual'.[9] Greene is not suggesting that the risks the drugs are used to 'manage' are fictitious. However, the continued expansion of their use depends on the ability of pharmaceutical companies to set the threshold for what is considered to be the risk of disease. Should a blood pressure reading of 140/90 be diagnosed as hypertension, or 130/80? The difference may appear negligible as regards a given individual, but for the pharmaceutical industry the difference is worth many billions of dollars. As Greene puts it, 'The diagnostic process is now as much a negotiation between the pharmaceutical industry and guideline-setting committees as it is a negotiation between doctor and patient'.[10]

For the bridge between marketing efficiencies, consumer perceptions and motivations for purchase to be completed, the abstract realm of symbolic production must also be linked to powerful, expandable emotions. Fear, and its antidote, risk reduction behaviour, has proven an ideal marketing vehicle because it permits the conversion of seemingly healthy, symptomless people into sick ones, in need of medication and constant measurement. Risk management has come to stand in for prevention, though the two are not the same. Both the risk management and the lifestyle models of pharmaceutical use call for long-term therapy.[11] This is the basis for 'blockbuster' drugs, products with annual sales of over $1 billion, which have competed successfully against the pursuit of both cures and strategies of prevention. The profits from blockbusters have come to rival those of all the other drugs combined in a pharmaceutical company's product line. In 1991 blockbusters accounted for 6 per cent of the overall pharmaceutical market. This figure tripled to 18 per cent by 1997, and in 2001 accounted for 45 per cent of the market.[12] The top ten drugs alone, constituting less than a quarter of one percent of the drugs available in a growing pharmacopeia, accounted for over $60 billion in annual sales in 2006.[13]

The industry finally claims an exclusive connection to the subjective experience of illness on grounds that it has an intimate understanding of quality-of-life issues, an aspect of the illness experience it alleges the medical profession disregards.[14] This is the segue to promulgating marketing-defined concepts of need, including risk management, lifestyle appeal, consumer choice, and a trust that the West's branded medicines are efficacious and the most advanced. Because winning over consumers entails gaining voluntary conformity from them, the challenge facing pharmaceutical marketers is how to meet human suffering on its home ground, i.e. in the subjective experience of illness, and to incorporate that into the depersonalised, privatised calculus of 'growing the market' for pharmaceuticals.

Risk management, lifestyle appeal, and consumer choice may sound quite removed from the concerns of much of the developing world: AIDS, tuberculosis, malaria, and cholera are not ordinarily targets of marketing because they are diseases suffered mainly by poor people, and/or because the drugs available to treat them are no longer on patent. However, many developing country (and increasingly affluent country) economies are typified by the coexistence of rich and poor, an inequality that extends directly to healthcare access. But developing country health budgets also increasingly face a two-tier health challenge. The indigent suffer from infectious and diarrheal diseases, malnutrition and the like, while their more affluent countrymen suffer from cardiovascular disease, cancer, allergies, depression and other 'diseases of affluence' – so called because their prevalence (and diagnosis) increase with economic prosperity.[15] As in any consumer product area, the affluent are the primary targets of marketing. However, in this case, it is public rather than personal budgets that are being accessed, and the demands of the wealthy have a way of taking precedence to those of the poor.

Pharmaceuticalisation II: policy initiative

If stimulating demand for pharmaceuticals in the wealthy nations drives the agenda for human resource extraction elsewhere, global marketing aspirations animate the campaign to influence the scientific, administrative and ethical standards by which health care is to be viewed domestically in any given locale. The ability to supply drugs to the global body, as it were, is contingent upon altering both the policies and attitudes regarding patented drugs.

Pharmaceuticalisation is promoted abroad by the lobbying efforts of PhRMA (Pharmaceutical Research and Manufacturers of America) and with the aid of industry-advocated trade mechanisms such as the ICH (International Council on Harmonisation). Pharmaceuticalisation has already had dubious effects upon public health efforts in many countries, particularly in the area of mental health. For governments facing structural adjustment and other imposed economic belt-tightening, an emphasis on pharmaceuticals appears a faster, often cheaper solution than clinical engagement and care giving. But like other neoliberal economic reforms, as a public health initiative pharmaceuticalisation also represents a giant step backwards from addressing the structural causes of disease prevalence.[16]

In his study of global health politics in Brazil, Biehl investigates the negotiation between the neoliberal state and market forces that results in the pharmaceuticalisation of public health in that country.[17] He reports on the transactions between the Brazilian government and the pharmaceutical industry in the effort to develop a biotechnology policy that would stanch the destruction being wreaked by AIDS. The Brazilian government managed both to 'challenge the patent and pricing structures of global pharmaceutical companies' and to coordinate an alliance of partners, including pharmaceutical companies, to accomplish some of its objectives.[18] Yet it is clear to Biehl how pharmaceutical companies 'engage in biopolitics, gaining legitimacy and presence in both state institutions and individual lives through drugs', and pharmaceuticalisation proceeds in Brazil as planned.[19] There may be all manner of public/private partnerships proposed and accepted by the Brazilian government, but in the end there remains a *competition* between business and government for the simple reason that many of their goals do not coincide.

This competition between business and public health goals was very evident to me in my investigation of the introduction of SSRI antidepressants in Japan in the early 2000s.[20] The elements of the ground-preparing pharmaceuticalisation programme, greatly aided by PhRMA's participation, included: (1) rhetorically accentuating the alleged deficiencies in the treatment of Japanese sufferers from mental disorders; (2) coordinating the efforts of supposedly competing firms to 'make the market'; (3) deploying transnational institutions such as ICH and patient advocacy groups to help impose global criteria for Japanese healthcare reform that served the pharmaceutical industry's interests; (4) provoking, through lobbying the Ministry of Health, Labor and Welfare, internal debates about healthcare reform and Japanese drug company competitiveness. These and related campaigns amounted to an attempt to influence an entire society's attitudes concerning treatment seeking and public provision in treating mental illness. While the putative aim of these activities was to introduce standards of global excellence to Japanese mental health care, the ulterior goal was to press for the privatisation of the pharmaceutical market so that the predominantly foreign purveyors of the new drugs would be free to install their accustomed system of marketing and pricing in the Japanese market.

Pharmaceuticalisation thus functions as a three-way bridge among the universalising assertions of biomedical science, the moral imperative to treat the world's sick, and the subjective experience of illness. The pharmaceutical industry claims privileged access to each of these domains. It boasts about how much it spends on R&D, and its enactment of clinical trials, and waves the frayed banner of twentieth century pharmacological successes, saying, 'See, we are the saviors of mankind!' This is simultaneously an ethical claim. And the industry coordinates efforts (among patient advocacy groups, for instance) to lobby public health authorities that hesitate to pay top dollar for the latest pharmaceuticals, rebuking them for withholding the fruits of progress from suffering constituents.

Resource extraction

Corporations have always sought to lower costs by searching abroad for low-cost labour and cheaper inputs for their manufacture. This was a driving motive behind colonialism. In the pharmaceutical industry, R&D costs have grown for a variety of reasons, among them the expanding uses to which clinical trials are put. For instance, a drug might be tested for many possible indications at once; if successful, this greatly expands the commercial potential of the drug. At the same time, as citizens in affluent countries have become overmedicated, they are less useful as trial subjects. Drug effects are best measured on 'treatment naïve' populations. Drug companies and their subcontractors therefore take much of their research to developing countries (and to down-and-out populations in the US[21]), where 'treatment naïve' subjects are plentiful and cheap.

Developing host countries may also be less equipped to enforce codes intended to safeguard research subjects. Contract research organisations (CROs) in such countries can often evade ethical codes. The crimes Pfizer was alleged to have committed in Nigeria when testing their drug Trovan in the 1990s are reminiscent of both colonial resource extraction and the 19th-century practice of 'exporting' inhumane labour practices abroad when they had been outlawed at home.[22] In the case of clinical trial research, the practice outlawed at home is the use of prisoner populations for drug testing.

The globalisation of clinical trials raises a number of thorny dilemmas. From a scientific standpoint, the use of research subjects in developing countries can be problematic because patients' medical histories are often incomplete. Criteria for evaluating drug effects may vary cross-culturally, a bias associated both with how local medical partners are accustomed to making diagnoses and with patient reporting habits. For drugs intended to treat neuropsychiatric conditions, for instance, the problems of cultural translation in diagnosis and results reporting can make a hash of the research.

The ethical-legal problems are more complex still. There is no clear legal precedent for foreign claimants successfully suing American or European companies when they have committed or participated in human rights violations abroad. The task of constraining pharmaceutical research subcontractors into ethical conformity has been left to the international community to deal with through such unenforceable pacts as the Helsinki Declaration, which offers guidelines for biomedical research involving human subjects. However, the existence of a universally accepted ethical code does not by itself ensure adherence to it. The translation of an ethics code into an ethics regulation is itself as tricky as any other translation of theory into practice in human society, and enforcing regulations is yet another problem.

Adriana Petryna has pointed out that the variability in the way ethical codes end up being applied in the real world (as contrasted with the prescriptive certainty of the written codes) opens up an indeterminate gap into which entire populations may fall. It is a gap that trial research companies and others can exploit.[23] And there is, moreover, no mechanism for obliging companies to make drugs affordable to the populations on whom they have been tested.

THE MISPLACED FAITH IN MARKET COMPETITION

One way of describing marketing's functional responsibility is that of bridging supply and demand – bringing into alignment the consumer's inclination to buy (broadly taken) with the corporation's requirement to sell, and overcoming structural market barriers that might inhibit the sale of one's products. In the case of pharmaceuticals, the distribution chain is especially complex because many of the intermediaries necessary to convey the product to the end user are not commercial actors, like those in the distribution channel for most other consumer products. Commercially-defined value must therefore somehow come to be equated with medical value. If the length of the supply chain is long enough, as it is for pharmaceuticals (and, of course, for global commerce generally), the work and expense of bridging supply and demand comes to overshadow those of other functions in the corporation. Marketing grows, and its habits and outlook become the focus of the corporation itself. In the pharmaceutical industry, we can point to the rise of blockbuster drugs two decades ago as the moment when the traditional research orientation of the large drug companies became completely subordinated to marketing.[24]

It should therefore not be surprising to learn that the medical merits of blockbuster drugs are mostly unremarkable. Merrill Goozner says, 'Three out of every four drug applications involve drugs that either replicated the action of medicines already on the market or were new formulations that at best added minor conveniences for patients and doctors'.[25] A 2006 US Government Accountability Office Report to Congress stated, 'Innovation in the pharmaceutical industry has become stagnant'.[26] Industry commentators are likewise cognisant of this decline in innovation and are fearful for the long-term profitability of pharmaceutical companies, a subject I will return to below.

The corollary of the scientifically uninspired quest for blockbusters is that marketing budgets have overtaken those of research and development (R&D). Marc-André Gagnon and Joel Lexchin conclude that the US pharma-ceutical industry spends nearly twice as much on marketing as on

R&D.[27] My research suggests that this figure must be revised sharply upwards because much of what is classified as R&D spending (including competitive drug trials, publication planning, and post-marketing surveys) is devoted to efforts to improve market share or to maintain hold on the profits associated with impending patent expiries. These can be labelled 'adjunct-to-marketing' R&D as opposed to 'exploratory' R&D activities. Together with 'me-too' drug research (replicating existing drugs with minor variations), adjunct-to-marketing R&D greatly overshadows the conduct of exploratory science in all the major pharmaceutical companies. Indeed, quibbling over the relative investment numbers of marketing vs. R&D may be beside the point, because realistically, the two have already been integrated under the direction of marketing.[28]

While the public seems not to question the notion that any product that succeeds in the market must be innovative, the reality is that the most successful pharmaceutical products today bear the mark not of scientific innovation but of effective marketing. Pfizer's Lipitor, for instance, was the sixth statin (cholesterol-lowering medication) on the market, but with an estimated $1.3 billion invested by Pfizer in 2002 alone (*one hundred* times the health budget for Haiti in the same year[29]) to increase the public's awareness of the dangers of hypercholesteremia, the entire statins market enjoyed double digit growth for half a decade.[30] Sales of Lipitor topped $14.3 billion in 2006. Awareness campaigns create a multiplier effect in health care; increased demand stimulates even more demand. This is one important cause of the spiralling costs of health care in markets such as the US where direct-to-consumer advertising is legal and widely employed.

Competition has become the primary focus for companies, and its yields are often not innovative products focused on consumer needs, but products whose virtue is that they bear differentiating characteristics from those marketed by other companies. A crowded ecology of competitors in the market, all of whom share comparable access to technology, managerial resources and methods for investigating the consumer's unmet needs, has brought about a competitor-directedness that is an inversion of the professed marketing goal to 'create, communicate, and deliver value to customers'.[31] The search for 'breakthrough' products is replaced by a 'structural hole' logic of unmet need-seeking that is as well satisfied by meaningless product/ brand differentiation as by real invention.

In this way, competition in the pharmaceutical industry has come to resemble brand-based rivalries in the 'fast moving consumer goods' (FMCG) industries such as toiletries, packaged foods and cosmetics. In fact, there is a rallying cry among pharmaceutical industry consultants that to maintain its profits the industry needs to emulate FMCGs. Thereby, the same inane and useless competition-borne innovation visible in the multi-billion dollar rivalrous extravaganza of 'the cola wars' comes to predominate also in the pharmaceutical industry. The 'statin wars', which is how the advertising-heavy rivalry among me-too cholesterol-lowering medications has been described, is the pharmaceutical equivalent to the cola wars. What comes to matter more than competition for drug innovation is brand distinctiveness, or 'brand value'. Brands are the perfect or pure example of marketing value as distinct from other more objective forms of value, in so far as a brand's importance lies entirely in consumer perceptions, and not in any tangible benefits of the product itself. If what current industry leaders say is an accurate barometer the pharmaceutical future portends more and not less emphasis on brands and marketing-based consumer segmentation.

There is another consequential attribute of industrial competition particular to the pharmaceutical industry because of the way it brings its goods to end-users. As pharmaceutical companies seek to broaden their marketplace to include new and ever larger client populations, the definition of who is to be regarded as a competitor has come to mean more than other firms offering similar products. The competition now includes regulators, payers, providers, patient-consumers and anyone else who poses an obstacle to successful sales. The underlying conception that drives this practice can be found in 'distribution channel management', in which the principle is that one key player, known to marketers as the 'channel captain', must control the chain from manufacturer to consumer.[32] In this respect, marketing authorises a predatory expansion that, by treating all publics as competitors to be wooed, subdued and incorporated into collaboration, often against their own interests, crowds out the possibility of true service and innovation being delivered. Just as the engagement with industrial competitors can be agonistic and secretive, if sometimes collaborative, the engagement with consumers and intermediaries en route to reaching them has also become covertly agonistic and evasive, even as the language used to describe these relationships is dipped in honeyed words such as 'trust', 'shared decision-making', 'value co-creation', and the like.

Finally, as suggested by the Japanese case cited earlier, competition between firms does not preclude oligopolistic collaboration within the industry. For physicians as for the public, the existence of several competing pharmaceutical companies serves as a specious guarantee that the race to a cure is genuine and unbiased, while also appearing to function as a bulwark against monopolistic power. However, as the perceived risk associated with competition from external stakeholders has grown, pharmaceutical companies have taken similar approaches to remove obstacles facing them in the marketplace, and the industry has become an arena in which outcomes are no longer the result of salutary rivalry with other firms, bearing the fruit of inevitably unpredictable but always innovative and progressively more affordable results. True competition and its purported benefits are often replaced by a form of intrinsic collaboration that has developed between corporations, a 'collaborate with your competitors – and win'[33] cartelisation that renders the commercial world an environment reliable for profit-taking. Sometimes the collective action results from the competitive, homogeneous field-effect of several firms simultaneously backing comparable products through corresponding marketing channels; sometimes these firms actually work in concert to establish the groundwork – the trade structures – for future sales, which will eventually proceed on a more purely competitive basis. As reported in my research on the new SSRI-class antidepressants in Japan: 'In the words of a manager at one of the pharmaceutical companies in question, "It takes a whole industry to make a market. . . . It's going to take all of us".'[34]

The work of an industry trade group such as PhRMA – whose worldwide mission is 'to conduct effective advocacy for public policies that encourage discovery of important new medicines for patients by pharmaceutical/ biotechnology research companies'[35] – produces a pattern of collaborative alliances among putative competitors that can be called 'competitive integration', and is a force as formidable as vertical integration.

EMERGING MARKETS AND MASS 'NICHEBUSTERS'

Many industry pundits express concern over the prospect of shrinking profits as blockbusters go off patent and few new drugs promising high profits are in the pipeline. This alarm may be premature. The recent proposal to medicate children for high cholesterol is an example of blockbuster extension with imminent fulfillment. On 7 July 2008 the *New York Times* reported: 'The nation's pediatricians are recommending wider cholesterol screening for children and more aggressive use of cholesterol-lowering drugs starting as early as the age of 8 in hopes of preventing adult heart problems.'[36] Long before parents are educated about good childhood nutritional practices, before funds are redirected into schools for improved physical education programmes, and certainly before the long-term effects of the use of statins on the young are understood, one might hazard the prediction that many American children will be placed on specially-patented cholesterol-lowering drugs.[37]

Nevertheless, there are two post-blockbuster era developments on the horizon. One is the rush to work out business plans in emerging markets. The so-called 'pharmerging countries' of Brazil, Russia, India and China are the current targets, because of their size and because of the rise of a globally affluent segment in each of them that can become profitable over-consumers of lifestyle and risk management medicines, i.e. mainstream blockbusters. Second, many industry executives are preparing for the age of 'personalised medicines', which are therapies targeted at specific individual disease profiles. The good news thus far about personalised medicines comes from their projected tendency to concentrate on diseases such as cancer rather than, say, erectile dysfunction or 'restless leg syndrome'. The bad news is that unchecked testing for disease markers will usher in a new wave of medicalisation that will contribute to our anxieties and to industry profits in equal proportion. In addition, the biotech industry, on which we are relying for discoveries, has a poor track record for internally-generated discoveries.[38]

Where there are objective cures, there is less ambiguity for the marketing professional to exploit. In the meantime, the pharmaceutical industry is preparing the way for a 'mass customisation' era of personalised medicine along marketing lines. *Next Generation Pharmaceutical*, a trade magazine, reports:

> Analyst Datamonitor, in its recent report From Blockbuster to Nichebuster, concludes that niche therapies will drive future drugs growth and incentivize R&D investment. Dependence on blockbuster-generated revenue is set to fall from 2004-2010 according to the report, as the industry turns to a 'nichebuster' strategy, utilizing increased licensing activity, R&D collaborations and small-scale M&A [merger and acquisition] deals to harness innovation and provide access to niche markets with a high unmet need. The shift into niche markets is helping drive a more personalized approach to therapy. Central to the development of the nichebuster model is the raised importance of personalized therapies, which is being driven by increased used of diagnostics. This trend is helping to clarify market segmentation and will boost the size of the total drug industry.[39]

Placing one's ear to the ground of industry conferences and trade publications, one can see the anticipated direction of personalised medicine: More integration of marketing and R&D,[40] which positions segmentation research as a precursor to more marketing-driven assessments of need; more diagnostic tests and strategic medicalisation; more industry consolidation (for example, to incorporate test-equipment firms); and the consequent expansion of the yawning chasm between those who have access and insurance coverage and those who do not.

REDEFINING VALUE IN HEALTH?

Any discussion aimed at realigning existing arrangements, much less granting oversight responsibility to governments, will be denounced by free market devotees as meddling in the private sector. Nevertheless, the point has been reached where neither the interests of public health nor the private consumer/ patient is being served by an industry that has, formally or otherwise, been entrusted to deliver a significant portion of our health treatments.

Distribution and consumption of pharmaceuticals are spread throughout the world. Discovery and dissemination, however, are highly concentrated in the West. Marketing-drivenness is entrenched at the core of the industry. No casual reform will root it out. Public health infrastructures around the world are burdened by the expense of drugs they may be obliged to purchase at patent-protected prices. Many lives have been sacrificed to the specious justification that firms must protect their profits, or they will be unable to continue the research necessary to discover new cures. Partnerships with drug companies aimed at reducing this burden, or even at cultivating domestic drug industries, may contribute to rather than hold in check the global marketing-driven juggernaut.

Journalists, academic researchers, and at last lawmakers are pressing the pharmaceutical industry to reform. In response, there is both retrenchment and apparent compromise. Retrenchment means propaganda to convince the public that the industry's priority is to heal the world, not make a profit from it. 'Industry branding', so called, is one such collective effort (and another instance of industry-wide collaboration rather than competition). Compromise takes two forms. One is image-boosting giveaways of free drugs and similar programmes designed to demonstrate good corporate citizenship. Drug giveaways have recently gained popularity as a means to improve corporate images in Europe and America, where the drug industry's reputation is said to be lower than that of the oil industry and just above that of tobacco.

In an enlightening paper that discusses Novartis Corporation's wrangle with the Indian government and citizen groups over the pricing of its cancer drug Glivec, Stefan Ecks takes a strong anti-market stance worth quoting in full:

> [G]lobal corporate citizenship is not a brake on free-wheeling capitalism, but rather a strategy of extending and accelerating it by new means. Different from what Bourdieu might have predicted, GCC is not 'a programme for destroying collective structures which may impede pure market logic', but a programme aimed at fostering collective structures that enhance profitability, such as pro-corporate patient activism. It does not destroy social bonds to give free rein to capitalism in all spheres of life, but it creates new social bonds to distract from less obvious market mechanisms... I think it would be more ethical by corporations to tone down the claim of being a 'good citizen' and to state in simple capitalist terms why they are doing what they are doing. If medicines such as Glivec are not 'free gifts' but part of a global pricing strategy, this should not be disguised through a rhetoric of good citizenship.[41]

The second apparent compromise follows the same masking pattern in a different way. This is deployment of what are called 'value co-creation' efforts, which is a putative attempt to include consumers in the design and marketing process for new pharmaceutical products. The up-to-date marketer is encouraged to regard value not as something created inside a company and then sold to outside constituents, i.e., consumers. Rather, value co-creation, according to marketing professors C. K. Prahalad and Venkat Ramaswamy, occurs in the interaction between company and consumer, 'Co-creation is about joint creation of value by the company and the customer'.[42] In light of the pharmaceutical trends described in this essay, we might prefer to view this new managerial buzzword for creating value as a source of 'productive consumption', to add a third sense to Marx's explanation of that expression in his *Grundrisse*.[43]

In a recent study of the pharmaceutical industry's attempts to enhance 'patient lifetime value' by improving compliance rates in drug therapies through a value co-creation campaign operating under the name 'shared decision-making', I concluded: 'The marketer's approach to shared decision-making regards the consumer's private considerations and behaviors as objects of intervention. The marketer is a *shareholder* in the consumer, not a healer.'[44] For as long as value continues to rest in something controlled ultimately by the producer of that value, 'value co-creation' remains only a camouflage for marketing-driven aspirations.

The most entrenched barriers to pharmaceutical company expansion, particularly outside the privatised United States, are the guardians of public health. Public health authorities control the approval and reimbursement evaluations for new drugs. If a national health bureaucracy or ministry of health somewhere determines that a company's patented drug is worth five cents instead of five dollars a pill, the effect on profitability is exactly as it seems. This predicament pertains to the publicly-insured portion of private healthcare markets as well, meaning that in the US, Medicare, Medicaid or the Veterans' Administration must be persuaded to adopt a high value attitude towards one's drug.

Thus confidence in the market mechanism is possible only if no discussion of power in the relation between public and private authority over health care and its provisioning is entertained. I believe there to be an inherent and unbridgeable gap between the respective goals and principles behind the two – a 'fundamental conflict between what is just and what is profitable'.[45] But a *de facto* overlap between the two spheres has emerged in institutional, resource and managerial dimensions, an overlap that has been embraced in the belief that combined, the two systems, public and private, can avail themselves of the best practices of the other for an enhanced outcome.

As a result the managerial techniques and outlooks of private industry have been widely adopted by public sector providers. Under the sway of managerial models, private non-profit providers, non-governmental organisations, foundations, governments and all manner of other social sector institutions have come to conceive of themselves as *strategic* enterprises operating in a *competitive* environment. In short, public sector administrators have been convinced to *think like a business*. They have become goal- rather than process-oriented and they have come to measure their success by market-oriented criteria of return on investment ('ROI') and customer satisfaction. The exchange of personnel and resources across public/private institutions further blurs the distinction between the two. The question thus becomes not whether we are speaking of private vs. public health care, but whether any given health-providing organisation enjoys the independence that will allow it to be devoted to the public good without substantial interference from ROI criteria, and whether it can deploy non-business- oriented governance and service models in its work.

NOTES

1   John Abramson, *Overdo$ed America: The Broken Promise of American Medicine*, New York: Harper Collins, 2004; Shannon Brownlee, *Overtreated: Why Too Much Medicine is Making us Sicker and Poorer*, New York: Bloomsbury USA, 2007; Greg Critser, *Generation Rx: How Prescription Drugs are Altering American Lives, Minds, and Bodies*, New York: Houghton Mifflin, 2005.

2   Paul Farmer, *Pathologies of Power: Health, Human Rights, and the New War on the Poor*, Berkeley: University of California Press, 2003.

3   Kalman Applbaum, *The Marketing Era: From Professional Practice to Global Provisioning*, New York: Routledge, 2004; David Healy, *Mania: A Short History of Bipolar Disorder*, Baltimore: Johns Hopkins University Press, 2008.

4   We can learn much from a commercial and geographical breakdown of these numbers, such as that generics comprise about 7 per cent of the market (but of growing importance in terms of sales volume) or that the US market accounts for about half of the world's pharmaceutical spending. There is insufficient space to explore these facts here.

5   OECD, *Pharmaceutical Pricing Policies in a Global Market*, Paris: OECD, 2008.

6   Steven Woloshin and Lisa M. Schwartz, 'Giving legs to restless legs: a case study of how the media helps make people sick', *PLoS Medicine* 3(4), 2006: p. e170. See also Ray Moynihan and Alan Cassels, *Selling Sickness: How the World's Biggest Pharmaceutical Companies are Turning Us All Into Patients*, New York: Nation Books, 2005.

7   Francoise Simon and Philip Kotler, *Building Global Biobrands: Taking Biotechnology to Market*, New York: Free Press, 2003, p. 147.

8   Mikkel Borch-Jacobsen, 'L'industrie pharmaceutique manipule Wikipédia,' *Rue89*, 7 April 2009, available from http://www.rue89.com. Jeffrey Light, 'Abbott Laboratories deletes safety concerns from Web', *Patients not Patents*, available from http://www.PatientsNotPatents.org.

9   Jeremy Greene, *Prescribing by Numbers: Drugs and the Definition of Disease*, Baltimore: Johns Hopkins University Press, 2007, p. viii.

10   Ibid., p. 219.

11   For a discussion of lifestyle drugs, see Kalman Applbaum, 'Pharmaceutical Marketing and the Invention of the Medical Consumer', *PLoS Med*, 3(4), 2006, p. e189.

12   http://www.mcareol.com/mcolfree/mcolfre1/visiongain/blockbuster.htm.

13   This estimate is based upon reports published by IMS Health and available at http://www.imshealth.com.

14   Annemarie Mol, *The Logic of Care: Health and the Problem of Patient Choice*, New York: Routledge, 2007.

15   M. Ezzati, S. Vander Hoorn, C.M.M. Lawes, R. Leach, W.P.T. James, 'Rethinking the "diseases of affluence" paradigm: global patterns of nutritional risks in relation to economic development.' *PLoS Medicine*, 2(5), 2008, p. e133.

16   Nguyen Vinh-Kim and Karine Peschard, 'Anthropology, inequality and disease: a review', *Annual Review of Anthropology*, 32, 2003, pp. 447-74.

17   João Biehl, 'Pharmaceuticalization: AIDS treatment and global health politics', *Anthropological Quarterly*, 80(4), 2007, p. 1085.

18   Ibid., p. 1102.

19   Ibid., p. 1093.

20   Kalman Applbaum, 'Educating for global mental health: American pharmaceutical companies and the adoption of SSRIs in Japan,' in A. Petryna,

A. Lakoff and A. Kleinman, eds., *Pharmaceuticals and Globalization: Ethics, Markets, Practices*, Durham: Duke University Press, 2006, pp. 85-111.

21 Carl Elliott and Roberto Abadie, 'Exploiting a research underclass in phase 1 clinical trials', *New England Journal of Medicine*, 358(22), 29 May 2008.

22 Joe Stephens, 'Panel faults Pfizer in '96 clinical trial in Nigeria', *Washington Post,* 7 May 2006.

23 Adriana Petryna, 'Ethical variability: drug development and globalizing clinical trials', *American Ethnologist,* 32(2), 2005, pp. 191-2.

24 Kalman Applbaum, 'Broadening the marketing concept: service to humanity or privatization of the public good?', in D. Zwick and J. Cayla, eds., *Inside Marketing*, Oxford: Oxford University Press, in press.

25 Merrill Goozner, 'GAO: drug innovation lags despite high drug prices', *Gooznews*, 19 Dec 2006, available from http://www.gooznews.com.

26 United States Government Accountability Office, 'New drug development: science, business, regulatory, and intellectual property issue cited as hampering drug development efforts', Washington: Government Accountability Office, November 2006, available from http://www.gao.gov.

27 M.A. Gagnon and J. Lexchin, 'The cost of pushing pills: a new estimate of pharmaceutical promotion expenditures in the United States', *PLoS Medicine*, 5(1), 2008, p. e1.

28 Kalman Applbaum, 'Is marketing the enemy of pharmaceutical innovation?', *Hastings Center Report*, Forthcoming.

29 Joia S. Mukherjee, 'Scaling up access to HAART in Haiti', 20 September 2003, available from http://www.impactaids.org.uk.

30 Sharon Reier, 'Blockbuster drugs: take the hype in small doses', *International Herald Tribune*, 1 March 2003. Ginal Kolata, 'Experts set lower low for levels of cholesterol', *New York Times*, 13 July 2004.

31 As defined by the American Marketing Association in its entry for 'Marketing' in the AMA Dictionary, available from http://www.marketingpower.com.

32 Kalman Applbaum, 'Getting to yes: corporate power and the creation of a psychopharmaceutical blockbuster', *Culture, Medicine and Psychiatry,* 33(2), 2009.

33 Gary Hamel, Yves L. Doz, and C.K. Prahalad, 'Collaborate with your competitors – and win', *Harvard Business Review on Strategic Alliances*, Boston: Harvard Business School Press, 2002.

34 Applbaum, 'Educating', p. 92.

35 http://www.phrma.org.

36 Tara Parker-Pope, 'Cholesterol screening is urged for young', *New York Times*, 7 July 2008.

37 Anticipating the failure to renew patents on statins by 'ever-greening' strategies, some of the big players appear to be preparing two alternate strategies. One is to lobby for converting the statins to over-the-counter status. This would enable marketers of drugs such as Lipitor and Zocor to switch to consumer brand strategies and thereby make a profitable end-run around generic competition. The second incipient plan is to lobby to have the statins delivered through public drinking water, in the same way that fluoride is.

38   See Merrill Goozner, *The $800 Million Pill*, Berkeley: University of California Press, 2004.

39   'The new pharma landscape', *Next Generation Pharmaceutical*, 6, December 2006, available from http://www.ngpharma.com.

40   As quoted from a 2002 pharmaceutical executive roundtable: 'More and more, marketing is backward integrating into the clinical trial process because the customer is becoming pat of it. The other trend is the forward integration of researchers into the new technologies on the marketing side.' Wayne Koberstein, Cavan Redmond and Larry Star, 'When worlds collide: the unleashed power of marketing/R&D collaboration', *Pharmaceutical Executive*, 1 September 2002, available from http://pharmexec.findpharma.com.

41   Stefan Ecks, 'Global pharmaceutical markets and corporate citizenship: the case of Novartis' anti-cancer drug Glivec', *BioSocieties*, 3, 2008, pp. 165–81.

42   C.K. Prahalad and Venkat Ramaswamy, 'Co-creation experiences: the next practice in value creation', *Journal of Interactive Marketing*, 18 (Summer), 2004, p. 8.

43   For a subtle discussion of the cultural dynamics of value co-creation, see Robert J. Foster, 'The work of the new economy: consumers, brands, and value creation', *Cultural Anthropology*, 22, 2007, pp. 707-31.

44   Kalman Applbaum, '"Consumers are patients!"': Shared decision-making and treatment non-compliance as business opportunity', *Transcultural Psychiatry*, 46(1), 2009, p. 124.

45   Barbara Rylko-Bauer and Paul Farmer, 'Managed care or managed inequality? A call for critiques of market-based medicine', *Medical Anthropological Quarterly*, 16(4), 2002, pp. 476-502.

US HEALTH REFORM
AND THE STOCKHOLM SYNDROME

MARIE GOTTSCHALK

The US healthcare system is exceptional in many ways compared to other developed countries. On average, the United States spends more than twice as much per capita on health care, yet nearly 50 million people are uninsured, and tens of millions more are grossly underinsured. The US ranks near the bottom in major health indicators like life expectancy and infant mortality, and public satisfaction with the healthcare system is extremely low. Heartbreaking stories of people scrambling to find affordable and adequate healthcare coverage while facing down serious, even life threatening, illnesses are common in the media.

In the face of these remarkable problems, the leading solution proposed by the Obama administration, top Democrats in Congress, and their supporters was remarkably modest. Time and again, major attempts to reform the US health system fall victim to the 'Stockholm syndrome' – like the famous Swedish bank hostages who became emotionally attached to their captors and even defended them after they were released. Held captive for so long by neoliberal ideas about how best to organise the US economy and society, many advocates of universal health care put competition and consumer choice at the centre of the latest major push for health reform. Dozens of major organisations close to the Democratic Party, including the AFL–CIO (the country's pre-eminent labour organisation), Moveon.org, and the Children's Defense Fund, mobilised on behalf of a breathtakingly modest solution: creation of a public health plan – essentially a nonprofit insurance company – to compete with the commercial health insurers. They abandoned the call for a 'single-payer' health system modelled after Canada's that many progressives have rallied around since the demise of the Clinton administration's Health Security Act. This push for a competitive public insurance plan indicates that faith in market-led solutions for health reform remains largely unshaken despite the recent financial collapse, which has prompted even former Fed chairman Alan Greenspan to publicly question the market *über alles*.

As the problems of the US health system have mounted over the last four decades, the vision of what is possible in healthcare reform continues to shrink. The enthusiasm for creating a nonprofit health insurance company to relieve the country's healthcare malaise was but the latest example. A closer look at the origins, development, and shortcomings of the Democrats' competitive public plan solution helps explain why many advocates of universal, affordable, high-quality health care continue to bite off less than they can chew.

THE COMPETITIVE PUBLIC PLAN PROPOSAL

The focus of the latest health reform debate was the creation of a new public insurance option for Americans under age 65 who lack employment-based health coverage. This group would be able to choose between a standard package of benefits offered by the public plan, or a comparable one provided by private insurers. Employers who do not offer insurance to their employees would pay a penalty tax to help cover the uninsured ('play-or-pay'). Lower-income Americans would receive subsidies or tax credits based on a sliding scale to buy into the public plan or one of the private ones. Those who remained uninsured would likely be fined (the so-called individual mandate). The progressive case for this was that the public plan would win hands down in a fair competition because commercial health insurers are so bloated by administrative waste, huge underwriting and marketing costs, and excessive executive compensation and profits. Tens of millions of consumers would vote with their feet, choosing the less costly yet also higher-quality public plan. This would force the commercial insurers to reduce costs and improve benefits and service, slowing the galloping rate of healthcare inflation.

Private insurers raised alarms that a public plan would not be competing on a level playing field and thus would ultimately drive them out of business. This subtly recast the debate over health reform. The focus shifted to how to make the public plan a 'fair' competitor and away from the enormous inequities of the under-regulated private insurance market in the United States that have contributed so significantly to the country's healthcare crisis. In order to neutralise charges of unfair advantage, some supporters of the public plan watered down the original proposal or bargained away (or shunned) key reforms needed to rein in insurers and providers. For example, one popular 'neutered' version of the public plan would have required the new public programme to abide by identical rules and standards that apply to private insurers.[1] It would have denied the new programme access to

Medicare's purchasing clout to bargain with providers or impose uniform reimbursement rates, two proven mechanisms for containing the costs of the decades-old government-run health programme for all elderly Americans.

Supporters of this 'hybrid' approach to reform created highly stylised versions of the relative strengths and weaknesses of the public and private sectors in the delivery of health care.[2] They extolled the public sector for its reported ability to contain costs and to pursue innovations that improve the quality of care. Meanwhile, they applauded the private sector for offering a range of insurance products and nimbly adjusting benefit packages to meet shifts in consumer demand. Glossed over were the enormous variations in how the public and private sectors actually deliver health care in the United States and abroad.

The highly stylised version of what public plans are best at doing was based on a select and idiosyncratic reading of the origins and development of Medicare, the public healthcare programme for senior citizens established in 1965. Under Medicare, the US government directly pays providers to care for people over 65 primarily from funds collected from a designated payroll tax, general revenues, and health premiums charged to the over-65s themselves. Medicare is heralded for its superior ability to retain wide access while containing healthcare expenditures through cost-saving innovations like the prospective payment systems introduced in 1983 and national fee schedules for physicians introduced in the 1990s. Left out of the story is that these innovations took decades to enact. The quid pro quo to get physicians and hospitals to end their jihad against Medicare was an agreement to reimburse them on a fee-for-service basis and to eschew imposing serious cost or budget controls. It was well understood at the time that this was a massive financial concession in aid of reaching a compromise. By the early 1970s, talk was already widespread about the runaway costs of Medicare and of a crisis in financing health care. In recent years, spending per enrollee in private plans has generally grown faster than in Medicare. But for much of its history Medicare has been a largely unregulated cash cow for providers.

Medicare is so politically and fiscally attractive because it is a very particular kind of public plan. Medicare has been able to spread risks broadly and maintain wide access for the simple reason that the government bluntly requires it to do so. Nearly everyone qualifies for Medicare upon reaching age 65, regardless of health status or income level. This has created at least some sense of social solidarity, given older Americans across the board a stake in defending a public healthcare system for the aged, and, until recently, avoided incentives to cherry pick healthier (and presumably cheaper) subscribers.

For public programmes, the devil is in the details. Medicaid, the means-tested healthcare programme for low-income Americans established alongside Medicare in 1965, has had a strikingly different trajectory. It has been far easier to starve Medicaid for funding because lower-income Americans do not enjoy the political clout of the elderly, all of whom fall under Medicare's protective umbrella. Despite improvements in Medicaid in recent years, it is still widely viewed as an expensive public programme that dispenses second-class medical care. When healthcare reformers talk about the superiority of the public approach, it is no wonder they talk mostly about Medicare, not Medicaid.[3]

The competitive public plan that reformers envisioned differed from Medicare in key ways that reinforced the current pathologies of the US health system and introduced new ones. First, supporters talked about the need for competition and choice. Yet the estimated 160 million American workers and their dependents who rely on employment-sponsored health benefits would probably not be free to choose the public plan. These captive consumers would likely only have the option to go public if their employers decided to move over to the public plan or gave up providing benefits altogether and paid the penalty tax. Even if the public plan turned out to be cheaper and better, employers would not necessarily make the switch. In the history of the development of US social policy, business leaders have often allowed their visceral ideological opposition to government programmes to trump their immediate bottom-line calculations. The fear is that permitting an expansion of the public sector in one area opens the door for government expansion in other areas. A number of large employers walked away from the Clintons' Health Security Act in 1993-94 for precisely this reason.

Another crucial factor is that some employers are, not surprisingly, large manufacturers of lucrative medical devices and other medical products. Would General Electric, whose second most important division is health care, be ready to funnel its employees into a government-sponsored plan with potentially enormous power to, say, reduce the costs and utilisation of MRI and x-ray machines, a multi-billion dollar business each year for the company? And how about the pharmaceutical companies? Furthermore, as much as employers begrudge how much they pay for healthcare coverage for their workers, many of them do not want to relinquish the paternalistic control that employment-based benefits give them over their workers. Welfare capitalism has deep roots in the evolution of labour-management relations in the United States. Even in the darkest days of the Depression, employers were loath to abandon job-based benefits and the power over workers they conveyed.[4]

In competing with private plans, the public plan should, in theory, be able to provide better benefits and services at lower costs because it presumably would not be saddled with high administrative, marketing, and executive compensation expenses and would not need to turn a profit for shareholders. But the public programme, with its superior benefits and initially lower costs, could end up becoming a magnet for sicker patients in need of costlier care. This would drive up its costs, prompting healthier people to flock to the less expensive private insurance options. Furthermore, private insurers are quite ingenious when it comes to tailoring their benefit packages, premium costs, and provider networks to discourage less healthy people from enrolling. The private Medicare Advantage plans introduced in 2003, which tend to attract healthier elderly Americans, are a stark reminder of this. Moreover, doctors and hospitals might balk at participating in the new public plan and might demand costly inducements to sign up, just as they did 45 years ago as a quid pro quo to support Medicare.

It is not obvious that the public plan could compete primarily on costs, quality, and service alone if insurance companies in the United States remain free to market and advertise their products with few restrictions.[5] One can imagine driving down the highway and seeing massive billboards paid for by private insurers with slogans like: 'Should Uncle Sam's plan tell your doctor what to do?' This could erode the public's confidence in the government's ability to solve the health system's pressing problems.

The competitive public plan option could also undermine public support for government intervention in social policy in other ways. It might end up pitting the captive consumers of employment-based private insurance against people enrolled in the public plan. It would be politically explosive if employees covered by private health insurance came to believe that they were providing huge subsidies to a superior public plan that they were not permitted to enrol in. For years, physicians and hospitals have compensated for lower Medicare and Medicaid reimbursement rates by shifting some of their costs onto patients covered by private insurance. Presumably private insurers would frame their marketing and political strategies around allegations of unfair cost shifting, putting the public plan on the defensive. Instead of cultivating a shared sense of social responsibility, as supporters had hoped, the public plan might end up fostering a zero–sum view of health reform. Advances in the public provision of health care would appear to be coming at the cost of unfairly squeezing people covered by private insurance. This would put the public plan on the defensive. The crucial role of private insurers in creating and sustaining such an inequitable health system would recede further to the margins of the public debate.

In short, under these conditions public plans may not necessarily be superior when it comes to developing cost-saving innovations. The real question is: under what conditions do the political stars line up to the point where both the government and the public are willing to use their considerable powers as the prime purchasers of health care to control the providers and insurers? The new public plan could look like the largely unregulated Medicare programme in 1965, or the semi-regulated Medicare programme in 2009, or today's underfunded Medicaid programme, or the healthcare equivalent of Fannie Mae and Freddie Mac, the quasi-public mortgage companies that were leading culprits in the subprime fiasco and the foreclosure crisis.

THE SINGLE-PAYER ALTERNATIVE

The competitive public plan option has split organised labour and other key groups. Just as was the case in the early 1990s, supporters of a single-payer plan continue to be some of the fiercest opponents of a minimalist approach to health reform. They essentially advocate vaporising the US health insurance industry and replacing it with a government-run programme modelled after Canada's system.[6] The government would pay most medical bills directly; doctors, hospitals, and other providers would operate within global budgets but remain in the private sector; and everyone would be entitled to a basic package of health benefits. The single-payer message has not changed much from the early 1990s, though supporters have been investing more effort this time around in mobilising organised labour and other groups to endorse their position. Hundreds of union locals and dozens of central labour councils and state labour federations have passed symbolic resolutions in favour of single-payer legislation, as have the international chapters of many major unions.

A single-payer system has much to recommend it. When the Congressional Budget Office analysed all the major health reform proposals then under consideration in 1993-94, it concluded that a single-payer plan was the only one likely to achieve universal coverage while saving money.

Earlier in his political career Obama spoke strongly in favour of a single-payer system. Today he acknowledges that if he were starting from scratch, a single-payer plan would be preferable but that the best option now is to build on the current system. In the opening months of the health reform debate, Obama, Senator Max Baucus (Democrat – Montana) – chairman of the pivotal Senate Finance Committee – and other leading political players sought to delegitimise single-payer advocates, or even exclude them from the debate. At the healthcare summit in March 2009 and other leading forums, they surrounded themselves with the 'men and women who made their careers killing healthcare reform', in the words of *The Washington Post*.[7] This strategy backfired. Baucus's move to arrest single-payers supporters (many of them doctors and nurses) demanding admission to a Senate roundtable on health reform created an uproar, as did Obama's initial guest list for his summit, which did not include any single-payer advocates.

Some key labour leaders publicly made polite noises about a single-payer system while disparaging it behind the scenes. Most national labour leaders put their energy and resources behind Obama's prescription early on, even though the president was stunningly vague on key issues. Some rallied around the public plan after convincing themselves that it really is a Trojan horse that will ultimately unleash a single-payer plan after enfeebling the private insurance industry. Others signed up because they consider themselves political realists and view the single-payer option as politically dead on arrival.

To their credit, single-payer advocates have drawn public attention to the extraordinary pathologies of the US health system, notably its gross lapses in care and coverage, excessive costs, and the billions of dollars squandered on administrative costs. They also have offered the most progressive tax proposals to finance universal health care. Held hostage for so long by a health system that is dysfunctional and cruel in many respects, it is not surprising that single-payer advocates want to essentially blow up the private insurance industry. But the fixation on the Canadian solution over the years may have come at the cost of ignoring the scandal of inadequate regulation of providers and insurers in the US healthcare system.

THE PROBLEM OF REGULATION

What fundamentally distinguishes the US healthcare system is the price of care not the amount of care.[8] President Obama and other would-be reformers have attempted to skirt an axiom of medical economics that is at the heart of the politics of health care: 'A dollar spent on medical care is a dollar of income for someone'.[9] Health reform to achieve universal, high-quality, affordable care is fundamentally a redistributive issue with high political and economic stakes. Meaningful cost control will require strong government leadership that sets targets or caps on medical spending. Competition is a weak, indirect way to contain costs. This is especially so in the absence of strong regulatory institutions.

Historically the United States has been shockingly unwilling to seriously regulate its private insurance industry. US health insurance companies have not just been under-regulated compared to private insurers overseas, but also compared to many other major industries in the United States. A hodgepodge of loose regulations at the state level enforced by ineffectual and sometimes corrupt state insurance departments govern the health insurance industry. On the eve of the last major push for health reform, the US House of Representatives issued a scathing report in the late 1980s denouncing the greed, incompetence, and profiteering of the health insurance industry and the lax state regulators who repeatedly looked the other way.[10]

Today the US insurance industry is gung-ho to be the stick to prod doctors and hospitals to get in shape with pay-for-performance standards and other cost-cutting and quality control measures. Insurers are outspoken advocates of greater transparency for physicians and hospitals so that the public is better able to scrutinise their performance and costs. But insurance companies stridently defend their rights to keep vital information about their own operations confidential. This has permitted them to strategically shape debates over health and other social policies by selectively making claims about costs and performance that are difficult to verify. As long as the private insurance industry is allowed to hide behind the cloak that these are business trade secrets, informed consumer choice – a key ingredient of market competition to contain costs – is a myth.[11]

Beginning in late 2008, US health insurers made what many commentators have billed as sweeping concessions on regulation. They signalled their willingness to accept all individual applicants, regardless of pre-existing health conditions. They also expressed their willingness to discontinue setting premium rates that are based on health status or gender, but only if the US Congress mandated that all Americans must carry health insurance – i.e., if all Americans were forced to buy their products. US insurers included some other whopping caveats. First, they would retain the option of setting rates based on age, geography, and family size in the individual market. This means that premium rates would continue to vary enormously, pricing many people out of the market. Insurers would also remain free to use their extensive marketing budgets and experience to attract healthier subscribers and discourage sicker people from seeking coverage. Insurers also made no promises to forego considering health status and other key factors in setting rates for small employers, one of the most profitable segments of the health insurance market.[12]

The proposed competitive public plan was supposed to force insurers to be more aggressive with providers in order to hold down costs and prices or else risk losing customers to the public plan. Obama repeatedly talked about the need to use the market to discipline insurers but did not make a strong case for tightly regulating them in the opening months of his Presidency. The administration even hailed the vague and largely unenforceable voluntary promises to cut costs that the US insurance industry and medical providers announced in May 2009 as a watershed in health reform. Obama's message was inconsistent. As healthcare reform was floundering in Congress by midsummer, the administration became more openly critical of the insurance industry after months of portraying it as a key ally.

Obama attempted to finesse the politically explosive issue of real cost containment by focusing on what one critic has called 'faith-based savings'.[13] The flagship proposal the president unveiled at his healthcare summit in March 2009 was the national adoption of electronic health records, which Obama said could save $80 billion annually. But medical experts dispute that electronic health records will yield sizable savings.[14] So does Peter Orzag. Or at least he did when he headed the Congressional Budget Office before becoming Obama's budget czar. Experts generally agree that preventive care and better disease-management programmes – two other cornerstones of the Obama effort – are good ideas that will improve the quality of life for many people. But most experts also agree that these measures are not likely to save much money any time soon – and might even drive medical expenditures up.

Supporters of the competitive public plan solution did concede that the insurance industry needs to be regulated more tightly, but this was not their main focus initially. Their emphasis on competition reinforced the idea that health care should be treated primarily as a private consumer good distributed by market principles. This displaced the idea that health care is a social good that needs to be organised around underlying principles of social solidarity, not market competition.

Advocates of the public plan squandered enormous political capital to get so little. They bent over backwards to convince the public and critics in the insurance industry that they would create a level playing field. This fostered the impression that the insurance industry has been playing fair and square all along. The terms of the debate shifted to the imaginary injustices that a mammoth public plan would inflict on a Lilliputian insurance industry that has historically been too weak and fragmented or too disinterested to put the cost-containment screws on providers. This revisionist portrait was completely at odds with the real role of the insurance industry in the US healthcare crisis, past and present.

The US insurance industry has been a shrewd behind-the-scenes political operator for well over a century. Each time healthcare reform has moved to centre stage, cries for more federal action have repeatedly ended up further entrenching the private insurance industry.[15] Fearing that the United States might copy Europe's burst of social insurance programmes during the Progressive era, US commercial insurers and business executives aggressively sought to develop corporate welfare schemes to blunt calls for more government action. Once the New Deal put security at the centre of American economic and political life, commercial insurers set out to redefine what security meant in ways that served their interests. They also sought to ensure that the private sector would be the main provider of that security – not public welfare programmes or nonmarket alternatives like union-backed healthcare centres or community health cooperatives.[16]

Three years ago, the industry's leading Washington lobbyist predicted that health care would top the domestic agenda in 2009 and that insurers needed a strategy based on more than just saying no. As head of America's Health Insurance Plans, Karen M. Ignagni positioned the industry as an ally of health reform, not its enemy, without making any serious concessions or revealing what the industry would do if Congress produced a bill it opposes. Ignagni was so successful that '[n]ot only are health insurers at the table, they're sometimes driving the debate'.[17] This was a remarkable accomplishment. After all, relatively few Americans have a favourable view of the health insurance industry, and profits at the ten largest publicly traded health insurance companies more than quadrupled between 2000 and 2007 while health insurance premiums soared and millions lost coverage.[18]

PHYSICIANS AS POTENTIAL ALLIES

The emphasis on insurers and the competitive public plan to police providers and bring down costs implied that US physicians and the US medical community are single-mindedly rapacious and are best controlled by the brute force of competition and market power. But the US medical community has the potential to be a constructive and creative force in healthcare reform. Nurses have been some of the feistiest advocates of a single-payer plan. And while physicians do not want to see their earnings cut, they also have other interests. It is no secret that there is no love lost today between physicians and insurance companies in the United States. Physicians simmer as they watch healthcare dollars eaten up by high administrative costs and as they deal with multiple private insurers second-guessing and micro-managing them at every turn. A 2009 study calculated that dealing with health plans costs physicians and their staffs $31 billion each year in lost hours – or about $68,000 on average per physician.[19] Doctors might be more willing to accept cuts in their incomes and fee schedules if they were assured that the savings did not flow into insurers' pockets but rather went to expand access, enhance healthcare quality, and improve the quality of life for doctors.

The alleged monumental shifts in the US health insurance industry on the question of health reform have overshadowed important real shifts in physician sentiment. Nearly 60 per cent of physicians recently surveyed now favour switching to a national health plan, up from fewer than half in 2002. 'Across the board, more physicians feel that our fragmented insurance system is obstructing good patient care, and a majority now support governmental legislation to establish national insurance as the remedy', according to one of the authors of the study.[20] Physicians for a National Health Program, one of the most outspoken organisations in favour of a single-player plan, has more than 15,000 physician members. Marcia Angell, former editor of the *New England Journal of Medicine*, a premier medical journal, is a leading voice on behalf of a single-payer plan. In January 2008, the American College of Physicians, the second largest physician organisation in the country, published a position paper recommending a single-payer plan as one viable option for reform. Furthermore, the historically conservative AMA is no longer the pre-eminent voice in health policy that it once was. The medical profession has splintered into a myriad of specialty associations. Today barely one-quarter of the country's physicians belong to the AMA, and younger doctors are shunning the association in record numbers. Furthermore, the medical profession is no longer the all-white male army of white coats it once was, as women and minorities increasingly fill its ranks.

Physicians, who were largely invisible in the healthcare battle 15 years ago, have slowly become more outspoken about the ills of the private insurance industry. Recently doctors turned the tables on private insurers and began rating health insurance plans. The AMA has focused public attention on the troubling consequences of the insurance industry's massive consolidation over the last decade or so. As of 2007, the top two insurance companies, WellPoint and UnitedHealth, together covered 67 million people, or 36 per cent of the national market for commercial health insurance. Thanks in part to the lax enforcement of anti-trust laws, most metropolitan areas are now dominated by two health insurers – and often just one.[21] According to the AMA, the 'physician's role is being systematically undermined as dominant insurers are able to impose take-it-or-leave-it contracts that directly affect the provision of patient care and the patient-physician relationship'.[22]

The US hospital and insurance industries have been undergoing major consolidations, but doctors remain one of the least-consolidated sectors of the US health system. Indeed, most doctors belong to practices with four or fewer physicians and with no clout to bargain with insurers. But there are a significant number of physician groups in the United States that are potentially large enough to own and operate their own health plans independently of insurers. Paving the way for them to do so by fostering self-regulatory associations of physicians or by modifying anti-trust legislation so physicians have more leverage vis-à-vis insurers may be important carrots to lure US physicians to accept uniform fee schedules, budget targets, and the like. Notably, physicians employed by California's Kaiser Permanente are the most satisfied doctors in California, according to survey data. Their satisfaction undoubtedly stems from having to deal with a single, non-profit insurance plan 'that is answerable to the medical group'.[23]

The AMA is widely blamed (not entirely justifiably) for single-handedly killing national health insurance in the 1930s, and again in the immediate postwar decades. This may help explain why some reformers are unable to envision a constructive and leading role for physicians in health reform. But this is a period of disarray and uncertainty among US doctors at a time when physicians' legitimacy with the public is plummeting because of their questionable ties to pharmaceutical companies and manufacturers of medical devices. Furthermore, physician impotence vis-à-vis insurance companies is growing. More doctors are realising that if they do not find a way to restore their public image and police their own members, someone else may take up the task, with less favourable results.

HEALTH CARE AND ECONOMIC HEALTH

The political agility of the insurance industry and the neoliberal cloud that has dogged US public policy for decades do not entirely explain why many advocates of universal health care lined up behind such modest proposals in such extraordinary times. Another key factor is the persistently unshaken belief that the healthcare issue needs to be framed primarily as an economic issue and that doing so will attract the allegedly crucial support from the business sector.

We are in the midst of an economic meltdown widely understood to be the result of breathtaking malfeasance by the financial sector and its political patrons. Yet President Obama and key advisers repeatedly single out healthcare costs as the leading threat to the country's long-term economic health.[24] Characterising health care as primarily an economic issue is costly. It fosters an exaggerated faith in the possibility of forging productive coalitions with business leaders and the insurance sector and a diminished interest in cultivating a wider social movement on behalf of universal health care. This is exactly what happened in 1993-94. It also distracts political and public attention away from arguably more dire threats to the economy, including the opaque bailout of the financial sector, the gargantuan military budget, and the grossly inequitable tax system. It also stokes public hysteria over the costs of Medicare and Social Security, paving the way for major retrenchments in these two central pillars of the US welfare state.

Top labour leaders – most notably Andrew Stern, president of the Service Employees International Union (SEIU), the nation's largest union – have echoed the administration's highly economistic view of healthcare reform. Stern's stance is quite similar to the pro-business position that John Sweeney (who stepped down as president of the AFL–CIO in September) manoeuvred the labour federation into when he was chairman of its healthcare committee in the lead-up to the battle over the Clinton plan in the early 1990s. Stern contends that no fundamental change in health care will 'arrive until American business leaders make the call for change'.[25]

Stern has been aggressively identifying the interests of the SEIU with the interests of the business sector in many high-profile business-labour coalitions and other activities. One of Stern's most controversial public dalliances was with H. Lee Scott, Jr. when he was chief executive officer of Wal-Mart. Despite Wal-Mart's dismal record on health benefits and its virulently anti-labour history, Stern argued that the bottom line provides compelling reasons for Wal-Mart and other large employers to be constructive allies in health reform.

In tapping big business as a key ally in the healthcare debate beginning in the late 1980s, much of organised labour took a stance quite similar to Stern's position today.[26] Labour leaders largely accepted the Fortune 500's definition of what was ailing the American economy and hence the American worker. Many of them jumped on the 'competitiveness' bandwagon. In their public statements, labour and business leaders regularly sang off the same song sheet. Their refrain was a simple one – higher medical costs were making American products less competitive in the international marketplace, which was severely hurting the US economy and the American worker.

Economists have raised numerous objections to the contention that escalating healthcare costs are imperilling US economic competitiveness and the overall health of the US economy. But their analyses have made little headway against the 'shared folklore' that employees' healthcare costs are pricing US products out of the market.[27] In his eagerness to woo business on the healthcare issue, Stern has been a leading purveyor of this simplistic folklore. He has promoted alarmist claims that the average Fortune 500 company is at risk of spending more on health care than it earns in profits.

Left out of the story is that spending on health care measured as a percentage of after-tax corporate profits declined steadily from 1986 to 2004 (except for the late 1990s due to a drop overall in corporate profits as the dot-com and high technology sectors went bust). More significantly, employer spending on wages and salaries and on total compensation as a percentage of after-tax profits has dropped precipitously since 1986, except for the 1998-

2001 period.[28] Although healthcare costs continue to escalate, employers have had great success at squeezing wages and other forms of compensation and shifting more healthcare costs onto their employees. Wages and salaries make up the smallest portion of the country's gross domestic product since the government began collecting such data in 1947. In 2006, on the eve of the subprime crisis and the economic meltdown, corporate profits were at their highest level in four decades.

To underscore the alleged severity of the healthcare cost crunch, Stern and some business leaders stress (as they did in the late 1980s and early 1990s), what US employers are paying out in direct costs for health care as compared with their foreign competitors. Over the years, the auto industry has been the designated poster child as auto executives and labour leaders bemoan how crippling medical expenses add $1,500 to the cost of each car manufactured by GM, while some of its competitors pay as little as $200 per vehicle.

But the focus on comparing what US companies pay *directly* for health care relative to their foreign competitors is often misleading. It ignores the higher indirect costs that many overseas firms and individuals shoulder due to higher corporate and personal income taxes to support more extensive public welfare states. This amount generally exceeds what even the most generous US firms spend on health care for their employees. The fact is that many firms in Europe and elsewhere have been highly competitive even though their workers have enjoyed more generous health, vacation, maternity, and other benefits. Moreover, in a number of countries, the direct healthcare costs paid for by corporations have been considerable.[29]

In the early 1990s, much of labour's political energy went into forging an elite-level deal between labour, business, and the government over health care. The defeated Clinton plan, which caused such an uproar with much of the business sector, called for larger employers to contribute a modest 7.9 per cent of their payroll to help pay for employees' health coverage. According to Drew Altman, president of the Henry J. Kaiser Family Foundation, 'You couldn't have done more to pay off corporate America than they did with the Clinton plan, but in the end, companies turned on it because it was viewed as a big government plan'.[30]

When business walked away from the table, there was no sustained grass-roots pressure to bring it back. The ingredients for that mobilisation had been squandered by promises that business would do right by workers on health care, even as it was engaged in a massive assault on workers in other areas, like the right to unionise and passage of the North American Free-Trade Agreement (NAFTA) in late 1993. Labour leaders repeatedly

portrayed business leaders as ready to do the right thing on health care
– until they weren't. There is a parallel here with the current situation.
The latest healthcare debate has unfolded simultaneously with the business
sector's vitriolic mobilisation against the Employee Free Choice Act, the
most important piece of US labour legislation in decades.

HARRY AND LOUISE GET ANGRY

The competitive public plan solution emerged from the doldrums of the
vanquished Clinton plan and out of a very particular reading of what went
wrong 15 years ago. In the revisionist account, the Health Security Act
was not defeated because Clinton came into office with a weak mandate,
elected with only 43 per cent of the vote. Nor because of strategic mistakes
his administration made and divisions within the Congressional Democratic
leadership. Nor because powerful interest groups, including within organised
labour, were at war with one another. Nor because Newt Gingrich and the
new ascendant conservative wing of the Republican Party had committed
themselves to the defeat of 'Hillarycare' at all costs. Nor because the tepid
support within the business community rapidly evaporated once Clinton
began looking like a one-term president due to missteps over gays in the
military, Somalia, etc.

In the revisionist account, Harry and Louise killed healthcare reform.
Harry and Louise were a white, middle-class – dare I say yuppie – couple
that starred in a series of commercials funded by the insurance industry. The
fictional Harry and Louise became famous – or infamous – as they sat around
their kitchen table fretting that the Clinton plan would force them to change
their current health benefits and maybe even switch doctors. The ghosts
of Harry and Louise have had a striking hold on the current health reform
debate. The mantra from President Obama, the SEIU's Andy Stern, Senator
Baucus, and other would-be reformers is that most Americans are basically
content with their health coverage and seek a uniquely American solution
that keeps the current system of employment-sponsored benefits largely
untouched. The biggest impact of the ad campaign then and now appears
to have been on elite policy and opinion makers, who have persistently
overestimated just how much Harry and Louise represented heartfelt popular
sentiment and how satisfied Americans are with the healthcare coverage
they have.[31]

Evidence continues to mount that Americans are profoundly dissatisfied
with their health system and are ready for major changes. In terms of public
satisfaction with its medical system, the United States is nearly last compared
with other developed countries (and dead last among public health experts

polled).[32] No wonder why. Since the demise of the Clinton plan, the wheels have come off job-based benefits. Some employers have eliminated health benefits altogether while others are persistently whittling them away. In 2008, only 60 per cent of all workers – or barely half of the total US population – were covered by employment-based health benefits. Those employers who do offer benefits have been offloading more of the costs onto employees through higher co-pays, deductibles, out-of-pocket expenses, and insurance premium costs.

It is no longer possible for most Americans to be six degrees of separation from the uninsured. With the official unemployment rate surpassing 8 per cent in February 2009, a Kaiser Family Foundation survey found that 52 per cent of people with employment-sponsored coverage were worried about losing it. Nearly 87 million Americans were uninsured at some point in the last two years. In California, nearly 40 per cent of residents under age 65 did. The foreclosure crisis has also riveted public attention on the enormous number of Americans – many of them middle-class people who had health insurance at the start of their illness – who go bankrupt and risk losing their homes because of medical debts. On the eve of the historic November 2008 election, a Commonwealth Fund survey found that four out of five US residents believe the nation's health system needs to be completely rebuilt or fundamentally changed. Asked whether they support national health insurance and a government guarantee of health care, overwhelming numbers of Americans routinely tell pollsters yes. One of the most surprising poll results came from a 2008 Harvard School of Public Health survey that directly asked whether a 'socialised medical system' would be better than the current one. Among those who said they had some understanding of this historically inflammatory phrase (82 per cent), a stunning plurality (45 per cent) said socialised medicine was preferable (39 per cent said it wasn't).

The minimalist approach to health reform does not tap into this smoldering public anger over the health system or into the explosive public outrage at the financial industry, the business sector, and their political patrons in Congress in the wake of the economic meltdown. The political futures of several Democratic barons in Congress, including Senator Christopher Dodd, Senator Charles Schumer, and Representative Charles Rangel, are clouded because of their close, see-no-evil ties to the banking and insurance industries nourished over the years by enormous campaign donations from these sectors. The healthcare sector spent nearly $1 billion in lobbying in 2007 and 2008 alone and has long ranked as one of the most powerful political forces, alongside the financial and energy sectors. Over the last four years, Senator Max Baucus, who became the most important member of

Congress on health reform after Senator Edward Kennedy became gravely ill, was the top recipient of campaign contributions from health insurers and drug makers. Notably, Baucus proudly co-authored the controversial 2001 tax cuts, the Bush administration's signature 'trickle-up' legislation.

These conflicts of interest run deep. UnitedHealth, one of the nation's largest insurers, now owns the Lewin Group, which once was considered a reliable independent analyst of trends in healthcare benefits and costs. David E. Nexon, who for two decades was Senator Kennedy's key staffer on health policy, became a top executive at Advanced Medical Technology, a leading trade association for the medical industry. Karen M. Ignagni, president of the main trade group for the insurance industry, ran labour's healthcare reform effort at the AFL-CIO in the early 1990s.

The time was ripe for an ambitious healthcare plan that fundamentally challenges these special interests. The economic meltdown has made legislators on both sides of the aisle in Congress particularly vulnerable to charges of shilling for the business sector. A revealing study of voter discontent conducted in 2007 by Democracy Corps on the eve of the financial crisis found that the most commonly chosen phrase to characterise what's wrong with the country was: 'Big business gets whatever they want in Washington'.[33] Obama's decision to seed his administration with many protégés of Citigroup's Robert Rubin made him vulnerable on this score. So did the choice of Nancy-Ann DeParle, who served as director of many large healthcare companies, as his health czar.

During the campaign, Obama said, 'It's time to let the drug and insurance industries know that while they'll get a seat at the table, they don't get to buy every chair'.[34] He also promised that if the insurance industry sought to block reform with another Harry and Louise blitzkrieg, he would go on the offensive. But in the formative months of the healthcare debate, Obama and his key advisers gave no public indication of their readiness to defend certain first principles – or even to define what those first principles might be.[35] To the consternation of some Congressional Democrats and healthcare reformers, they appeared willing to accept a grossly watered down public plan or maybe even to abandon the public plan altogether as a concession to conservatives. They did not proclaim universal coverage as a fundamental goal and were noncommittal on a mandate requiring employers to pay for a portion of their employees' health benefits. The administration quickly retreated from proposals to fund health reform by levying higher taxes on upper-income earners. Instead, it began talking favourably about taxing employees' health benefits to raise money for health reform. This was a key feature of Senator John McCain's healthcare platform that Obama had denounced during the 2008 campaign as an unfair tax on middle-class Americans. During the presidential campaign, Obama promised to 'take on' the pharmaceutical industry. But his concessions to drug companies as the health reform battle unfolded surprised and alarmed some leading Democrats in Congress.[36]

The Obama administration and much of the leadership of the Democratic Party have responded to the healthcare crisis much as they have responded to the financial crisis. They have taken extreme care not to upset the basic interests of the powerful insurance industry and segments of the medical industry and not to raise fundamental questions about the political and economic interests that have perpetuated such a dysfunctional health system. The biggest surprise is how the leadership of organised labour and many supposedly progressive groups have unquestioningly followed Obama and Congressional Democrats on health care. As a consequence, they may be squandering an exceptional political moment. If the Obama administration can get away with such a massive government role in the bailout of General Motors, Chrysler, and Citibank, garnering public support to bring about the demise of the for-profit health insurance industry should not be impossible.

There are not many times in American history when the previous administration and ruling party have been so thoroughly discredited, as were former President George W. Bush and the Republican Party. Or when the princes of the financial sector have been 'stripped naked as leaders and strategists', in the words of Simon Johnson, a former chief economist at the International Monetary Fund.[37] The Depression was one of them. This is another. As the billionaire financier Warren Buffet said a couple of years ago: 'There's class warfare, all right, but it's my class, the rich class, that's making war, and we're winning'.[38]

President Franklin D. Roosevelt came into office at an exceptional moment in 1933. Four years into the Depression, the Hoover administration was thoroughly discredited, as was the business sector. FDR recognised that the country was ready for a break with the past as he symbolically and substantively cultivated that sentiment. But the break did not come from FDR alone. Massive numbers of Americans mobilised in unions, women's organisations, veterans' groups, senior citizen associations, and civil rights organisations to push FDR to switch course. Faced with deep public mistrust and contempt of business after the 1929 stock market crash, leading American corporations invested heavily in winning back the public trust. Over the next few decades, they spent lavishly on public relations and company-based propaganda campaigns directed at their employees to reassure America that capitalism was indeed good and that too much of the state was, well, socialism.

The Obama administration and leading Democrats have sought a minimalist solution rather than seizing the exceptional political moment to strike out in a bold new direction in health policy. If they calculated that the political conditions were not fortuitous to secure a single-payer plan, at least they might have pushed for a seriously regulated insurance system. Failure to attempt even that is perilous for the cause of universal health care and for their political futures. The president and the Democrats risk looking in a couple of years like Herbert Hoover and the Republicans on the eve of their historic 1932 defeat rather than FDR and the Democrats on their march to a triumphant re-election in 1936.

Would-be reformers who have fought so doggedly to essentially create a nonprofit health insurance company do not recognise the potential of this political moment. It is not 1993-94 all over again. These would-be reformers remain under the spell of the Stockholm syndrome and identify too closely with insurers, the medical industry, and their political patrons. Identifying too closely with one's captors is risky. When the window opens, you don't make a run for it. Indeed, you may not even notice the opening.

NOTES

1   Len M. Nichols and John M. Bert, 'A modest proposal for a competing public health plan', Washington, D.C., New America Foundation, March 2009. See also the remarks by Senator Charles E. Schumer (D-N.Y.) in Robert Pear, '2 Democrats spearheading health bill are split', *The New York Times*, 30 May 2009.

2   See, for example, Jacob S. Hacker, 'The case for public plan choice in national health reform: key to cost control and quality coverage', Washington, D.C., Institute for America's Future, 2008, p. 1.

3   One notable exception is Michael Sparer, 'Medicaid and the US path to national health insurance', *New England Journal of Medicine* 360(4), 22 January 2009, pp. 323-25.

4   Jennifer Klein, *For All These Rights: Business, Labour, and the Shaping of America's Public-Private Welfare State*, Princeton: Princeton University Press, 2003; and Sanford M. Jacoby, ed., *Masters to Managers: Historical and Comparative Perspectives on American Employers*, New York: Columbia University Press, 1991.

5   Although private insurers play a significant role in many European countries, they have been restricted in their promotional advertising, and direct-to-consumer advertising of prescription drugs has been banned in the European Union. Lawrence D. Brown and Volker E. Amelung, '"Manacled competition": market reforms in German health care', *Health Affairs* 18(3), May/June 1999, p. 82; and Uwe E. Reinhardt, '"Mangled competition" and "managed whatever"', *Health Affairs*, 18(3), May/June 1999, p. 93. As the clout of

multinational insurance companies, for-profit hospital chains, pharmaceutical companies, and much of the medical industry have increased worldwide, these and other regulations are increasingly under threat by a strident push for more market competition. See Christoph Hermann's essay in this volume.

6   For a succinct comparison of the major health reform proposals under discussion, see 'Focus on health reform: side-by-side comparison of major health reform proposals', The Henry J. Kaiser Family Foundation, available from http://kff. org.

7   Ceci Connolly, 'Ex-foes of healthcare reform emerge as supporters', The Washington Post, 6 March 2009, p. A-2.

8   Claims that the US medical tab is so high because Americans are comparatively unhealthy or use comparatively more medical services are largely mistaken. Americans actually tend to see a physician less often, to spend fewer days per year in the hospital, and to take fewer prescription drugs. Gerald F. Anderson, Uwe E. Reinhardt, Peter S. Hussey, and Varduhi Petrosyan, 'It's the prices, stupid: why the United States is so different from other countries', Health Affairs, 22(3), May/June 2003.

9   Theodore Marmor, Jonathan Oberlander, and Joseph White, 'The Obama Administration's options for health care cost control', Annals of Internal Medicine, 150(7), 7 April 2009, p. 485.

10   Jill Quadagno, One Nation Uninsured: Why the US Has No National Health Insurance, New York: Oxford University Press, 2005, p. 169.

11   Diane Archer, 'Making health care work for American families: saving money saving lives', Statement, US House Committee on Energy and Commerce, Subcommittee on Health, 2 April 2009.

12   Reed Abelson, 'Health insurers balk at some changes', The New York Times, 3 June 2009.

13   Jonathan Oberlander, 'Miracle or mirage? Health care reform and the 2008 election', Leonard Davis Institute, University of Pennsylvania, 10 October 2008.

14   Jerome Groopman and Pamela Hartzband, 'Obama's $80 billion exaggeration', The Wall Street Journal, 11 March 2009.

15   Quadagno, One Nation Uninsured, p. 75; and Klein, For All These Rights.

16   Klein, For All These Rights, pp. 3-6.

17   Erica Werner, 'Lobbyist ready for feverish effort', Washington Times, 26 May 2009.

18   For more on public opinion about the insurance industry, see USA Today, Kaiser Family Foundations, and Harvard School of Public Health, 'The public on prescription drugs and pharmaceutical companies', March 2008, p. 8, available from http://kff.org. On insurance industry profits, see Health Care for America Now, 'Premiums soaring in consolidated insurance market', May 2009, p. 7, available from http://healthcareforamericanow.org.

19   Lawrence P. Casalino, Sean Nicholson, David N. Gans, et al., 'What does it cost physician practices to interact with health insurance plans', Health Affairs, 4 May 2009, available from http://content.healthaffairs.org.

20   Personal e-mail correspondence with Ronald T. Ackermann, 12 June 2009.

21 Emily Berry, 'Most metro areas dominated by 1 or 2 health insurers', 9 March 2009, available from http://www.ama-assn.org.

22 American Medical Association, Private Sector Advocacy Unit, *Competition in Health Insurance: A Comprehensive Study of US Markets, 2007 Update*, Chicago: American Medical Association, 2007.

23 Alain C. Enthoven and Wynand P. M. M. van de Ven, 'Going Dutch – managed-competition health insurance in the Netherlands', *New England Journal of Medicine*, 357(24), 13 December 2007, p. 2423.

24 Sean Lengell and Jon Ward, 'Senators set out to meet health care goal; Obama aims for end of year', *The Washington Times*, 6 March 2009, p. A-1; and Ezra Klein, 'The number-cruncher-in-chief', *The American Prospect*, January/February, 2009, p. 17.

25 Comments made at 'A Brookings Institution-New America Foundation Forum: Employment-based health insurance: a prominent past, but does it have future?', Brookings Institution, Washington, D.C., 16 June 2006, available from http://www.brookings.edu, p. 15.

26 For more on organised labour and health policy, see Marie Gottschalk, *The Shadow Welfare State: Labour, Business, and the Politics of Health Care in the United States,* Ithaca: Cornell University Press, 2000.

27 Uwe E. Reinhardt, 'Health care spending and American competitiveness', *Health Affairs,* 9(4), Winter 1989, p. 6.

28 For more details on the relationship between profits and healthcare costs, see Marie Gottschalk, 'Back to the future? Health benefits, organized labour, and universal health care', *Journal of Health Politics, Policy, and Law*, 32(6), December 2007, pp. 923-70.

29 'The cost of employment-related health benefits as a percentage of payroll is nearly 50 per cent greater in Germany than in the United States, but little is heard about this'. Mark Pauly, *Health Benefits at Work: An Economic and Political Analysis of Employment-Based Health Insurance*, Ann Arbor: University of Michigan, 1997, p. 119.

30 Joe Nocera, 'Resolving to reimagine health costs', *The New York Times*, 18 November 2006, p. C-1.

31 Mollyann Brodie, 'Impact of issue advertisements and the legacy of Harry and Louise', *Journal of Health Politics, Policy, and Law*, 26(6), December 2001, pp. 1353-60.

32 Robert J. Blendon, Minah Kim, and John M. Benson, 'The public versus the World Health Organization on health system performance', *Health Affairs*, 20(3), May/June 2001, Exhibit 1, p. 16.

33 See Paul Krugman, 'Big table fantasies', *The New York Times*, 17 December 2007.

34 Jay Newton-Small and Aliza Marcus, 'Obama, following rivals, unveils health plan', Bloomberg.com, 29 May 2007.

35 See, for example, Richard Wolf, 'Sebelius, DeParle ready to tackle health care overhaul', *USA Today*, 1 June 2009.

36 Alicia Mundy and Laura Meckler, 'Drug makers score early wins as plan takes shape', *Wall Street Journal*, 17 July 2009.

37   Simon Johnson, 'The quiet coup', *Atlantic* Online, May 2009, available from http://www.theatlantic.com.

38   Ben Stein, 'In class warfare, guess which class is winning', *The New York Times*, 26 November 2006.

THE MARKETISATION OF HEALTH CARE IN EUROPE

CHRISTOPH HERMANN

In contrast to the United States and other parts of the world, the financing and provision of health care in Europe is still very much based on public planning and the services are mostly delivered by public organisations, or private organisations that are not aiming to maximise profits. Surveys show continuously strong support for this system. With few exceptions citizens are rather critical of privatisation and marketisation in healthcare provision, and they have good reason to be. The public system not only ensures that the vast majority of citizens have access to health care, but comparisons with the US also show that the public provision of health care is cheaper than in private for-profit systems.[1] However, despite the obvious superiority of public healthcare systems, the public nature of healthcare provision in Europe has been challenged through a series of reforms that amount to what can best be described as the marketisation of health care. Such developments include the introduction of purchaser-provider relationships, the establishment of internal markets, competition between different providers, performance-oriented compensation, individualisation of risks, outsourcing, the use of public-private partnerships, and the sale of public hospitals to private investors. While these reforms have officially been introduced to cut costs and improve efficiency, they have primarily served to create healthcare markets which promote inequality among patients and healthcare workers and erode the public nature of healthcare provision.

THE EVOLUTION OF PUBLIC HEALTH CARE IN EUROPE

The financing and provision of health care in Europe has always involved a variety of institutions and actors, some of whom were public, and others private. What makes the situation even more complicated is the fact that in several European countries there are also important non-profit private actors.[2] And even where private providers predominate, as is the case with non-hospital care in many countries, they are mainly independent physicians who may earn a reasonable income but are not necessarily maximising profits. But what makes health care a public service, and what distinguishes Europe – at least western Europe – from the United States is that it is funded out of taxation and/or a compulsory insurance system; profit-maximising actors play a subordinate role, and the state plays a crucial role in planning and overseeing the system. In the United States, in contrast, almost 15 per cent of the population lack any health insurance and almost 75 per cent of those insured are covered by voluntary private insurance, mostly attached to their place of work.[3]

The compulsory character of the European healthcare system had two different roots and hence has taken two basic forms. One was the Bismarck model, named after the German chancellor who introduced social insurance in the nineteenth century, where contributions are deducted automatically from salaries and paid into social insurance funds, along with contributions by employers and the state.[4] The other model, named after Beveridge, the mastermind behind the reorganisation of the British welfare system after 1945, was funded by tax revenue collected by the state. The Bismarck model has prevailed in continental Europe, while Britain, the Nordic countries and some southern European states have adopted versions of the Beveridge system. Both systems incline to some degree of redistribution, as high income-earners normally pay higher taxes and higher social insurance contributions.[5] In both cases the state played a critical role in expanding the proportion of the population that had access to health care.

During the second half of the twentieth century European states continually enlarged their responsibility for the healthcare sector through a variety of measures, including the planning of supply, the funding of research and innovation, the regulation and training of medical professions, the establishment and control of medical standards and, not least, the extension of healthcare funding. 'More or less as a universal trend, health care throughout Europe entered into what may be called the *public domain*. A by-product of this development was the rollback of the private sector in healthcare spending and, in some countries, healthcare provision'.[6] The creation of the National Health Service in Britain after the Second World War involved the takeover and integration of 1,143 voluntary and 1,545 municipal hospitals.[7] Patients with private insurance were offered the choice of being treated in NHS 'pay beds' (for which the physicians could directly charge the patients or their insurers, while the NHS received some compensation for the accommodation amd nursing and technical services), or going to a private hospital. In any case during the 1950s and 1960s their numbers were rather low. Similarly, the creation of heavily subsidised outpatient clinics in Sweden in the late 1960s meant that private practice virtually 'dried up', although patients could still visit private doctors.[8] Public healthcare spending increased continuously during the post-war years. This was not perceived as a serious problem as long as GDP increased at the same pace.

DRIVERS OF HEALTHCARE RESTRUCTURING

Technological and organisational innovations, decentralisation, the need for new skills and qualifications, as well as a growing awareness of patients' rights and the availability of better information, have certainly all played a role in the restructuring of the healthcare sector in the past three decades, but the most important driver of change has been the wish to contain costs. All European countries experienced difficulties covering increasing healthcare costs in the 1970s after the end of the long post-war boom. With economic recession, GDP growth was exceeded by the acceleration of healthcare costs, due to the possibility of more and more interventions as medical knowledge expanded, increasingly expensive equipment and medication, as well as growing needs and expectations. As a result a growing proportion of public budgets was spent on health care. In several countries the recession was also followed by a change in government: neo-conservative parties came to power that had promised tax cuts. This was part of a new neoliberal agenda which aimed at 'rolling back the state' in favour of private initiative and capital. The prime example was Margaret Thatcher's project in Britain, but more moderate forms of economic austerity were also introduced in other European countries, including Sweden. Economic austerity in fact became a major goal of the European Union, and especially of those member states which joined the Growth and Stability Pact with its 3 per cent cap on budget deficits.[9]

The combination of tax cuts and budgetary austerity not surprisingly resulted in a financial crisis in public healthcare systems. This not only concerned the tax-based systems, but also countries with social health insurance schemes. In the latter case hospital infrastructure was often funded by the local government while the costs of treatment were covered by the insurance funds. In federal systems such as Germany it was initially the municipalities that felt the strongest pressure to cut costs. However, in recent years the federal states (Länder) have also increasingly sold hospitals to private investors who promised to make long overdue investments.[10] Social insurance funds also came under pressure, as they had difficulty in increasing the premiums paid by workers, who were already suffering from stagnating wages, while their total income was reduced by continuously high rates of unemployment and the growing number of workers in non-standard forms of employment, who did not pay premiums.[11] However, the same politicians who had introduced tax cuts also promoted the privatisation of health care as a solution to the healthcare funding crisis. Private healthcare providers, they maintained, could deliver the same if not better services at lower prices, thereby relieving the pressure on public budgets.

A second major driver behind the transformation of the healthcare sector has been multinational healthcare companies and the large amount of financial assets in search of profitable investment opportunities in health care. These assets have shrunk as a result of the 2008/2009 financial crisis, but they are still a powerful driving force: despite the crisis in public budgets and cost-containment efforts, the healthcare sector is expected to grow strongly in the future. What makes the healthcare sector so interesting for private investors is that the business is non-cyclical. Other sectors may suffer from a decline in demand, but patients need medical treatment regardless of the world economic outlook. As a result a growing number of multinational health companies have been pushing for liberalisation and privatisation, while companies from outside the health sector (e.g. private equity funds and facilities management firms) are increasingly investing in healthcare projects in order to add additional streams of income to their otherwise cyclical businesses.[12] The increasing importance of health care as a profit-making sector can also be seen in its important role in the WTO talks on a General Agreement on Trade in Services.[13]

HEALTHCARE RESTRUCTURING AND MARKETISATION

In the privatisation literature, authors often make a distinction between liberalisation and privatisation. While liberalisation refers to the introduction of competition, i.e. the admission of more than one provider for the same service, allowing customers to choose between different suppliers, privatisation involves the transfer of assets from public to private ownership. In reality, however, these are only two extremes in a rather complex and fluid process in which the nature of the provision of public services is altered.[14] This is particularly true for social services, where markets and competition cannot easily be installed, and where the sale of public assets to private investors may not be easy for political reasons.[15] In such cases, supporters of liberalisation and privatisation often look for alternative methods to achieve similar effects. The healthcare sector stands out because it comprises a wide range of processes that amount to a shift towards marketisation, including the introduction of buyer-purchaser relationships and prices, the pricing and individualisation of risks, the introduction of choice and consumer behaviour and the introduction of private business management tools and goals, as well as the greater involvement of private actors through public-private partnerships, or privatisation.[16]

All these developments have in common that they contribute in one way or another to the creation of healthcare markets, which itself is a precondition for the commodification of health care.[17] Although the changes vary between countries and between different areas of healthcare provision, they can nevertheless be grouped into those affecting the financing of health care and others affecting its provision.

Changes in healthcare financing

While total healthcare spending has increased in the 1990s after a temporary slowdown in the 1980s, the proportion of public health care expenditure as a percentage of total health expenditure decreased in the majority of European countries between 1980 and 2005.[18] Among the countries that experienced the greatest proportional reductions are Sweden, the Netherlands, Spain, Greece and the new member states in Central Eastern Europe (CEE). However, while in Greece public healthcare spending accounts for barely more than 43 per cent of total healthcare spending, in Sweden the proportion is still 84.6 per cent and therefore among the highest in Europe.[19] The relative decrease in public healthcare spending went hand in hand with the increasing importance of private health insurance. Today private health insurance schemes are particularly important in the Netherlands, where in 2005 they accounted for at least 23 per cent of total healthcare financing, followed by France and Germany, where private insurance covered 13 and 10 per cent of total spending respectively.[20]

Private insurance schemes are generally more important in countries with Bismarck–type social insurance funds. Some of these systems exclude particular groups, which are then dependent on private insurance, or they allow certain groups to choose between public or private insurance.[21] In these cases private insurance functions as a *substitute* for public health insurance. However, rather than substituting for public insurance, private insurance schemes are more often *supplementary* to the public system, covering services excluded from, or not fully covered by, the public system, or for co-payments (fees payable by patients). Such schemes play an important role in France, where in 2000 85 per cent of the population were covered by supplementary health insurance; in the Netherlands, where more than 60 per cent had additional private insurance; and in Belgium, where the proportion was somewhere between 30 and 50 per cent.[22]

The growing importance of supplementary health insurance in Europe is reinforced by another important trend: the 'de-listing' of treatments and medication hitherto covered by public health insurance. The classic case in all countries is dental care, which is now largely financed by private insurance or by out-of-pocket payments (sometimes euphemistically called 'cost-sharing'). Except for the Netherlands and France (the only country where they have decreased since 1980), out-of-pocket payments are in fact more important than private insurance in closing the financial gap left by diminishing public resources.[23] They are particularly important in Belgium, Italy, Portugal and Spain, where in 2005 they accounted for more than 20 per cent of total health expenditures.[24] Out-of-pocket payments have also become an important source for covering healthcare costs after the regime change in central and eastern Europe. In Hungary and Poland in 2005 they accounted for 26 per cent of total health expenditure.[25] However, in addition to formal co-payments, patients in some central and east European countries are also expected to pay 'informal' fees, and patients in public hospitals pay 'tokens of gratitude' for adequate treatment.[26]

In addition to increasing competition from private insurers, in some countries public or social health insurance funds have been forced to compete with each other for customers. In the Netherlands the government introduced a reform of the insurance system in 2006 enabling insurance holders to switch insurers (public or private) and to select between individual insurance plans. The government hopes that patients will profit from competition between insurers, who are expected to lower premiums and expand coverage in order to protect or expand their market share. In turn, insurance funds are allowed to negotiate special contracts with particular healthcare providers and require their clients to seek treatment at particular facilities where they can negotiate better terms.[27] These changes have already triggered further liberalisation in the hospital sector, including a plan to lift the existing ban on for-profit hospital care in 2012.[28]

While the introduction of competition between different insurance funds is typical of social insurance fund systems, in tax-based systems an important trend has been a division between those charged with funding services, and those providing them – the so-called 'purchaser-provider split'. The objective is on the one hand to improve control over spending, and on the other to increase the autonomy and responsibility of the healthcare provider in the interest of efficiency. In the British case this entailed a far-reaching reorganisation of the NHS as an 'internal market'. Hospitals and some community health services were organised into semi-autonomous 'trusts', and hospital trusts were no longer granted fixed annual budgets but were expected to win contracts from decentralised 'commissioning' organisations (the 'purchasers'), acting for the Department of Health.[29] The autonomy of a growing number of hospitals has since been further increased through making them 'foundation trusts', no longer accountable to the Department of Health but to a new healthcare market regulator: foundation trusts are allowed to generate income through establishing commercial arms or engaging in joint commercial ventures with private companies, and to borrow funds on the private financial market. It is intended that all NHS trusts will eventually have foundation status.

There are similar developments in other Beveridge-type health systems. In Sweden regional councils have created separate purchasing organisations for the funding of local hospitals, while the hospitals were granted more auto-nomy. In contrast to the British system, where hospitals have retained a special legal status (trusts and foundation trusts) even though they are expected to act more and more like independent businesses, in Sweden and other countries public hospitals have been converted into public limited companies. Having the legal status of private businesses has in turn facilitated the emergence of larger hospital networks, cooperation with private businesses and in some cases even the sale of public hospitals to private investors.[30] The system of funding itself has also been altered in connection with the separation of funding and provision. In most European countries hospitals have been given global budgets for infrastructure maintenance and investment, with the effect that hospitals are forced to set spending priorities. On the other hand, compensation for the costs of treatments is increasingly based on flat-rate payments set for each procedure and category of patients (Diagnosis-Related Groups), rather than for the costs actually incurred in treating a particular patient. DRG systems have increasingly become a way to put pressure on hospitals to reduce costs through a reduction of the average length of stay in hospital – since compensation is the same regardless of the actual length of stay there is a financial incentive to discharge patients as early as possible. About a quarter of physicians interviewed in a German hospital said they believed that patients were often discharged too early.[31]

In sum, the changes in healthcare financing, although not necessarily entailing a shift from a public to a private system, have profoundly altered the way health care is delivered in many European countries.

Changes in healthcare provision

While changes in financing have had a lasting effect on the provision of health care, the consequences have not necessarily been the same every-where. In a number of countries cost containment led to a wave of decentralisation, with hospitals becoming increasingly independent. This, for example, has been an important element in successive healthcare reforms in Sweden.[32] In other countries the need for rationalisation had the opposite effect, with smaller hospitals being integrated into larger units or larger, centrally-controlled hospital networks. As a result of a wave of hospital mergers in Belgium, including mergers between public and private non-profit organisations, more than half of all hospitals have disappeared since 1981.[33] In Germany, 10 per cent of all hospitals have been closed since 1990, eliminating 134,232 hospital beds.[34] While the reduction in hospital bed numbers can partly be explained by technological developments such as day surgery, and the fact that smaller hospitals have often found it difficult to afford increasingly specialised and expensive medical equipment, the process has been accelerated by the financial problems caused by the changes in the funding schemes described earlier.

The most radical form of privatisation in healthcare provision is the sale of public hospitals to private investors. A number of countries have experimented with the privatisation of public hospitals. One of the oldest hospitals in Sweden, Saint Görans Hospital in Stockholm, with about 1,500 workers, was privatised in 1999. It is now owned by the Swedish healthcare multinational Capio. Several other hospitals, most of them in the Stockholm region, have been turned into independent commercial organisations, although they are still owned by regional governments. In 2002 this trend was, however, put on hold with the adoption of the 'Stop Law' initiated by the Social Democrats, prohibiting the sale of further hospitals to for-profit owners.[35] In Austria, two public hospitals have been sold to private investors.[36]

But Germany stands out as the one country in Europe where the sale of public hospitals has been carried out on a large scale and in a systematic way.[37] Between 1991 and 2004 the number of private hospitals in Germany increased from 14.8 to 25.4 per cent of the total, while the share of public hospitals decreased from 46 to 36 per cent (the rest consisting of private non-profit institutions). Private for-profit hospitals tend to be smaller. In 2004 the public sector still accounted for 52.8 per cent of all hospital beds and employed nearly 60 per cent of all hospital workers.[38] Yet more recently Germany has faced a number of stunning takeovers involving large and prestigious hospitals, including the takeover in 2005 of the seven local hospitals of the city of Hamburg (*Landesbetrieb Krankenhäuser*) with 5,688 beds, and in 2006 the university clinics of Marburg and Gießen with more than 2,400 beds.[39] The wave of hospital privatisation is expected to continue. It is estimated that by 2020 between 40 and 50 per cent of German hospitals will be in private hands.[40]

While in western Europe large public hospitals have been privatised, in central and eastern Europe new private hospitals have been built. In the Czech Republic the number of private hospitals grew from 64 in 2000 to 122 in 2007, and in Poland from 38 in 2000 to 153 in 2006.[41] These hospitals mainly treat patients who have private insurance, or sufficient personal funds, which means that only a small proportion of the population can afford them. In Poland in 2006, for example, private clinics (profit and non-profit combined) accounted for only 5.6 per cent of all hospital beds.[42]

The purchaser-provider split and the increasing autonomy given to hospitals have been complemented by internal restructuring. In the British case, hospital departments became individual 'cost centres' charging for each completed procedure (significantly augmenting administrative work). This created a financial incentive to invest in the most profitable parts of a hospital, even if it was not the most important from the point of view of the local population's health needs. Hospitals, or in some cases single units within hospitals, were increasingly obliged to 'assess all [their] costs as if [they] stood alone, like a small or medium-sized business'.[43] The creation of internal markets is a widespread development affecting hospital organisation across Europe.

The growing fragmentation of healthcare services and the introduction of prices paved the way for outsourcing and public-private partnerships. Initially outsourcing was limited to secondary services such as cleaning, portering and catering, gradually followed by more and more sophisticated services such as information technology and accounting. In recent years, however, an increasing number of medical services have been contracted out to the private sector.[44] In Britain the government started a programme to set up new treatment centres specialising in a number of fairly standardised types of non-emergency surgery such as hip replacements. The idea was that the high degree of specialisation and the elimination of interruptions caused by emergency work would allow these centres to operate more efficiently and thereby help to reduce waiting times for elective surgery. The first treatment centres were operated by the NHS, but in 2002 the government started to invite private healthcare companies to establish additional so-called 'independent sector' – in practice, private for-profit – treatment centres (ISTCs). The official rationale was that the private sector would bring in additional capacity and perform the procedures 'at competitive unit costs' – the implication being that they would be cheaper than the NHS. In July 2007, 24 ISTCs operated by seven companies were up and running. [45]

But far from helping to reduce costs, there is strong evidence that the cost of treatments in privately-run treatment centres has been higher than the standard tariffs paid to NHS hospitals for the same procedures. Similarly, the predicted contribution of additional capacity turned out to be misleading. While private operators of independent treatment centres were initially barred from hiring NHS staff, the rules have been relaxed and qualified staff drawn from NHS hospitals, rather than brought in from elsewhere as initially envisaged, while the loss of patient income to the private centres destabilised NHS hospital finances.[46] The real aim of the ISTC programme can be seen in retrospect to have been to use the public's concern over waiting times to break the previous taboo on introducing private companies into the provision of NHS clinical care. The programme eventually evolved into a so-called 'Extended Choice Network' of some 150 private hospitals and clinics that now treat NHS-funded patients, and was also quickly succeeded by the extensive introduction of private firms into the provision of primary care in England.

Long-term outsourcing contracts can also result in what is described as Public Private Partnerships (PPPs). Like outsourcing, PPPs have become increasingly popular in the organisation of health care provision. PPPs can take different forms. In Austria, for example, several public hospitals are run in cooperation with private hospital companies and a number of new hospitals with private involvement are planned.[47] One regional government disclosed plans to hire a private hospital company to manage its 21 provincial hospitals, with a total of some 13,000 employees. The plan had to be abandoned because of public resistance, but one of the bidders received a well-remunerated multi-year consultancy contract. The city of Vienna's Hospital Association has recently established a joint venture with the regional social insurance fund and a private non-profit hospital with the aim of building a new dialysis centre. Because the centre will be managed by the private partner its employees will be covered by the less expensive (and so less favourable) private hospital collective agreement.

A special form of public-private partnership is the private finance initiative (PFI). Private capital has been involved in building (or refurbishing) and maintaining public hospitals in a number of countries, and notably in Spain, but nowhere has this policy has been pursued more vigorously and systematically than in the UK.[48] The role of the private partners in PFI projects includes not just financing but also the design and construction of hospital buildings as well as the operation of services such as maintenance, catering, cleaning and security. Once the facility is up and running, the PFI consortium charges the public contractor – typically an NHS hospital trust – an annual fee during the 25- to 30-year lifetime of the project.

Since 1997 nearly all new NHS hospitals in England have been financed under the PFI.[49] The main argument made in favour of the PFI is that it allows the public sector to transfer risk to private capital, in particular making sure that project costs and deadlines are met. There are doubts about the transfer of risks, partly due to the questionable way in which the risks have been calculated, but also in view of the long duration of PFI contracts, which in several cases have had to be re-negotiated in order to adapt them to changing circumstances, causing additional costs. Furthermore, in contrast to government claims there is no evidence that private-sector involvement actually reduces time- and cost-overruns in hospital construction.[50] Above all there is substantial evidence that total PFI costs are significantly higher than if the same project had been financed by regular public borrowing.[51] The higher-than-expected yearly payments affect the provision of services, as hospitals struggling to meet their obligatory leasing payments have to cut services.[52] The average reduction of hospital beds in the first wave of hospitals entering into PFI projects was 30 per cent, while the number of clinical staff was cut by 25 per cent.[53]

A corollary of commercialistion in the European hospital sector is the emergence of European healthcare multinationals. In Germany it has resulted in the formation of four major private hospital chains through a series of mergers and acquisitions.[54] The largest takeover so far took place when the dialysis-specialist Fresenius acquired the Helios group in 2005. Fresenius operates more than 2,000 dialysis centres around the world. Helios owned 58 hospitals with 15,800 beds and 27,000 employees.[55] Foreign investors were also attracted by the privatisation of German hospitals. The Swedish Capio Group acquired Deutsche Kliniken GmbH in August 2006, and then in November of the same year a majority shareholding in Capio was bought by the British private equity fund Apax. As well as owning Saint Görans Hospital in Stockholm, Capio operates hospitals and other health institutions in at least five other EU member states. In Spain Capio is the largest private hospital operator, and in France Capio Santé is the second largest. In the UK the company owns 21 hospitals. Capio's new owner Apax also holds shares in the South African healthcare giant Netcare. In Europe Netcare is primarily active in Britain as the owner of the largest private hospital operator, BMI Healthcare, with 49 hospitals. Apax and Nordic Capital also own shares in the French private hospital chain Vedici. However, Vedici and Capio Santé still fall considerably short of the 206 hospitals owned by Générale de Santé, the largest private hospital operator in France and one of the largest in Europe. In addition there are also a number of healthcare firms that have focused their activities on Central Eastern Europe. Swedish Medicover, for example, offers private insurance and private healthcare services. It is active in Poland, Romania and the Czech Republic. Another example of western healthcare companies reaching into central and eastern Europe is Euromedic. Although the company headquarters is in the Netherlands it is owned by the American private equity funds Warburg Pincus and GE Capital. Euromedic operates in twelve countries, including Hungary, Bosnia-Herzogovina, Romania, the Czech Republic, Croatia and Russia.

THE ROLE OF THE EUROPEAN UNION

Member states have always been reluctant to cede their control over social and health policies to the European Union. With regard to health care, the European Treaty only mentions public health and demands that Community action and national policies should 'be directed towards improving public health, preventing human illness and diseases, and obviating sources of danger to human health'. (Article 152, §1). Otherwise the EU has no mandate to interfere in national healthcare systems. However, the freedom of member states to design and administer their national health services increasingly conflicts with the 'four freedoms' that are the cornerstone of the European integration process: the free movement of goods, persons, capital and services. While member states have argued that health care is not an economic activity and should therefore not be subjected to economic rules, the European Court of Justice has repeatedly stated the opposite by judging in favour of patients who have gone to another country for treatment and applied for public reimbursement at home.[56] The European Commission followed this interpretation by including rules on cross-border health services in the 2004 draft directive on services in the internal market (which became widely known as the Bolkestein Directive). Not least because of the strong public support that exists for non-commercial healthcare services, the directive met fierce resistance with a series of large public demonstrations and protests across Europe in 2005. The European Parliament subsequently voted to completely remove health care from the scope of the directive, and the Commission conceded this in early 2006.

At the same time, however, the Commission announced that it would propose a separate directive on health services. Since then the Commission has come forward with at least two proposals. Its latest proposal, of July 2008, focuses solely on cross-border health care, although only a very limited number of patients so far go abroad for treatment.[57]

It is telling that the legal base for this draft directive is exclusively derived from the internal market provision (§95) of the European Treaty.[58] The Commission argues that access to cross-border health care will greatly expand the choices of patients in Europe. Notwithstanding the small number of patients who up to 2008 had sought treatment outside their home countries, the directive is important because it addresses the more fundamental question of whether healthcare systems should be planned and administered by public organisations, or should be left to be shaped by market forces. Cross-border health care poses a serious threat to healthcare provision because it erodes the capacity of national, regional and local governments to plan it. With the promotion of cross-border health care, demand will be increasingly dependent on external factors which member states themselves cannot control or even influence (such as, for example, the healthcare budgets of neighbouring countries). Conversely, the possibility of sending patients abroad may induce some countries to export their healthcare problems to others. Rich western European countries may attempt to solve their financing problem by sending patients to southern or eastern Europe, where treatments are significantly cheaper, while the populations of these countries in turn may be deprived of medical attention if the available resources are increasingly used to treat well-paying patients from abroad.

At the same time it must be questioned whose choices will increase as a result of being able to go to another country for treatment. Those who leave their home country for health treatments are most likely those who are able and accustomed to travel and live abroad, and who have families that can accompany them. Obviously, these are people at the upper end of the income scale. In contrast the choices of those who are not mobile, for language and cultural reasons, and who are dependent on neighbourhood support, may actually shrink as a result of local services becoming increasingly under-funded. Such patients will tend to be on low incomes.[59] Hence liberalisation and deregulation of health care in Europe will likely fuel differences between countries and within countries, undermining the solidarity on which European healthcare systems are built.

While promoting cross-border health care provision, the European Union is also increasing pressure on member states to reform their national healthcare systems. Because it cannot do so directly it uses the open method of coordination (OMC) initially invented to streamline European social and employment policies.[60] In a nutshell, the open method of coordination is a mode of governance based on the identification and dissemination of 'best-practice' examples. It is also a 'soft-law' approach. Countries are only advised to introduce certain measures; they cannot be forced to implement them. But because each national health system is a unique and extremely complex arrangement it is very difficult if not impossible to develop a set of common benchmarks to compare and evaluate them. Similarly problematic is the idea that a measure adopted in one system will have the same effect in a different institutional environment in another country.[61] Because of these difficulties, the only viable criterion of comparison for the European Commission is the impact on public budgets. Accordingly, it regards healthcare reforms as successful if they help to reduce costs or to shift costs from public to private funding, no matter what the consequences may be for the quality and accessibility of health care. Guideline No 2 of the Broad Economic Policy Guidelines for 2005-08 states that 'Member states should, in view of the projected costs of ageing populations ... reform and re-enforce pension, social insurance and health care systems to ensure that they are financially viable, socially adequate and accessible'.[62] In reality, however, financial viability as perceived by the European Council and the Commission renders healthcare services increasingly inadequate and limits access for low income earners.

CONCLUSION

Marketisation of health care in Europe takes a variety of forms. Changes that can be associated with the shift towards a market-based provision of health care include the reduction of the share of public financing in total healthcare financing and, related to this, the increasing role of private insurance schemes and out-of-pocket payments; competition between different insurance providers, including competition between social insurance funds; a split between funding and provision of health care; the increasing autonomy of healthcare providers coupled with growing competition between providers and flat-rate-based compensation; decentralisation and concentration; the sale of public hospitals to private investors and the building of new private hospitals; and the creation of internal markets, outsourcing, PPP and the PFI. In several countries, these changes have been introduced on the basis of the claim that they will increase patients' choice. In all countries they were meant to reduce healthcare costs. But the effect of the reforms has been not so much a reduction of costs as a shift from public to private healthcare spending. Increasing healthcare costs – in most countries the proportion of GDP spent on health care has continued to increase – are not considered a problem as long as they do not weigh on public budgets. The shift from public to private healthcare financing is not least the result of pressure from the European Union to reduce public deficits and to streamline national healthcare policies.

The most notable consequence of the shift towards private healthcare financing is the erosion of the redistribution built into the Bismarck and Beveridge systems of public healthcare financing. Private insurance premiums and out-of-pocket payments are the same for all citizens regardless of their income, with the effect that as a proportion of their income private healthcare premiums and out-of-pocket-payments are substantially higher for people on low incomes. However, marketisation not only amplifies inequality, it may also actually increase total expenditures. Research shows that private insurers have significantly higher administration costs than their public counterparts.[63] Given their higher costs, it is difficult to see how private insurers can offer better coverage for less money unless they are allowed to offer different premiums to different risk groups. This again disadvantages those who are already at the bottom of the income scale. In the same way private hospitals can be more efficient than public operators mainly because they specialise in highly standardised low-risk procedures, while the more complicated cases are left to the public system. While private investors have therefore focused on small hospitals, the recent takeovers in Germany are attempts to make profits out of larger general hospitals. It is not clear yet if this strategy will pay off, but the input of long overdue investment, the reduction of staff numbers and the subsequent intensification of work, the payment of lower wages to nurses and non-managerial and non-medical personnel, as well as a move to outsource as many internal services as possible, have helped private owners to rapidly cut operational deficits.[64] In addition to evidence from individual privatisation cases, national statistics show that private hospitals in Germany tend to operate with lower ratios of staff to beds. In 2007 the average ratio in private for-profit hospitals was 25 per cent lower than in public hospitals.[65] The lower staff-to-patient ratio naturally increases the intensity of work (in hospitals the potential for greater rationalisation, other than in administration, is very limited). The intensification of work is typically accompanied by a greater division of labour, with the result that patients are confronted with frequently changing staff members, easily giving them the impression – perhaps with reason – that they are not being properly looked after. Not surprisingly five out of the six privatised hospitals in Hamburg were among the lowest-ranked clinics in a 2007 patient survey.[66] The introduction of the PFI in British NHS hospitals has had a similar effect, with the important difference that in order to pay for their up to 70 per cent higher-than-expected PFI costs, NHS hospitals not only cut staff but also reduced bed numbers.

In any case, while the effects of marketisation on quality and access remain debated, it is clear that private capital has profited in many ways from the marketisation and commodification of health care in Europe. Profits derive from holding shares in the new European healthcare multinationals, from private-public partnerships, including the UK's now notorious Private Finance Initiative, from outsourced services, from the provision of highly standardised elective surgery and the treatment of well-off patients with private insurance, as well as from supplementary private insurance schemes that cover additional expenses and the costs of 'de-listed' services, while the basic and larger costs are covered by public funds or by the provision of new private insurance plans that charge customers according to the potential health risks they are carrying.

NOTES

Research for this essay was conducted as part of two EC-funded European research projects – Privatisation and the European Social Model (PRESOM) and Privatisation of Public Services and the Impact on Productivity, Employment and Service Quality (PIQUE). I am grateful to all the colleagues who participated in the projects, especially to Christine André. The usual disclaimer applies.

1   According to OECD Health Data, the US spent 15 per cent of its GDP on health care in 2006 whereas the 'old' EU 15 (15 western European countries) spent on average only 9 per cent. In terms of dollars per capita the US spent more than twice the average of the EU 15.

2   In Belgium and the Netherlands most hospitals are private non-profit, mostly affiliated with one of the major churches.

3   Robert Mills and Shailesh Bhandari, 'Health Insurance Coverage in the United States 2002', US Census Bureau, September 2003, available from http://www.census.gov. Michael B. Katz, *The Price of Citizenship. Redefining the American Welfare State*, New York: Metropolitan Books, 2001, p. 266ff.

4   Richard Saltman and Hans Dubois, 'The Historical and Social Base of Health Insurance Systems', in R. Saltman, R. Busse and J. Figueras, eds., *Social Health Insurance Systems in Western Europe*, London: Open University Press, 2004.

5   In the case of social insurance funds, some countries have a maximum contribution rate: above a certain income the contributions remain the same even for rich people.

6   Hans Maarse, 'The Privatisation of Health Care in Europe: An Eight-Country Analysis', *Journal of Health Politics, Policy and Law*, 31(5), 2006, p. 982 (italics in original).

7   John Lister, *The NHS after 60. For Patients or For Profits?*, London: Middlesex University Press, 2008, p. 27.

8   Mike Dent, *Remodelling Hospitals and Health Professions in Europe*, Houndmills Basingstoke: Palgrave Macmillan, 2003, p. 51.

9   Christoph Hermann, 'Neoliberalism in the European Union', *Studies in Political Economy* 79, 2007.

10   Gabriele Gröschl-Bar and Niko Stumpfögger, 'Krankenhäuser', in T. Brandt et al., eds., *Europa im Ausverkauf. Liberalisierung und Privatisierung öffentlicher Dienstleistungen und ihre Folgen für die Tarifpolitik*, Hamburg: VSA Verlag, 2008, p. 168.

11   Both developments have resulted in a continuously falling proportion of wages as a percentage of GDP. See Simone Leibner, 'Pragmatic Change in Social

Insurance Countries? Assessing Recent Health Care Reforms in Germany, the Netherlands and Austria', Paper presented at the ESPAnet Conference, Vienna, 20 - 22 September 2007. See also Alois Guger, Markus Materbauer and Ewald Walterskirchen, 'Alternative Ansätze zur Finanzierung des öffentlichen Gesundheitswesen', *Kurswechsel* Heft 2, 2007.

12   Jane Lethbridge, 'Strategies of Multinational Health Care Companies', in M. Mackintosh and M. Koivusalo, eds., *Commercialisation of Health Care: Global and Local Dynamics and Policy Responses*, Houndmills Basingstoke: Palgrave Macmillan, 2005. David Hall, 'Multinational Corporations and the Pattern of Privatisation in Healthcare', in Kasturi Sen, ed., *Restructuring Health Services*, London: Zed Books, 2003.

13   Sarah Sexton, 'Trading Healthcare Away: the WTO's General Agreement on Trade and Services (GATS)', in Sen, *Restrucuturing Health Services*. Kai Mosebach, 'Gesundheit als Ware? Managed Care, GATS und die "Amerikanisierung" des deutschen Gesundheitssystems', *Prokla*, 132, 2003.

14   David McDonald and Greg Ruiters, 'Rethinking Privatisation: Towards a Critical Theoretical Perspective', in *Public Service Yearbook 2005/2006*, Amsterdam: Transnational Institute, 2006.

15   There are, however, cases in Germany where public hospitals have been sold to private investors despite fierce resistance from local populations, and despite a majority of citizens voting against privatisation in local ballots. See Nils Böhlke, 'The Impact of Hospital Privatisation on Industrial Relations and Employees: The Case of the Hamburg Hospitals', *Work Organisation Labour & Globalisation*, 2(2), Autumn 2008.

16   Jaime Baquero Vargas and Carmen Pérez, 'La Mercantilización de la Sanidad', *Revista Economía Crítica*, 6, 2007.

17   Stewart Player and Colin Leys, 'Commodifying Health Care: The UK's National Health Service and the Independent Treatment Sector Programme', *Work Organisation Labour & Globalisation*, 2,(2), Autumn 2008, pp. 11-12; and Colin Leys, *Market-Driven Politics: Neoliberal Democracy and the Public Interest*, London: Verso, 2001, p. 84.

18   Exceptions are Austria and Portugal, where public expenditures as a proportion of total expenditures actually increased between 1980 and 2005. This was also true, from the late 1990s, in the UK, due to the Labour government's large increases in funding for the NHS, especially after the year 2000.

19   Data from OECD Health Data 2007. See Christine André and Christoph Hermann, 'Privatisation and Marketisation of Health Care Systems in Europe', in Frangakis et al., eds., *Privatisation Against the European Social Model*, Houndsmills Basingstoke: Palgrave Macmillan, forthcoming.

20   Ibid.

21   Jürgen Wasem et al., 'The Role of Private Health Insurance in Social Health Insurance Countries', in: R. Saltman, et al., eds., *Social Health Insurance Systems*.

22   Ibid.

23   Out-of-pocket-payments include direct payments (payments for goods and services that are not covered by insurance), co-payments (insured patients are

required to cover parts of the costs for treatment and medication, which is also referred to as user charges), and informal payments for preferential treatment. See Nadia Jemiai, Sarah Thomson and Elias Mossialos, 'An Overview of Cost Sharing for Health Services in the European Union', *Euro Observer*, 6(3), Autumn 2004.

24   André and Hermann, 'Privatisation and Marketisation'.

25   Ibid.

26   Wieslawa Kozek, 'Liberalisation, Privatisation and Regulation in the Polish Healthcare Sector/Hospitals', November 2006, available from http://www. pique.at.

27   Hans Maarse and Ruud Ter Meulen, 'Consumer Choice in Dutch Health Insurance after Reform', *Health Care Analysis* No 14, 2006.

28   Hans Maarse, 'Health reform – one year after implementation'. *Health Policy Monitor*, May 2007, http://www.hpm.org/survey/nl/a9/1.

29   Allyson Pollock, *NHS plc: The Privatisation of Our Health Care*, London: Verso, 2005.

30   Monika Andersson, 'Sweden', *Sozialpolitik in Diskussion* No 5 (Privatisierung von Gesundheit – Blick über die Grenzen), 2007, p. 69.

31   Sebastian Klinke and Rolf Müller, *Auswirkungen der DRGs auf die Arbeitsbedingungen, das berufliche Selbstverständnis und die Versorgungsqualität aus Sicht hessischer Krankenhausärzte*, ZES-Arbeitspapier No 4/2008, University of Bremen, p. 91.

32   Dent, *Remodelling Hospitals*, p. 52.

33   Koen Verhoest and Justine Sys (2006): 'Liberalisation, Privatisation and Regulation in the Belgian Healthcare Sector/Hospitals', Report produced for the PIQUE project, http://www.pique.at/reports/pubs/PIQUE_ CountryReports_Health_Belgium_November2006.pdf.

34   Schulten, 'Germany', p. 36.

35   Andersson, 'Sweden', p. 63.

36   Martin Rümmele, 'Die Privatisierung von Gesundheitseinrichtungen und ihre Folgen', *Kurswechsel* 2, 2007, p. 40.

37   Maarse, 'The Privatisation of Health Care', p. 996. Nils Böhlke et al, eds., *Privatisierung von Krankenhäusern. Gegenstrategien aus gewerkschaftlicher und zivilgesellschaftlicher Perspektive*, Hamburg: VSA Verlag, forthcoming.

38   Schulten, 'Germany', pp. 37-8.

39   Gröschl-Bahr and Stumpfögger, 'Krankenhäuser'.

40   Schulten, 'Germany' pp. 39-40.

41   Ibid., p. 9.

42   Ulrike Papouschek und Nils Böhlke, *Strukturwandel und Arbeitsbeziehungen im Gesundheitswesen in Tschechien, Deutschland, Polen und Österreich*, FORBA - Working Life Research Centre, Vienna, 2008, p.15-16.

43   Pollock, *NHS PLC*, pp. 110ff.

44   Ibid., pp. 45-46.

45   Stewart Player and Colin Leys, *Confuse & Conceal: The NHS and Independent Sector Treatment Centres*, Monmouth: Merlin Press, 2008, pp. 5ff.

46   Player and Leys, 'Commodifying Health Care', pp. 14-15.

47   Ines Hofbauer, 'Österreich', *Sozialpolitik in Diskussion*, 5, pp. 31-2; Rümmele, 'Die Privatisierung von Gesundheitseinrichtungen'.

48   On Spain see Marciano Sánchez Bayle, 'La privatización y los nuevos modelos de gestión en sanidad', *Revista Economía Crítica*, 6, 2008.

49   In Wales and Scotland, where regional parliaments have become responsible for health policy as a result of devolution, enthusiasm for the PFI in the hospital sector has been less (see Lister, *The NHS after 60*, pp. 209ff). In particular the Scottish government has shown a growing willingness to re-examine existing PFI projects, whereas in England the authorities have repeatedly refused to disclose essential information (Allyson Pollock, 'Finance Capital and Privatisation', public lecture, Vienna, 23 April 2009). In general, many if not quite all of the privatisation measures described here for the UK apply to England only.

50   Allyson Pollock, David Price and Stewart Player, 'An Examination of the UK Treasury's Evidence Base for Cost and Time Overrun Data in UK Value-for-Money Policy and Appraisal', *Public Money & Management*, 27(2), April 2007.

51   Jean Shaoul, Anne Stafford and Pam Stapleton, 'The Cost of Using Private Finance to Build, Finance and Operate Hospitals', *Public Money and Management*, 28(2), April 2008, p. 103.

52   Mark Hellowell and Allyson Pollock, *Private Finance Public Deficts. A Report on the Cost of PFI and its Impact on Health Services in England*, Edinburgh: Centre of International Public Health, 2007.

53   Pollock, *NHS PLC,* p. 59.

54   Gröschl-Bar and Stumpfögger, 'Krankenhäuser', p. 168. Schulten, 'Germany', p. 40.

55   The frequent takeovers of hospitals in Germany alerted the Federal Cartel Office, which has repeatedly objected to the sale of public hospitals to particular buyers. In the case of Hamburg, for example, the new owner Asklepios was ordered to resell one of the seven hospitals to a competing private hospital provider (Schulten, 'Germany', p. 45).

56   Dorte Sindbjerg Martinsen, 'Towards an Internal Health Market with the European Court', *Western European Politics*, 28(5), 2005; and Wolfram Lamping, 'Europäische Integration und Gesundheitspolitik. Vom Paradiesvogel zum Prestigeobjekt', *Kurswechsel*, 2, 2007.

57   European Commission, 'Proposal for a Directive on the Application of Patients' Rights in Cross-Border Healthcare', July 2008, available from http://ec.europa. eu; and see Klaus Dräger, 'Bolkestein durch die Hintertür. EU-Richtlinie zu grenzüberschreitenden Gesundheits-diensten', *Sozialismus*, 12, 2008.

58   An attempt to expand the legal basis of the directive by referencing public health as a second source for the legitimacy of the proposed measures was voted down in the European Parliament on 23 April 2009.

59   Dräger, 'Bolkestein durch die Hintertür'.

60   Hans-Jürgen Urban, 'Wettbewerbskorporatismus und soziale Politik. Zur Transformation wohlfahrtsstaatlicher Politikfelder am Beispiel der Gesundheitspolitik', Marburg, Forschungsgruppe Europäische Integration (FEI), Study Number 21, 2005, pp. 65-70.

61   Thomas Gerlinger and Hans-Jürgen Urban, 'From Heterogeneity to Harmonisation? Recent Trends in European Health Policy', *Cadernos Saúde Pública*, 23 Sup 2, 2007.

62   European Commission, 'European Economy No 4/2005, The Broad Economic Policy Guidelines (For the 2005-08 Period)', p. 40.

63   Sarah Thomson and Elias Mossialos, 'Voluntary Health Insurance in the European Union', European Observatory on Health Systems and Policies, 2004, p. 100. Available from http://www.euro.who.int.

64   Gröschl-Bar and Stumpfögger, 'Krankenhäuser', p. 169-73.

65   Ibid. p. 170; Statistisches Bundesamt, 'Grunddaten der Krankenhäuser 2007' (Fachserie 12, Reihe 6.1.1), Table 2.3.3 (Personalbelastungszahlen nach Krankenhaustypen), Wiesbaden, 2008.

66   Böhlke, 'The Impact of Hospital Privatisation', p. 128.

CONTRADICTIONS AT WORK: STRUGGLES FOR CONTROL IN CANADIAN HEALTH CARE

PAT ARMSTRONG AND HUGH ARMSTRONG

The history of health care is in many ways a history of struggles for control of the work involved. These struggles have typically been highly gendered and racialised as well as class-based, with contradictory and complex consequences for both the care work and different workers. Indeed, some methods of managerial control are derived from reforms that have been fought for by workers, or have been built on their strategies. The nature and results of these struggles have changed over time and with place, shaped by global as well as local pressures. They have also changed with efforts to commodify health services, driven by profit-seeking and ideological motives, alongside management strategies introduced from the commercial sector into the organisation of healthcare work in the non-profit health services that remain. But there are real limits to the application of such strategies in health services, limits set not only by the organised resistance of healthcare workers but also by the nature of the work itself.

Prominent in recent changes has been the introduction of new technologies, especially information technologies. Although they increase precision and reduce waste, these technologies can also serve to restrict the scope for the exercise of independent judgement, and fragment care. Narrow approaches to 'productivity' and 'efficiency' are invoked by managers seeking to compress work time, whether through traditional Taylorist intensification initiatives or through flexibilisation initiatives introduced in response to the inevitable peaks and troughs in healthcare needs.

These initiatives are often introduced in the name of evidence-based medicine (EBM), with its claim to having the right practitioner do the right thing at the right time and place. Although no one would advocate health care interventions that ignore or flout the available evidence, Timmermans and Berg have persuasively argued that the EBM movement makes uncritical assumptions about the virtues of standardisation.[1] Feminists meanwhile have revealed how work intensification and flexibilisation are gendered and racialised processes.[2]

As in Western Europe, health care in Canada has, at least until recently, largely escaped many of the forms of managerial control developed in the for-profit industrial sector. In this essay we focus on Canada, not because it is a special case but because it provides a concrete example of processes at work in many countries, and because context matters, with each country demonstrating some unique features.

THE EVOLUTION OF THE DIVISION OF LABOUR IN CANADIAN HEALTH CARE

Health care is about human life. All of us are current or potential users of healthcare services. Yet the risks and consequences of care can be enormous, making claims for skill and scientific certitude particularly appealing. These claims can be used to expand control by healthcare workers as well as undermine it. There are vigorous debates about the extent to which a commitment to saving human life, as opposed to securing a profitable monopoly, motivated doctors to seek control over who could do what in medicine. What is clear is that in Canada as elsewhere doctors gained much of their monopoly power in the mid-nineteenth century, well before there was a firm scientific basis for most aspects of medical practice. Given the belief in scientific progress in 'the age of reason' and the continuing guild dominance of crafts, Canadian doctors – who were and remain for the most part self-employed practitioners – established the guild-like Canadian Medical Association that used its class connections to acquire state-supported control over admission to the profession, the acquisition of medical skills and the right to autonomous practice, regulated loosely by other doctors.

Their power as a profession then helped doctors establish methods that were more effective and science-based, and also ensured the dominance of white males over the growing number of other healthcare workers. Although nuns and a range of other women defined as unskilled provided care in hospitals and homes, formally trained nurses did not graduate until the end of the nineteenth century. At the beginning of the twentieth century, there were over 19 doctors for every nurse in Canada, and the doctors were able to determine nurses' conditions of practice. Basically, nurses were assigned tasks doctors did not want to do and carried them out under doctors' direction. Unlike doctors, most nurses have always been wage workers, but like doctors they were later to shed some essential tasks to others.

Until the Second World War, the bulk of nursing work was actually done without pay by female student nurses, who lived in residences where they were carefully supervised by matrons. Because no regulations prevented the firing of women when they married or became pregnant, the relatively small numbers of graduate nurses who stayed in nursing were single women who managed other women. These nurses, not surprisingly, sought to imitate the doctors by forming their own guild-like organisations in an attempt to assert control and gain rewards as well as recognition for their skills. Unlike the doctors' organisations, however, theirs were not autonomous and, while seeking to establish the regulation of skills, they did so under doctors' direction. And unlike the doctors, nurses were saddled with the prevailing ideas about women's natural caring skills and devotion to care work as a motivating force, ideas that were reinforced by their explicit subordination to doctors. But they followed the example of the doctors in seeking to shed some of their tasks as a means of establishing their skills and status, and to do so in a way that allowed them to direct the workers who took over those aspects of their work.

Like many other countries, Canada emerged from the Second World War with a greatly expanded healthcare labour force and a growing demand for healthcare services as well as an expectation that these would be provided through public means. Hospitals were owned primarily by non-profit charitable or religious organisations or by municipalities. Payment for doctors and hospitals came from individuals or insurance companies, and much hospital insurance was run on a non-profit basis. There were very few privately-owned facilities and none with shareholders. There was little effort to introduce methods from the commercial sector, both because most doctors were in solo practices and because there was a strong cultural ethos, supported by them, that health care was about altruism more than financial gain. Indeed, doctors' incomes were generally quite low, the largely female hospital labour force had low wages and much of the work was still done by unpaid student nurses.

The gradual and uneven introduction of public health insurance – begun in 1947 with the hospital insurance introduced in Saskatchewan by North America's first social democratic government, and finally realised federally only in the mid-1960s – largely left this system in place, simply making the government the single payer for services that doctors judged to be necessary. Although doctors did not collectively resist public involvement in hospital services, they staged the infamous doctors' strike when the Saskatchewan government moved in the early 1960s to install a universal medical programme. Claiming that this would make doctors public employees, they appealed to the public on the grounds that government control and the loss of their autonomy would entail health risks. Although the strike was defeated, the combination of pressures from the doctors and from patients fearing for their lives ensured that the new system would be based on public payment for private practice, and this was reinforced when the Saskatchewan initiative led first to a Royal Commission and then to the federal programme introduced a few years later.[3]

Under Canada's federal system, responsibility for health care rests primarily with the provincial (and territorial) governments. The federal role – aside from supporting health research, overseeing food and drug safety, screening immigrants and visitors for health risks, and providing health care to Aboriginal peoples – is to fund a share of the hospital and other medical costs borne by the provinces. By offering, initially, to pay half the costs of 'medically necessary' hospital and medical services, in return for the provinces respecting broad principles of universal coverage, equitable access, comprehensiveness (of services within hospitals and doctors' offices), portability (between provinces) and public administration (of each provincial payment scheme), the federal government made an offer that by 1971 not even the most conservative of provincial governments could refuse.

The new federal system gave rise to an enormous expansion in health services, while also amounting to what the venerable Canadian healthcare historian, Malcolm Taylor, appropriately called a blank cheque to doctors, who continued to be paid on a fee-for-service basis.[4] Attempts to control expenditures directly through constraining doctors' fees have consistently failed, with doctors continuing to use strike threats and public appeals about health risks effectively. As jobs expanded in nursing and women won the right to stay in their jobs after marriage and pregnancy, nurses began demanding decent wages and working conditions. They tried to follow the doctors' lead to claim power as a profession but were less successful in part because doctors restricted the scope of what nurses could do, in part because of their gender and in part because they were already employees. In 1973 the Supreme Court sided with the Service Employees International Union (SEIU) in deciding that the Saskatchewan Registered Nurses Association could not act as a union negotiating wages because its board of directors included nurses in management positions.[5] This decision contributed significantly to the formation of nurses' unions, although many of these new unions still retained the notions and labels of professional associations, as well as traditional ideas about women's skills. The unionisation of nurses contributed to rising costs as exploitative wages, or none at all for students, were replaced by relatively decent pay.

At the level of the hospital or other institution, managers embraced the demands coming from doctors and nurses to shed aspects of their work to less skilled workers as a means of cutting costs and increasing control over some workers by assigning more of the work to those defined as unskilled. Most of these new workers – personal support workers, home care aides, housekeepers, dietary aides, clerical and laundry workers – were women, and many were from racialised and/or immigrant communities, making them particularly vulnerable to exploitation. They also began organising into unions, reducing the impact of the further division of labour on costs and control. In spite of the increasing fragmentation of work and the increasing use of substitute labour, in the foundational years of the Canadian health system the means of institutional control were quite specific. Doctors rather than managers retained much of the power. Health care was primarily delivered as a public good by non-profit organisations and by self-employed doctors working mainly in solo practices, with at most a single employee to assist them. Rather than reduce the power of doctors, the new public investment in health care supported and even increased it as the demand for care rose with access. It also substantially increased their incomes.

Science and technology also tended to enhance, rather than undermine, doctors' control as they helped them deliver better care and reinforced their claim that their work rested on scientific knowledge and their skill in applying it. Attempts to decrease doctors' fees largely failed, partly for this reason and partly because they were highly organised. Nurses, although they never enjoyed the same autonomy and control, also managed to carve out particular skill areas as well as improve their conditions of work. The nature of health care assisted both doctors and nurses in their efforts to avoid managerial control, and so did the idea that healthcare work was different from the other sectors of the economy. It was an idea supported by the state through the granting of monopolies over specified areas of medical practice to the various health professions, based on the notion of protecting the public from unskilled care. This degree of professional control was made more acceptable by the non-profit nature of the service, removing it from the pressures that for-profit organisations faced even as the development of universal access increased demand for medical services.

RESTRUCTURING FOR CONTROL

Since the 1970s all this has been consistently challenged. With the end of the post-war boom, rising public debt and growing budget deficits, powerful forces within and outside the state began to talk about a 'high cost spiral' and of a general fiscal crisis.[6] The federal government initiated bitter and complex negotiations with the provinces to restructure the cost-sharing arrangement. From 1977 on, the federal contributions were reduced and made more predictable, while the provinces gained more flexibility in how they were allocated. For their part, the provinces began to adopt managerial control strategies taken from the commercial sector.

Equally important, health services were increasingly seen as an untapped source of profit. Transforming care into profit-making investor-owned services could help solve the crisis in capital accumulation. Multinational corporations began pressuring the provincial governments to open up services, at times finding enthusiastic support within the state. Not only should health care be organised like a business, they argued, wherever possible it should become one. Trade agreements, such as NAFTA in North America and the TRIPS and GATS treaties that became globalised under the World Trade Organization rubric, served to increase the pressure on states to open their public services to foreign investment, transferring elements of care into commodities for market exchange. Health care was held to be ripe for change, with business and business practices leading the way and worker autonomy and the lack of managerial control seen as the problem.

Health care is labour-intensive: in Canada labour costs are estimated to consume between 60 and 80 per cent of health care budgets.[7] As of 2005, registered nurses (RNs) made up 34 per cent of the professional and technical health labour force. Licensed practical nurses (LPNs; in some provinces called registered practical nurses) made up another 9 per cent, as did doctors. The rest were in a vast array of over 30 smaller occupations, ranging from dentists to ambulance attendants, from midwives to medical lab technicians.[8] Missing from this count of healthcare workers are most of those labelled 'ancillary', ranging from laundry workers to clerical workers, from personal support workers to food service workers, and well beyond. In total, their numbers in the healthcare sector are broadly equivalent to those in the professional and technical categories.[9] Their numbers are however significantly understated, as many of them doing healthcare work are classified as being in other industries, if their work has been contracted out to for-profit firms.[10] Finally, there are the multitudes who perform unpaid, 'informal' work in health care. Although their numbers are yet more difficult to estimate, the Canadian Cancer Society and the Canadian Caregivers Coalition suggest that if those providing homecare were to be switched to paid homecare at the current (low) rates of pay, the annual bill would be $25 billion, or more than Canada spends on doctors.[11]

Not only are healthcare labour costs high, but the autonomy of doctors in particular has given them considerable power to determine what services patients receive, and thus what the state must pay for. For all these reasons reducing the costs of healthcare labour became a key policy issue from the 1970s onwards. Driven by corporate pressures, neoliberal ideology and rising costs, the provinces gradually introduced many business management strategies, from work reorganisation and time compression to the employment of lower-cost workers and the introduction of labour-saving technologies. But these methods have enjoyed only limited success in reducing costs or increasing managerial control, in part because their proponents have failed to understand that health care is not a business like the rest, and in part because of the considerable power within health care of those who actually do the work. We shall now see how these contradictions play out with respect to doctors, nurses and ancillary workers.

DOCTORS

Doctors remain a self-regulating profession with a mandate from government that supports this independence. It is still the case today that public money pays for private practice through fees negotiated with the provincial medical associations. The doctors' negotiating strength continues in large part because of their ability to appeal to the public's concern for their health. Although most Canadian doctors are not employees, they are not owners of profit-making businesses either. They are paid on a fee-for-service basis by the state and in most provinces are required to be either completely in or completely out of the public payment system. They may not charge patients for services that are covered by the public insurance system. Although the provincial regulatory authorities or colleges that are responsible for registration, complaints, education and discipline have come under criticism for failing to protect the public, their only major concession has been to include some non-physicians on their governing boards.[12] Once granted registration by this body, a doctor remains free to bill the provincial government for all medically necessary services, unless either a disciplinary hearing by the college in question removes the licence or the doctor's annual membership fees go unpaid.

Although the state has gradually reduced the area of practice controlled by doctors alone, allowing some other professions such as 'nurse practitioners' to perform tasks previously reserved for doctors, they still have a wide scope and considerable control over the areas (of practice and of location) in which they work. This is in part why efforts to increase control by reducing the number of doctors trained in Canada, and threatening to import more foreign-trained doctors, has had little impact. In an effort to reduce supply and thus costs, the provinces did agree to cut the number of places in medical schools by 10 per cent, starting in 1993, but this turned out to be a largely futile effort.[13] With doctors controlling so much of the work, very few nurse practitioners were hired and the result was mainly a shortage of doctors. The presence of foreign-trained doctors (just over 20 per cent of the total) has had little impact either, given that the medical profession has a great deal of say over who gets to practice, and given that these foreign-trained doctors, whose education the Canadian state did not have to pay for, are nevertheless paid at the same rates as those trained in Canada.[14]

Indeed, government policy has not proven very effective in either reducing costs or increasing control over doctors' work. Fees have continued to rise, partly as a result of doctors' appeal to the public and their threats of work action. Moreover, whenever the real dollar value of fees is reduced, as happened across Canada between 1972 and 1984 and especially in Quebec between 1972 and 1976, doctors increased their billings by equivalent amounts by seeing more patients and providing more complicated services.[15] It is important to note, however, that there is a difference between this speed-up response and one driven by the search for profit by investors. Doctors in Canada who choose to work more slowly will still make a good income. Almost all doctors work for themselves, with no shareholders intent on speeding up the work in order to realise a profit.[16]

Given that most doctors are in private practice, hospitals have not had much direct control over doctors either, although hospitals do decide who has admitting privileges.[17] This partly reflects the dramatic reduction in hospital beds. While acute care bed ratios have been falling across the OECD, Canada had 2.8 acute care hospital beds per 1000 population in 2005, well below the OECD average of 3.9.[18] This trend has had the effect of indirectly controlling doctors. Some hospitals have substituted salaried hospital doctors for family physicians in an effort to fill gaps, promote more integrated care, and increase their control over physicians' work. The employment of such salaried doctors has been limited, however, both by opposition from family physicians and by the fact that doctors' fees are paid directly out of the government's health insurance fund; the global budgets given to hospitals cover all other costs of care, but not doctors' fees.[19] So if a hospital pays for a doctor it does not get reimbursed unless it has made a special arrangement with the state.

Thus while state funding practices have contributed to doctors' independence by paying most of them on a fee-for-service basis, government cutbacks and reorganisation have limited doctors' control, not least by reducing the overall number of hospital beds and forcing doctors to accommodate their practices to the scarce resources. Equally important, the restructuring of hospitals into giant organisations has been combined with an enhancement of managerial power, increasingly exercised by those trained in the for-profit sector rather than by doctors, as in the past.

The reduction in beds is, in turn, related to other indirect forms of control. Time, timing and tempo have been altered, especially when combined with a move to 'evidence-based medicine' (EBM). Evidence-based medicine originated with a group of academics and practising physicians at Ontario's McMaster University in the early 1990s.[20] It appealed to doctors' claims to have scientific grounds for their work as well as to their desire to improve care. Although its protagonists were undoubtedly committed to improving patient care, it was promoted within a context of neoliberal cost-cutting and control strategies. The emphasis in EBM is on using the rigorous evaluation of evidence to develop practice guidelines and treatment protocols, as well as performance indicators that would allow doctors to make informed decisions for specific patients. But the notion, encouraged by EBM, of identifying the right person to do the right thing at the right time, fit very well with efforts to control how doctors practise – what they do with each patient and how long they take to do it.

In Canada, it was difficult for governments and managers to use practice guidelines and treatment protocols directly to control doctors. But they have done so indirectly by supporting organisations such as Ontario's Institute for Clinical Evaluative Sciences to produce reports that could provide the basis for performance indicators, which in turn could be linked to fee payments. Doctors are increasingly required to justify their orders for hospital stays on the basis of standardised protocols. With, for example, evidence suggesting that replacement knee operations require three hospital days, doctors are under pressure to justify any longer stay. However, there are limits to such pressure created by the very real differences in patients' bodies and by the fact that patients are active, rather than simply passive, in their own care. Some people simply do not recover sufficiently from knee replacements to be discharged in three days, or may not do all the exercises that would make them ready to leave.

Although Canadian hospitals are not under pressure from investors to produce a profit, they are under pressure from provincial governments to control costs and managers tend to have an ideological commitment to market principles. And they do have the ability to appeal to the public, using the EBM approach, arguing that more efficiency is needed to save a system characterised as under threat. The wait times strategy provides a telling example. The public has been bombarded with stories about horrendous wait times for care. There is undoubtedly a problem here, one which concerned doctors and managers have been seeking to address through a variety of strategies. But the problem has been exaggerated by those seeking to make a profit through the provision of care in investor-owned facilities, and by those seeking to limit doctors' power. Governments have appealed to the public over the heads of the doctors, using concern about wait times to support strategies for reducing doctors' control and for moving to for-profit services. Wait times have been used as a justification for taking the management of wait lists for surgeries and tests out of the hands of individual physicians and making them the responsibility of public health authorities. In Saskatchewan, where the doctors' strike was all about retaining their autonomy, and which they largely managed to secure despite the introduction of the public health insurance system, surgeons today must participate in the provincial registry of patients waiting for surgery in order to book their operations in a hospital.

The wait times issue has also been used to pressure doctors to work in multi-disciplinary pre-surgery centres where their labour is more visible and coordinated with the work of other staff, some of whom are doing work previously done by doctors alone. Based on the argument that valuable time was wasted in preparing surgeries for the preferences of individual surgeons, new protocols have been developed to standardise preparation, speed up the switching of patients among surgeons, and allow 'swing' operating rooms that permit no down-time. Not only surgical procedures but also clinical practices have been standardised to eliminate 'previously idiosyncratic variations', such as individual surgeons' preferences among alternative prosthetic devices.[21] Technology has assisted in this approach. New techniques in cataract surgery, for example, lend themselves to production-line efficiencies without loss of quality.[22] In the context of new government wait-time guarantees that require a speed-up in service, and with the stick of evidence-based medicine, hospitals and clinics have been reorganising care in ways that significantly reduce the power of individual doctors.

Most of these strategies have been introduced in the public sector, where profit plays no role. To some extent the strategies are in response to the claim that the commercial sector is more efficient, and they do help to impose a more uniform structure on a historically diversified system, which is one reason these strategies have received support from the public. It may indeed be useful to reduce doctors' independent control in order to make care more effective and accessible. But the emphasis on wait times not only reduces doctors' power over these areas, it also fundamentally alters the way care work is approached overall. This is not always in the best interests of patients, and shifts power from doctors to management, just as more care is becoming for-profit by being moved out of the hospital setting to long-term residential care, as well as to clinics of various sorts, and to homecare.

NURSES

The largest single occupational group in the health sector consists of nurses: registered nurses (RNs) and licensed practical nurses (LPNs). Although still hampered by traditional ideas about women and care, their strong unions and professional organisations have been able to protect at least some of their skills and their conditions of work from new managerial control practices.[23] At the same time, however, appeals to nurses' professionalism and commitment, as well as the constraints on those among them who are also caring for their families, have made nurses complicit in and even promoters of some of these strategies.

As the transfer of some nursing work to lower-paid workers defined as less skilled reached its limits, hospital managers started to look to Taylorist techniques to increase control over nursing work and speed it up. Nursing work was examined to determine the individual tasks required and then to determine how each task could be timed, recorded and reorganised. Many nurses accepted or even embraced this approach, convinced that such an examination would demonstrate that they were overworked and would lead to more staffing as well as more recognition. It quickly became obvious, however, that the purpose was to speed up the work and reduce staff. Even when the figures showed that more staff were needed, nurses found the numbers were simply recalculated to show that what initially took 120 per cent of their time now took only 80 per cent.[24]

These task measurement techniques were combined with computerised patient classification and patient information systems. These systems, like the work measurement ones, were sold as ways of improving patient care. They were not initially resisted by the majority of nurses, who believed these methods would improve patient care by standardising it on a scientific footing. The appeal to science was particularly attractive to nurses seeking to demonstrate the scientific nature of their own work. The appeal to their concern for patient welfare through these classification systems also allowed management to introduce what were in effect indirect forms of control over nursing work.

These measurement systems also reflected and reinforced an increasing emphasis on only the most acute aspects of care being the proper work of hospitals, and even of many public health services.[25] This redefinition of the work of hospitals fits/ well with government efforts to reduce government involvement in, and payment for, health care, because the federal government's prohibition against doctors' charging fees directly to patients is restricted to charges for 'medically necessary' doctor and hospital services. Once Canadians leave the doctor's office or the hospital, they are no longer guaranteed coverage by universal public health insurance.

The narrower definition of hospital care opens up services to both fees and more for-profit involvement. Many hospitals have been closed, on the grounds that new methods of treatment and of work organisation mean that fewer beds were required. Others have been amalgamated, based on business plans that assumed that this created economies of scale in the private sector and would do the same in the health sector. Governments justified these moves to the public not only as a way to improve efficiency but also as a way to save taxpayers money and so save the public system. For nurses the result was dramatic: in Ontario alone, between 1994 and 1999 more than 5,000 nurses lost their jobs.[26]

There was some justification for promoting patient tracking and standard ways of classifying patients as means of improving the quality of care. Similarly, new and less invasive technologies that made it possible to dramatically shorten patient stays and to do more day surgery also improved care for many. However, as Jacqueline Choiniere makes clear in her study of these technologies, when 'treatment becomes rationalized or objectified in this manner, it is much easier to monitor', and managers are particularly interested in monitoring the nurse along with the patient.[27] Managers acquire greater control over the distribution and pacing of the work and are able to justify staff cutbacks. What had been defined as unproductive time is reduced and staffing levels are adjusted to match with precision what are inherently uneven levels of demand for care. Nurses employed full-time are increasingly 'floated' around the hospital, shifted to other areas if the indicators suggest there are too many nurses in one area. So, for example, while in the past fewer babies being born on one afternoon might mean a nurse could provide additional instruction to a new mother or even have a cup of tea, fewer babies now meant fewer nurses, even in the middle of a shift. In addition, more nurses are hired as part-time or casual staff, intended to be at work only during peaks in demand. Meanwhile, new definitions of care and new technologies mean that hospitals serve only the sickest patients. This too intensifies the workload, especially when combined with flexibilisation, and staffing levels dependent on standardised calculations of the time required for care.

At the same time as hospitals were introducing these measurement systems for patient classification and nursing work, by the 1990s many governments and managers were more explicit and open about adopting new work organisation strategies developed in the manufacturing sector. As an advisory body to the Ontario government put it, the 'health sector can learn a great deal from modern management science – particularly from Japanese and

American experiences in the total quality management of individuals and organizations', based on the assumption that such practices were 'equally applicable to manufacturing or service operations'.[28] The manager of one major Canadian hospital even went so far as to claim that these techniques were *more* applicable to hospitals 'because the practices of the majority of health care professionals are value-based on concepts of services, care, and compassion for the sick and injured'![29] Here managers were using the specific nature of health services to justify the introduction of new forms of work organisation, appealing to workers' notions of professionalism and compassion. Total Quality Management (TQM) and similar schemes were promoted as a way to improve quality through focusing on the work processes, on self-managed teams, on training rather than monitoring and on taking pride in the work. Many nurses bought into the schemes because these approaches did seem to support both their autonomy and their ideas about the work. Whatever the motivations of managers and nurses, in the context of a focus on cutbacks and the TQM emphasis on the elimination of variation, which contradicted both the principle of professional autonomy and the promotion of innovation, nurses found themselves multi-tasking rather than multi-skilling in ways that reduced their control over and pride in their work.[30]

During the 1990s many nurses once again sought to improve their power and status by imitating what they saw as the doctors' methods. They began emphasising the evidence base of their work, supporting the setting up of graduate programmes in nursing across the country that emphasised nursing theory and scientific research. In many jurisdictions, nurses were successful in their efforts to make a university degree, rather than college or hospital-based education, the requirement for entry. These objectives were not without controversy among nurses. A significant number argued that nurses should continue their long tradition of practising hands-on care and should not try to become mini-doctors. At least one jurisdiction, Manitoba, continues to resist the move to making university graduation a mandatory requirement for entry to nursing. Ironically, the shift to higher nursing qualifications as a route to enhanced power and status, following the doctors' example, has come just as doctors' power is being somewhat curtailed. Equally important, the nurses failed to recognise that much of the doctors' power came from their class and gender, the era when they were organised, and their establishment-oriented politics, rather than primarily from science and degrees. What the move to higher qualifications did do, however, was make it harder for working-class women to enter nursing, given that entry required significant tuition fees and longer periods of training without income.

Some nurses have been transformed into wage labourers, employed to produce profits. Although most hospitals are still non-profit organisations – and even those operated as public/private partnerships keep nurses in the public side – they did begin to rely heavily on temporary help agencies to fill gaps in services. Some nurses are willing to work in these agencies for a variety of reasons. Although working for a temporary help agency pays less and offers fewer benefits it does allow nurses to control their time and choose their workplace. Some opt for agency work as a means of managing their unpaid work at home, but many now do so because it has increasingly become the only way to get work, as full-time employment for nurses becomes scarcer. These nurses are 'just-in-time' workers, creating profits for private companies that bear few of the responsibilities or risks in the actual management and delivery of health care.[31]

'Temp agencies' are not the only for-profit companies that have established a foothold in the provision of health care in Canada. As patients are sent home quicker and sicker, more care work must be provided at home. Much of it is done (or at least is assumed will be done) by women relatives or friends without pay. This shedding of paid labour from the healthcare system is based on the presumption that any woman can do the work involved, which also makes it harder for the women who are paid to do the work to claim it is skilled work. It gives healthcare managers some flexibility in shedding labour when they are denied the resources needed to pay for the service. The public money that is now spent on paying workers to provide care in the home is increasingly channelled to for-profit companies. In Ontario, the government introduced in 1995 a competitive bidding process for the delivery of home care services and actively encouraged private companies to seek contracts. This meant that the nurses, as well as the personal support workers and therapists, became potential sources of profit. It also meant that all employers providing care in people's own homes were motivated to hire workers on lower salaries, to eliminate job security and benefits, to make employment precarious and to speed up the work. Data from Ontario show that, in the five years after managed competition was introduced, the wages of licensed practical nurses dropped by over two dollars an hour; notably, however, those in the not-for-profit sector were paid more than those in the for-profit sector.[32] RNs fared better, in part because the legally-defined scope of their work meant they could not as easily be replaced by other paid workers, but those in the for-profit sector still earned close to three dollars an hour less than those in the not-for-profit sector, and most of the jobs were in the for-profit sector.[33] The Ontario government had a similar programme for the for-profit delivery of long-term residential care. By 2005-06, 62 per cent of the 88,874 beds in Ontario's long-term care facilities were owned by for-profit companies.[34]

Although many nurses initially accepted or even supported attempts to measure their tasks and to standardise the work through the patient classification systems, the sceptics among the nurses increased as the uses to which these methods were put became increasingly obvious. Some left the country to seek jobs elsewhere and many left nursing altogether. Their unions launched research and publicity campaigns, as well as grievance procedures, to limit the increasing managerial control over their work and the privatisation of services. They have also appealed to the public, relying on the high levels of support that nurses continue to enjoy. Their unions and professional organisations were relatively successful in restricting the use of foreign-trained nurses as a reserve army. As of 2006, only about 8 per cent of nurses employed in Canada were foreign-trained. This is comparable to the proportion of foreign-trained nurses in the UK, and about half the proportion found in the US.[35] A few nurses have also been able to carve out some space from doctors' areas of work as nurse practitioners. These are advanced practice RNs with additional education in health assessment, diagnosis, and the management of illness and injury. In the last decade or so, they have been permitted to take over some responsibilities of doctors, notably in ordering and interpreting certain tests and in prescribing selected drugs. As yet, however, they account for only 0.5 per cent of the RN workforce.[36]

At the same time, some forms of standardised practice have given nurses the authority to do some things without seeking instructions from doctors. And they were successful, during the boom years of the early twenty-first century, in restoring some of the lost full-time jobs. But they have been less successful in expanding or even maintaining areas of autonomy for the majority of nurses. Methods of managerial control adopted from the for-profit sector have been eroding nurses' control over the pacing and order of work, directly via the reduction of nurse:patient ratios, and indirectly as a result of shorter patient stays. New technologies, such as self-administered medications, have taken some work away from nurses, as have efforts by LPNs to increase the scope of their work into areas once reserved for RNs. And RNs are increasingly required to teach women to do nursing work at home without pay, a process that further undermines RNs' claims to have special skills and threatens their legally defined scope of practice.

ANCILLARY WORKERS

From a managerial perspective, the control strategies taken from the for-profit sector have been most successful in reducing costs for the lowest paid workers, although it should again be noted that those who work in the public health sector earn more than those in similarly-labelled jobs in the private sector.[37] The first step involved defining many of these jobs as not being part of health care, even though a wide body of research shows that cleaning, laundry, food and paper work are critical components in health care and that team work is essential to good care.[38] Increasingly, from the 1970s on, official documents talked about 'hotel services' within hospitals, and the 'unskilled labour' involved.[39] This redefinition was made easier by the fact that most of the workers were women, dismissively described as doing just what women could do naturally. Many were from racially defined and immigrant populations as well.

On the basis of this redefinition, and of unsubstantiated claims about the greater effectiveness and efficiency of the for-profit sector, hospitals began contracting out the so-called ancillary work to multinational firms providing services to hotels and other businesses. These workers became producers of surplus value, as corporations such as Compass, Sodexho and Aramark recorded huge profits from taking over these services from the public sector. In some cases, companies were contracted to cover just one aspect of work, such as cleaning. In other cases companies took over all the services defined as not being part of 'clinical' health care, including the managerial functions related to them. Such major takeovers were often done through public/private partnerships of one kind or another.

In classical capitalist fashion, these companies used technology to reduce their reliance on labour and increase control over workers. Laundry, for example, was centralised in processing centres where machines did much of the work. Food was centrally prepared in capital-intensive plants and delivered over long distances, then reheated in delivery carts with the trays sent back for cleaning.[40] Information technologies allowed both the speed-up of clerical work and greater employer control. Cleaning was more difficult to mechanise, especially in patients' rooms, although it could be centrally controlled through the use of information technology. But managers mainly relied on other means to reduce labour costs and increase control. Cost savings were achieved by using Taylorist techniques to measure the tasks, determining what needed to be done, for how long and how, without much consultation with workers. Tasks were carefully specified and required to be done in shorter time periods, by fewer workers. Managers not only worked remaining employees harder but also paid them less and increased control in part through making employment precarious.

This neo-Taylorism went to an extreme in British Columbia, resulting in enormous losses of pay, benefits and job security for the overwhelmingly female and often racially-defined workers.[41] In order to privatise the services, in 2002 the government also tore up existing collective agreements, over the strenuous objections of the unions involved. The unions used the Canadian Charter of Rights and Freedoms to successfully challenge, in a case finally heard by the Supreme Court in 2007, the government's failure to bargain in good faith and to fulfil an existing contract, in the process establishing an important right for all workers.[42] Even apart from this victory, however, it became obvious that cleaning hospitals required not only considerable skills but also attention to the specific nature of the work. The irregular nature (or regular irregularity) of much of the work in health care, the particular skills needed for this, the crucial importance of the specialised cleaning required for germ-free conditions, and the importance of effective teams were all undervalued and underestimated. After cleaning services were privatised in British Columbia in 2003, nursing staff were forced to contact regional call centres to request extra cleaning services whenever spills or other accidents occurred, common incidents in hospitals that were not considered in contracts that specified work assignments suited to regular, measurable tasks. The new division of labour not only took nurses away from their work, reducing efficiency and causing delays, but also undermined the past practices of nurses working cooperatively with other staff when such incidents happened.

Contracting out ancillary work also meant that hospitals no longer took responsibility for the ongoing training of cleaning staff in infection control protocols. Under the terms of at least one commercial contract, the corporation concerned charges up to $57 an hour over and above its contracted price to provide any more intensive cleaning that might be required as a result of a superbug outbreak.[43] Yet research brought together by the Canadian Union of Public Employees shows that well-trained in-house teams, appropriately supported by decent wages and working conditions, are central to preventing such superbugs from taking hold.[44] As the cleaning firms cut back on hours and on training they have been repeatedly cited by the Workers Compensation Board for failure to adequately train workers, and the incidence of superbugs has increased. Between May and October 2008, 'investigators cited Compass for its failure to provide adequate health and safety training to workers; train workers in the safe use of toxic cleaning agents or in dealing with spills of hazardous substances; keep records of health and safety incident investigations, and have an exposure plan for workers who are exposed to materials contaminated with blood'.[45]

Similar legal, research and collective bargaining strategies have been used across the country to resist and even in some cases reverse the contracting out of ancillary work.[46] Research on rising illness and injury rates, as well as on the declining quality and increasing risks for patients, has been used to muster public support in opposition to these practices. In 1995, there was enormous public support for an illegal strike of healthcare laundry workers in Alberta, prompting the government to back down on planned cuts to health spending.[47] And in 2000 Manitoba unions successfully rallied public support to reverse the contracting out of food services.[48] It is difficult to imagine such support for strikers and unions operating in the private, for-profit sector outside health services, yet another indication of the particular nature of health services.

It would be wrong to exaggerate the extent to which either worker resistance or the nature of health care work has prevented the imposition of control mechanisms, and some forms of control that have been imposed are very difficult to reverse. For example, once hospitals have dismantled their kitchens and laundries, outsourcing the services involved, it is very hard to rebuild them. Some opposition has simply led to new contract controls rather than the reversal of service commodification. Some laws have not been enforced or contracts upheld. Equally important, many healthcare and other public sector employers have adopted business strategies to control labour, and is much harder to rally public support for resisting this form of privatisation.

But it would also be wrong to ignore the extent to which even the most vulnerable workers have resisted control, or to minimise the skilled and particular aspects of these jobs in health care. Indeed, even as unemployment rose with the onset of the global economic crisis in late 2008 employers were finding it difficult to find people to do the work.[49]

CONCLUSION: UNPAID LABOUR AND
THE STRUGGLE TO CONTROL HEALTH CARE WORK

As hospitals define their mission ever more narrowly, and send their patients home 'quicker and sicker', more and more work is being shifted to those who provide unpaid health care.[50] Meanwhile, more individuals survive infancy and childhood with severe chronic conditions, and more individuals live, albeit with varying care needs, well into their 80s or 90s; this is to be celebrated, but it does impose increased homecare obligations. Although it is no simple matter to distinguish social care from health care, the distinction is not particularly important to the caring relationship, especially when the lessons from the social determinants of health are taken into account. Personal and environmental hygiene, good nutrition, exercise, companionship and so on all contribute to health promotion and disease prevention. Care work is intimately linked to these and other determinants. The unpaid care work that results is critical in simple numerical terms. In Canada, it is estimated that over 70 per cent of all care is provided by unpaid labour,[51] a considerable majority of it performed by women. Unpaid labour is also critical because the threat of shifting even more care work to the home to be undertaken without pay is yet another means of controlling paid care workers.

The ways in which the neo–Taylorist impact on health care is shifting the burden to unpaid labour has potential to create a new basis for solidarity between the general public and healthcare workers. Struggles over labour control take specific forms in health care, shaped not only by its particular characteristics but also by gender, class and race. The nature of health care has allowed workers to appeal to the public's support for health care and their fear of ill heath as a means of strengthening the workers' case in these struggles. To be sure, governments have also appealed to the public on the same grounds to justify both neo–Taylorism and privatisation. Equally important, the specific nature of healthcare work, and especially the female-dominated labour force and its association with 'natural' female attributes, has allowed governments to shift work from paid employees to unpaid, mainly female workers at home, and to rely on healthcare workers' altruism within the paid sector. But as with neoliberalism in general, this kind of appeal from governments in the area of health care may be reaching its limits.

Until recently, doctors were mainly white men, largely from middle-class families, who used their privileged position to promote a division of labour that allowed them to shed the less attractive tasks involved in health care. They were able to increase their power as specialists, while retaining their position as the primary decision-makers, and were paid handsomely for the medical work that was determined and controlled by them. But the recent attempts by governments to use indirect forms of control to limit doctors' autonomy and power, challenging the doctor-determined division of labour by allowing others to do more of the tasks that were previously their exclusive preserve, mean that although doctors may have been the last and least affected, they are nonetheless certainly experiencing a loss of control today. And this loss of control, happening just when the majority of new doctors graduating from medical schools are women, and more are from immigrant communities, has the potential for the first time to ally doctors explicitly with popular struggles in health care.

Similarly the only partial success of the nurses – in good part because they were women – in emulating doctors' past strategies, has meant that managers have been even more successful in measuring, timing, compressing and flexibilising nurses' task. But this provides an even stronger basis for potential alliances than is the case with doctors. And the ancillary workers hired to take up the tasks shed by nurses have been the most privatised and proletarianised, with their work increasingly defined as being outside of health care. The fact that this has been supported by notions of the unskilled tasks associated with female-dominated work as well as racialised and/or immigrant workers, and by the assumptions that the work can be shifted to unpaid, mainly female workers at home, has produced a reaction inside the health sector and out that has already allowed healthcare unions to score some significant victories on their behalf. As we have seen, this has sometimes enjoyed notable public support, and this has been most recently demonstrated by the high public profile of the Ontario Health Coalition's grass roots mobilisations through town-hall assemblies and popular referenda in communities right across Ontario. As the burden of care in increasingly shunted to the household, while hospital care is increasingly industrialised, the possibilities for combining healthcare workers' struggles with popular activism to extend and democratise public health care is greater than ever.

NOTES

1   Stefan Timmermans and Marc Berg, *The Gold Standard: The Challenge of Evidence-Based Medicine and Standardization in Health Care*, Philadelphia: Temple University Press, 2003.

2   See for example Cynthia Coburn, *Gender and Technology in the Making*, London: Sage, 1993; Carla Freeman, *High Technology and High Heels in the Global Economy*, Durham: Duke University Press, 2000.

3   David Naylor, *Private Practice, Public Payment*, Montreal: McGill-Queen's University Press, 1986.

4   Malcolm Taylor, *Health Insurance and Canadian Public Policy*, Montreal: McGill-Queen's University Press, 1987.

5   Janet Kerr, 'The emergence of nursing unions as a social force in Canada', in Kerr and Janetta MacPhail, eds., *Canadian Nursing: Issues and Perspectives*, Toronto: McGraw-Hill Ryerson, 1988, pp. 211-12; see also Pat Armstrong and Linda Silas, 'Taking power: making change and nurses' unions in Canada', in Marjorie McIntyre and Carol McDonald, eds., *Realities of Canadian Nursing: Professional, Practice, and Power Issues*, Philadelphia: Wolters Kluwer Health, 2009, pp. 316-36.

6   See Taylor, *Health Insurance*, p. 423 as well as James O'Connor, *The Fiscal Crisis of the State*, New York: St. Martin's Press, 1973.

7   Conference Board of Canada, *Unleashing Innovation in Health Systems: Alberta's Symposium on Health*, Ottawa: Conference Board of Canada, 2005, p. 15.

8   Canadian Institute for Health Information (CIHI), *Canada's Health Care Providers, 2007*, Ottawa: CIHI, 2007, Fig. 3.2.

9   Pat Armstrong, Hugh Armstrong and Krista Scott-Dixon, *Critical to Care: The Invisible Women in Health Services*, Toronto: University of Toronto Press, 2008, p. 17.

10 Pat Armstrong, Hugh Armstrong and Kate Laxer, 'Doubtful data: why paradigms matter in counting the health-care labour force', in Vivian Shalla and Wallace Clement, eds., *Work in Tumultuous Times*, Montreal: McGill-Queen's University Press, 2007, pp. 326-48.

11 Carol Goar, 'The high price of unpaid caregiving', *Toronto Star*, 13 May 2009.

12 In Ontario, for example, at least 13, but no more than 15, of the 32 to 34 members must be non-physicians. College of Physicians and Surgeons of Ontario, 'About Council' at http://www.cpso.on.ca.

13 The cut had been recommended by M.L. Barer and G.L. Stoddart in *Toward Integrated Medical Resource Policies for Canada*, a 1991 report prepared for the Federal/Provincial/Territorial Deputy Ministers of Health. Their many other recommendations on the reorganisation of healthcare provision were however largely ignored.

14 In 2007, 22 per cent of Canada's close to 64,000 practicing doctors were foreign-trained. Their share has been slowly and steadily declining since the mid-1970s.

15 Milton Terris, 'Lessons from Canada's health program', *Technology Review*, February-March 1990, p. 31.

16 Investor-owned walk-in clinics, day surgery clinics and diagnostic centres are starting to make their presence felt in some provinces, but numbers remain small.

17 Just over a third of family physicians in Canada have such privileges, leaving the majority without access to their patients when they are admitted to hospital. College of Family Physicians of Canada, 'Family physicians caring for hospital inpatients: a discussion paper', 2003, available from http://www.cfpc.ca.

18 From 1980 to 1998, for example, the average annual decline was 1.7 per cent, and it has continued to decline in Canada and in all but 5 of the other 27 OECD countries for which there are data between 2000 and 2004 or 2005. OECD, 'How does Canada compare', *Health Data 2008*, Paris: OECD, 2008, p. 2; *Health at a Glance, 2001*, Paris: OECD, 2001, p. 26; *Health at a Glance, 2007*, Paris: OECD, 2007, Table A.4.5a.

19 Galt Wilson, 'Are inpatients' needs better served by hospitalists than by their family doctors?', *Canadian Family Physician*, 54(8), 2008, pp. 1101-03.

20 Milos Jenicek, 'Evidence-based medicine: Fifteen years later. Golem the good, the bad, and the ugly in need of a review?', *Medical Science Monitor*, 12(11), 2006, RA241-51.

21 Alicia Priest, Michael Rachlis and Marcy Cohen, *Why Wait? Public Solutions to Cure Surgical Waitlists*, Vancouver: Canadian Centre for Policy Alternatives, 2007, p. 15.

22 Ibid., p. 17.

23 Sioban Nelson and Suzanne Gordon, eds., *The Complexities of Care: Nursing Reconsidered*, Ithaca: Cornell University Press, 2006.

24 Pat Armstrong et al., *Take Care: Warning Signals for Canada's Health System*, Toronto: Garamond, 1994.

25 Reflecting this redefinition of hospital responsibilities, a major 2002 report on the future of health care in Canada called for the expansion of state support for homecare, albeit in just three 'priority areas': post-acute care, interventions for mental health clients with 'occasional acute period[s] of disruptive behaviour', and palliative care. Roy Romanow, *Building on Values: The Future of Health Care in Canada. Final Report*, Ottawa: Canadian Government Publishing, 2002, pp. 176-77.

26 Registered Nurses Association of Ontario and Registered Practical Nurses Association of Ontario, *Ensuring the Care Will Be There*, Toronto: Authors, 2000, p. 63.

27 Jacqueline A. Choiniere, 'A case study of nurses and patient information technology', in Pat Armstrong, Jacqueline Choiniere and Elaine Day, *Vital Signs: Nursing in Transition*, Toronto: Garamond, 1993, p. 63.

28 Ontario Premier's Council on Health Strategy, *Achieving the Vision: Health Human Resources* Toronto: Premier's Council, 1991, p. 5.

29 Philip Hassen, *Rx for Hospitals: New Hope for Medicare in the Nineties*, Toronto: Stoddart, 1993, p. 63.

30 Pat Armstrong et al., *Medical Alert: New Work Organization in Health Care*, Toronto: Garamond, 1997.

31 Leah Vosko, *Temporary Work: The Gendered Rise of a Precarious Employment Relationship*, Toronto: University of Toronto Press, 2000.

32 Dara Zarnett et al., 'The effects of competition on community-based nursing wages', *Healthcare Policy*, 4(3), 2009, pp. e129-144, Table 1.

33 Ibid.

34 See Catherine-Rose Stocks-Rankin, 'Who cares about ownership? A policy report on for-profit, not-for-profit and public ownership in Ontario long-term care', Masters Dissertation, Centre for International Public Health Policy, Edinburgh University, 2008, p. 30; and Statistics Canada, *Residential Care Facilities, 2005/2006*, Ottawa: Minister responsible for Statistics Canada, 2007, Table 1-7, p. 30.

35 CIHI, *Canada's Health Care Providers,* p. 109.

36 CIHI, *Regulated Nurses: Trends, 2003 to 2007*, Ottawa: CIHI, 2008, p. 44.

37 Pat Armstrong and Kate Laxer, 'Precarious work, privatization, and the health-care industry: the case of ancillary workers', in Leah Vosko, ed., *Precarious Employment: Understanding Labour Market Insecurity in Canada*, Montreal: McGill-Queen's University Press, 2006, pp. 115-38.

38 Pat Armstrong, Hugh Armstrong and Krista Scott-Dixon, *Critical to Care: The Invisible Women in Health Services*, Toronto: University of Toronto Press, 2008.

39 Marjorie Griffin Cohen, 'Do comparisons between hospital support workers and hospitality workers make sense?', Report prepared for the Hospital Employees Union (CUPE), Burnaby, 2001.

40   Canadian Union of Public Employees, 'Fact Sheet – Shared food services', 11 July 2003, available from http://cupe.ca.

41   Marjorie Griffin Cohen and Marcy Cohen, *A Return to Wage Discrimination: Pay Equity Losses Through Privatization in Health Care*, Vancouver: Canadian Centre for Policy Alternatives, 2004.

42   Health Services and Support-Facilities Subsector Bargaining Assn. v. British Columbia, 2007 SCC 27, [2007] 2 S.C.R. 391, 8 July 2007.

43   Canadian Union of Public Employees, 'Privatization deal slashes hospital cleaning', 25 February 2008, available from http://cupe.ca.

44   Canadian Union of Public Employees, 'Health care associated infections: a backgrounder', 2 March 2009, available from http://cupe.ca.

45   49 Hospital Employees' Union, 'WCB issues orders to VIHA's cleaning contractor', 7 January 2009 news release. The inspection reports were accessed at http://www.heu.org on 16 January 2009.

46   See, for example, CUPE Local 145 v. William Osler Health Centre [in Brampton, Ontario], March 2006.

47   Darcy Henton, 'Klein backs down on cuts to health care', *Toronto Star*, 23 November 1995.

48   Canadian Union of Public Employees, 'Fact Sheet'.

49   Carol Kushner, Patricia Baranek and Marion Dewar, *Home Care: Change We Need*, Toronto: Ontario Health Coalition, 2008, p. 6, available from http://www.web.net.

50   See Armstrong, Armstrong and Scott-Dixon, *Critical to Care,* and Mario R. Dal Poz, Yohannes Kinfu, Sigrid Dräger and Teena Kunjumen, 'Counting health workers: definitions, data, methods and global results', Geneva: World Health Organization, 2006, p. 8.

51   S. Stobert and K. Cranswick, 'Looking after seniors: who does what for whom?', *Canadian Social Trends,* Autumn, 2004, pp. 2-6.

MATERNAL MORTALITY IN AFRICA:
A GENDERED LENS
ON HEALTH SYSTEM FAILURE

PAULA TIBANDEBAGE
AND MAUREEN MACKINTOSH

The 2005 report of the UN *Millennium Project Task Force on Child Health and Maternal Health*, and subsequent UN reports on maternal health, make grim reading.[1] With barely five years to go to 2015, the target set for the fifth Millennium Development Goal (MDG), reducing the Maternal Mortality Ratio (MMR – the ratio of deaths from childbearing to all live births) by three quarters between 1990 and 2015, remains far beyond the reach of many low-income countries. To achieve a reduction of 75 per cent, the annual decline in the MMR between 1990 and 2005 should have been 5.5 per cent. With the actual average annual decline estimated at less than 1 per cent over these years, it is apparent that many countries cannot reach the target.

Worse, the average annual decline to date masks huge global inequalities. WHO data show an especially alarming situation in low-income countries. In Sub-Saharan Africa, the MMR has been declining on average by only about 0.1 per cent a year.[2] Developed regions now have an MMR of 9 deaths per 100,000 live births – fewer than one birth in ten thousand (0.9) results in the mother's death. This contrasts shockingly with 100 times that death rate in Sub-Saharan Africa, where the MMR is estimated at 900 per 100,000 live births. The lifetime risk of maternal death in Sub-Saharan Africa – that is, the chance that a 15-year-old woman will die of maternal causes – was estimated at 1 in 26 in 2005, and in Niger, the worst case, 1 in 7. In Ireland, the lowest-risk country, it was 1 in 48,000.

Why is this happening? What does this terrible crisis of maternal mortality and associated ill health tell us about the state of health systems in much of Sub-Saharan Africa? These very high maternal death rates are not only a crisis requiring urgent attention; they also provide a 'gender lens' that illuminates the discriminatory gendered structure of health systems and health policy, and tell us a great deal about the roots of the crisis in the economics of health systems.

GENDER, POWER AND HEALTH SYSTEM COMMERCIALISATION

Gender permeates social institutions and is an organising principle of social life. Feminist economists and health campaigners such as Gita Sen and her colleagues have develop.ed the concept of a 'gender lens' as a gendered perspective from which to analyse the structured inequalities between men and women embedded in health systems.[3] Concepts of health and illness, roles and expectations, and the patterns of access to resources that shape health-seeking behaviour, are all highly gendered. The maternal mortality crisis provides us with such a gender lens on current health system failure.

We concentrate on the experience of Tanzania, which is far from the worst case in Sub-Saharan Africa, but our arguments have much wider relevance in Africa and elsewhere, especially in so far as health system commercialisation is centrally implicated in maternal mortality. The UN *Millennium Project Task Force Report* cited above accepted that health systems are institutions deeply embedded in wider social and economic forces. The report advocated 'power mapping' to identify where the power lies to address the crisis of exclusion and impoverishment associated with many low-income health systems. Health systems in Africa as in much of the world reflect the huge, gendered social inequalities of the wider society, including gendered hierarchies among staff, and extremely unequal quality and access for higher and lower social classes.[4] Gender and social class interact to create a situation where low-income, low-status women, those with the greatest needs, have the least access to care.[5]

Key gender-differentiated aspects of health systems in many African countries, that are known to be implicated in failures of provision, include staffing and the availability of medicines. Equally structured by gender, but less often understood to be so, is health system commercialisation, the process by which healthcare provision has increasingly become a commoditised, fee-based service market.[6] Charges for both publicly and privately provided services create a barrier to access in time of need and generate further impoverishment. Exclusion from health care thereby becomes not only a generator of poverty but also a defining aspect of the experience of being poor.[7] To be sent away from a health facility without care when you or a child is ill is truly to know how poor you are. These pressures can bear particularly hard on women, who form the majority of users of the health system since they are responsible also for bringing children for care; who may lose out in household debates over competing uses of income; and who may lack independent access to cash.

Market relations of buying and selling are generally analysed as if they are gender-neutral, but this is misleading. Diane Elson draws a useful distinction between social and economic relations that are 'gender ascriptive', such as kinship relations, and those which are not, but are nevertheless 'bearers of gender'.[8] Economic relationships through the market are of this second kind. Gender roles and norms shape the network of social relationships that support market trading in contexts of incomplete information and unwritten contracts. They also support the property rights that underlie market trading and influence economic behaviour.

However, while the gendered nature of market relationships has been established, the concept appears to have been little applied to commercialised – i.e. market-based – health systems. We have found little robust research or policy effort applied to an integrated assessment of the effects of the market-based supply of health care on women's health and female impoverishment. And we have looked in vain for analyses of the methods – the exercise of social and economic power – through which charging for health care becomes in practice a gendered activity. Healthcare transactions are not one-off market events: they are shaped by information, expectations, experience, norms of behaviour and incentives, all of which evolve over time through market interaction and competitive pressures.[9] Gender interacts with economic inequality to ensure that healthcare commercialisation, and the newly-emerging market relationships it sets up between health providers and those in need of health care, are immediately constituted as gendered economic processes.

THE MATERNAL HEALTH CRISIS IN TANZANIA

Estimates of the MMR in Tanzania vary widely, but are all alarmingly high. Tanzanian government survey data show an *increase* from an estimated 529 per 100,000 live births in 1996 to 578 in 2004/05.[10] Other estimates are higher. In 2000, the WHO and other UN bodies estimated the MMR in Tanzania at 1,500 per 100,000 live births, ranking Tanzania in third position among 13 countries that accounted for 67 per cent of all maternal deaths globally;[11] in 2005 the WHO estimate was 950 (Table 1). Whichever estimate we take, the crisis of high maternal death rates is replicated across much of the subcontinent. Of the 14 countries estimated to have an MMR of at least 1,000 per 100,000 live births in 2006, 13 were in Sub-Saharan Africa. In Kaputa, Zambia, maternal mortality estimates calculated using a sisterhood method[12] in 1995 were 1,549 per 100,000 live births.[13]

Table 1: Estimates of MMR, births attended by skilled health personnel, and health expenditure: selected countries in Sub-Saharan Africa[14]

Country	MMR (2005)	Births attended by skilled health personnel (per cent) (1996-2004)	Health expenditure (2003)	
			Public (per cent of GDP)	Per Capita (PPP US$)
Tanzania	950	46	2.4	29
Cameroon	1,000	62	1.2	64
Chad	1,500	16	2.6	51
Congo	740	–	1.3	23
Guinea	910	55	3.2	98
Lesotho	960	60	4.1	106
Malawi	1,100	61	3.3	46
Rwanda	1,300	31	1.6	32
Zambia	830	43	2.8	51
Botswana	380	94	3.5	373
South Africa	400	84	3.2	669

Within countries, the burden of maternal mortality is generally unequally distributed, with striking inequalities by area of residence and socio-economic status. In Tanzania, inequalities in access to maternal health care during delivery by area of residence (rural vs. urban), by education level and by wealth status clearly suggest that the MMR will be higher among poor, less-educated women living in rural areas. As Table 2 also shows, more educated women and women in the better-off 20 per cent of households (as measured by assets owned) are far more likely to give birth in a health facility (public, private or voluntary) than other women. Rural areas are poorer and less well served: a far higher percentage of live births take place at home in urban than in rural areas. The implication is that disadvantaged rural women face a higher risk of maternal mortality than better off, more educated women in urban areas.

Table 2: Tanzania: per cent distribution of live births in the five years preceding 2005 according to background characteristics[15]

	Health Facility			
Background characteristic	Public	Voluntary	Private	None
Residence				
Urban	71.5	4.0	5.5	18.9
Rural	29.7	2.8	6.5	60.9
Mother's education				
No education	26.6	1.7	3.8	67.5
Primary incomplete	35.2	1.9	4.9	57.8
Primary complete	41.4	3.7	7.8	47.0
Secondary+	71.3	6.3	7.3	14.9
Asset quintile				
Lowest	25.6	2.1	4.4	67.5
Second	30.1	2.2	4.5	63.1
Middle	28.7	3.2	7.0	61.1
Fourth	42.6	1.9	9.4	46.1
Highest	73.0	6.6	6.8	13.3

For the 47 per cent of women estimated to deliver in health facilities, there are again inequalities in quality of care.[16] Better-off women and women with more education are likely to be assisted by more qualified medical personnel. The proportion of women in urban areas who were assisted by a nurse or midwife (67.2 per cent) was more than twice that of women in rural areas (30.2 per cent). This again suggests that the MMR is likely to be higher among less educated poor rural women, and some evidence supports this conclusion directly. Research using a sisterhood method estimated the MMR in a remote regions of Tanzania (Kigoma) at 606 per 100,000 live births, and in the most remote part of the region at 757.[17] In another rural district, a 1998 study estimated the MMR at 961 per 100,000 live births, much higher than the estimated national average.[18]

Disparities in MMR by socio-economic characteristics are not unique to Tanzania: in other countries too, poverty is associated with higher MMR.[19] In Chad and Niger survey data show a 14-fold difference between the better off and the poor in access to skilled assistance at birth. In Ethiopia the rich were 28 times more likely than the poor to be attended in delivery by a skilled health worker. Beyond Africa, a similar picture has been observed, even in middle-income countries. In India the better-off were seven times as likely as the poor to be attended by a skilled health worker.[20] Explanations of high maternal mortality must therefore incorporate social and economic inequality, linking deprivation to lack of health system access and to other problems affecting maternal health.

THE IMPORTANCE OF HOSPITAL CARE

Maternal mortality is generated by the interaction between household and individual health-seeking and the capabilities and behaviour of providers of care. Delays in making decisions to seek maternal health care, and lack of financial resources to meet the costs of transport, and of health services once at the health facility, contribute to many maternal deaths. And a mother's arrival at a health facility in time, even with money for fees, is not in itself sufficient to assure the safety of mother and child: essential supplies and medication must be available, including those for emergency obstetric care. All of these factors are too often lacking.

The health facility infrastructure in Tanzania is dominated by lower-level facilities, mainly dispensaries, and it is there that most of the population, including pregnant women, first seek health care. Services provided for pregnant women at dispensaries include antenatal care and delivery.[21] Lower-level facilities are however less likely to provide good quality maternal health services, in terms of appropriate infrastructure, skilled personnel and equipment. Dispensaries and many health centres lack the necessary equipment to handle complications during pregnancy and delivery. Hospitals, which generally are better equipped and staffed with more qualified personnel, are few. Referral linkages between hospitals and lower level facilities are weak, yet active collaboration between referral levels is essential for effective maternal health care.[22]

All this has translated into Tanzania's unacceptably high MMR, as so many women die of obstetric complications. Available evidence for Tanzania and other low income countries shows that access by all pregnant women to good quality hospital care is the key to reducing maternal deaths. It is a necessary condition for reducing deaths resulting from direct obstetric causes, which according to the WHO account for 80 per cent of maternal deaths in Africa. Haemorrhage is the leading cause, accounting for 33 per cent of maternal deaths; sepsis is another major cause.[23] The importance of achieving more effective access to hospital cannot be overemphasized.

Yet most pregnant women in Tanzania seek antenatal care in lower-level facilities (dispensaries and health centres), most of which often lack basic supplies and medicines and have severe shortages of staff with the skills to handle complications during pregnancy and delivery. According to the 2006 *Tanzania Service Provision Assessment (TSPA)* survey, only 10 and 9 per cent of antenatal care providers had training in complications of pregnancy and risk pregnancies respectively.[24] A very low proportion of the facilities surveyed could conduct any basic diagnostic tests (e.g. 18 per cent could test for anaemia, 20 per cent for urine protein , 18 per cent for urine glucose and 20 per cent for syphilis). The medicines situation was even worse: only 8 per cent of facilities providing antenatal care had in stock all the medications needed for treating common complications and infections. Only 5 per cent of the facilities had Caesarean-section services: no dispensaries, and only 13 per cent of health centres, offered this service, compared with 90 per cent of hospitals. Other studies show similar findings, with lower-level public health facilities having severe shortages of medications and laboratory equipment.[25]

Either lower-level facilities must be strengthened in terms of skilled human resources, availability of drugs and essential supplies and equipment, or access by all pregnant women to hospital-level care must be assured. The *Millennium Project Report* identifies the key elements of high quality delivery care as (i) a skilled attendant at delivery, (ii) access to emergency obstetric care in case of a complication, and (iii) a working referral system to ensure that women who experience complications reach emergency obstetric care in time.[26] The report argues that a health system with these three elements could ensure that maternal mortality ceased to be a public health problem. It shows that some countries whose health systems fare quite well on the three listed elements have managed to reduce their MMR significantly.

Unfortunately, the Tanzanian health system scores poorly on all these elements. There is evidence of major delay in transferring pregnant women with complications from lower to higher level facilities; improper diagnosis and management of cases such as anaemia and hypertension; and inadequate treatment.[27] As concerns referral, there is a strong contrast with some other countries, including Honduras and Sri Lanka, where the success of programmes to reduce maternal mortality has been attributed among other things to organized ambulance services.[28] In Tanzania in 2007 less than 10 per cent of health facilities covered by one survey had transport for referral purposes, despite the importance of hospital-level life-saving emergency care.[29] A study in Northern Tanzania shows a significantly lower risk of maternal death (325 per 100,000 live births) for respondents attending antenatal clinics close to hospitals than for those attending more distant clinics (561 per 100,000 live births), while the lifetime risk of maternal death was 1 in 42 for the former as compared to 1 in 25 for the latter. [30] Access to hospitals is an absolutely key factor in reducing maternal mortality.

GENDER-DISCRIMINATION, MARKETS AND POVERTY: A LETHAL MIX

If hospital-based intervention is so important for tackling the appalling level of maternal death and disability just catalogued, why are these interventions so unavailable to women in Tanzania? What are the key health system failures and why do they occur? There appear to be three major interlinked problems.

First, the health system at all levels is quite commercialised. That is, access is fee-based, and there are markets for services and essential medicines at all levels of the system. Antenatal consultations are generally free of charge in the government sector, but they may well involve payment for medicines and supplies such as syringes.[31] In the private for-profit and NGO sector charges may not be imposed for consultation, but charges are made for supplies. And any charges must be paid on top of travel costs.

However, antenatal care at dispensaries is the most accessible level of the system, with the lowest entry charge and widespread provision, and access to antenatal consultation and check-up is quite widespread. It is at later stages of pregnancy and at higher levels of care that charges become a major barrier to access. Table 3 shows average official payments – not including informal payments such as bribes – in the late 1990s for 107 women in Mtwara seeking maternity care. Actual payments varied greatly, and in one case the total cost (including informal payments) of antenatal hospitalisation reached the equivalent of US$41 – in a district where the average *annual* female earnings were the equivalent of US$110 at the time.

Table 3: Average direct costs of maternity care in hospitals (US$ equivalents of Tanzanian shillings) (costs at health centres and dispensaries in brackets)[32]

	Service fees	Drugs	Supplies	Travel Cost	Total
Antenatal consultation	–	–	0.20(0.20)	–	0.20(0.20)
Antenatal hospitalisation	1.50	0.70	2.90	1.60	6.70
Normal delivery	1.60	–	1.50(0.20)	2.80(1.60)	5.90(1.80)
Complicated delivery	1.60	0.80	1.50	2.80	6.70

Women have great difficulty in paying these charges. There is an exemption system, but it works poorly for women.[33] Of women interviewed in the above study, most were small farmers and 45 per cent had no personal cash income at all. Finding 20 cents for an antenatal consultation might be possible, but further treatment and hospital care could well be out of reach. Furthermore women coming for admission had to be accompanied by someone to support them, adding to the travel and time-loss costs. And these interviewees were already self-selected as more likely to be able to pay. They were among those who had come to facilities for care and treatment; those who stayed at home were not included in the study.

In urban areas people at all levels of income rely largely on private for-profit and NGO health facilities for all types of care. These are small businesses, relying on fees and charges.[34] They charge for medication and supplies and for consultations, except in some cases for antenatal care. Their charges for delivery and for in-patient care will generally – though not always, especially in the case of some faith-based facilities – be above those of government facilities. Prices respond to market pressures, to low ability to pay and to the facilities' struggle for financial viability. It is a commercialised system of care where, except for antenatal consultations, women have to strive to find money to purchase the care they need. Many fail.

Yet the literature on maternal death and maternal morbidity in Africa barely discusses charging and the commercialisation of health care, and evidence is almost completely lacking.[35] A mid-1990s study reported a sharp drop in hospital antenatal consultations when charges were introduced.[36] Since women are known to seek hospital care if they know the pregnancy is risky, this is likely to have a disproportionate effect in increasing risk.

It seems likely that charges also have a disproportionately severe impoverishing effect on women of childbearing age. Women have responsibility for childcare in health and illness, and often need to borrow from others in the immediate or wider family or draw on tiny savings or sell assets such as farm animals to pay maternity charges. Women are likely to have lower incomes than men, and for a low-income household finding cash for charges is dispiriting, may be impossible and can cause conflict. There is a lack of good empirical work on maternity charges and their gendered implications.[37]

The second main reason why the system fails women is that government hospitals – the more affordable option – are inadequate to the task of emergency obstetric care. They are too few, too far from most people's homes, while the intermediate-level health centres do not function effectively in dealing with obstetric emergencies. The reasons for this major failure are numerous and interlocking, but they include an inherited health system structure that was focused on a few large hospitals rather than a dispersed 'cottage hospital' network of the kind that has been successful in Sri Lanka. There has also been a failure to build up and sustain health centres – the intermediate level between dispensaries and hospitals – to fill the gap, for a variety of reasons rooted partly but not exclusively in resource constraint. And there has been a very heavy concentration by donors on supporting primary care, associated with (in the case of the World Bank) a narrow definition of public health, focused on 'public goods' such as vaccination.[38] This combination of factors has meant that government's own limited funds have been spent on trying to keep public hospitals functioning in the face of very high demand.

The result is the inaccessibility of emergency obstetric care documented above. Geographically situated largely in towns, facilities capable of providing it are distant from many people's homes, and Tanzania is geographically very large relative to the size of its population, with poor or very poor rural roads and over half of the population still rural. The last twenty years have seen the polarisation between dispensary and hospital services grow worse.

This policy outcome is profoundly gendered. Since maternal death rates cannot be brought down without skilled obstetric intervention, and since emergency hospital services are less crucial for many other aspects of adult health care, the health system structure described is highly damaging to the health needs of women of child-bearing age. A gender bias against the health needs of women is built into the public sector health system structure. Furthermore, the relative inaccessibility of hospital care for the poor has been widely used, not to argue for more dispersed and widely accessible hospitals, but to argue for *further* concentration of spending at the primary level, the level where poor pregnant women with the need for emergency care are all too often trapped.[39] This apparently illogical but influential argument is revealed by the maternal health 'lens' as profoundly discriminatory against the health needs of women.

The third major factor in the failure of the system to save so many women from death in childbirth is that even the hospitals that are available lack staff and supplies, as documented above. Many lack even basic antibiotics, but aid funding for essential medicines – which has increased very sharply since 2004 – has largely ignored the needs of maternal health, focusing instead on HIV/AIDS, TB and malaria. As a result, the broad availability of essential medicines appears to have risen little in Tanzania since 2004.[40] As of 2006, only 11 per cent of government health facilities offering delivery services had all essential supplies for delivery, and only 5 per cent had all essential supplies for serious complications.[41] Staffing levels and staff attitudes are also particularly poor in maternal health care: there is a severe shortage of trained midwives; conditions of work can be poor and even dangerous; pay rates are low; and there are recurrent problems of a culture of poor and even abusive attitudes to women in obstetric wards which also discourage attendance and care-seeking.[42] The picture adds up to a lack of priority for maternity care, and especially emergency care, that is deeply gender-discriminatory.

These three problems interact and reinforce one another, creating a cumulative and apparently worsening cycle of discriminatory effects. This can be seen most clearly by considering referral. The clinical literature emphasises the importance of rapid and effective referral for emergency obstetric interventions. Yet in Tanzania all three major structural factors identified as problematic militate against proper referral mechanisms. Commercialisation has meant in effect that referral as a formal mechanism has almost ceased to exist. People may be 'told to go' to hospital, and sometimes referral letters may be written, but patients experience this process as another facility that requires payment, where they often start from scratch again, and often not with a fully qualified staff member. Unsurprisingly, in these circumstances patients with conditions they perceive as severe 'bypass' lower levels, saving funds for the hospital level. If hospital is unaffordable, the patient will not go, preferring to 'die at home', as some of our interviewees in the late 1990s put it. If people have gone first to a private dispensary they may be badly received at a public hospital, and hence may not speak of their earlier visit. The facilities form a fragmented market, not an integrated referral system.[43]

The concentration of hospital care in large public urban hospitals compounds the referral problem since they are more expensive than small-scale units would be likely to be – in fees and travel costs – and physically inaccessible in emergencies. Not all low and middle-income countries have taken this route. Comparative research on public spending on health in Asia showed that 'in Malaysia and Sri Lanka many hospitals are small in scale and not particularly well equipped. But their wide geographic distribution makes them accessible to the rural poor'.[44] The same study makes the point that where public hospital provision is very restricted it is more likely to be 'captured' by a cash-strapped middle class than better funded and more geographically distributed hospital provision. Thus there is likely to be a cumulative interaction between funding, health system structure and the political economy of resource use. In the maternal healthcare case, better-distributed hospital care in terms of social class is also less gender-discriminatory: better distribution by class and gender reinforce each other.

International policy too has reinforced the crisis of maternal health by the lack of priority assigned to medicines and supplies for obstetric care.

International health policy has combined much 'gender talk' with a failure to assess the gendered implications of, for example, international funding initiatives for medicines for specific illnesses, or the bias against funding hospitals. The lack of medicines and supplies worsens working conditions in hospitals, undermines staff morale, raises their incentives to demand 'informal' fees and raises costs to women who have to buy their own supplies from commercial sources – or stay away.

CONCLUSION

The crisis represented by appalling maternal death rates in Africa is deep-rooted. It arises and persists, not as a result of a single failing that can be identified and corrected, but out of a set of deep-rooted and long-standing health system structures, policy assumptions and funding activities. Each of these, as the *Millennium Project Task Force* authors emphasised, responds to power: to tackle the underlying problems requires an acceptance that health systems are core social institutions, and demands negotiation of sustainable redistributive reforms that lessen structural gender disadvantage.[45]

This is a huge challenge – which is why the prognosis for meeting the Millennium Goal for reducing maternal deaths is so gloomy. Some commentators indeed see improvements in emergency obstetric access as unlikely to be achieved and concentrate on seeking non-hospital ways to lessen risk.[46] Creating accessible emergency obstetric intervention requires a series of interlocking actions, all of them challenging. It is necessary to cease the virtual silence on the commercialisation of health systems and its consequences, and to tackle the problem of how the out-of-pocket fee-for-service system is to be replaced by access without payment barriers to emergency and other essential care; to restructure the health system to bring emergency obstetric care closer to those who need it; and to rethink international funding priorities on a less gender-discriminatory basis, which requires, as a first step, a gender assessment of those priorities.[47]

Sri Lanka, with a different history of public health provision and a different health system structure from that in Tanzania and many other African countries, and very low fees in public hospitals, had by 2005 managed at quite a low level of national income per capita – and despite economic and political crisis – to get maternal death rates down to about 43 per 100,000 live births.[48] It can be done. Access to emergency care that saves a mother's life is a human right, and this principle should be the starting-point for policy priorities to address the international 'collective badge of shame' represented by the scale of avoidable maternal death in so many low-income countries such as Tanzania.[49]

NOTES

We thank the INNOGEN research centre at the Open University, funded by the UK Economic and Social Research Council, for financial support; and Abhishek Chakravarty and Suleiman Mbuyita for research assistance in the form of reviews of the international and Tanzanian literature.

1   Lynn P. Freedman, Ronald J. Waldman, Helen De Pinho, and Meg E. Wirth, *Who's got the power? Transforming Health Systems for Women and Children,* UN Millennium Project Task Force on Child Health and Maternal Health, London: Earthscan, London, 2005.

2   WHO, UNICEF, UNFPA, World Bank, *Maternal Mortality in 2005: Estimates developed by WHO, UNICEF, UNFPA and the World Bank,* Geneva: World Health Organisation, 2007.

3   Gita Sen, Asha George and Piroska Östlin, 'Engendering health equity: a review of research and policy', in Gita Sen, Asha George and Piroska Östlin, eds., *Engendering International Health,* Cambridge: MIT Press, 2002.

4   Commission on the Social Determinants of Health, *Closing the Gap in a Generation,* Geneva: World Health Organisation, 2008; WHO, *The World Health Report 2003: Shaping the Future,* Geneva: World Health Organisation, 2003.

5   A. Iyer, G. Sen, and P. Östlin, 'The intersections of gender and class in health status and health care', *Global Public Health,* 3(S1), 2008; Maureen Mackintosh and Paula Tibandebage, 'Gender and health sector reform: analytical perspectives on African experience', in S. Razavi and S. Hassim, eds., *Gender and Social Policy in a Global Context: Uncovering the gendered structure of 'the social',* Basingstoke: Palgrave, 2006.

6   Maureen Mackintosh and Meri Koivusalo, eds., *Commercialisation of Health Care: Global and Local Dynamics and Policy Implications,* Basingstoke: Palgrave, 2006.

7   Paula Tibandebage and Maureen Mackintosh, 'The market shaping of charges, trust and abuse: health care transactions in Senegal', *Social Science & Medicine,* 61(7), 2005.

8   Diane Elson, 'Gender awareness in modelling structural adjustment', *World Development,* 23(11), 1996.

9   Tibandebage and Mackintosh, 'Market shaping'.

10   See the Tanzania Bureau of Statistics reports, *Tanzania Demographic and Health Survey 1996,* Calverton: Bureau of Statistics, 1997 and *Tanzania Demographic and Health Survey 2004-05,* Dar es Salaam: National Bureau of Statistics, 2005, both available from http://www.measuredhs.com.

11   WHO, UNICEF, and UNFPA, *Maternal Mortality in 2000: Estimates developed by WHO, UNICEF and UNFPA,* Geneva: World Health Organisation, 2003.

12   In the sisterhood method, a random sample of women are interviewed about their adult sisters; they are asked whether their sisters are living or dead, and if any of them ever died during pregnancy or within six weeks of delivery.

13   F. Le Bacq and A. Rietsema, 'High maternal mortality levels and additional risk from poor accessibility in two districts of Northern Province, Zambia', *International Journal of Epidemiology*, 26(2), 1997.

14   WHO et al., *Maternal Mortality in 2005*; UNDP, *Human Development Report 2006. Beyond scarcity: Power, poverty and the global water crisis*, New York: UNDP, 2006.

15   Only the most recent birth in the five years preceding the survey. Tanzania Bureau of Statistics, *Tanzania Demographic and Health Survey 2005*.

16   Ibid.

17   G. Mbaruku, Fred Vork, Dismas Vyagusa, Rex Mwakipiti and Jos van Roosmalen, 'Estimates of maternal mortality in western Tanzania by the sisterhood method', *African Journal of Reproductive Health*, 7(3), 2003, available online from http://www.bioline.org.br.

18   J. Macleod and R. Rhode, 'Retrospective follow-up of maternal deaths and their associated risk factors in a rural district in Tanzania', Bagamoyo district office, unpublished paper, 1998.

19   W.J. Graham, A.E. Fitzmaurice, J.S. Bells and J.A. Cairns, 'The familial technique for linking maternal death with poverty', *Lancet,* 363(9402), 3 January 2004.

20   Freedman et al., *Who's got the power?*.

21   This is referred to in the United States as 'prenatal' care.

22   S.F. Murray and S.C. Pearson, 'Maternity referral systems in developing countries: Current knowledge and future research needs', *Social Science & Medicine*, 62(9), 2006.

23   K.S. Khan, D. Wojdyla, L. Say, A. Gülmezoglu and P. Van Look, 'WHO analysis of causes of maternal death: A systematic review', *Lancet,* 367(9516), 2006; F. Font et al., 'Maternal mortality in a rural district of South Eastern Tanzania: An application of the sisterhood method', *International Journal of Epidemiology,* 29(1), 2000.

24   Tanzania National Bureau of Statistics, *Tanzania Service Provision Assessment Survey 2006, Preliminary Report (TSPA)*, Calverton: Bureau of Statistics, 2007, available from http://www.nbs.go.tz.

25   A survey was undertaken in 2007 by the CMI (Chr. Michelsen Institute), and the NIMR (National Institute for Medical Research) and REPOA (Research on Poverty Alleviation) in health facilities in nine rural districts of Tanzania on issues of health worker availability, performance and motivation. Preliminary analysis by P. Tibandebage and W. Lindeboom of data from the unpublished survey shows that 67 per cent of public health facilities in the sample did not have laboratories for basic diagnostic tests. Tibandebage and Lindeboom, 'Performance enhancing factors at the health facility level: Preliminary findings', Paper presented at a research workshop on 'Health Worker Motivation, Availability and Performance in Tanzania', 24-25 September 2008, Dar es Salaam, Tanzania.

26   Freedman et al., *Who's got the power?*.

27 E. Urassa, S. Massawe, G. Landmark and L. Nystrom, 'Operational factors affecting maternal mortality in Tanzania', *Health Policy and Planning*, 12(1), 1997.

28 M.M. Koblinsky and O. Cambell, 'Factors affecting the reduction of maternal mortality', in Koblinsky, ed., *Reducing maternal mortality: Learning from Bolivia, China, Egypt, Honduras, Indonesia, Jamaica and Zimbabwe*, Washington: World Bank, 2003.

29 Unpublished CMI/NIMR/REPOA survey 2007; estimates from initial data analysis by Tibandebage and Lindeboom, 'Performance enhancing factors at the health facility level'.

30 B.E. Olsen, S.G. Hinderaker, M. Kazauru, R.P.B. Terje, P. Gasheka and G. Kvale, 'Estimates of maternal mortality by the sisterhood method in rural Northern Tanzania: a household sample and an antenatal clinic sample', unpublished paper, 2007.

31 M. Kowalewski, P.G.M. Mujinja and A. Jahn, 'Can mothers afford maternal health care costs? Users' costs of maternity services in rural Tanzania', *African Journal of Reproductive Health*, 6(1), 2002, available online from http://www.bioline.org.br.

32 Ibid.

33 P. Nanda, 'Gender dimensions of user fees: implications for women's utilisation of health care', *Reproductive Health Matters*, 10(20), 2002.

34 Paula Tibandebage, Haji H. Semboja, Phares G.M. Mujinja and Henock Ngonyani, 'Private sector development: the case of private health facilities', *ESRF Discussion Paper*, No. 26, Dar es Salaam, April, 2001; Maureen Mackintosh and Paula Tibandebage, 'Competitive and institutional constraints on innovation, investment and quality of care in a liberalised low income health system', *European Journal of Development Research*, 19(1), 2007.

35 A literature review by Abhishek Chakravarty found very little systematic empirical assessment of the effect of fee charging on maternal health care access, but a consensus that user fees for health care in general do discourage use. See also Nanda, 'Gender dimensions'.

36 A.K. Hussein and P.G.M. Mujinja, 'Impact of user charges on government health facilities in Tanzania', *East African Medical Journal*, 74(12), 1997.

37 R. Tolhurst, Y.P. Amekudzi, F. Nyonator, S. Bertel Squire and S. Theobald, '"He will ask why the child gets sick so often": The gendered dynamics of intra-household bargaining over healthcare for children with fever in the Volta Region of Ghana', *Social Science & Medicine*, 66(5), 2008.

38 World Bank, *World Development Report 1993. Investing in Health*, Washington: World Bank, 1993.

39 Ibid.

40 Data from WHO-supported medicines price and availability surveys in Tanzania, summarised in Maureen Mackintosh and Phares G.M. Mujinja, 'Markets and policy challenges in access to essential medicines for endemic diseases', *Journal of African Economies*, Special AERC issue, forthcoming.

41 Tanzania National Bureau of Statistics, *TSPA 2006*.

42 Authors' fieldwork.

43   Maureen Mackintosh and Paula Tibandebage, 'Inclusion by design: rethinking health care market regulation in the Tanzanian context', *Journal of Development Studies*, 39(1), 2002.

44   Owen O'Donnell et al., 'The incidence of public spending on health care: comparative evidence from Asia', *World Bank Economic Review*, 21(1), 207, p. 109.

45   Freedman et al., *Who's got the power*; Lynn Freedman, 'Achieving the MDGs: health systems as core social institutions', *Development* , 48(1), 2005.

46   Ndola Prata, Amita Sreenivas, Farnaz Vahidnia and Malcolm Potts, 'Saving maternal lives in resource-poor settings: facing reality', *Health Policy*, 89(2), 2009.

47   Hilary Standing, 'Gender and equity in health sector reform programmes: a review', *Health Policy and Planning*, 12(1), 1997.

48   WHO et al., *Maternal Mortality in 2005*.

49   Lynn Freedman, 'Using human rights in maternal mortality programs: from analysis to strategy', *International Journal of Gynecology & Obstetrics*, 75(1), 2001.

BETWEEN OBESITY AND HUNGER: THE CAPITALIST FOOD INDUSTRY

ROBERT ALBRITTON

We live in a world capable, in principle, of providing a diverse and healthy diet for all, and yet one quarter of its people suffer from frequent hunger and ill health generated by a diet that is poor in quantity or quality or both. Another quarter of the world's population eats too much food, food that is often heavy with calories and low on nutrients (colloquially called 'junk food'). This quarter of the world's population risks diabetes and all of the other chronic illnesses generated by obesity. In Mexico, for example, 14 per cent of the population have diabetes, and in India, 11 per cent of city-dwellers over 15.[1] In the US it has been estimated that one-third of the children born in the year 2000 will develop diabetes – a truly sad prospect, given that most of this is entirely preventable.[2] Study after study in recent years has come to the conclusion that the single most important factor in human health is diet, and diet is something we can shape.

Cheap food is important to capitalism because it allows wages to be lower (and thus profits to be higher) and yet leave workers with more disposable income available to buy other commodities. For these and other reasons, early in the history of capitalism, the food system became tied to colonialism, where various forms of forced or semi-forced labour were common. After the civil war ended slavery in the US, the domestically-produced food system came to rest primarily on the family farm. But after the Second World War the increasing mechanization and chemicalisation of agriculture favoured larger farms. In the early 1970s the US Secretary of Agriculture Earl Butz got Congress to pass a programme of subsidies that rewarded high yields. As a result, the larger the farm and the higher the yield, the larger became the subsidy. Nearly all the subsidies went to large farms, and for a few basic crops: tobacco, cotton, corn, wheat, and eventually soy. Moreover the large farms that could benefit the most from mechanization and chemicalisation became increasingly subservient to the gigantic corporations that supplied the inputs and bought the outputs of these factory farms.[3]

This situation remains essentially unchanged today. In 2005 alone the US government spent over \$20 billion in agricultural subsidies (46 per cent of this went for corn production, 23 per cent for cotton, 10 per cent for wheat, and 6 per cent for soybeans).[4] The largest 10 per cent of the farms got 72 per cent of the subsidies and 60 per cent of all farms got no subsidy at all. For the most part, fruit and vegetable crops received no subsidies, and the same could be said for most small and medium sized farms. In short, the subsidy program rewards the large yields that result from very large, highly industrialized farms.

Today, while there are still many family farms in the US, the older mixed family farm that utilized manure from its animals to fertilize the land, and practised crop rotation and other techniques to control pests, has been largely wiped out. The giant capitalist farm of today is dependent on cheap oil and government subsidies. David Pimentel, professor of ecology at Cornell University and a globally recognized expert on food systems and energy, has argued that if the entire world adopted the American food system, all known sources of fossil fuel would be exhausted in seven years.[5] At the same time, utilizing such huge amounts of petroleum-based chemicals (fertilizers and pesticides) would not only contribute enormously to global warming, but also would make our toxic environment even more toxic.

In this short essay most of my examples come from the US, because, as the most hegemonic capitalist power in the world, it has done the most to shape the global food system. But I don't want to give the impression that there is one tightly integrated capitalist world food system. Even in the US, capitalism has not entirely subsumed the whole food system, and while there are few places in the world untouched by capitalism, its degree of hegemony may vary a great deal. Still, up to the present, capitalism has been the single strongest force shaping the global food system, and much of that shaping power has flowed outward from the US.[6]

THE PROFITS OF OBESITY

It is scandalous that in the academic world many professors of economics still teach the doctrine of consumer sovereignty when it is so clear that on the contrary, corporations are the far greater sovereign force. Coca-Cola, for example, is the most universally recognized brand name, and is one of the world's largest and most profitable corporations. But Coke got this way with a little help from its friends. According to food political economist Raj Patel:

> ... the US taste for Coca-Cola was first chorused in the theatre of the Second World War. The drink itself wasn't given away during the conflict, but General Marshall went to great lengths to make sure that it was freely available to buy wherever US troops were stationed. The Coca-Cola Company was exempted from sugar rationing [Pepsi was not] so that it might produce a drink that came, for US soldiers, to signify the very lifeblood of the country.[7]

According to nutritionist Marion Nestle, Americans consume on average 31 teaspoons of added sugars a day, 40 per cent of which comes from soft drinks.[8] American teenage boys drink on average 800 12-ounce cans of soft drink a year, while the standard soft drink in vending machines has gone from 8 to 12 to 20 ounces (on average there are 15 teaspoons of sugar in a 20-ounce bottle).[9] No wonder the number of overweight children in the US has tripled since 1980. Given that fat and sugar constitute 50 per cent of the caloric intake of the average American, it is also not surprising to find that over two-thirds of all Americans are overweight, while the very obese (at least 100 pounds overweight) are the fastest-growing group.[10] Obesity is a risk factor for many chronic diseases, but is most closely connected to diabetes. In the seven years from 1997 to 2004 type 2 diabetes increased 41 per cent in the US. Globally the six-fold increase in cases of diabetes since 1985 almost exactly parallels the global increase in high fructose corn syrup (HFCS) consumption.[11]

The ideal food ingredient for profit purposes is something that is cheap and that consumers crave. Sweetness is the most desired taste to the point that many if not most people can easily be caught up in an 'excessive appetite' for it.[12] A craving for sugar is widespread, and recent tests suggest that sugar may be addictive.[13] It also happens that many of the widely used sugars in the food industry are among the cheapest inputs to food processing. The cheapness of HFCS makes soft drinks – that typically consist of artificial flavour, artificial colouring, water, and HFCS – among the most profitable commodities produced by the capitalist food industry.[14] A common way of classifying foods contrasts calorie density to nutrient density. While some foods may be both calorie dense and nutrient dense, food that we usually call 'junk food' tends to be very high in calories relative to nutrients.[15] Many soft drinks contain lots of calories but no other nutrients whatever.

The addictive quality of sugar can be compared to that of cigarettes. In part because of the marketing power of corporations like Philip Morris, cigarette smoking is now common amongst children as young as thirteen in places like Latin America, the former Soviet Union, China, and India, and it is estimated that over one billion people will die from smoking cigarettes in the twenty-first century.[16] But the so-called 'obesity pandemic' with its frequent sugar fix may end up damaging more lives than the rapid spread of smoking cigarettes amongst the youth of developing and post-communist societies. Tobacco often kills after the age of sixty, while sugar attacks the teeth of the young and may in many cases be the main cause of obesity and all of its related chronic illnesses throughout life.[17]

Warren Buffet, among the top five richest men in the world, once said: 'I'll tell you why I like the cigarette business. It costs a penny to make. Sell it for a dollar. It's addictive. And there's fantastic brand loyalty.'[18] One could say that the same for sugar. It is very cheap and it produces a craving, and in the case of Pepsi and Coca-Cola there is often strong brand loyalty too – a sure formula for fabulous profits in the food industry. It should also be noted that the cost of food inputs (in many cases of 'value added' processed foods) constitutes a small fraction of the total price. This is certainly the case with soft drinks, as it is also for most breakfast cereals. For example, the grain in a 12 ounce box of cereal that sells for $3.50 may only cost 25 cents.[19] The rest of the $3.50 reflects the costs of transporting, processing, packaging, and retailing, plus a very sweet profit.

It happens that the sugars, fats, and salts that are so central to junk food, are not only the foods that humans most crave, but also are among the cheapest food inputs. With such cheap inputs it is tempting to increase portion sizes, since the increased cost to the consumer of the larger portion then becomes almost pure profit. While McDonalds led the way, the entire food industry has now followed. Many studies show that as portions get larger, people eat more, and since food itself is a small portion of the costs in food items like french fries, or soda pop, much of the extra cost to the consumer of larger portions is pure profit for the fast food outlet. Indeed, the difference between what the farmer gets and the final selling price of food items sometimes reaches obscene proportions as when on average the potato farmer gets 2 cents out of an order of fries that sells for $1.50.[20] No wonder some burger chains have found it profitable to serve larger and larger orders of fries.

In response to recent criticisms, fast food chains have made a few cosmetic changes, but overall their commitment to deliver large portions of junk food cheap is continuing. For example, in the summer of 2008, Pizza Hut began to aggressively market its new one pound P'zone pizza and dipping sauce, which contains 1,560 calories (the average daily intake of calories should be 2,100 calories) and twice the recommended daily intake of sodium. [21]

Indeed, salt consumption in the US increased by a striking 20 per cent over the ten-year period between 1992 and 2002.[22] Salt itself is not fattening, but it does increase thirst, which in the US is very often slaked by high calorie soft drinks or beer. Further, salt contributes to high blood pressure, a major risk factor in heart disease and strokes. It has been estimated that reducing salt consumption by half in the US would prevent 150,000 deaths a year.[23]

The growth of meat and dairy consumption, with their saturated fats, along with the conversion of various vegetable oils into trans fats, have also contributed to the obesity epidemic and other health problems. The percentage of fat in the average American diet increased from 19 per cent in 1977 to 40 per cent in 2005.[24] French fries drenched in fat and salt constitute 25 per cent of all vegetables consumed in the US,[25] and the per capita consumption of cheese has nearly tripled since 1970.[26]

And this meatification and junkification of diet is now spreading to the rest of the world with dire long term consequences to human and environmental health. The world's poorer countries already carry immense burdens of infectious diseases. Now they have to contend with the junkification of their diets, plus increased tobacco use, both of which have escalated the incidence in these countries of chronic illnesses such as diabetes, heart disease, and cancer.

The United Nations International Codex Alimentarius Commission, which sets international food norms, is heavily influenced by the food industry. This influence was demonstrated at its November 2006 meeting where it was proposed to lower the limit of sugar in baby foods from the existing 30 per cent to 10 per cent. The proposal was defeated by the combined forces of the European and American sugar industries.[27] In a similar case, the UN's World Health Organization (WHO) and Food and Agriculture Organization (FAO) proposed, in their 2003 report, *Diet, Nutrition and the Prevention of Chronic Diseases*, a guideline, widely supported by nutritionists, that recommended that added sugars should not exceed 10 per cent of daily calorie intake. This was too much for the US sugar industry to swallow, and they threatened to lobby Congress to cut off its $400,000 annual funding of the WHO and FAO if they did not remove the offending norm from their report.[28] Under the circumstances, it was hardly surprising, if nevertheless still shameful, that the UN bodies gave in.

According to Patti Randall, policy director of Baby Milk Action Group, 'A bottle-fed baby consumes 30,000 more calories over its first eight months than a breast-fed one. That's the calorie equivalent of 120 average size chocolate bars.'[29] 'Several research studies have shown correlations between bottle-feeding and subsequent obesity', which is what would be expected given the early age at which tastes may be formed.[30] And yet despite these findings, baby formula is aggressively marketed around the world. The soy lobby in the US has convinced the government to buy its soy formula and give it away to mothers on welfare – despite the fact that giving a baby soy formula with its powerful oestrogen is equivalent to an adult woman taking 5 birth control pills a day.[31]

At the same time, because the American sugar industry is protected by high tariffs blocking the import of sugar, it can charge consumers up to three times the going international price, which typically amounts to a subsidy of $1-3 billion a year.[32] This subsidy paid by American consumers of sugar is given to very large and profitable corporations that grow a crop high in calories and low in other nutrients (refined sugar typically has no other nutrients), a crop that consumed in large quantities endangers the health of the world. At the same time, sugar laden food is marketed with a vengeance.[33]

'Brand loyalty from cradle to grave' is the aim of current marketing strategies that seem to be achieving just that. Toddlers are requesting brands early in life, with 60 per cent of American children under two watching television (and with 26 per cent having their own television!).[34] According to Schor, children request on average over 3,000 products a year.[35] The food brands that can tap into the human craving for sugar, fat, and salt the earliest end up being the big winners, for kids' number one spending category (at one-third of the total) is sweets, snacks, and beverages.[36] American children get on average over 25 per cent of their total calorie intake from snacks,[37] and 50 per cent of their calories from sugars and fats added to their food.[38] The incidence of diabetes among children and teenagers is to say the least alarming: besides the one-third of the babies born in the US in the year 2000 who are likely to become diabetic, about 6 per cent suffer from fatty liver disease,[39] and about 25 per cent have risk factors, such as elevated blood pressure, for heart disease.[40]

The private sector has developed numerous marketing strategies for getting at the impressionable minds of today's youth by exploiting the underfunding of schools. McDonalds and other fast food chains utilize sets of toys made by children in China to entice American children to want to come back repeatedly in order to complete their set. [41] The hunger and exploitation of children in one part of the world feeds 'the toxic food environment' offered children in another part, where soft drink companies gain exclusive 'pouring rights' in educational institutions in return for a modest monetary contribution, junk foods find their ways into cafeterias in similar fashion, and some schools even receive free televisions for having students watch ten minutes of news and two minutes of commercials a day on Channel One in the US. [42] Since so much of this advertising is for junk foods, it would indeed appear that so long as this continues – however many pledges we hear today to turn around the massive increase in healthcare spending in recent decades – we may expect an even greater expansion of healthcare spending in the future. [43]

THE HUNGER OF CAPITALISM

Almost as a hallmark of its dysfunctionality, the same capitalist food system that produces obesity also produces hunger, which in terms of immediate suffering is far more serious than obesity. One of the UN's Millennium Development Goals is to reduce hunger from the previous 800 million (in 2000) to 400 million by the end of 2015. Yet, since this goal was enunciated, the number of hungry people in the world has *grown*, to over a billion.

Why is it that the term 'obesity epidemic' has wide currency and 'starvation epidemic' does not? One reason is that capitalists would rather not call attention to hunger, because its widespread existence stands in such jarring contrast to the 'chicken in every pot' pretensions of capitalism. A second reason is that to medicalise starvation with the term 'epidemic' seems out of place in connection with something so obviously connected, except for natural disasters, to institutions of human design. A third reason is that capitalistic rationality dictates profit maximisation, and the 'starvation sector' of the economy is not one where profits can be made. A fourth reason is that from the point of view of distributive justice or of ethics, the global massacre that is starvation is totally preventable and totally unjustifiable.

Defenders of the capitalist system might point out that hunger and starvation have always been problems, and that we must accept them as we do the law of gravity. But we have the knowledge and technical means to provide a good diet for everyone in the world, and failing to do so stems from radically unjust institutions of distribution. Good intentions continually arise from the grass roots, but more often than not they get deflected away from altering the capitalist institutions that lie at the base of the hunger and starvation. Hunger is basically a problem of poverty, a poverty created primarily by capitalism, colonialism, imperialism, racism, and patriarchy.

Agriculture remains the main source of income for 2.5 billion people, 96 per cent of them living in developing countries. In the late 1970s the World Bank and International Monetary Fund developed increasingly invasive structural adjustment policies (SAPS) which set conditions for developing countries to get further loans, or get better repayment schedules for existing loans, in response to the capitalist-generated 'debt crisis'. Many of these countries were forced to develop export-oriented cash crops to pay off debts. With many tropical countries expanding their export crops (such as tea, coffee, tobacco, sugar, flowers, peanuts, cotton, and cocoa) at the same time, the resulting glut on the market produced falling prices. Given that agriculture is the weightiest sector in the economies of over 80 developing countries, the result was devastating. According to Peter Robbins, 'The collapse of tropical commodity prices represents the most formidable obstacle to efforts to lift huge numbers of people out of poverty and yet, mysteriously, the problem has received almost no attention from the world's mainstream media'.[44] For example, by 2002 coffee prices were 14 per cent of their already low 1980 price, while cocoa had fallen to 19 per cent and cotton to 21 per cent. Is it really so surprising that a class-biased media would neglect such phenomena?

Worse still, while one might think that coffee farmers would be better off if the price of coffee went up this does not necessarily follow. Kraft and Nestlé, which control 49 per cent of the roasting, are among the small number of importers and roasters that control 78 per cent of the total revenues received from selling coffee.[45] History has shown that when the price of coffee increases it is the large corporations that rake in extra profits, while the money received by the direct producers changes little if at all; just as when the price of coffee falls, it often does not fall for the consumer, the large corporations grabbing the difference.[46]

Developing countries cannot compete with crops grown in the US or Europe because they are so highly subsidized. The North American Free Trade Agreement (NAFTA) between Canada, Mexico, and the US has had a similar impact on Mexico as SAPs and the 'green revolution' have had in other parts of the world. During the first ten years of the agreement, 1.7 million Mexicans were displaced from agriculture largely as a result of highly subsidised US food commodities (especially corn) flooding into Mexico.[47] Because US corn farmers receive on average half of their income in subsidies, they can sell their corn on the international market under the cost of production and still make a profit. For instance, in 2002 US corn cost $2.66 a bushel to produce and was sold on the international market for $1.74 a bushel.[48] Many of the Mexican farmers displaced by the dumping of cheap US corn into the Mexican market crossed the border to the US. Before the NAFTA 7 per cent of the 900,000 migrant farm workers in the US were undocumented. Ten years later 50 per cent of the 2 million migrant farm workers in the US were undocumented.[49]

The struggle of farm households is not limited to developing countries. By 1990 20 per cent of farm households in the US had incomes that put them below the poverty line.[50] And with up to 20,000 family farms shutting down each year, many low income farm families no longer farm.[51] These trends largely account for the fact that the average Iowa farmer is now approaching 60, and that suicide is the leading cause of death amongst US farmers, three times higher than for the population as a whole.[52]

It is the rising incidence of hunger and starvation among children that bodes so ill for the future. More than 18 per cent of hungry people are children under five, and many of them do not make it to five. For those who do survive, physical and/or mental stunting affects 31 per cent of all children in developing countries.[53] Current trends indicate that soon one billion people in the world will suffer impaired mental development because of malnutrition.[54] According to the FAO, malnutrition plays a role in more than 50 per cent of the annual 12 million deaths of children under five.[55] In developing countries 25 per cent of men and 45 per cent of women have anaemia, which is also far more dangerous to women, of whom an estimated 300 die during childbirth each day.[56] Clearly gender relations that disadvantage women play a huge role in the continuation of global poverty. A more thorough analysis of global poverty would need to make gender issues much more visible.

The UN estimates that 1.2 billion people live on less than $1 a day, while 2.8 billion, or 40 per cent of the world's population, live on less than $2 a day.[57] When food prices spike, as they did in the first half of 2008, the survival of many of these 2.8 billion people is jeopardised, as many of them were already spending 90 per cent or more of their income on food. The deepening global depression has since reduced all commodity prices, including food, but the price of food has still gone up 28 per cent since 2006.[58] Though many prices may fluctuate in the short term, there are several reasons why the price of food is bound to go up in the long run unless some radical changes are made.

- Fertile land that could grow food crops is being utilized for non-food crops, including tobacco, agro-fuels, illegal drugs, and trees for pulp and paper.
- Fertile land is being lost to suburban sprawl, golf courses, roads, parking lots, and mega shopping malls.
- Land is being degraded by industrial farming techniques.
- Global warming will sharply decrease crop yields due to higher temperatures and extreme weather.[59]
- The globalisation of a meat-based diet will divert food grains to animals.

- Speculators, seeing all of these pressures on the global food supply, will bid up the price of basic grains on commodity futures markets.

All of this adds up to rising food prices and increasing hunger for nearly half of the world's population. It is unlikely that the poor farmers who produce the food will benefit much from higher prices, since they will mostly be skimmed off by the transnational corporations that control the international trade and processing.

THE IRRATIONALITY OF CAPITALIST RATIONALITY

What could be more foolhardy than placing food, the basis of all human flourishing, in the hands of giant corporations, which are obliged to pursue profits in order to further enrich an elite of wealthy stockholders? Indeed, within the framework of existing company law, units of capital must continually attempt to expand by maximizing profits, no matter what the social or environmental costs. The absurdity of our capitalist economic system emerges clearly when our understanding is not blinded by the ideology of market fundamentalism. The two basic institutions of our capitalist system are corporations and markets, and without radical reform neither has the capability of rationally responding to the mounting crises that we face now (and will increasingly face in the future) as the ecological and energy crises compound the economic crisis. Immense corporations whose decisions affect everyone in the world are fundamentally only accountable to a small number of wealthy shareholders, and even to them only in accord with the narrow criteria of profit maximisation. Markets, that in theory are supposed to satisfy social needs, treat enormous and ever-mounting social costs as 'externalities' that corporations can ignore and simply pass on to taxpayers, or to future generations.

In India, Coca-Cola's bottling companies are running down aquifers that farmers desperately need to irrigate crops.[60] Banana corporations have knowingly exposed third world workers to highly toxic pesticides, because the companies figured that they would not have to pick up any medical bills and because poor people desperate for jobs abound, so that sick or dying workers can always be replaced.[61] Meatpacking companies prey upon the vulnerability of undocumented workers, paying them low wages and speeding up the line to the point where injuries become routine.[62] Sugar companies oppose a norm which would lower the 30 per cent sugar now allowed in baby foods to 10 per cent.[63] Giant feedlots (Confined Animal Feeding Operations or CAFOs) pollute the surrounding earth, air, and water with foul odours and toxic substances.[64] Highly subsidised and therefore profitable ethanol producers buy up much of America's corn crop (as much as 50 per cent in the near future, on current predictions), and, as a result, raise the cost of food while the world's poor starve.[65] Cocoa farmers in Ivory Coast receive so little for their crop that some have had to turn to child slavery in order to survive.[66]

All of the above examples are taken from our actually existing capitalist system of food provision, and what needs to be emphasized is that they are all perfectly rational from the point of view of profit-maximising capitalism. But this only confirms the extreme irrationality of capitalist 'rationality', and the urgent need to bring about radical changes via democratic long-term planning from the local level to the global. It is precisely because today's global capitalist food system promotes both hunger and obesity while at the same time undermining the earth's capacity to support us, that we need to fight to replace it at every link of the food chain with a system that is democratically planned to meet the human need for nutritious food and ensure that everyone has access to it, while at the same time leaving the environment – in so far as this is possible, given the damage already done – in an improved state for future generations.

NOTES

1   B. Popkin, 'The world is fat', *Scientific American*, September, 2007, pp. 94-5; 'By 2020, 7 million Indians may die of lifestyle diseases', *Times of India*, 24 September 2007.

2   Cited in M. Pollan, *The Omnivores Dilemma*, New York: Penguin, 2006, p. 102.

3   Another aim of Butz's subsidies was that by enabling the dumping of basic grains on international markets at below cost of production, the growing US balance of trade deficit could be lessened, and developing countries would become more dependent on the US for food.

4   'Uncle Sam's teat', *The Economist*, 9 September 2006, p. 35.

5   Cited in R. Manning, 'The oil we eat', *Harpers*, February, 2004.

6   For a much more inclusive analysis of how the current food system is integrated into global capitalism in ways that undermines not only human and environmental health, but also social justice and democracy, see my recently published book: *Let Them Eat Junk: How Capitalism Creates Hunger and Obesity*, London: Pluto Press, 2009 and Winnipeg: Arbeiter Ring Press, 2009.

7   Raj Patel, *Stuffed and Starved: Markets, Power, and the Hidden Battle for the World Food System*, Toronto: Harper Collins, 2007, p. 258; see also B. Popkin, *The World is Fat*, New York: Avery, 2009, p. 59.

8   M. Nestle, *What to Eat?*, New York: North Point Press, 2006, pp. 321, 327.

9   Global Dump Soft Drinks Campaign, http://www.dumpsoda.org, 2007. See also, Center for Science in the Public Interest, 'Consumer groups in 20

countries urge Coke and Pepsi to limit soft drink marketing to children', 3 January 2008, available from http://www.cspinet.org/new/index.html.

10 J. Schor, *Born to Buy*, New York: Scribner, 2004, p. 35. See also E. Schlosser, *Fast Food Nation*, New York: Harper Collins, 2002, p. 53; G. Gardner and B. Halweil, 'Overfed and underfed, the global epidemic of malnutrition', *Worldwatch Institute*, paper no. 150, March, 2000.

11 T. Philpott, 'How the feds make bad-for-you-food cheaper than healthful fare', 22 February 2006, available from http://www.grist.org.

12 J. Orford, *Excessive Appetites: A Psychological View of Addictions*, Toronto: Wiley, 2001.

13 See C. Colantuoni, 'Evidence that intermittent, excessive sugar intake causes endogenous opioid dependence', *Obesity Research*, No. 10, pp. 478-88; See also 'A survey of food', *The Economist*, 13 December, 2003, p. 16.

14 HFCS constitutes 50 per cent of all caloric sweeteners in processed foods. There is considerable debate over whether or not HFCS is more likely to cause diabetes than other sugars. There is some evidence that high levels of HFCS consumption may contribute to heart attacks, kidney and liver disease, high blood pressure, systemic inflammation and increased formation of cell-damaging free radicals. Two things are well established: never has the level of fructose consumption in the human diet increased so rapidly and to such a high level, and HFCS does not trigger the body's satiation reflex as much as other sugars. P. Roberts, *The End of Food*, New York: Houghton Mifflin, 2008, pp. 97-8. T. Talago, 'Too poor to avert diabetes', *Toronto Star*, 27 December 2007, p. A27.

15 Popkin, *The World is Fat*, pp. 33-4.

16 A. Brandt, *The Cigarette Century*, New York: Basic Books, 2007, pp. 451, 459, 486-7.

17 I. Loefler, 'No sweet surrender', *British Medical Journal (BMJ)*, 330(7495), 2005.

18 Brandt, *The Cigarette Century*, p. 448.

19 Roberts, *The End of Food*, p. 37.

20 Schlosser, *Fast Food Nation*, p. 117.

21 A triple thick 32 ounce milk shake has 1,110 calories. J. Wells, 'Chewing the fat about what's really in fast food', *Toronto Star*, 29 January 2005, p. L1. See also *Toronto Star*, 1 September 2008.

22 *Economist*, 'A Survey of food', p. 9.

23 Nestle, *What to Eat?*, p. 367.

24 G. Critser, *Fat Land: How Americans Became the Fattest People in the World,* New York: Houghton Mifflin, 2003, p. 32.

25 Ibid., p. 75.

26 Nestle, *What to Eat?*, p. 63.

27 Ibid.

28 G. Dyer, 'Sugar lobby copies big tobacco', *Toronto Star*, 29 April 2003.

29 F. Lawrence, 'Sugar rush', *Guardian*, 15 February 2007.

30 Ibid.

31   F. Lawrence, *Eat Your Heart Out: Why the Food Business is bad for the Planet and your Health*, London: Penguin, 2008, p. 283.

32   *The New Internationalist,* No. 363, December, 2003, p. 23.

33   The health of workers on sugar plantations also needs to be considered. There are approximately 650,000 field workers on American-owned sugar plantations in the Dominican Republic, where in 2004 they received on average $2 for a twelve hour day working in the hot sun cutting cane. See Brian McKenna's documentary film, *Big Sugar* (2005), produced by Galafilm.

34   S. Linn, *Consuming Kids: Protecting Our Children from the Onslaught of Marketing and Advertising*, New York: New Press, 2004, p. 49.

35   J. Schor, *Born to Buy*, p. 20.

36   Ibid., p. 23.

37   Popkin, *The World is Fat,* p. 33.

38   Gardner and Halweil, 'Overfed and underfed', p. 15. See also M. Nestle, *Food Politics*, Berkeley: University of California Press, 2002, p.175.

39   This condition can lead to cirrhosis, liver cancer, and liver failure. A. Johnson, 'Liver disease plagues obese adolescents', *Associated Press*, 9 November 2008, available from http://abcnews.go.com.

40   Center for Science in the Public Interest, 'Obesity on the kids' menus at top chains', 4 August 2008, available from http://www.cspinet.org/new/index.html.

41   McDonalds, for example, sells or gives away more than 1.5 billion toys a year. Most are made in China, often by children paid as little as 20 cents an hour. See E. Schlosser and C. Wilson, *Chew On This: Everything You Don't Know About Fast Food*, Boston: Houghton Mifflin, 2006, p. 59.

42   K. Brownell and K. Horgen, *Food Fight: The Inside Story of the Food Industry, America's Obesity Crisis, and What You can Do About It*, New York: McGraw-Hill, 2004, pp. 86-8.

43   J. Califano, *High Society: How Substance Abuse Ravages America and What to do about it,* New York: Public Affairs, 2007, p. 80.

44   P. Robbins, *Stolen Fruit*, Halifax: Fernwood, 2003, p. 3.

45   World Vision (2006), 'Slave to coffee and chocolate', available from http://www.worldvision.com.au.

46   J. M. Talbot, *Grounds for Agreement*, New York: Rowman & Littlefield, 2004, p. 115.

47   P. Rosset, *Food is Different: Why We Must Get the WTO out of Agriculture,* Halifax: Fernwood, 2006, p. 62.

48   Patel, *Stuffed and Starved*, p. 74.

49   C. Ahn, M. Moore and N. Parker, 'Migrant farmworkers: America's new plantation workers', *Backgrounder*, Food First, 10(2), available online via http://www.foodfirst.org.

50   T. Weis, *The Global Food Economy: The Battle for the Future of Farming*, Halifax: Fernwood, 2007, p. 83.

51   P. Rosset, *Food is Different*, p. 49.

52   *The New Internationalist*, 2003, No. 353, p. 10.

53 P. Pinstrup-Andersen and F. Cheng, 'Still hungry', *Scientific American*, 297(3), September 2007, pp. 96-8.

54 T. Lang and M. Heasman, *Food Wars: The Global Battle for Mouths, Minds, and Markets*, London: Earthscan, 2004, p. 61.

55 Cited in Pinstrup-Andersen and Cheng, 'Still hungry', p. 101.

56 Ibid., p. 98

57 FAO, *The State of Food Insecurity in the World 2006*, Rome: FAO, 2006, p. 32.

58 J. Berger & J. Jowitt, 'Nearly a billion people worldwide are starving, UN agency warns', *The Guardian*, 10 December, 2008, p. 1.

59 E. deCarbonnel, 'Catastrophic fall in 2009 global economy food production', available from http://www.marketskeptics.com; see also T. Engelhardt, 'What does economic "recovery" mean on an extreme weather planet?', 18 February 2009, available from http://www.countercurrents.org.

60 'Campaign to hold Coca-Cola accountable', *India Resource Center*, available at http://www.indiaresource.org/campaigns/coke.

61 N. Berube, 'Chiquita's children', *In These Times*, May 2005.

62 This has occurred throughout the US meatpacking industry. See S. Striffler, *Chicken, The Dangerous Transformation of America's Favourite Food*, New Haven: Yale University Press, 2005, p. 8; S. Parker, 'Finger-lickin bad', 21 February 2006, available from http://www.grist.org; Schlosser, *Fast Food Nation*, p. 174.

63 Lawrence, 'Sugar rush'.

64 The smell of CAFOs is repellent, and schools near to CAFOs have a higher incidence of asthma. S. Cox, *Sick Planet: Corporate Food and Medicine*, London: Pluto Press, 2009, p. 71. One study found that 25 per cent of hog house workers had breathing obstructions that could cause long-term lung damage. See T. Pawlick, *The End of Food*, Toronto: Greystone, 2006, p. 132.

65 L. Brown, 'Distillery demand for grain to fuel cars vastly understated: world may be facing highest grain prices in history', *Earth Policy Institute*, Paper No. 5, January 2007, available from http://www.earth-policy.org.

66 C. Off, *Bitter Chocolate*, Toronto: Random House, 2006.

TV MEDICAL DRAMAS: HEALTH CARE AS SOAP OPERA

LESLEY HENDERSON

'Medicine is drama, doctors are human,
and patients are trouble or troubled'.[1]

The medical drama occupies an extraordinary position in contemporary television. The format attracts multiple awards (*ER* became the most nominated series in TV history, earning 122 Emmy nominations and 22 Awards) and breaks new ground in television aesthetics (*St Elsewhere* popularised pedeconferencing – the 'walk and talk' tracking shot to signify the supposedly frenetic pace of hospital life). The genre is economically important, too, as medical dramas consistently attract large audiences with 'gold dust' demographics for advertisers – the notoriously elusive 18–49 years. These programmes deliver high drama but also convey important messages about health and illness, often highlighting political issues which are neglected in television news and documentary formats. Thus the humanitarian crisis in the Darfur region of Sudan – underreported by the US news media – was brought to *ER* viewers through characters Dr John Carter and Dr Gregory Pratt, who were depicted working in a refugee camp trying to protect their patients from the Janjaweed militia (series 12, 2006). As these fictional scenes were being transmitted to global audiences, George Clooney – formerly *ER*'s Dr Doug Ross – spoke out at public rallies to stimulate support for American intervention in Darfur, thus blurring the lines between drama and the material world still further.[2] Shows such as *House MD* are dissected in meticulous detail by fans and medical professionals on websites filled with endless analysis of the plausibility of plot and procedure.[3]

The medical drama is a commercial product that not only reflects our socio–cultural and economic environment but also illuminates wider changes in broadcasting culture. Why are medical dramas important? How do they relate to other fictional genres, such as police series and TV soaps? What sorts of messages are conveyed in medical dramas, and what are omitted?

What is their influence on public understandings concerning health care?

There is little doubt that in recent years we have witnessed an increased medicalisation of the mass media: medical-related stories appear more frequently than ever in press and television outlets. This is driven in part by an increase in health-related PR, and in a multi-channel, multi-platform environment there are also more spaces where health and illness issues can be aired. Entire cable channels are devoted exclusively to our wellbeing and numerous internet websites offer instant access to health information and celebrity gossip that is also often health-related. Emerging television formats such as lifestyle and physical 'make-over' shows also provide opportunities for audiences to witness intensely personal moments and have sparked debate concerning their overly voyeuristic nature.[4] At the same time there has been an increasing 'soapisation' of the media in general, with documentary formats appropriating popular techniques from television soap opera. Medical and police drama series (commonly termed 'cops and docs') dominate television viewing schedules, and although strictly defined as being within the drama-series genre (being produced as self-contained episodes to be watched, in theory, in any order) they do now share many of the characteristics of soap opera serials, interweaving multiple plots with a continuous core cast and concluding with 'cliff-hanging' plot twists. Almost all US TV series are now soap operas, 'since storylines stretch across several episodes and there is a sense of a long story being slowly unfolded as seasons go by'.[5]

The dominance of medical and police drama in television schedules has sparked a serious concern that such relatively cheap and formulaic programming is displacing other more challenging 'quality' drama. Indeed the 'soapisation' of the media in general is seen as a negative consequence of increased competition for audiences and the proliferation of channels. The rise in 'reality television' shows, the decline in resources allocated to documentary programming, and the alleged 'feminisation' of news media (move towards lighter, human interest, interpretation based stories) suggest that broadcasting is in crisis and becoming ratings-led to the detriment of more challenging programming. Shifts in news media from the public to the private realm (replacing expertise with the 'raw testimonies of experience') have been accompanied by a simultaneous blurring of the boundaries between fiction and reality in television drama.[6]

The routine portrayal of 'hard' subject matter in prime time 'entertainment' slots, and the impact of this on audiences, have sparked a lot of discussion about the cultural role of television drama. Yet these formats and their reach in terms of audiences are highly desirable to health charities, lobbying groups and even governments — all of whom consider television drama to be a useful conduit of policy messages.

The explosion in PR generally, and concerning health and illness issues in particular, means that there is significant competition between charities to place information posters and leaflets in background shots. In soap opera scenes the positioning of such posters, leaflets or message-carrying mugs is not just beneficial to the charity which receives wider exposure but also arguably adds authenticity and realism to a hospital scene or a primary health clinic. These details function as visual referents, just like domestic details in characters' homes; dishes in the sink, photographs on a mantelpiece.[7] Story lines win awards for ground-breaking representations: so the Channel 4 soap opera *Brookside* was awarded the first National Childbirth Trust baby friendly award for portraying breastfeeding positively, by showing (very unusually for British television) a baby suckling at her mother's breast.[8] In 2002 *EastEnders* received a Mental Health Award for sensitively portraying Kat Slater as she contemplated suicide after breaking her silence about childhood sexual abuse.[9]

But there is an ambiguous relationship between seeking the public profile which a soap story can confer and simultaneously policing these stories, and production teams are frequently criticised for what is said to be the negative impact of their story lines on the public. The soap opera *Brookside* was criticised for showing a terminally ill woman begging her family to end her suffering because her doctor failed to provide sufficient pain relief. The British Medical Association and the Director General of the Cancer Research Campaign criticised the portrayal of carers of people with cancer being forced to buy drugs on the street. Resisting the efforts of medical organisations, charities, lobby organisations and indeed governments to promote policy initiatives seems to have become an established part of the producer's role. The former executive producer of *Coronation Street*, David Liddiment, has commented that 'soap, corporate agendas and politicians make a heady mix best avoided'.[10]

Nonetheless drama with a social message has developed a unique position in television culture, so much so that fictional programmes may themselves become events with social and material consequences.[11] In the UK, *Cathy Come Home* (1966) focused public attention on the plight of the homeless. In the US, audiences reportedly cheered as Helen Hunt's character launched a vitriolic attack on her HMO in the film *As Good As It Gets* (1997).[12] More recently the powerful film *John Q* (2002) featured Denzel Washington as the underinsured father of a critically ill son and highlighted the issue of managed care in the US. In the same year the Kaiser Family Foundation organised a public forum, *John Q Goes to Washington,* which drew together drama writers, academics and representatives from the American Association of Health Plans to debate the role of entertainment TV in shaping public perceptions. A survey found that as many as seven in ten of those Americans who had watched this film believed that insurers refuse to pay for treatment 'a lot of' the time.[13] The potential of television drama and soap opera to shift and focus public opinion means that these formats are subject to intense lobbying by diverse groups keen to have their issues incorporated into story lines.[14] At the same time, these programmes generate vital revenue, and producers are inevitably constrained by the competing and at times conflicting interests of network/channel sponsors/advertisers and audiences. It seems clear, however, that fiction can be a powerful tool for social change and is increasingly recognized as such.

A BRIEF HISTORY OF THE EVOLVING MEDICAL SOAP

From paternalistic and compassionate ...

In the early days of medical drama television fiction was seen as important to preserving and enhancing the reputation of the medical profession. The popular UK drama *Dr Finlay's Casebook* (1962-71) and the US shows *Dr Kildare* (1961-1966), *Ben Casey* (1961-66) and later *Marcus Welby MD* (1969-76) presented a dominant view of dedicated doctors willing to move beyond their professional boundaries to help their patients and motivated not by financial reward but by a noble calling. These TV doctors have been described as 'psychological brokers', or 'necessary outsiders', in that their central role was to help patients resolve the internal dramas or conflicts that were generated by their illness.[15] These programmes centred on the medical hero (embodied in the modern but compassionate *Dr Kildare*) who was concerned with the lives of his patients to the extent that he was willing to sacrifice financial rewards and personal relationships. As Vandekieft notes, at this time medicine was becoming more reliant on high-tech science, which dramatically improved treatment but also raised its cost, with serious consequences for patient-doctor relations in the US:

> as physicians' incomes rapidly increased, and the profession fought
> to preserve traditional fee-for-service medicine, many viewed the
> profession as avaricious and uninterested in public health.[16]

Television audiences were, then, often watching the type of doctors they desired rather than ones who bore a close similarity to their actual healthcare professionals. The TV doctors were infallible, had endless time to spend with few patients and were not financially driven (in the eponymous medical drama Dr. Marcus Welby 'never argued with his partner about money, the commonest problem in American medical partnerships').[17] As Anne Karpf commented:

> the more rushed real-life doctors become, the more leisurely the pace of their fictional counterparts. And the same went for money: as American medicine became increasingly profit orientated, with tales of impecunious patients being turned away from casualty, American medical dramas depicted a medical practice where fees were almost never discussed, and patients never rejected because of their inability to pay.[18]

These programmes received an official 'stamp of approval' from organised medicine. The American Medical Association (AMA) Advisory Committee endorsed *Dr Kildare* and *Ben Casey*, and the American Academy of Family Physicians (AAFP) collaborated with the producers of *Marcus Welby*. Although the extent to which such institutions could control the content of programmes is debatable, this was nonetheless a useful collaboration, and these largely positive fictional portrayals were regarded as supporting AMA interests in preserving private medicine and resisting state provision of health care.[19]

These programmes were also being screened during a period of enormous social change in the US and Europe, with the birth of the civil rights and feminist movements. In this context their role was to reassert social stability. As Karpf noted, 'the white male tele-doctor made good the damage and healed the hurt, the doctor shows offered reassurance that the system could succour and patriarchy provide'.[20] The reassuring medical drama was also exemplified by the UK television show *Emergency Ward 10* (1957-67), which was developed with the aim of 'overcoming the pre-war attitude of the British public of hospitals as institutions, places to be avoided at all costs'.[21] The programme used ideas from the Ministry of Health and was praised by the British Medical Association for helping to allay public fears about hospital treatment. At the same time, however, as Joseph Turow argues, by presenting a utopian view of health care such programmes began a trajectory of medical drama in which audiences assume that health care is a limitless resource.[22]

... to working on the front line

Despite the widespread cynicism and disillusionment with the 'establishment' that marked the 1960s and 1970s on both sides of the Atlantic there appeared to be little public desire in those years to tune into medical shows that portrayed the institutional failings of the medical system in any detail. One programme which did attempt to highlight the shortcomings of medical bureaucracy in radical ways, *Medical Story* (NBC, 1975) was a ratings failure. This became seen as a warning to producers contemplating a more overtly political approach to medical drama. As Turow argues, although American audiences were disenchanted with the establishment they were not yet ready to think of themselves as 'pawns in struggles within the medical bureaucracy and between doctors and lawyers'.[23] In other areas of the mass media (and certainly in academic medical sociology) the flaws in the medical establishment were being very clearly illuminated with critical accounts of medical negligence and law suits, rising healthcare costs, and patronising doctor–patient relations but little of this was depicted in medical drama.[24]

By the early 1980s, however, when medical dramas reappeared it was with a reworked formula and a new critical edge. In the US the ensemble series *St Elsewhere* (NBC, 1982-8) represented a new wave of hospital drama, taking its cue from the police series *Hill Street Blues* and the Korean war black comedy *M*A*S*H* (CBS, 1972-83) in presenting a more subversive, irreverent take on powerful institutions. This was a very different setting from earlier programmes: *St Elsewhere's* seedy inner city hospital was characterised by peeling wallpaper and dark corridors. Here there was no obvious hero, and although doctors were the main focus, rather than the patients, these doctors had personal problems, and unlike their earlier counterparts they were not necessarily in control of their environment. [25]

This vision of health care did not provide viewers with reassurance. New medical dramas such as *Casualty* (BBC One, 1986-)were now keen to present the hospital not as 'sanctuary' but rather ' an extension of the street, a rough street at that, in which medical miracles were rare and damage limitation was often the best that could be achieved'.[26] Producers Paul Unwin and Jeremy Brock originally developed the programme under the working title *Front Line*, reflecting their jaundiced view of the National Health Service. Their original programme outline began with these words, 'In 1945 a dream was born in the National Health Service. In 1985 that dream is in tatters'.[27] This uncompromising approach fitted with a swathe of other socially realistic drama that was emerging at around the same time, such as G.F. Newman's four-part series 'The Nation's Health' (1983) which was a didactic attack on Western medicine and characterised doctors as self-serving and the NHS as 'diseased, class-ridden and doomed'.[28]

From the outset *Casualty* was devised not only as a mainstream Saturday evening family show but also explicitly as a campaign vehicle to counteract the cuts that were being made in the National Health Service (NHS) by Margaret Thatcher's neoliberal government. The programme was criticised by the Conservatives as being like 'a Labour Party meeting'[29] and it formed part of a new wave of social problem television with the British soaps *EastEnders* (BBC1, 1985-) and *Brookside* (Channel 4, 1982–2003) winning new audiences of men and younger people by focusing on gritty issues such as drug addiction, alcoholism and rape. In *Casualty* these problems were as likely to affect the staff as the patients and the programme was controversial in depicting accident and emergency personnel turning to alcohol, popping pills or smoking heavily to cope with the severe pressure of NHS conditions.[30] *Casualty* is now the longest-running emergency room drama and has consistently drawn praise for producing fairly challenging story lines in a number of areas. A major study of images of mental distress in UK media highlighted the fact that *Casualty* was one of the very few programmes to critique the way in which mental illness was depicted as culturally constructed (thus the programme is not just sympathetic towards people deemed to be mentally ill but goes further in that it explores the social definition of behaviour that is labelled 'irrational').[31]

Notably, background research for *Casualty* has gone well beyond reading newspaper cuttings or medical journals but also draws on practical experience and medical expertise. Writers have visited hospital departments to observe patients and discuss cases with medical staff. A script-editor for the programme has explained that a 'research drama' like *Casualty* 'has to have that credibility about it. We would always encourage new writers to go to a casualty department anywhere in the country'.[32] The programme script writers have not only been encouraged to identify their own contacts in the medical or social services profession, much as news journalists do, but have also been supported by regular medical advisers on the programme. An experienced script writer describes getting 'my first commission and then [I] went off and researched it in my local hospitals, Guy's [Hospital], Greenwich, I just spent a night and observed, watched cases, talked to the nurses'. The programme also paid a consultancy fee to a gynaecologist to advise her about a future termination story line. *Casualty* has regular medical advisers who are embedded within the production, checking story lines for inaccuracies, and script deadlines are flexible enough to allow for their advice to have an impact, As a script-editor explained:

> We have three medical advisers so they are on hand and obviously at the (initial) stage it is very important that the medical advisers give the stories the thumbs up. Often we would have cases where a

medical adviser would say 'this would never happen' so obviously we chuck the story out. Every single stage goes to a medical adviser for checks on dialogue. Once we've had all the medical notes back and the producer's notes and the script editors notes we then have a meeting with the writer and they go away and re-write again. Even when a script has been finalised there are usually changes. A doctor might say 'Well actually he wouldn't say or do that'.

MONEY AND MEDICINE

The ER era

Perhaps more than any other medical drama the highly-regarded and influential US series *ER* (NBC, 1994-2009) can be considered to embody the characteristics of 'the new hospital dramas' which are distinctive in their 'foregrounding of body trauma as spectacle, the intensification of the genre's melodramatic dimensions and the exploitation of the narrative adaptability of the long-running serialised-series form'.[33] The programme was developed by the late Michael Crichton who worked on the original TV pilot and series with Steven Spielberg. Crichton had trained as a physician, although he did not practise medicine, and he had clear ideas about developing a medical show that conveyed the hectic pace and raw feel of his casualty training. The programme centres on an ethnically diverse group of doctors, nurses and medical students working in County General, a fictional public hospital in Chicago. This teaching environment allows for the discussion of diverse social problems and the show has often used the doctors themselves as representatives of social problems. Thus Dr Abby Lockhart is a recovering alcoholic, Dr John Carter becomes addicted to painkillers, and Dr Jeanie Boulet contracts HIV from her sexually promiscuous husband.[34] The programme has been critically acclaimed on a number of counts (not least the innovative camera work that has become the norm in medical dramas) and is even said to play an important role in medical training:

> Students update their medical vocabulary as they recognize the acronyms, drug names, and diagnoses being tossed around the fictional emergency room.... Interestingly, the total time that a student could spend watching weekly episodes of ER over 4 years rivals the duration of a typical emergency medicine rotation at most schools.[35]

The show has been subjected to considerable scrutiny and despite its well-researched production base can for example use only generic drug names lest drug companies become associated with any negative side effects the drugs used in the programme appear to have. This highlights the tensions between creative staff, the network, and the sponsors, and raises potential problems involved in the blurring of 'realistic' content and commerce. In fact, although praised for its fast-moving plots and the emotional resonance of its personal story lines *ER*, like many earlier shows, has been criticised for presenting an idealised version of contemporary American health care. As Cohen and Shafer (2004) argue:

> This is the one hospital in America that hardly ever asks about insurance status. On ER, health care is as good and as accessible as it gets, reflecting a viewing audience's dream perception, not reality.[36]

The bioethicist George Annas has commented that the programme is successful because of a combination of sex, violence and youth. 'The real star of this show is the fourth American standby, money; and it is money's remarkable absence that makes it the star.'[37]

An analysis of prime time US medical dramas found that the shows referenced hospital administrators, lawyers, government agencies, insurance companies and Health Maintenance Organisations (health insurance companies or HMOs). Although every reference to HMOs was found to be negative, the problem of the people with no insurance at all was absent from these programmes.[38] Despite the institutional differences between the US and UK healthcare systems, it is interesting to note that the shows discussed earlier share common characteristics in terms of what is discussed and omitted. Thus blame and criticism is directed towards NHS bureaucrats and hospital managers (*Casualty, Cardiac Arrest, Holby City*) or alternatively towards the inadequacies of HMO (*Scrubs, ER*). Where reference is made to health care as limited it is personified in specific characters such as Dr Lisa Cuddy (Dean of Medicine and Hospital Administrator in *House MD*) or Dr Bob Kelso (Chief of Medicine in *Scrubs*), who are frequently pitted against the committed physician who is always willing to break rules to gain the best care for the patient (Dr Perry Cox in *Scrubs)* or to arrive at the perfect diagnosis (Dr Gregory House in *House MD*). Since in these programmes only 'money grubbing hospital administrators (the fall-back "black hat" characters in medical drama) believed in fiscal restraint',[39] this suggests that these contemporary programmes have more in common with the early doctor shows than we might imagine.

In fact, even more recent reworkings of the medical drama format are perhaps less critical than is often assumed. It is also worth noting that where *Medical Story* failed to attract audiences in the 1970s, the drama-comedy *Scrubs* (NBC, 2001–) has a committed following, not least among the medical profession who see it as an accurate depiction of their brutal training experiences.[40] The programme makes frequent (albeit humorous) references to patients' insurance status, legal disputes, the greed of powerful drug companies, the commodification of health care and also the ultimate futility of the practice of medicine.[41] These issues are softened and packaged in a surreal, fantasy format as seen through the eyes of overworked junior medical staff, particularly Dr 'JD' Dorian.[42] Studies suggest that (particularly younger) viewers are prepared to watch difficult material concerning socially sensitive topics if it is presented within a soap opera or drama rather than a documentary or news broadcast. Perhaps only a comedic and fantasy-led approach allows audiences to engage with the downsides of the healthcare system.

Health and illness in television soap opera

Medical dramas share many characteristics with the television soap opera, and health and illness storylines also feature regularly in more traditional soap opera formats. Sometimes these deal with common illnesses such as cancer (once rarely mentioned but now dealt with by many programmes), or conversely, extremely rare illnesses, unknown to audiences and medical practitioners alike. As with medical drama these soap story lines are constantly policed for accuracy. Thus daytime US soaps have been criticised for presenting an overly optimistic portrayal of coma,[43] and in the UK a *Coronation Street* story, which featured the plight of an older character, Alma Halliwell, who missed two cervical smear tests and was then diagnosed with inoperable cervical cancer, was criticised heavily by public health researchers for the panic it induced. [44] During the transmission of the story there were 300 extra calls a week to the cancer charity, CancerBACUP, and the peaks in the calls matched directly the twists in the story line.[45] As a direct result of the story an additional 14000 smear tests were performed in the North West of England alone (just 2000 of these were for women whose test was overdue or who had had no previous smear test). The panic resulted in local laboratories being overwhelmed, costs to the NHS were significant, and in the view of public health researchers, scarce health care resources were overburdened.[46]

Despite or even *because of* such controversies, stories of illness and disease are popular with drama production teams. These strong story lines propel the narrative forward and have a 'far reaching cultural consequence extending far beyond the biological fact of illness itself'.[47] Health story lines are important within the soap genre because they attract large and loyal audiences and generate 'gossip' and extended discussions on other media formats. As a member of the *EastEnders* production team explains:

> A lot of illnesses do, it sounds awful, but do translate quite readily into quite strong dramatic material and everybody in the audience will have or know someone who has had that experience of going to the doctor, waiting for the results and dealing with being in hospital. It is an incredibly difficult situation (but) the whole experience whether you've been through it or not, everyone can identify with.[48]

The process of selecting an illness for soap is influenced by a production team's perceptions of their audiences. For example, the choice of breast cancer reflected the same team's concern that the disease the story focused on should be easily and swiftly understood by viewers, and have a resonance with audiences:

> If you say MS, motor neurone disease or ME − what does that mean? We would need to set up explaining a whole host of things about the disease process for people to understand. (But) you say 'cancer' and the viewers say 'Yes I know what you're talking about'. Cancer is in the language.[49]

It is worth examining the origins and development of the *EastEnders* breast cancer story (scenes first appeared in 1996). Although it was devised at the suggestion of a script-writer in a regular Story Conference session, the programme took expert advice on storyline visuals from a variety of sources and anticipated few problems. The production team believed that Peggy Mitchell should take on the breast cancer story for several reasons. She had the 'right mentality' for this particular story theme which was about 'a woman who discovers a lump and then refuses to accept there's anything wrong'. An added factor was that in choosing 'Peggy' the programme could avoid appearing too 'issue driven' and a strong breast cancer story line could be used as a device to expand and develop her characterisation. Many soap opera viewers are used to anticipating 'issue' story lines from clues in the characters' behaviour, but the causes of breast cancer are not easily attributable to particular risky behaviour which made it unpredictable that Peggy would get it. As an *EastEnders* production team member explained:

> If you take a character who smokes and they get lung cancer that would seem too issue driven. The great thing about a character like Peggy is [her breast cancer was] quite unexpected. At the time there were lots of other issues in her life. She was a character who [audiences] had only really seen pulling pints behind the bar. Suddenly she was in a new environment in a hospital and had a huge medical crisis to go through so that allowed the character to grow and expand in many ways.[50]

The repetitive nature of soap, with its core of established characters, may allow a level of identification and empathy that is not possible to engender in other formats. The structure of the television serial facilitates 'coming to terms' with an issue over time and can include important emotional dimensions such as ambivalence, confusion, anger and denial. Health stories can be revisited at a later date (as Peggy's cancer can and does return) and the soap opera can feature those who are often marginalised from wider media accounts (this powerful matriarch character provided a useful counterpoint to the images of the young female cancer survivors which dominated media reporting of the topic).

CONCLUDING REMARKS: LEARNING FROM TELEVISION?

As James Curran rightly points out, media entertainment facilitates public engagement at an 'intuitive and expressive level in a public dialogue about the direction of society' and is in this respect an integral part of media's 'informational' role.[51] Yet this does not mean that such programmes can or should be judged on their 'accuracy' or 'truth' – although inevitably, as we have seen, it is precisely this that generates conflicts and arguments between programme makers and those who lobby the producers of such formats. Ultimately, of course, the demands of entertainment and drama are prioritised over more accurate but less visually exciting elements, and in some circumstances this has important consequences.[52] In comparison to other lobbying organisations or social institutions, the medical profession has significant power over representation and even the more radical portrayals do not attack the underlying causes of illness, such as social origins or structural health inequities. The medical profession has a visibility and presence in television entertainment that many other professions are unable to match.[53]

The impact of health stories in television soap opera and medical drama is assumed to be significant but has been relatively understudied. Indeed in comparison with the numerous analyses of the content of such programmes there has been remarkably little research that seeks to examine how audiences respond to and make sense of messages. In the mid-1990s I was involved in a study designed to explore the role of medical drama in encouraging 'inappropriate attendance' at the Accident and Emergency departments of UK hospitals. It was striking that far from perceiving 'A and E' as a glamorous and exciting place, populated with attractive medical staff, the vast majority of participants saw it rather as dirty, chaotic and frightening. Reasons for increased attendance did not in their view involve any expectation that people would encounter the sort of excitement seen on their television screens, but ranged from the limited opening hours of their General Practitioner clinic to more general health fears fuelled by media and public health advertising. Yet some fans also said that these programmes can give an accurate representation of the pressures and strains experienced in their local hospitals. As one participant explained:

> What do you call [the character in Casualty] with the white hair? You see him having arguments with the guy who's running the [hospital] that they need more funds but they'll not give them the funds for the beds. That gives you a bit of insight into what's going on in [my local hospital] Stobhill or down in the Victoria [hospital], of why they've not got beds and why they've not got more nurses.

The participants in this study clearly had no difficulty in distinguishing between television fiction and the material world, yet this does not mean that such programmes cannot and do not influence public understandings concerning health and illness.[54] Media images and messages conveyed in television drama can help shape audiences' ideas about, for example, the epidemiology of certain diseases, and as noted earlier the format of television drama may pose real moral ambiguities and ethical dilemmas quite appropriately.[55] TV drama can engage audiences emotionally and the issues can be effectively personalised, 'Instead of bill numbers and budget figures, health policy issues are portrayed through the lives of characters the viewer cares about'.[56]

The intensification of competition for audiences is likely only to increase and medical soaps provide relatively cheap ways of ensuring the survival of any channel. As new twists on the medical soap are sought we are likely to witness novel hybrid programmes that include a health dimension (such as the popular forensic science police/medical mix). This makes it all the more unfortunate that the medical drama has failed to take on more complex and possibly less audience-pleasing elements of the realities of health care. Health policy experts/analysts tend not to be involved in the TV drama production process. This is in marked contrast to the valued role played by physicians, who check scripts and advise the team on technical accuracies and whose input is considered vital in conferring credibility on a medical drama or soap. On the whole, therefore, contemporary audiences are neither educated about their healthcare system nor invited to become engaged in health policy debates. Yet the privatisation drive of the past two decades or more is now reaching deep into clinical work and the consequences of this could well provide script writers with fresh ingredients for dramatic and gripping storytelling. The creative challenge remains, more than ever at a time of health care marketisation and economic crisis, 'to find compelling ways to invite viewers behind the scenes of the corporate and governmental politics that shape all healthcare workers' approaches to life and death in a range of settings. There is drama in much of that, and comedy, too. There may well even be high ratings'.[57]

NOTES

In May 2008 I was involved in my own medical emergency and I would like to take this opportunity to thank my colleagues and friends in Social Sciences, Brunel University and at the London School of Hygiene and Tropical Medicine for their support. I am particularly grateful to Simon Carter, Gill Green, Charlie Davison, Lorna Henderson, Klara Ekevall, Greg Philo, James Curran, Julian Petley, Bob Franklin, Chris Rojek, Sanjay Sharma, Monica Degen, John Tulloch, Emma Miller, Mike Michael, Judy Green, Nicki Thorogood, Simon Lewin, Jo Green, Holly Powell Kennedy and Nick Wooding.

1   These are the results of a content analysis study of *Chicago Hope* and *ER*. See Gregory Makoul and Limor Peer, 'Dissecting the doctor shows: a content analysis of *ER* and *Chicago Hope*', in Lester D. Friedman, ed., *Cultural Sutures: Medicine and Media*, London: Duke University Press, 2004, p. 258.

2   The programme producers invested considerable resources in these scenes reportedly costing around $7 million. Very little attention had been paid to the same issue in television news with just 10 minutes coverage from the 3 main US evening news bulletins in the previous five months. This discussion is extended in Chapter 1 of Lesley Henderson, *Social Issues in Television Fiction*, Manchester: Edinburgh University Press, 2007.

3   Distinct elements of each episode are rated separately – the medical mystery; final diagnosis; the medicine and the soap opera each receive respective scores: http://www.politedissent.com/archives/2077.

4   See *Living Television* coverage of the final weeks of *Big Brother* contestant Jade Goody who received her cervical cancer diagnosis during filming and was filmed through radiotherapy treatment until shortly before she died at the age of 27 in March 2009.

5   Jostein Gripsrud makes this point in *Understanding Media Culture*, London: Arnold, 2002, p. 301.

6   Graham Murdock, 'Rights and representations: public discourse and cultural citizenship', in J. Gripsrud, ed., *Television and Common Knowledge*, London: Routledge, 1999, p. 14.

7   Christine Geraghty, *Women and Soap Opera: A Study of Prime Time Soaps*, Cambridge: Polity Press, 1991, p. 38.

8   See Lesley Henderson, Jenny Kitzinger and Josephine Green, 'Representing infant feeding: content analysis of British media portrayals of bottle and breast feeding', *BMJ (British Medical Journal)*, 321(7270), 2000, pp. 1196-8.

9   See Henderson, *Social Issues in Television Fiction*, Chapter 3 'family secrets'.

10   David Liddiment, 'Why street cred matters', *Guardian*, 19 September, 2005, p. 1.

11   John Tulloch, *Television Drama: Agency, Audience and Myth*, London: Routledge, 1990, p. 124.

12   Cited in Marc R. Cohen and Audrey Shafer, 'Images and healers: a visual history of scientific medicine', in Lester D. Friedman, ed., *Cultural Sutures: Medicine and Media*, London: Duke University Press, 2004, p. 211.

13   Detailed reports are available at the Kaiser Family Foundation website under the heading 'John Q Goes to Washington: health policy issues in popular culture': http://www.kff.org. There is also some evidence that European viewers of *ER* see the show as highlighting the financial differences in US and French/UK healthcare systems, Solange Davin, 'Healthy viewing: the reception of medical narratives', *Sociology of Health and Illness*, 25(6), 2003, pp. 662-79.

14   The educational soap opera is not discussed here but it is used to carry health promotion messages in developing countries and with hard-to-reach communities. Many of these message-led storylines are linked directly to government public health campaigns and typically cover topics such as family planning, AIDS prevention and TB. These projects are not always successful with more 'television savvy' audiences who react badly to didactic messages, nor are they popular with TV professionals who see their role in a more creative light. For discussion see Henderson, *Social Issues in Television Fiction*, pp. 18-21.

15   Gregg Vandekieft, 'From city hospital to ER: the evolution of the television physician', in Friedman, ed., *Cultural Sutures*, 2004, p. 221.

16   Ibid., p. 218.

17   Anne Karpf, *Doctoring the Media*, London: Routledge, 1988, pp. 184-5.

18   Ibid., p. 188.

19   Joseph Turow, *Playing Doctor: Television, Storytelling and Medical Power*, Oxford: Oxford University Press, 1989, pp. 71-2.

20   Karpf, *Doctoring the Media*, p. 191.

21   Ibid., p. 183.

22   Joseph Turow, 'Television entertainment and the US health-care debate', *Lancet*, 347, 4 May 1996, pp. 1240-3. Here Turow reiterates that economic and health care policy issues are not discussed adequately in medical drama.

23   Turow, *Playing   Doctor*, p. 189.

24   See Clive Seale, *Media and Health*, London: Sage, 2002, p. 145-6.

25   Vandekieft, 'From city hospital to ER', p. 226.

26   Hilary Kingsley, *Casualty: The Inside Story*, London: BBC Books, p. 8.

27   Ibid., p. 8.

28   Ibid., p.10.

29   Karpf, *Doctoring the Media*, p. 192.

30   Within the medical profession *Cardiac Arrest* (1994-6) is considered to be a far more accurate portrayal of hospital life. This bleak account of working in the NHS focuses mainly on a small group of young doctors who are left to fend for themselves as their older more cynical superiors prioritise their own private health care practices. Tony Garnett advertised in the *BMJ* for an interested medic to work on a sitcom, and senior house officer Ged Mercurio responded and wrote the programme (under the ironic alias John MacUre) while working 56 hour shifts. In episode one 'Welcome to the House of Pain' we see the new houseman discussed disparagingly: 'His first day and he thinks he's sodding Dr Kildare!'. The wards are termed 'the alamo' and the consultants ruthlessly bully and exploit those below. Mr Simon Betancourt sneers: 'Junior doctors are like cattle. House them in crumbling flats, pay them a pittance and they daren't bite the hand that writes their references' (Series 1, Episode 5, 'Turning out the Light').

31   The classic fictional account in this area is of course *One Flew Over the Cuckoos Nest* (novel by Ken Kesey, 1962, film 1975, UA/Fantasy). See Greg Philo, ed., *Media and Mental Distress*, London: Longman, 1996.

32   Quotations are from interviews with Lesley Henderson and discussed in *Social Issues in Television Fiction*.

33   Jason Jacobs, *Body Trauma TV: The New Hospital Dramas*, London: BFI, 2003, p. 29.

34   Heterosexual risk was similarly highlighted in the soap operas *The Young and the Restless*, *All my children* and *Another World* all of which featured women with HIV/AIDS. In *EastEnders* (BBC1) Mark Fowler was forced to confront his own prejudice against gay people and intravenous drug users when he contracted HIV heterosexually. These stories represent an important commitment to social realism and were developed to counter public misconceptions of the disease as a 'gay plague'.

35   Michael O Connor, 'The role of television drama *ER* in medical student life: entertainment or socialisation?', *Journal of the American Medical Association (JAMA)*, 280, 2 September 1998, pp. 854-5.

36   Cohen and Shafer, 'Images and Healers', p. 212.

37   George Annas (1995) quoted in Vandekieft, 'From city hospital to ER', p. 230.

38   Joseph Turow and Rachel Gans, *As Seen on TV: Health Policy Issues in TV's Medical Dramas. A Report to the Kaiser Family Foundation, 2002, July*, Menlo Park: Henry J. Kaiser Family Foundation, 2002.

39   Ibid., p. 230.

40   Ibid., p. 231.

41   The programme's humour is typically dark and focused mainly on sex and death. Dr Perry Cox is a key figure in the show and acts as reluctant mentor to 'JD' and other junior doctors. Cox is committed to patient care and is also deeply cynical of those who seek to profit from those in poor health. For example he launches an attack on Julie, the seductive pharmaceutical sales rep, thus, 'Would you like to know the real dirty, dirty little secret? It's that your drug is so damn good that you guys went ahead and put about a 600% mark up on it. But hey the only ones that get hurt are the sick people right? And since your company damn sure doesn't care about them, and you're part of the system well that means you don't care either and that's pretty much what's making me sick, that's all' ('My First Step', Season 2). Dr Cox also exemplifies the frequently bleak outlook of the show in the following exchange with surgeon 'Dr Christopher Turk', 'Life is pointless Gandhi and I'm gonna let you into a little secret. The only thing more pointless than life itself is being a doctor. I mean bottom line you spend 8 years and 200Gs trying to get through med school and what do you have to show for it? A diploma on your wall and a bullseye on your back', ('My Female Trouble', Season 4).

42   Chief of Medicine Bob Kelso is more complex than he first appears. Although seen amongst the hospital staff to make harsh and unpopular decisions we viewers witness him in moments of private regret and see more compassionate elements to his choices. Thus for example in 'My Jiggly Ball', Season 5, 2006, he chooses to treat a rich man rather than a poor one with the same condition. The rich man's donation allows Kelso to reopen a prenatal health facility for low income women which was closed due to budget constraints.

43   David Casarett, Jessica M Fishman, Holly Jo MacMoran, Amy Pickard and David A Asch, 'Epidemiology and prognosis of coma in daytime television dramas', *BMJ*, 331(7531), 2005.

44   Soap stories are often a hook for press coverage and her swift screen death triggered a front page story in *The Sun* newspaper, J. Kay and H. Bonner, 'Alma: I'm so Angry with Corrie', 18 June 2001, in which the actor accused the production team of cynically 'cashing in on cancer'.

45   Rachel Hardyman and Geraldine Leydon, 'Media influence behaviour', *BMJ*, 326(7387), 2003, p. 498.

46   Andy Howe, Vicci Owen-Smith and Judith Richardson, 'Television programme makers have an ethical responsibility', *BMJ*, 326(7387), 2003, p. 498.

47   Ien Ang, *Watching 'Dallas': Soap Opera and the Melodramatic Imagination*, London: Methuen, 1985, p. 66.

48   This and subsequent quotations from script writers are taken from a series of interviews with TV production personnel conducted by Lesley Henderson. This story is discussed in *Social Issues in Television Fiction*, p. 80.

49   Ibid, p. 78.

50   Ibid, p. 82.

51   James Curran, 'Mass media and democracy: a reappraisal', in J. Curran and M. Gurevitch. eds., *Mass Media and Society*, London: Edward Arnold, 2000, p. 102.

52   See Henderson, *Social Issues in Television Fiction*, Chapter 5 'Casting the Outsiders: Mental Distress' for a discussion of how production priorities of pace and drama may work against balanced accounts of mental illness.

53   The social work profession has serious problems with its public image and is either ignored in TV drama or presented as populated by faceless bureaucrats. See Lesley Henderson and Bob Franklin, 'Sad not bad: images of social care professionals in popular British TV drama', *Journal of Social Work*, 7(2), 2007, 133–153.

54   The results of this study are discussed in Greg Philo and Lesley Henderson, 'Why go to Casualty? Health fears and fictional television', in Greg Philo, ed., *Message Received*, Harlow: Addison Wesley Longman, 1999, pp. 93–105.

55   Lesley Henderson and Jenny Kitzinger, 'The human drama of genetics: "hard" and "soft" media representations of inherited breast cancer', *Sociology of Health and Illness*, 21(5), 1999, pp. 560–78.

56   Vicky Rideout quoted in Kaiser Family Foundation news release, 'TV medical dramas address health policy issues', 16 July 2002, available from http://www. kff.org.

57   Joseph Turow and Rachel Gans-Boriskin 'From expert in action to existential angst', in Leslie J. Reagan, Nancy Tomes, Paula A. Treichler, eds., *Medicines Moving Pictures,* Rochester: University of Rochester Press, 2007, p. 280.

CUBA'S HEALTH POLITICS
AT HOME AND ABROAD

JULIE FEINSILVER

Over the past fifty years Cuba has constructed a healthcare system lauded by international experts and the envy of developing countries – and some developed ones. Despite considerable economic hardships, Cuba provides free universal coverage for its own population, and has developed country health indices at a dramatically lower cost. In addition, it is a global leader in providing medical aid and education to other countries through its 'medical diplomacy' programme of South-South collaboration. From its initial days in power, Cuba's revolutionary government also evinced a strong ideological commitment to the duty to help other nations in an effort to repay a debt for the external support it received during the revolution. As a result, the provision of medical aid – the basis for medical diplomacy – to other developing countries has been a key element of Cuba's international relations ever since the revolution, as first exemplified by the medical brigade sent to assist Chile in coping with the great earthquake of May 1960.

Although most governments supported the World Health Organization's initiative of 'Health for All by the Year 2000' when it was announced in 1978, few have paid more than lip service to this ideal. By contrast, the Cuban revolutionary government has had an overwhelming preoccupation with health from the outset – almost two decades before the WHO initiative. The underlying philosophy has been that health is a basic human right and a responsibility of the state. Moreover, the Cuban approach to health is holistic (physical, mental and social); it sees health as linked to the material environment in which each person lives and not only focuses on the patient as a whole person but also integrates prevention, cure and rehabilitation.

More than any other government, Cuba's leaders consider health indicators, particularly the infant mortality rate and life expectancy at birth, to be measures of government effectiveness. As a result, the health of the population becomes a metaphor for the health of the body politic. This constantly focuses government attention on both health conditions and the determinants of health. This unusual concern for the health of the population has proved politically beneficial because of its contribution to the regime's legitimacy and, therefore, survival. And on the international level it provides the foundation for a distinctive brand of medical diplomacy, which improves relations with other countries and garners prestige and influence (symbolic capital), and trade and aid (material capital) for Cuba.[1]

CUBA'S HEALTH IDEOLOGY

A fundamental ideological premise of the Cuban government since the 1959 revolution has been that medicine alone could not improve the population's health. This required a significant socioeconomic transformation to eliminate the problems of underdevelopment. Health sector reform, therefore, was only one part of a larger societal transformation which included universal free education, a guaranteed minimum food ration, very low-cost housing and universal social security, among other things. The guiding principles of the reform were: 1) equality of access to services, 2) a holistic approach to health (which required interdisciplinary teams to implement programmes), and 3) community participation in health initiatives.

Equality of access refers to a myriad of factors, including legal, economic, geographic and cultural access to health care. The right to health, and the state's obligation to provide health services, were enshrined in the constitution. Economic access meant universal free services for all. Geographic access required a major redistribution of facilities and personnel to reach all citizens, no matter where they lived. Cultural access meant a decrease in the social class and educational differences between physicians and their patients. This was done through open enrolment for medical education and by training and as far as possible stationing doctors in their home provinces. Open enrolment was ideologically appealing, but also necessary in order to train enough new doctors, in view of the exodus of approximately half of the country's existing doctors shortly after the triumph of the revolution.

Popular participation was envisioned as a means of involving the public, through their community-based organisations (Committees for the Defense of the Revolution, Federation of Cuban Women, trade unions, student organizations), in the planning, administration, implementation, and monitoring of health service delivery, in conjunction with local level health workers and institutions. Despite the rhetoric and initial government desire, community participation has primarily meant the implementation of government health initiatives, and this has been done with great success. It has extended the reach of the healthcare workers and reduced the cost of service delivery. Importantly, popular participation has given the public an opportunity not only to take matters into their own hands and see that they could solve some of their own problems, but also it has given them an education in certain health matters. This has been an important part of the government's general efforts to enhance individual and community self-reliance, and a step toward community cohesion.

THE EVOLUTION OF THE CUBAN HEALTH SYSTEM

Ongoing reform has been a key characteristic of the Cuban health system. During each decade there has been a reassessment of progress and problems, and adjustments have been made accordingly in response to changing health, social, economic and political priorities over the half-century of the Cuban revolution. What follows is a brief discussion of those changes, decade by decade.

The 1960s: the establishment of a national health system

To achieve universal free health care, the Cuban revolutionary government began its health sector reform almost immediately after taking power in 1959. This decision was based on three important factors: 1) the revolutionaries' experience of the abject poverty of much of the rural population, and their provision of medical care for the population living in areas under their control during the revolutionary war; 2) the example of pre-revolutionary mutual aid societies that provided pre-paid (HMO-like) medical services to their members; and 3) the espousal of social medicine by progressive physicians in one of the two pre-revolutionary Cuban medical societies (the Cuban Medical Federation). Given these factors, the logical first step was to form the Rural Health Service in January 1960, thereby establishing medical care in the periphery where little or none had previously existed. To staff this service, new medical school graduates were required to serve in it for one year upon graduation.

Beginning in 1964 health centres were converted to polyclinics, each serving a population of between 25,000 and 30,000. These geographic areas were further subdivided into health sectors, with one internist per 5,000 adults, one obstetrician/gynaecologist for every 3,000 to 4,000 women over age 15, and one paediatrician for every 2,000 to 3,000 children under age 15. A nurse trained in the corresponding discipline completed each basic team. Services were standardised and norms and methods laid down centrally. By 1967, the government had radically restructured the three health subsystems (public, mutual aid society prepaid plans, and private) into a regionalised and hierarchically organised National Health System, providing referrals from one level of care to the next and, most importantly, free universal coverage.

The 1970s: medicine in the community

Although decentralised medical education began in 1968 it did not truly take off nationally until the mid-1970s with the official introduction of medicine in the community and the conduct of part of each student's medical education in a polyclinic. Medicine in the community was meant to be the ultimate realisation of the ideological commitment to health as more than just the absence of disease. It deployed the medical teams from the polyclinic into the community to attend the populations they were responsible for in their homes, day-care centres, schools and places of employment. Importantly, the medical teams began their work by doing an in-depth diagnostic of the health conditions and determinants of health of their respective populations; developing a database of information on morbidity, mortality and immunisations; assessing needs and resources available; and selecting at-risk groups for targeted interventions. These diagnostics were to be updated and discussed by the medical staff and community representatives every two months, but this was often not done. By 1978 there was an evident disconnect between theory and practice with regard to the expected benefits of the medicine in the community model, particularly disease prevention, a reduction in the use of hospital emergency rooms for primary care, and continuity of care.[2]

The 1980s: the family doctor programme

The inability of the 'medicine in the community' model to solve the problems mentioned above led to a reassessment and further decentralisation, this time to the block level through the Family Doctor Programme, which was first piloted in 1984. The intent was to further project the health systems' resources into the community by putting a doctor and nurse team on every city block and by sending teams out to the remotest communities. Their task was (and still is) to aggressively investigate and monitor the health of the whole population, not just the infirm; to promote wellness; to detect risk factors; to prevent and cure disease; and to provide rehabilitation services. These were not new mandates, but it was thought they would be fulfilled better if the medical team lived in the community and provided care 24/7. Moreover the population's morbidity and mortality structures had changed from the diseases of poverty to diseases of development, requiring greater attention to health promotion, disease prevention, and chronic degenerative disease management.

This new model of health care provided a family doctor and nurse for every 120 to 150 families or about 600 to 700 people. Back-up was provided by an extensive network of health facilities of increasing levels of technological sophistication, from the polyclinic (with upgraded facilities) to tertiary care hospitals and research institutes. At the same time, emergent biotechnology and pharmaceutical industries were developed and later began to supply the system. Although the Ministry of Public Health provided norms for the whole family doctor programme, there was considerable flexibility about implementing them and great encouragement to the teams to spend more time seeing people in their normal environment rather than in the office. This was and is particularly important because of the emphasis on health education to alter unhealthy lifestyles and on the promotion of physical fitness, particularly among the elderly.

The family doctor also acts as a patient-advocate for those referred to the next level(s) of care and manages their care after they are discharged. The fact that patients can be monitored so closely means that every bed in Cuba is now potentially a hospital bed. This greatly facilitates continuity of care, patient compliance, and recuperation and rehabilitation, and at the same time decreases associated costs. Data for 2007 indicate that 99.7 per cent of the country was covered by 32,548 family doctors working in 14,007 family doctors' offices. Only Holguin and Santiago de Cuba provinces had slightly less than 100 per cent coverage.[3]

Based on the practices of the some of the world's best medical schools, both the structure and the curriculum of Cuban medical education were revised to produce the new type of medical professional required to meet growing domestic and international needs and goals. This meant a qualitative improvement in medical education, a curriculum change to a biological systems perspective as opposed to the traditional disciplinary focus, the creation of a specialisation in Comprehensive General Medicine (Family Medicine), and an integrated teaching, patient care and research approach to community-based medical education. All medical students, with very few exceptions, were (and still are) required to do a three-year residency in Comprehensive General Medicine first, even if they elect to do another residency later. Family doctors complete their residencies while on the job, where they conduct research on primary healthcare issues and attend seminars at the neighbourhood polyclinic where they are on call once a week. In the case of doctors located in remote areas, the professors go to groups of them, rather than the reverse as is the case elsewhere.[4]

Although the Family Doctor Programme may be criticised as involving an excessive medicalisation of natural processes such as childbirth and being costly to operate, sometimes coercive (women at high risk are sent to maternity homes prior to childbirth, or convinced to abort an unviable fetus), and possibly even a form of social control, data indicate that the programme has had various beneficial effects. For example, more effective prevention, which resulted in decreased hospitalisations, surgery, and emergency room use; lower morbidity and less use of medication among the elderly; and overall better patient compliance. All of this has led to decreased costs. More importantly, it has led to a considerable reduction in the infant mortality rate in rural areas, improved general health indices and, according to Ministry survey data, greater patient satisfaction.[5] The programme also provides a sense of relief and security for patients as well as their families, which in turn leads to greater government legitimacy. Whether the benefits of this programme outweigh the social and other costs remains debated. However, the financial costs of training and employing family doctors and establishing simple offices for them are much lower in a society where the state controls the economy (and therefore employment and compensation) and the education system, and can produce more doctors than otherwise would be required and direct them to work wherever they are needed.

At the same time that great emphasis was being placed on primary care, the government also made considerable investments in the expansion and upgrading of its hospital network and the chain of specialised and high-technology research institutes, including the development of internationally significant biotechnology, genetic engineering and pharmaceutical research and production capacity.[6] Cuban doctors and medical scientists quickly learned sophisticated techniques and pioneered new ones. Cuba's biotechnology, genetic engineering, and pharmaceutical research facilities began to develop products that would eventually replace imports and provide hard currency earnings from their export. At the same time, the government invested heavily in the mass production of physicians specifically for its medical diplomacy programmes.

The 1990s: adjusting to economic crisis

The dissolution of the Soviet Union and the Eastern Bloc led to what Cubans called the 'special period'. As trade relations collapsed at the beginning of the 1990s the economy went into a tailspin. For decades Cuba had relied on the international socialist division of labour and subsidised trade or fair terms of trade. Suddenly, basic necessities were no longer available or if they were, it was only at world market prices in convertible currency. This situation was exacerbated by the long-standing US trade embargo, which continued to force Cuba to purchase supplies from much more distant countries, greatly increasing their final cost. The Cuban government estimates that this decreased its purchasing power by between 20 and 30 per cent.[7]

What had been problematic all along, such as shortages of some basic medicines and disinfectants, among other supplies, reached crisis proportions during the special period. All types of inputs for the medical system, including replacement parts for equipment, basic pharmaceutical ingredients, and infrastructure components, became extremely scarce. At the same time food supplies were also seriously decreased, making the population more vulnerable to disease. This dire situation left the Ministry of Public Health (MINSAP) with only one real option, to develop a strategy to improve operational efficiency in an effort to ensure the sustainability of the system.

MINSAP strategy, therefore, gave priority to the further development, deepening and/or expansion of a series of measures already in effect, which were not necessarily originally conceived for the purpose of cost containment even though that was one of their results: 1) health promotion and disease prevention, 2) traditional or natural products medicine and alternative therapies, 3) decentralisation, 4) community participation, and 5) epidemiological surveillance. For example, emphasis on health promotion and disease prevention had been a priority for decades, and one of the reasons for constant system reform. Greater use of natural products medicines and alternative therapies such as acupuncture and ozone therapy also had begun in the 1970s, but new emphasis would now be placed on their standardisation, reliability and ability to replace allopathic treatments.

Decentralisation too had begun much earlier with the administrative subordination of the municipal level health facilities to the Municipal Assemblies of Peoples Power (local government), which was supposed to, but did not always, facilitate coordinated cross-sector activities and community participation. The new decentralisation approach adopted the international 'Healthy Cities' approach. By 1998 almost half of all Cuban municipalities belonged to the National Network of Healthy Municipalities, which encourages healthy living activities in schools, workplaces, markets, penitentiaries, and cooperative centres. This effort further required the community, both as individuals and as a group, to take greater responsibility for their own and their community's health. Finally, as a result of an optical neuropathy epidemic in 1993, epidemiological trend analysis units were created to improve the existing surveillance system and provide early warnings of disease outbreaks.[8]

Moreover, in response to the rapid deterioration of many health facilities, the lack of management capacity in a number of health units, and patient dissatisfaction with services, MINSAP indicated that it would revitalise the hospitals' operational aspects (and also downsize them, because a large number of hospital beds were no longer needed); give family doctors greater problem-solving capacity and some material improvements; and increase coverage, access and the quality of care. MINSAP would also seek external funding to bolster the work of state-of-the-art research institutes and clinical facilities. Change was necessary, but it had to be efficient.[9]

Despite the severe economic crisis the Cuban government ratified two basic principles of its public health system: the health system would continue to be government financed (free for the user), and it would provide universal coverage as a basic human right. Government health expenditures per capita had risen considerably over the years, but most particularly as the overall economic situation of the country deteriorated. The government correctly acted in a counter-cyclical fashion by increasing health allocations as a percentage of the state budget, with the exception of 1991 when there was a slight decrease. Between 1994 and 2000, government health expenditures increased by 59 per cent, with wages comprising the largest item. Central government spending fell as municipal government spending rose, as a result of increased decentralisation and an even greater focus on primary care.[10] However, the crisis vastly diminished the convertible currency portion of the budget that was available for healthcare financing: from 1990 through 1996 it fluctuated between one third and one half of the 1989 pre-crisis amount in US dollars.[11] This left the system's infrastructure and equipment in dire condition, except for what was used for health tourism (visitors coming to Cuba for treatment) and therefore earned hard currency that could be reinvested in the ailing public health system.

The twenty-first century: focusing on results

Economic recovery – a good deal of which can be attributed to the deepening of Cuba's strategic alliance with Hugo Chavez' Venezuela – allowed the Cuban government to begin to rebuild its broken health infrastructure. After a decade of neglect plans were drawn up to rehabilitate the more than 400 polyclinics island-wide, as well as at least 50 tertiary care institutions (hospitals and specialised institutes), and upgrade their technology. At the same time, approximately one-third of Cuban doctors went to Venezuela to provide health services in an oil-for-doctors exchange. Meantime, however, both the state of disrepair of the not-yet-upgraded facilities and the shortage of doctors in some areas in a country that has prided itself on having the highest rate of doctors per capita in the hemisphere (three times as many doctors per capita as the United States in 2005),[12] has led to considerable discontent.

Another problem that had become important by the twenty-first century was the greying of the population. As MINSAP planners reassessed the system, using evidence from their statistical databases and the comprehensive diagnostic of the health status of each community and sub-sector, it became clear that the population in some areas required some different services, based on their epidemiological profile, rather than simply following centrally-determined programmes. As a result, it was decided to make services more flexible, depending on local needs. To test this approach, a pilot programme was established in one Havana polyclinic, which was given greater human and material resources in an effort to improve health outcomes while actually reducing costs. The polyclinic has once again become the cornerstone of the health system as well as a key medical teaching facility (policlínico universitario), while the family doctor programme is being revamped primarily to conduct health promotion and disease prevention activities.[13]

Although from the outset of the revolution the Cuban government focused on ameliorating rural–urban and other disparities and has made enormous strides in this endeavour, some differences have remained. Recognition of continued inequalities in health led to the design of a system to monitor equity in the delivery of health services, in health outcomes, and in the determinants of health.[14] This is part of an increased emphasis on achieving results in terms of health outcomes (i.e., infant mortality, life expectancy, absence of disease, etc.), which always has been a priority, and not just outputs (such as the number of physician visits, vaccinations, clinical interventions, etc.). Outcomes, however, may depend as much or more on improved sanitation and nutrition (both of which deteriorated in the 1990s) as on increased and/or re-focused health service delivery. Greater equity in the determinants of health will have to be assessed in the coming years.

And in fact this is part of the government's long-term comprehensive plan for improving the determinants of health for the ten-year period from 2006 to 2015. This plan's risk-based approach utilised data collected in the Second National Survey of Risk Factors and Non-transmittable Diseases, conducted in 2004, as well as other routinely produced data sets. Among other things, it identified important environmental and behavioural factors that contribute to ill health but are not within the purview of the health system to ameliorate, such as unstable and aging potable water and sewerage infrastructure. Because health is inter-sectoral, it was recognised as incumbent upon the Ministry of Public Health to demonstrate the health effects of situations and conditions lying beyond its control and advocate their amelioration. Importantly, the plan sets out the strategic direction and objectives, the programmes, targets, organisation and functions, as well as the requirements for monitoring and evaluation at all levels of the system, based on results and impact.[15] Once again adjustments can be expected as data from implementation of the plan are analysed.

MEDICAL DIPLOMACY

Since 1960 Cuba has provided medical aid to other countries despite the immediate post-revolution flight of nearly half of the island's doctors and any domestic hardship this caused. The medical brain drain contributed to the government's decision to reform the health sector, revamp medical education, and vastly increase the number of doctors trained. These factors combined made possible a large-scale commitment to medical diplomacy and lent credibility to Cuba's aid offers by demonstrating success on the ground in establishing and managing health systems, reducing mortality and morbidity rates, and training the necessary human resources. By the mid-1980s Cuba was producing numbers of doctors well beyond its own needs, specifically for its internationalist programme. The latest available data (2007) indicate that Cuba has one doctor for every 155 inhabitants, a ratio unparalleled anywhere.[16]

Cuba as a medical power

Perhaps as a portent of things to come, even during the 1970s and 1980s Cuba implemented a disproportionately larger civilian aid programme in Africa (particularly medical aid) than its more developed trade partners, the Soviet Union, the east European countries, and China. This quickly generated considerable symbolic capital for Cuba, which translated into political backing in the United Nations General Assembly, as well as material benefits in the case of Angola, Iraq and other countries that could afford to pay fees for professional services rendered (although the charges were considerably below international market rates).[17]

The value of Cuban medical diplomacy for the beneficiaries is clear. Over the past almost fifty years, Cuba's conduct of medical diplomacy has improved the health of the less privileged in developing countries while improving relations with their governments. Cuban medical teams had worked in Guyana and Nicaragua in the 1970s where governments were leftist, but by 2005 they were implementing their Comprehensive Health Programme in Latin American and Caribbean countries that, with the exception of Bolivia and Venezuela, were not. Those countries are Belize, Dominica, Guatemala, Haiti, Honduras, Nicaragua, and Paraguay. In 2000 Cuban medical teams worked in El Salvador to control a dengue epidemic, using their community participation model. Even the Salvadoran military collaborated with them.[18] They had also established two Comprehensive Diagnostic Centres, one on the island of Dominica and one on Antigua and Barbuda. In 2008 both Jamaica and Suriname's health systems were bolstered by the presence of Cuban medical personnel.[19] Throughout the years, Cuba has also provided free medical care in its own hospitals for individuals from all over Latin America, and not just for the Latin American left.

During the 1970s and early 1980s Cuba undertook very large civilian aid programmes in Africa to complement its military support to Angola and the Horn of Africa. With the withdrawal of troops and the geopolitical and economic changes from the late1980s onwards, Cuba's programme was scaled back, but remained in place.[20] Having suffered a post-apartheid brain drain (white flight), South Africa began importing Cuban doctors in 1996. In 1998 there were 400 Cuban doctors practising medicine in townships and rural areas and in 2008 their number had increased slightly to 435. Later, the focus changed. Now (2009) 138 Cuban specialists work in 47 clinics and hospitals in eight of South Africa's nine provinces.[21] South Africa also finances some Cuban medical missions in third countries. Agreements were reached in 2004 to extend Cuban medical aid to the rest of the African continent and to deploy over 100 Cuban doctors in Mali. A similar agreement was planned for Rwanda. Cuban doctors have worked or are working in some thirty African countries and in most cases are implementing their Comprehensive Health Programme there. Cuban medical teams also have worked in such far-flung places as East Timor and the Solomon Islands, neither of which might be considered to be among Cuba's strategic areas of interest.

Overall, since 1961, Cuba has conducted medical diplomacy with 103 countries, deploying 113,585 medical professionals abroad.[22] As of April 2008 over 30,000 Cuban medical personnel were collaborating in 74 countries across the globe.[23] Cuban data indicate that Cuban medical personnel abroad have saved more than 1.6 million lives, treated over 85 million patients (of which over 19.5 million were seen on 'house calls' at patients' homes, schools, jobs, etc.), performed over 2.2 million operations, assisted 768,858 births, and vaccinated with complete dosages more than 9.2 million people.[24] Cuban medical aid has affected the lives of millions of people in developing countries each year. Moreover, to make this effort more sustainable, over the years more than 50,000 thousand developing country medical personnel have received free education and training either in Cuba or by Cuban specialists engaged in on-the-job training courses and/ or medical schools in their own countries. Today, approximately 25,000 developing-country scholarship students are studying in Cuban medical schools, alongside a group of 110 less-privileged American students. Even more are studying medicine in their own countries through Cuba's Virtual Medical School.

Since Cuba sent its first medical brigade abroad in 1960 it has utilized medical diplomacy to win the hearts and minds of aid recipients. Medical diplomacy has been a critical means of gaining prestige and goodwill which can be translated into diplomatic support and trade or aid. It has been a way of projecting Cuba's image abroad as an increasingly developed and technologically sophisticated country, and this is important for the country's symbolic struggle as David versus the Goliath of the United States. The success of Cuba's medical diplomacy has been recognized by the World Health Organization and other United Nations bodies, as well as by numerous governments, at least 103 of which have been direct beneficiaries of Cuba's largesse. It also has contributed to support for Cuba and rebukes for the United States in the United Nations General Assembly, where for the past 17 consecutive years Members voted overwhelmingly in favour of lifting the US embargo of Cuba. In fact, only Israel, Palau and the Marshall Islands have supported the US position in recent years.[25] Furthermore, Cuba's medical diplomacy was a key topic raised by Latin American and Caribbean leaders in their meetings with President Obama at the Summit of the Americas in April 2009, and one of the reasons why those same members of the Organization of American States voted in June 2009 to readmit Cuba.

Since 1960 Cuba has also been quick to mobilise well-trained disaster relief teams for many of the major disasters in the world. Among its recent activities were medical brigades dispatched to Indonesia after the May 2007 earthquake, Peru after the December 2007 earthquake, Bolivia after the February 2008 floods and China after the May 2008 earthquake.[26] Cuban medical missions also provided post-disaster preventive and curative care in post-tsunami Indonesia and post-2005-earthquake Pakistan. Cuba sent Pakistan a team of highly experienced disaster relief specialists, comprising 2,564 doctors (57 per cent), nurses and medical technicians.[27] The team brought with them everything they needed to establish, equip, and run those hospitals. The cost to Cuba was not insignificant. Two of the hospitals alone cost half a million dollars each. In May 2006, Cuba sent 54 emergency electrical generators as well.

In the past Cuba has also provided disaster relief aid to more developed countries as well as those that are less developed and this has garnered considerable bilateral and multilateral symbolic capital for Cuba. Beneficiaries include Armenia, Byelorussia, Moldavia, Iran, Turkey, Russia and the Ukraine, as well as most Latin American countries. For example, over a nineteen-year period, 20,000 children from Russian, Ukraine, Byelorussia, Moldavia and Armenia were treated free of charge in Cuba, mostly for post-Chernobyl radiation-related illnesses.[28] Cuba even offered to send over 1,000 doctors as well as medical supplies to the United States in the immediate aftermath of Hurricane Katrina. Although the Bush administration declined the offer, the fact that it was made by a small developing country that had suffered almost a half century of US hostility was highly symbolic.[29]

The Cuba-Venezuela-Bolivia connection

It is ironic that in 1959 Cuba unsuccessfully sought financial support and oil from Venezuelan president Rómulo Betancourt. It would take forty years and many economic difficulties before another Venezuelan president, Hugo Chávez, would provide the preferential trade, credit, aid and investment that the Cuban economy desperately needed. This partnership is part of Venezuela's Bolivarian Alternative [to the US] for the Americas (ALBA) to unite and integrate Latin America in a social justice-oriented trade and aid bloc. It has also created an opportunity to expand Cuba's medical diplomacy reach well beyond anything previously imaginable, beyond even Fidel's three-decade-long dream of making Cuba into a world medical power.[30]

By far the largest Cuban medical cooperation programme ever attempted is the present one with Venezuela. The oil-for-doctors trade agreements allow for preferential pricing for Cuba's exports of professional services in return for a steady supply of Venezuelan oil, joint investments in strategically important sectors for both countries, and the provision of credit. In exchange, Cuba provides medical services for un-served and under-served communities in Venezuela: the agreement is for 30,000 medical professionals, 600 comprehensive health clinics, 600 rehabilitation and physical therapy centres, 35 high technology diagnostic centres, 100,000 ophthalmologic surgeries, etc. In addition, the agreement provides similar medical services, on a smaller scale, in Bolivia, at Venezuela's expense.[31]

To contribute to the long-run sustainability of these programmes Cuba agreed to train 40,000 doctors and 5,000 healthcare workers in Venezuela and to provide full medical scholarships to Cuban medical schools for 10,000 Venezuelan medical and nursing students. An additional and later agreement includes the expansion of the Latin American and Caribbean region-wide ophthalmologic surgery programme (Operation Miracle) to perform 600,000 eye operations over a ten-year period. To handle some of the demand and to reduce the strain on facilities at home, Cuba established fifty small eye surgery clinics in Venezuela and Bolivia as well as clinics in Ecuador, Guatemala and Mali, to handle both local cases and others from neighbouring countries.

Cuba's second largest medical cooperation programme is with Bolivia. By February 2008 the Cuban medical brigade in Bolivia had 1,921 collaborators, as they are now called, of whom 1,323 were doctors, the remainder being paramedics, technicians and other personnel.[32] In July of the same year Cuban health personnel were working in 215 of Bolivia's 327 municipalities, including remote rural villages. It was reported that over the two-year period of medical diplomacy in Bolivia, Cuban doctors had saved 14,000 lives, conducted over 15 million medical exams, and had performed eye surgery on approximately 266,000 Bolivians and their neighbours from Argentina, Brazil, Paraguay and Peru.[33]

Additionally, Cuba offered Bolivia 5,000 more full scholarships to educate doctors and specialists as well as other health personnel at the Latin American Medical School (ELAM) which Cuba established in Havana after the 1998 Central American hurricanes. ELAM was developed as a means of helping other countries produce community service-oriented medical personnel to make their own health systems sustainable. As a result, ELAM also makes Cuba's medical diplomacy sustainable. In 2006, there were some 500 young Bolivians studying at the school (about 22 per cent of the total foreign scholarship student body) while another 2,000 had started the pre-med course there. The six-year medical school programme is provided free for low-income students who commit to practise medicine in under-served communities in their home countries upon graduation. In the 2006-2007 academic year, 24,621 foreign medical students were enrolled at ELAM.[34] Between 2005 and 2008, the school graduated 6,575 medical professionals from 56 countries, of whom 6254 were doctors.[35]

In 2006 Venezuela opened a second Latin American Medical School, jointly with Cuba, to provide free medical training to at least 100,000 physicians for developing countries over the next ten years, using the community-based medical education model pioneered in Cuba in the 1980s that saw the professors going to the students rather than the reverse. Going beyond past practice, the new medical education model is based on students being immersed in the clinical setting (in the mornings) as of the second year, initially as observers. This is supplemented by both classroom training (in the afternoons) by a Cuban medical professional and the use of specially prepared distance-learning materials, such as lectures on DVD and CDs by top Cuban medical professors and a dedicated website for the Virtual Medical School (Universidad Virtual de Salud or UVS). The UVS was established in 2006 as a means of mass-producing community-based family doctors by further extending Cuba's free medical education system beyond the capacity of its existing physical facilities. It also enables students to live, study and work in their own communities, which greatly decreases costs. At the same time, these students progressively provide assistance to the Cuban medical personnel attending their low-income communities, which further extends the services provided and decreases costs. Moreover, this model of community-based medical education produces doctors who are committed to working in their own and/or other poor communities. This type of training is now being provided not only in Venezuela (in 2008 there were about 23,000 students in the Mission Sucre school of Integral Community Medicine), but also in Cuba itself alongside traditional medical education, as well as in Bolivia, Guinea Bissau, Equatorial Guinea, Gambia, Guatemala, Honduras and Nicaragua, among other countries.[36]

There are concerns about the mass production of doctors and the quality of this new type of medical education. Medical associations in much of Latin America and the English-speaking Caribbean question whether those who graduate from the UVS are really qualified as doctors. They have also resisted the certification of ELAM graduates, although the latter have gained recognition in various countries. Because their training is focused on primary care, it is difficult for some graduates to pass medical boards that require the deeper knowledge needed for hospital-based practice without specific exam preparation or further training; exam success rates in the English-speaking Caribbean have not been high. This could also be a function of the graduates' socioeconomic status, and poorer prior education than that of traditional medical school students. Some US graduates of ELAM are however said to have passed the US Foreign Medical School Graduates exam.[37]

In this connection it is worth remembering that about 95 per cent of the medical problems for which patients see their primary care physicians in any country are problems these doctors can handle and for which they are trained. The issue may therefore not be so much whether ELAM graduates are competent to manage primary level patient care, but whether competitive barriers are being defended that produce doctors who are over-trained for what they actually do most of the time. Despite the controversy over credentials, both the humanitarian and the symbolic benefits of the programme are enormous. Moreover, the political benefits could be reaped for years to come as students trained by Cuba, with some financial aid from Venezuela, become health officials and opinion leaders in their own countries. Some of the 50,000 foreign scholarship students who have trained in Cuban universities as doctors and nurses since 1961 are now in positions of authority and increasing responsibility in their home countries.[38] With the plan to train 100,000 new doctors by 2015, this potential influence on health care in the developing world would increase rapidly.

The benefits and risks of medical diplomacy
The economic benefits of Cuba's medical diplomacy have been very significant since the rise of Hugo Chávez in Venezuela. Trade with and

aid from Venezuela in a large-scale oil-for-doctors exchange has bolstered Cuba's ability to conduct medical diplomacy and helped keep its economy afloat. Earnings from medical services (which includes the export of doctors) equalled 28 per cent of total export receipts and net capital payments in 2006 – US$2,312 million – a figure greater than that for both nickel and cobalt exports and tourism.[39] The export of professional services (primarily but not exclusively medical) accounted for 69 per cent of Cuba's 2008 balance of trade in services (US$8.2 billion), which helped offset its balance of goods deficit (US$10.7 billion).[40]

The financial costs to beneficiary countries are relatively low because the Cuban government pays the doctors' salaries and the host country or Venezuela pays for airfares and stipends of up to US$150 per month plus room and board.[41] This is far below the costs of recruitment in the international marketplace, although it can still be a strain on cash-strapped economies such as Haiti's. Perhaps more important are the non-monetary costs, and the risks, which are significant. Cuban doctors serve the poor in areas in which no local doctor would work, make house calls a routine part of their medical practice, and are available free of charge 24/7. This is changing the nature of doctor-patient relations in the host countries. As a result, they have forced a re-examination of societal values and the structure and functioning of the health systems and the medical profession within the recipient countries. In some cases, such as in Bolivia, Guatemala, Honduras and Venezuela, this different way of practising has resulted in strikes and other protest actions by the local medical associations who feel threatened by these changes, as well as by what they perceive to be competition for their jobs.

The costs for Cuba, however, are more complicated, partly because of the government's long-term investment in the education of medical personnel. Although Cuba pays the doctors' salaries, the pay scale is very low. In Cuba, doctors earn the equivalent in Cuban pesos of about US$25 per month. While abroad, they earn much more, in some cases up to ten times their Cuban salary.[42] When they return to Cuba their salaries double, to the equivalent of US$50 per month and they get access to certain otherwise unobtainable goods.[43] Since the Venezuelan agreement began, a significant amount of the cost for Cuba has been covered by Venezuela, both for medical services and education in Venezuela, and that provided to third countries. Previously, these were fully funded by Cuba. Money is fungible and any aid Cuba receives could be channelled to this area.

A recent added cost has been that of the state's investment in the education and development of professionals who defect from Cuban medical diplomacy programmes in third countries. Material conditions of life in Cuba are very difficult and salaries are a fraction of those that can be earned abroad. More importantly, doctors earn a fraction of what less well-educated Cuban tourist industry workers earn, leading some to moonlight in various tourist-related jobs.[44] Despite education and values that promote socialist ideology, and a real concern for improving the lot of those they serve, after fifty years of pent-up demand at home and difficult conditions in the host countries too, some Cuban doctors find that defection is their preferred option.[45] A little stimulus from the Bush administration contributed to the estimated 1,000 doctors who are reputed to have defected in recent years.[46] Under the August 2006 Cuban Medical Professional Parole Program, Cuban doctors serving abroad are granted fast-track asylum processing and almost guaranteed entry into the United States.[47] Although this programme has encouraged more defections and has even provided a reason for some Cuban doctors to go abroad in the first place, some have found that they are held in limbo in Colombia or other points of arrival, without the promised fast-track visa approval and with little or no money.[48] Hard data are not available on the number of defections, but Cuban planners build in a 2 to 3 per cent defection rate, which would be about 600 to 900 doctors based on current numbers.

Any thaw in the relations between Cuba and the US under the Obama administration may make defection less likely. That would radically change economic conditions on the island, and eventually could even lead to US insurance companies' willingness to reimburse US citizens for less costly medical procedures performed in Cuba. Of course, normal relations would also allow for medical professionals' exchanges and/or legal immigration without the hardship of defection and the consequences for families remaining behind.

CONCLUDING REFLECTIONS:
STRENGTHS AND LIMITATIONS

Two important strengths of the Cuban health system are its flexibility and the rapidity with which it can adjust to changes in health conditions and needs, medical technology, and international good practice, as well as domestic and/or international economic or political exigencies. The key facilitating factors have been political will and a vision of the future in which the health of Cubans would compare favourably with that of the US population, at least on key indicators. Certainly as compared with other countries with more complex polities and economies, the ability and willingness to make substantial changes to the health system every decade has been striking.

As mentioned at the beginning of this essay, the Cuban government uses key health indicators to measure (metaphorically) the health of the body politic. These key indicators, the infant mortality rate and life expectancy at birth, are used as proxies for socioeconomic development because of the many and varied inputs in their composition. Despite its economic difficulties Cuba rates very highly on both indicators.

Cubans acknowledge the shortfalls in their health system and publish statistics that show fluctuations in the most important health indices, particularly the infant mortality rate at birth and the under-five-mortality rate. They also admit the periodic deterioration of various morbidity and mortality rates subsequent to outbreaks of disease or to economic difficulties that have led to suboptimal nutrition and/or sanitation. With the economic crisis of the 1990s the infant mortality rate rose slightly in 1994, then fell and rose again, finally resuming a downward slope in 2006 when it reached a rate of 5.3 per 1000 live births, which would be enviable in the most developed countries. Movements in the under-five-mortality rate paralleled that of the infant mortality rate.[49]

Of course, many factors contribute to the low infant mortality rate, some of which, like female education, are outside the remit of the Ministry of Public Health (although education is another area where Cuba excels). One factor has authoritarian aspects: the health system's intense focus on infant mortality has led to the Ministry insisting that childbirth take place in a health system facility. To make this possible maternity homes were established where women with high-risk pregnancies, or who live far from an appropriate institution in which to give birth, are sent one to two months prior to their due dates to ensure a safe delivery. While this is viewed as positive by health officials both within Cuba and by many abroad, some Cuban women object to being sent away from their homes and families for that length of time. Moreover abortion is encouraged where the viability of the fetus is questionable. In these matters there is little or no choice because any infant death is the subject of careful scrutiny by Ministry officials.

Universal health care, of course, is a key contributor to Cuba's remarkable health outcomes, and is itself a major achievement of the Cuban revolution. Cuba's enviable doctor-population ratio and its network of health facilities provide the necessary means to carry out the government's policies and programmes. In keeping with the rationalisation of facilities and ever-increasing focus on preventive medicine, in 2008 there was a further decrease in the number of hospitals to 219 and an increase the number of primary care facilities to 499 polyclinics, 335 maternity homes and 156 homes for the aged.[50]

But even more important than numbers of physicians and medical facilities is the willingness to experiment, to assess the system's strengths and weaknesses and to make changes. The current system may be over-medicalised and too costly for strict emulation, but aspects of it can serve as a model for others to adapt to their own circumstances. In that regard, it has had traction with the World Health Organization as well as with Venezuela and other countries receiving Cuban medical aid, many of which are implementing Cuba's Comprehensive Health Programme.

Community participation has also contributed to Cuba's ability to produce better health indicators. It was critical for the success of mass vaccination campaigns, rural and urban sanitation drives, mass screening of women for cervical cancer, the early detection of pregnancy, the provision of prenatal care, blood and organ donations, and the dengue fever campaigns. Not only did community participation have a positive effect on health promotion and the reduction of disease, making possible a vastly expanded coverage of campaigns, but it also led to quicker and less costly results, community self-reliance, and greater social cohesion. The political significance of social cohesion generated by community participation should not be underestimated.

The overarching limitations of Cuba's health system are not specific to the health system, but belong rather to the economy as a whole: shortage of money and access to physical inputs and supplies. The latter is very much affected by the US embargo. As a result, the Cubans have become very adept over the years at doing more with less. However, there are very serious limitations resulting from inadequate resources. Although some infrastructure rehabilitation and equipment replacement have been undertaken recently, much remains to be done to repair all that crumbled during the special period. Medicines and other basic supplies and inputs into the system are still in short supply, forcing both doctors and patients to find an unofficial or black market way of getting them ('*resolver*'). Favours and gifts are commonplace forms of appreciation for doctors who must work very hard for very little, and investments in future treatment.[51]

Insularity resulting from the limited accessibility of basic telecommunications and the inability to travel abroad freely also slows progress, although the Ministry makes both locally and internationally produced medical journals and texts available online through the Pan American Health Organization's Virtual Health Library, as well as through its own efforts. Scarce resources limit computer and cell phone accessibility. Despite all these limitations, the health system has been capable of producing good results on key indicators by investing in what matters most to achieve them. It has targeted and prioritised resource allocation to assure essential services for women, infants and children, and (in recent years) senior citizens, within the context of universal coverage.[52] And the population has found ways of getting needed medicines and supplies through family abroad, foreign donations, purchase at dollar facilities for tourists, barter with friends and colleagues, and purchase on the black market, among other means.

The Cuban model cannot be transferred wholesale to another country. However, as already noted, it offers valuable lessons, particularly for countries with less developed private sector provision of care. One is that it pays to emphasise disease prevention and health promotion, in terms of both health outcomes and cost containment. This is hardly surprising, but without a public health system it is unlikely that these will be given sufficient attention because of their lower profitability for private sector providers. It is even more cost-effective to prioritise and target health promotion activities at women and children (particularly maternal-infant care), the elderly, and those with, or at risk of, chronic diseases. Prevention and targeting require planning, which in the Cuban case is extensive and based on detailed health conditions diagnostics of geographic areas conducted by family doctors, resulting in a national database that provides good epidemiological trend data, facilitating data-driven health policy decision-making. This type of community diagnostic and constant update is facilitated by Cuba's single-payer, regionalised, hierarchically-organised healthcare delivery system. Disease prevention and health promotion can be prioritised and certain populations targeted without the extensive service delivery network that Cuba has, and without the same rigorous planning. It is more difficult, less accurate, and the outcomes are likely to differ, but it can be done.

Although community-based medical education is conducted by a number of medical schools in industrialised as well as less developed countries, the depth of insertion into the community and the curricula differ. The mass production of doctors and their deployment to the remotest areas of the country as well as to every city block under the family doctor programme is not feasible for most countries, perhaps not even for Venezuela. However, the new type of community-based family doctor that is being trained using the tutorial method, coupled with distance learning, could make possible a far larger scale of medical training. There would be repercussions with regard to accreditation and the acceptance of credentials by local medical associations, and some type of negotiated non-threatening settlement would have to be achieved. Popular participation could be organised via willing NGOs, although their coverage and modus operandi would differ from that of Cuban mass organizations because of their differing political structures and relationship to the government.

A final reflection concerns the already mentioned increased dissatisfaction on the part of Cuba's own population, as medical staff go abroad, leaving some local health facilities and programmes with insufficient staff (or medicines and supplies), despite the impressive ratio of qualified doctors to population. A population accustomed to having a doctor on every block is finding that waiting times are now longer for some procedures, and that where doctors are overworked, the quality of care declines. Recognising this problem, in April 2008 Raúl Castro announced a reorganization of the Family Doctor Programme at home to create greater efficiency. This has meant rationalising the number and dispersion of Family Doctors offices, while increasing the official hours of operation for those outside Havana. Operating hours would also to be extended in Havana when a sufficient number of medical staff became available.[53] Despite some improvements, if insufficient attention is paid to the domestic health system it could contribute to a de-legitimisation of the regime. That said, the Cuban health system's limitations have often been overcome by the inventiveness and adaptability of both the doctors and patients within it.

NOTES

1   For a full discussion of the history, ideology and organisation of the Cuban health system, and its medical diplomacy and biotechnology development, see Julie M. Feinsilver, *Healing the Masses: Cuban Health Politics at Home and Abroad*, Berkeley: University of California Press, 1993.

2   Ibid., pp. 37-40.

3   Médicos de la familia y cobertura según provincias, *Anuario Estadístico de Salud 2007*, Fuente: Registro de profesionales de la salud y Dirección de Atención Primaria, 2007, http://bvs.sld.cu. Coverage was reorganised in late 2007, but data are not yet available. There were 673 fewer family doctors in 2007 than 2006, which could be due to a number of factors such as natural attrition, further specialisation, system rationalisation or defection while abroad.

4   Feinsilver, *Healing the Masses*, pp. 117-18.

5   Ibid., pp. 40-41, 44-47.

6   Ibid., pp. 58-62, 122-55.

7   'La Reforma Del Sector de la Salud', available from http://www.dne.sld.cu.

8   Pan American Health Organization (PAHO), *Health in the Americas 2007*, Washington: PAHO, 2007, available from http://www.paho.org.

9   Ibid.

10   Table 87, 'Ejecución del presupuesto y gasto por habitante 1959, 1960, 1965, 1970 – 2006', Año anuario 2006, Fuente: Registros administrativos de la Dirección Nacional de Finanzas y Contabilidad.

11   República de Cuba, Dirección Nacional de Estadística del Ministerio de Salud Pública, *Sistema Nacional de Salud Políticas, Estrategias y Programas*. Havana,

Cuba, December 1998. 'La Reforma Del Sector de la Salud'.

12 PAHO, *Health Situation in the Americas. Basic Indicators 2007*, p. 4.

13 Republica de Cuba, Ministerio de Salud Pública, *Proyecciones de la Salud Pública en Cuba para el 2015*, Havana: Editorial Ciencias Médicas, February 2006, p. 64.

14 Abelardo Ramírez Márquez and Cándido López Pardo, 'A Monitoring System for Health Equity in Cuba', *MEDICC Review*, 7(9), Nov/Dec 2005, available from http://ww.medicc.org.

15 Ministerio de Salud Pública, *Proyecciones*.

16 Republica de Cuba, Oficina Nacional de Estadísticas, *Anuario Estadístico de Cuba 2007 (Edición 2008)*, Table 19.3, available from http://www.one.cu.

17 Feinsilver, *Healing the Masses*, Chapter 6, 'Cuban Medical Diplomacy' (on comparison with the former Soviet bloc and China, see pp. 159–160).

18 Interview with Carlos Lovo, Advisor to the Salvadoran Minister of Health at that time, Washington, 30 April 2009.

19 Cuban Cooperation, Website of the Cuban Governmental Cooperation in the Health Sector, http://www.cubacoop.com (available in Spanish and English); and 'Cubans to help boost local health sector', *Jamaica Observer*, 10 May 2008.

20 Feinsilver, *Healing The Masses*, Chapter 6.

21 'Cuban medical cooperation in South Africa highlighted', *Cuba Direct* (on-line), 26 May 2009, available from http://emba.cubaminrex.cu.

22 http://www.cubacoop.com.

23 *Prensa Latina*, 11 April 2008.

24 http://www.cubacoop.com.

25 AFP, 'Massive UN vote in support of lifting US embargo on Cuba', 29 October 30 2008.

26 http://www.cubacoop.com.

27 Ibid.

28 Aleksei Aleksandrov, 'Health care: The secrets of Cuban medicine', *Argumenty i Fakty* (mass-circulation weekly), Moscow, 17 September 2003, reprinted in *World Press Review*, 50(12), 2003; and 'Over 20,000 children from Chernobyl rehabilitated in Cuba,' *Caribbean Net News*, 2 April 2009, available from http://www.caribbeannetnews.com.

29 Feinsilver, 'La diplomacia médica cubana: cuando la izquierda lo ha hecho bien [Cuban medical diplomacy: When the left has got it right]', *Foreign Affairs en Español*, 6(4), 2006, pp. 81–94. The English version is available from http://www.coha.org.

30 Feinsilver, 'Cuba as a world medical power: the politics of symbolism', *Latin American Research Review*, 24(2), 1989, p. 1; and *Healing the Masses*.

31 Feinsilver, 'Médicos por petroleo: la diplomacia médica cubana recibe apoyo de sus amigos [Oil-for-Doctors: Cuban medical diplomacy gets a little help from a Venezuelan friend]', *Nueva Sociedad*, 216(July–August), 2008, available in both English and Spanish from http://www.nuso.org; and Feinsilver, 'La diplomacia médica cubana'.

32 Dr. Miriam Gran Álvarez, 'Estructura de la BMC', 1 February 2008, available from http://colaboracion.sld.cu.

33   'Report on Cuban healthcare professionals in Bolivia', *Periódico 26*, 16 July 2008, available from http://www.periodico26.cu.

34   http://www.cubacoop.com.

35   *Prensa Latina*, 4 August 2008.

36   Interviews with Doctors Félix Rigoli and Eduardo Guerrero, PAHO, Washington, 30 April 2009; UVS website http://www.uvirtual.sld.cu; Steve Brouwer, 'Fidel's WMDs versus Bush's WMDs: World medical doctors are more powerful than weapons of mass destruction', 14 November 2008 and 'WMDs – World Medical Doctors – now being produced in Venezuela', 13 November 2008, both posted to the blog site, *Venezuela Notes*, and available at http://www.venezuelanotes.blogspot.com; and 'Cuba: More Doctors for the World', *MEDICC Review,* 14 April 2008, available from http://www.medicc.org.

37   Personal communication from Saul Landau, whose daughter was one of those who passed the FMG in the US, 8 May 2009.

38   *Prensa Latina*, 11 April 2008.

39   Embassy of India (Havana), 'Annual Commercial & Economic Report-2006', No.Hav/Comm/2007, 13 April 2007.

40   Carmelo Mesa-Lago, 'The Cuban economy in 2008-2009: Internal and external challenges, state of the reforms and perspectives', International Seminar on Cuba, Tulane University and Centro de Investigación y Adiestramiento Político Administrativo, San Jose, Costa Rica, 3-4 February 2009 (to be published in a book edited by Paolo Spadoni).

41   Interview with Dr. Félix Rigoli, PAHO, 30 April 2009.

42   Tal Abbady, 'Hundreds of Cuban medical workers defecting to US while overseas', *South Florida Sun-Sentinel*, 10 October 2007 (posted at http://www.coha.org).

43   Elise Andaya, 'The Gift of health: Socialist medical practice and shifting material and moral economies in post-Soviet Cuba', *Medical Anthropology Quarterly* (forthcoming, 2009).

44   Ibid. and Pierre Sean Brotherton, 'We have to think like capitalists but continue being socialists: Medicalized subjectivities, emergent capital, and socialist entrepreneurs in post-Soviet Cuba', *American Ethnologist*, 35(2), May 2008.

45   Abbady, 'Hundreds of Cuban medical workers defecting'.

46   The nature of the activity of defection makes valid estimates difficult. Neither Homeland Security nor the State Department's Cuba Desk would provide any information and said that they did not have that data. Abbady cites Rep. Lincoln Diaz-Balart's office indicating that 1,000 Cuban doctors have come to the US under a special programme announced in 2006.

47   US Department of Homeland Security, US Customs and Immigration Services, 'Fact Sheet: Parole for Cuban Medical Personnel in Third Countries', 19 September 2006.

48   Mike Ceasar, 'Cuban doctors abroad helped to defect by new us visa policy', *World Politics Review*, 1 August 2007.

49   Oficina Nacional de Estadisticas, *Anuario Estadistico 2007*, Table 19.21.

50   Oficina Nacional de Estadisticas, *Panorama 2008,* Table 19.4.
51   On the disparity between rhetoric and practice and the nature of doctor-patient relations in the Cuban health system, see Pierre Sean Brotherton, 'Macroeconomic change and the biopolitics of health in Cuba's special period', *Journal of Latin American Anthropology*, 10(2), 2005; Brotherton, 'We have to think like capitalists'; and Elise Andaya, 'The gift of health'.
52   María Isabel Domínguez, 'Cuban social policy: principal spheres and targeted social groups', *Latin American Perspectives*, 36(2), March 2009.
53   Feinsilver, 'Médicos por petroleo [Oil-for-Doctors]'.

CHINA'S DOUBLE MOVEMENT IN HEALTH CARE

SHAOGUANG WANG

The concept of a 'double movement' is adopted from Karl Polanyi, in his seminal 1944 book, *The Great Transformation*. In Polanyi's view, 'the idea of a self-adjusting market implied a stark utopia. Such an institution could not exist for any length of time without annihilating the human and natural substance of society; it would have physically destroyed man and transformed his surroundings into a wilderness'.[1] The extension of the 'self-regulating' market, he thought, was bound to provoke a countermovement aiming at protecting society against 'the ravages of this satanic mill'.[2] Polanyi's thesis is helpful in understanding the great transformation in health care in China over the last sixty years.

HEALTHCARE UNDER MAO

Prior to the foundation of the People's Republic in 1949, most Chinese had no access to healthcare services. As the vast majority of people earned barely enough to subsist and survive, malnutrition presented a grave threat to their health, and endemic diseases were prevalent. The country's infant mortality rate was as high as 250 per thousand[3] and average life expectancy barely 35 years, roughly on a par with the US level in the 1780s.[4]

Soon after the People's Republic was established, the central government held the First National Health Work Conference, which laid down the 'workers, peasants and soldiers' oriented healthcare guidelines. The first and foremost objective of healthcare then was to turn a countryside 'without doctors and drugs' into a countryside 'with doctors and drugs'.[5] Even during the Korean War, the new government made rapid progress in developing rural medical organizations. The number of county-level health institutions rose from 1,400 in 1949 to 2,123, by the end of 1952, covering over 90 per cent of the nation's regions.[6] Throughout Mao's era, China placed great emphasis on egalitarian principles. The government made enormous efforts to establish a healthcare system that could provide all citizens with access to basic health services at an affordable price.

In urban areas the healthcare financing system consisted of two schemes: (1) the Government Insurance Scheme (GIS) for all government employees (including retirees), disabled veterans, college teachers and students, and employees of non-profit organizations; and (2) the Labour Insurance Scheme (LIS) for employees (including retirees) of all state-owned enterprises (SOE) and some collective enterprises. The beneficiaries of the GIS received largely free outpatient and inpatient health services, except for a small number of items, such as a registration fee, tonic medicines and plastic surgery. Moreover, there were avenues through which coverage could be extended to members' dependants. The LIS provided its members with benefits similar to those provided by the GIS, and reimbursed half of all medical expenditures for their immediate dependants.[7]

The GIS was financed and administered by governments at various levels, while the LIS was financed by enterprises' welfare funds and administered by each individual enterprise.[8] Thus, despite the name 'insurance', the GIS was actually a self-insurance scheme with no risk-pooling across localities, and the LIS a self-insurance scheme with no risk-pooling across work units. In other words, GIS members' medical benefits theoretically depended on the tax revenues available in their particular administrative region, and LIS members' benefits were tied to the profitability of their particular enterprise. This implied that medical benefits might vary vastly from region to region and from enterprise to enterprise. In reality, however, no such differences existed prior to the economic reform because, thanks to the 'soft budget constraints' that existed under the planned economy, the central government served as the payer of last resort for all outstanding health bills and the whole system functioned as if there were a nationwide pool.

As for service provision, for several decades urban China maintained a three-tiered structure of healthcare delivery. Medium-sized enterprises normally ran their own clinics to provide their employees with free outpatient services; enterprises with more than 1,000 employees tended to operate their own hospitals; while city hospitals provided inpatient services for medium-sized enterprises, and all health services for small enterprises and the uninsured. All health institutions were publicly-owned. Government budgets directly or indirectly subsidised most of their recurrent costs (e.g., salaries of health personnel and equipment), their remaining revenue coming from fee-for-service activities. Regulated by the government, prices for medical services as well as drugs were universally set below cost so that even the poor and uninsured could afford them. Whenever health institutions ran deficits they could ask for more subsidies from the government. On top of that, the government was also responsible for their capital investments.

In rural areas China developed a quite distinctive medical system that had two key components: the Cooperative Medical Scheme (CMS) for health financing, and 'barefoot doctors' for service provision. The CMS was financed from three sources: 'healthcare fees' (RMB 0.5 to 2 per year) paid by villagers, the village's collective welfare fund, and medical proceeds (mainly charges for medicines).[9] Rural residents who participated in the CMS were entitled to receive such benefits as free visits at the village clinic, free drugs, or copayment for drugs, at the village clinic, and copayment for referred hospital visits and for hospitalization.[10] By the end of Mao's era, the CMS had been adopted by 92.8 per cent of production brigades (e.g., villages) nationwide, covering 85 per cent of the rural population (Figure 1).[11]

Figure 1: The Proportion of Villages Adopting the CMS (1955–2008) [12]

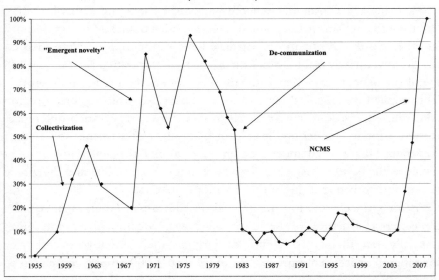

'Barefoot doctors' were farmers who received a brief period (from a few months to more than a year) of basic medical and paramedical training and worked in villages to promote hygiene, preventive health care and family planning, and to treat common illnesses. They referred seriously ill people to township and county hospitals. They were able to keep medical costs to an affordable level for three reasons. First, government provided funding to defray their training costs and for them to acquire essential medical equipment. Second, barefoot doctors worked both as farmers and as doctors, often spending as much as 50 per cent of their time in the field; and their income was only slightly higher than that of other villagers. Third, they were actively engaged in gathering, growing, harvesting and making Chinese herbal medicines and in applying acupuncture (herbal medicines and acupuncture were normally provided free of charge).

Both the CMS and the barefoot doctors reflected an approach to health care that was egalitarian, grassroots-based, decentralised, de-professionalised, 'low-tech', economically feasible, and culturally appropriate. Together, the two components ensured that the people's basic health needs were met.

Thus, on the eve of the economic reform, China's healthcare system provided inexpensive and equally accessible medical care for virtually all urban residents and most rural residents, although the quality of medical services was not then very high.[13] In the mid-1970s, China was not an affluent country but universal healthcare coverage helped to make it possible for the country to achieve significant improvements in people's health. Average life expectancy surged from 35 years before the Liberation to 68 years in 1980, while the infant mortality rate fell from approximately 250 per thousand before the Liberation to less than 34 in 1980.[14] China's medical services then were internationally recognised for fairness and accessibility, and became a model for the entire developing world.[15] The Nobel laureate economist Amartya Sen is by no means an uncritical admirer of Mao. However, he acknowledged that Mao's China enjoyed 'a large and decisive lead over India' in terms of the health status of its people.[16]

THE MOVEMENT TOWARD THE MARKET

In 1979 China embarked on market-oriented reforms. Since then its economy has grown on average by 9.9 per cent a year and the living standard of its people has improved markedly. The rapid growth of the economy has no doubt increased the total resources available to pursue better health for all citizens. When we examine China's health performance, however, the picture does not appear to be as thrilling as the growth in GDP and even in spending on health. Though life expectancy continued to grow and the child mortality rate continued to drop, progress slowed down considerably. Some may think that once life expectancy approaches seventy years, further gains are bound to come more slowly. Yet trends in other parts of the Asia-Pacific region indicate otherwise. From 1980 to 1998, for instance, China's average life expectancy rose by merely two years, but Australia, Hong Kong, Japan, New Zealand and Singapore, which had started from higher bases, increased their average life expectancy by four to six years. Sri Lanka, whose base had been similar to China's in 1980, increased average life expectancy by five years. Similar disparities can be seen in changes in infant mortality rates.[17] Even the Development Research Centre (DRC), a leading policy think tank directly under the State Council (China's Cabinet), openly admitted that the country's health reform up to the turn of the century was 'not successful', or even an outright 'failure'.[18]

Why, with higher disposable income per capita, better nourishment, and a bigger proportion of its national income devoted to health and health care, has China's health performance been so disappointing during the reform era? Determinants of health outcomes are of course multifarious, encompassing social, cultural, economic, and other factors. A possible culprit is mounting socioeconomic inequality. Over the last 25 years, a series of empirical studies, across both a wide range of countries and within industrialized nations alone, have related socioeconomic inequality to morbidity, mortality, and life expectancy. They all come to a consistent finding that the less equitable a country is, the less favourable its health outcome is.[19] The key message seems to be unequivocal: inequality is bad for national health, whatever a country's absolute material standard of living.

China used to be an egalitarian society, with income inequality well below the world average. However, the reforms of the 1980s through the 1990s drastically widened the gaps between regions, between urban and rural populations, and between rich and poor households in both urban and rural China. These inequalities are overlapping and interrelated. By the beginning of the new century the growing inter-regional, inter-personal, and rural–urban income differentials together made China's overall income distribution much more unequal than ever before in the history of the People's Republic. Such a steep rise in inequality in such a short period may have been gravely harmful to the nation's health, whatever the mechanisms underlying this relation may have been (e.g. the psychological effects of relative deprivation, the breakdown of social cohesion, and the like).

A more direct determinant of sluggish health improvement perhaps has to do with the government's reluctance and/or inability to spend on health. The pre-reform healthcare system was affordable and equitable primarily because it was based upon social norms that favoured equity. Underlying the reforms was a paradigm shift in ideology. Rather than equity and security, Chinese policy-makers now gave top priority to rapid aggregate economic growth. Their obsession with the fastest possible GDP growth rates made them ready to tolerate a certain degree of inequity and to sacrifice some basic human needs, including health care. Behind all the measures of healthcare reform introduced in the 1980s and 1990s lay an unstated premise: the market was more efficient than the state in allocating health resources. Faith in market forces gave the state an excuse to retreat from its roles as the funder and provider of health care. Indeed, in those two decades the state tried hard to give up its responsibility for healthcare financing and provision and expected societal actors to pick it up.[20] At that time, the Chinese leadership appeared to have intentionally or otherwise embraced the 'trickling down' hypothesis advocated by neoliberal economists: as long as the economic boom continued all citizens, rich or poor, would eventually be able to afford their health care out of their own pockets.

Among the first casualties of the ideological shift was rural health care system. As early as the second half of 1978, cracks had emerged in the CMS. *Document 37* issued by the Chinese Communist Party Central Committee on June 23 barred communes and brigades from 'allocating and transferring human, financial and material resources to conduct non-productive construction' and requested them to 'cut non-productive expenditures'.[21] Subsequently, some localities began to treat cooperative health care as a system of 'the poor eating the rich' and 'adding to the farmers' burdens'. As a result, 'the rural cooperative medical services drastically declined in some Northeastern provinces and were blown away by a gust of wind even in many brigades that had a solid economic basis ... As cooperative medical services were shut down, barefoot doctors were dismissed as non-productive personnel or brigade clinics were contracted to barefoot doctors who assumed sole responsibility for profits or losses; in many brigades, the peasants found it difficult and expensive to see a doctor'.[22] Other provinces reported similar problems.[23] In 1980, for instance, 'the cooperative medical services of many brigades were halted or ground to a standstill' across Henan Province so that some people issued a strong appeal for urgent action to salvage the CMS.[24] Nationally, the proportion of brigades covered by the CMS fell from 92.8 per cent in 1976 to 52.8 per cent in 1982, a 40 per cent drop in six years.

As a result of the official abolition of the People's Communes in 1983, the rural CMS collapsed like an avalanche and its coverage plunged to 11 per cent (Figure 1). By 1985, the number of villages that were still practising the CMS had decreased to 5 per cent. In the mid- to late-1980s, cooperative medical services still existed in the areas of suburban Shanghai and southern Jiangsu, where the collective economy was still strong.[25] Elsewhere, however, such services were retained in only a few localities, such as Macheng County of Hubei and Zhaoyuan County of Shandong.[26] As the CMS broke down, the vast majority of village clinics became privatised and the user-pay medical system became dominant again.

Why did the once world-renowned rural CMS decline so swiftly after reform? The most important reason was the change in the economic basis on which the CMS operated. Only under the institutional environment of a collective economy could the funds for cooperative medical services be drawn and retained directly from the collective economy so as to ensure a smooth financial path. After the household responsibility system was put in place, the collective economy became very weak or even non-existent in most villages, except in a few regions where collective township and village enterprises (TVEs) flourished. It was therefore no longer feasible in most localities to support cooperative medical services by collecting and retaining collective public welfare funds. The importance of a collective economy can be seen in the 40 per cent decrease in CMS coverage in 1983, when the People's Commune system was abolished. In the 1980s, while national cooperative medical services shrank, the rural cooperative medical coverage of southern Jiangsu was still kept at a level of more than 85 per cent, but this could hardly be sustained in the 1990s when the collectively owned TVEs there were restructured through 'privatization'. The experience of southern Jiangsu confirms that a collective economy was the backbone of the traditional CMS.

In addition, as a result of the breakdown of the collective economy, most villages could no longer afford to pay barefoot doctors reasonable salaries and had no alternative but to sell or contract out village clinics to individual doctors, offering them the motivation to seek profits. Meanwhile, it was no longer possible to collectively grow, gather, and make Chinese herbal medicines after the land had been allocated to individual households. Eventually, in early 1985, Health Minister Chen Minzhang announced the official abolition of the name 'barefoot doctor'.[27]

Another reason was that for much of the 1980s China's top leaders decided to let the rural CMS take its own course. Some health officials even openly advocated dissolving the CMS and contracting out village clinics to barefoot doctors. They asserted that this was an 'inevitable trend' of development.[28] When the CMS collapsed, they took pleasure in such misfortunes, saying, 'This is a great progress'. They believed that 'the user-pay medical system is here to stay for some considerable time in China'.[29]

For the urban healthcare system the turning point came in the mid-1980s when the market-oriented reforms accelerated. As reform deepened, market ideology steadily infiltrated the urban health sector, becoming the effective guiding principle of healthcare reform. Official documents dealing with health reform were imbued with such buzzwords as 'private initiative', 'market incentive', 'competition', 'choice', and 'individual responsibility'. Behind all these trendy catchphrases lay an unstated premise: the market would increase the efficiency of resource allocation, including health resources.

The economic reform steadily ruined the base of the GIS–LIS financing system. As mentioned before, the GIS and LIS were locality- and unit-based self-insurance schemes that could only function under the condition of 'soft budget constraint'. Decentralisation and marketisation, while giving local governments and state-owned enterprises (SOEs) greater operational autonomy, imposed stern fiscal discipline on them. The shift from 'soft budget constraints' to 'hard budget constraints' effectively dismantled the de facto nationwide risk pool and made it much more difficult for individual SOEs and local governments to finance employees' health care.

Starting in the early 1990s workers' medical benefits became increasingly tied to the profitability of the firms responsible for their health coverage. Facing mounting competitive pressures prompted by the economic reform, nonprofitable SOEs could often not continue paying the fixed percentage of wages needed to preserve sufficient medical insurance funds, thus jeopardising workers' access to health care. Moreover, due to the downsizing and bankruptcy of SOEs, millions of workers lost their jobs. As a result, they effectively lost health insurance cover. Even profitable firms might favour lower social insurance burdens in order to stay competitive. The problem was compounded by the rapid rise of the non-state sector. Not required to provide their employees with medical benefits, the upsurge of private and foreign invested firms further threatened access to healthcare coverage for workers and their dependants.

The economic reform also gradually crumpled the financial base of the GIS financing system. Fiscal decentralisation shifted an increasing share of social expenditures to sub-national governments and thus created pressures on them to meet such costs from locally-generated revenues. Increased fiscal autonomy was beneficial for governments in relatively advanced regions, and particularly good for governments in regions along the east coast that formerly had to remit revenues to the central government. In contrast, the weakened fiscal transfer capability of the central government hurt underdeveloped regions. Handicapped by their poor natural endowment and thin tax bases, governments in inland areas could often not afford to provide adequate health services for their employees. Combined with growing regional economic disparities,[30] the unequal distribution of fiscal resources across local authorities gave rise to huge gaps in the provision of health care. Although the GIS was nationally mandated, from the early 1990s onwards medical benefits began to vary vastly between different administrative jurisdictions, depending on the funds available to their respective governments.

In order to extend health insurance to the non-state sector, and to pool large health risks beyond individual firms and individual localities, the government began in the 1990s to experiment with a range of new health insurance schemes. Eventually, in 1999, a new Basic Medical Insurance System for Urban Employees emerged to replace the two old urban healthcare schemes.

Unlike the GIS and LIS, which had been solely financed by employers (SOEs or the government), financing for the new system was based on joint contributions from employers and employees. The new system extended its scope along two dimensions. First, it required all employees (including retirees) to participate, no matter who they worked for – government agencies, SOEs, collective-owned enterprises, private firms, or otherwise. Second, risk-pooling was no longer limited to individual work units. Rather, a citywide health insurance for catastrophic diseases was built up to cover all units within the jurisdiction. Together, the broad coverage and city-wide pooling were expected to minimize adverse selection (that is, the danger that only people with higher health risks might participate) and to establish a reliable mechanism that could share the health risks of retirees, and of the employees of loss-making firms, among all the firms in the area.

However, employees' dependants were no longer covered. Also excluded were the self-employed, workers in informal sectors, and migrant workers. Whereas the coverage of health insurance was nearly universal for the urban population at the onset of economic reforms, by the end of 2003 only roughly half of urban residents were insured. Were migrants to be counted in, the rate of coverage would be even lower.

Ideological shift aside, the economic reform also critically enfeebled the government's ability to deliver social welfare even if it so desired. At the core of Deng Xiaoping's reform programme was decentralisation. The massive fiscal decentralisation implemented between 1978 and 1993 might have been instrumental in generating high economic growth in those years, but it also significantly weakened the government's extractive capacity. In the 18 years between 1978 and 1995, the ratio of total government revenue to GDP fell from 31.2 per cent to around 10.7 per cent (Figure 4). Moreover, the central government's share in overall government revenues declined. Even compared to low-income countries, the extractive capacity of the Chinese government in general, and of the central government in particular, was rather weak.[31] With so little at its disposal, the central government simply could no longer afford to serve as the payer of last resort in health care.

The government's unwillingness and inability to shoulder the responsibility of primary health care for all is evident in Figure 2. Before the economic reform, the government's fiscal allocation and social insurance accounted for more than 80 per cent of the country's total health expenses. In the course of the economic reform, however, both the fiscal allocation and social spending dropped dramatically, reaching a nadir at the beginning of the new century. By 2001, the share of the government's allocation in total health spending had decreased to 15.93 per cent, and the share of social insurance to 24.1 per cent. Their combined share was barely 40 per cent. The shrinkage of the governmental allocation and social insurance caused a skyrocketing of peoples' out-of-pocket payments. In 1975, Chinese people's out-of-pocket payments had only accounted for 16 per cent, but by 2000-2001 it had increased to nearly 60 per cent. In other words, China's healthcare system effectively became a system funded mainly by private sources, while public sources only filled up the blanks here and there. This transformation fundamentally shifted the responsibility for health care from government and society to individuals. By the beginning of the new century, China's reliance on out-of-pocket payments exceeded that of most countries in the world. Even compared only to developing countries, China was still an outlier, which meant that China's healthcare system became one of the most commercialised in the world.[32]

Figure 2: Structure of Total Health Expenditure

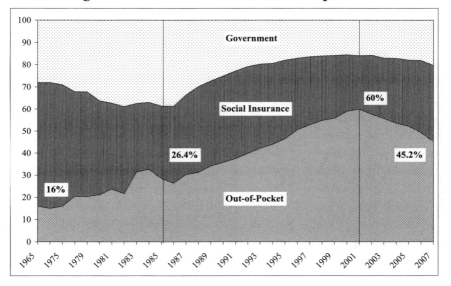

Whether health costs are borne by individual or by public sources is certainly not just a question of whether money comes out of the left pocket or the right. When medical costs are primarily borne by public sources, even poor people may enjoy a minimum level of health care. When health costs are primarily borne by individuals, however, the distribution of income and wealth largely determines who has access to necessary health care, because the market only serves the consumers who are capable of paying the bill. Relying on the free market to finance and provide health care would inevitably lead to reduced access to health services for the poor and the vulnerable. This was precisely what happened in China. The marketisation of health care was particularly detrimental to the wellbeing of the poor. While the rich could enjoy first-class medical care by international standards, the poor were often forced to endure minor health problems and put off dealing with major health conditions.

Based on data from four national health services surveys conducted by China's Ministry of Health from 1993 through 2008, Table 1 shows rates of foregone medical care (outpatient and inpatient). Evidently, the marketisation of health care created access barriers for many people.

Table 1: Rate of Foregone Medical Care Due to Cost Concerns from 1993 to 2008

	Foregone Outpatient Care Due to Cost			Foregone Inpatient Care Due to Cost		
	Total	Urban	Rural	Total	Urban	Rural
1993	5.2	1.8	6.7	20.1	10.7	24.6
1998	13.8	16.1	12	21	17.7	25.1
2003	18.7	20.7	17.7	20.7	15.6	22.8
2008	5.69			14.7		

There was a marked rise in the percentage of people not seeking care for economic reasons. In 1993, only a tiny fraction of urban residents (1.8 per cent) who reported feeling sick during the two weeks prior to the interview did not seek outpatient treatment due to cost concerns. The ratio quickly climbed to 16.1 per cent in 1998 and 20.7 per cent in 2003.[33] The proportion of rural residents who were sick but did not seek outpatient care due to cost concerns also increased continuously from 6.7 per cent in 1993 to 17.7 per cent in 2003.

The proportion of urban and rural residents who reported having refused to be hospitalised against professional advice in the year before the interview also rose between 1993 and 1998. The most important reason for not seeking inpatient care was, again, fear of being unable to pay hospital fees. Inability to pay was the reason given by 10.7 per cent of urban patients who refused to be hospitalised when they should have been in 1993; the ratio soared to 17.7 per cent in 1998, before falling to 15.6 per cent in 2003.

Marketisation of medical services started in rural areas in the 1980s and only became pervasive in the cities during the mid-1990s. Therefore, as early as 1993, about a quarter of rural residents who refused inpatient care did so due to cost concerns. Thereafter the ratio remained around this level.

Table 1 shows that the growing financial burden engendered by market-oriented health reform prevented a large segment of the population from accessing the existing healthcare services. Furthermore, a comparison of the survey results for 1993, 1998 and 2003 demonstrates how quickly income became a critical factor in deciding who received healthcare services and who did not. In 1993, income level did not seem to have played a significant role in determining whether or not one sought outpatient care. In fact, the proportion of urban residents who reported feeling sick but not seeking care was higher in the middle three income quintiles than in the lowest quintile, and the difference between the lowest and highest quintile was almost negligible. After 1998, however, low income became a factor that severely limited urban residents' health seeking behaviour. By 2003, nearly two-thirds of the lowest quintile did not seek outpatient care while only 45.2 per cent of the highest quintile did the same. With regard to inpatient care, a gradient by income quintile was already visible in 1993. By 2003, the gradient had become much steeper (Table 2). Among rural patients, income had already been decisive in 1993, but the income-related inequality in foregone health care grew stronger in 1998 and 2003.[34]

Table 2: Proportion of Urban Residents 'Not Seeking Care' by Income Quintile

Income Quintile Year	Lowest	II	III	IV	Highest
	Not seeking outpatient care in the last two weeks%				
1993	37.50	42.70	40.20	39.40	35.90
1998	49.10	46.10	44.10	45.50	39.90
2003	60.20	57.70	54.20	51.20	45.20
Year	Not seeking inpatient care in the last year%				
1993	31.67	23.84	22.42	21.04	16.87
1998	46.80	42.60	33.00	29.00	27.40
2003	41.58	32.30	22.73	28.23	17.18

When the poor were forced to endure minor diseases and delay treatment of major ones, minor health problems could become major ones, and major health problems could lead to the loss of the ability to work. The vicious cycle of 'illness due to poverty' and 'poverty due to illness' became a prominent social problem in urban China around the turn of the century. Massive medical bills or the loss of the ability to work brought many people's standard of living below the poverty line. When the Ministry of Health conducted its 'Second National Health Services Survey' in 1998, disease and injury had not yet become a major cause of poverty in large cities: less than 2 per cent of people living below the poverty line attributed their misfortune to 'illness or disability'. But in medium- to small-sized cities, about 10 per cent of poor people were poor because of illnesses or disability. By 2003 the percentage of illness-caused poverty reached a quarter of the total urban poor (Figure 3). Evidently, at that time one case of major illness could sink a once well-off family into dire straits and make a poor family absolutely impoverished.

Figure 3: Illness and Disability as Causes of Poverty (per cent)[35]

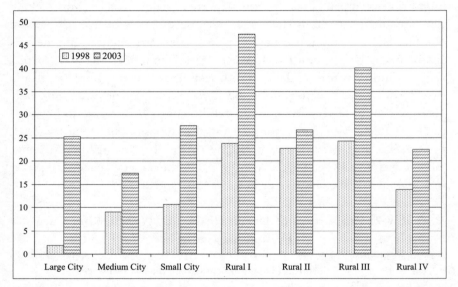

The same national health services surveys found that the role of illness in aggravating poverty was more pronounced in rural China. The 'Second National Health Services Survey' in 1998 had already found that disease and disability were a major cause of rural poverty. By the time China conducted its third survey in 2003, a third (33.4 per cent) of rural poor families had at least one member with a chronic disease or disability. By that time illness had become the single most important cause of rural poverty.[36] The heart-rending saying of rural people − 'we don't fear being poor, just getting sick' − stemmed precisely from the serious threat that illness poses not just to poor people's health but to their very livelihoods.

The data shown above indicate that behind China's macro-level economic prosperity there was a relatively large segment of poor households that could not access existing health care. When they were sick, they did not dare see a doctor; when they were seriously ill, they did not dare enter hospital; and when they were hospitalised they rushed out before they were well, afraid of being crushed by the heavy financial burden.

THE COUNTER-MOVEMENT

Karl Polanyi is absolutely right when he argues that a fully self-regulating market is a brute force, because creating a self-regulating market economy requires that human beings and the natural environment be turned into pure commodities, which assures the destruction of both society and the natural environment. Although China experienced perhaps the highest economic growth in the world in the 1980s and 1990s, the blind pursuit of high GDP growth rates gave rise to a host of serious problems. Such problems were perhaps not pronounced at the initial stage of reform, but as time went by they became increasingly evident and by the late 1990s some problems became critical. Around that time people's livelihoods became almost completely dependent on markets. Since markets only served people who were financially solvent, ordinary workers and farmers had much less security than before. In their view, the burdens imposed on them by market forces were too heavy, even unbearable.

In this context the golden banner of market reform became tattered and the consensus on it was broken. The classes of people whose interests were hurt, or who were insufficiently enriched in the previous round of reform, no longer lent unreserved support to new market-oriented reform initiatives; on the contrary, they fretted about every move labelled with the terms 'market' and 'reform' for fear of getting hurt again. These people generally believed that China's reform had gone astray and that it was time to stress economic and social development in a coordinated way. Prompted by this uproar there arose a protective countermovement aiming at enabling people to maintain 'a livelihood without reliance on the market'.[37] The government began to move gradually away from the reform strategy that had been based on the 'Washington Consensus' and to adopt what Stiglitz calls the 'second generation reform', concerned as much with human security and distributive justice as with economic growth.[38] Since 2002 the government has put more and more money into safety-net building in general, and health care in particular (Figure 2). The share of individual out-of-pocket payments in China's total health expenditure plunged, from 60 per cent in 2001 to about 45 per cent in 2007, the latest year for which data is available. It is expected the ratio will further decline to around 30 per cent in few years.

The counter-movement in the area of healthcare surfaced first in rural China in 2002. As early as the late 1980s, the Chinese government had already pledged to the World Health Organization that China would fully improve primary health care in rural areas by 2000.[39] To this end, the government set itself the mission of 'restoring and rebuilding' the rural CMS. During the entire 1990s, however, the government still wanted to avoid responsibility for financing the system because at that point it was experiencing the most horrendous financial crisis: the government's fiscal revenue as a percentage of GDP barely exceeded 10 per cent, and the proportion of the central government's fiscal revenue in GDP was merely 5 per cent (Figure 4). At that time, even if the government did not shirk responsibility for the farmers' health security, it was financially incapable of funding the cooperative medical scheme.

Figure 4: Chinese Government Fiscal Revenue/Expenditure as a Percentage of GDP

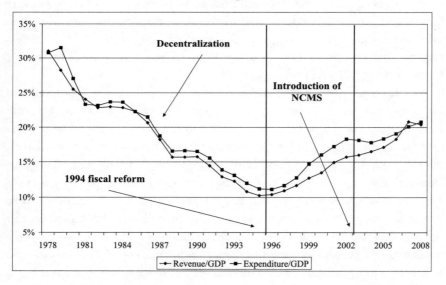

For this reason, throughout the 1990s, the government still insisted that the rural CMS should 'raise funds primarily from individual contributions, supplemented by collectively pooled subsidies and supported by government policies'. As a result, after a decade-long endeavour, the rural CMS was not restored as anticipated and its coverage remained below 10 per cent. Worse yet, even such a poor coverage base risked being eroded, thereby falling prey to a vicious circle of 'start-retreat-collapse-restart', 'getting started in the spring, going bust in the fall'.[40]

The tax-sharing reform initiated in 1994 swiftly reversed the perilous declining trend of the government's extractive capacity. As shown in Figure

4, by 2002 the Chinese government's fiscal revenue as a percentage of GDP rose to 16 per cent, while the central government's fiscal revenue as a proportion of GDP rose to 9 per cent. Only by that time did the government gain the fiscal capability to fund the rural cooperative medical scheme. Thus a drastic change in the government's rural healthcare policy at that time came as no surprise.

In October 2002, the government adopted a new approach towards the rural CMS. In a jointly promulgated *The Decision on Further Boosting Rural Healthcare Endeavor*, the Central Committee of the Chinese Communist Party and the State Council declared that the country would gradually set up a 'New Cooperative Medical System' (NCMS) and ultimately expand it to cover all rural residents by 2010. [41] The main difference between the NCMS and the traditional CMS lies in public financial involvement: in addition to an annual contribution from participating rural residents (RMB 10 per head in 2003, RMB 20 per head in 2008), the central and local treasury offer a specific amount of annual subsidy for each NCMS participant (RMB 20 per head in 2003, RMB 40 in 2005, and RMB 80 in 2008). [42] In addition, the *Decision* pledged to provide medical assistance for poor rural residents who could not afford to pay. [43]

The injection of public funds has vigorously pushed forward the rapid development of the NCMS, in stark contrast with past practice (as shown in Figure 1, above, on the trends from 1955 to 2008). In 2003, when the Ministry of Health conducted its Third National Healthcare Service Survey, the rural CMS only covered 9.5 per cent of the rural population. Five years later, by the end of 2008, the NCMS had covered nearly all administrative villages in the whole country, with 815 million participants, accounting for 91.5 per cent of China's rural population.[44] Thus, after nearly sixty years of development through several twists and turns, the cooperative healthcare system finally reached an all-time high.

In urban China, various medical insurance schemes have also developed very fast since 2002 (Figure 5). The number of active employees who joined the Basic Medical Insurance System for Urban Employees, for instance, multiplied from 18.78 million in 1998 to 200.48 million in 2008. It should be noted that this basic medical insurance scheme also covers retirees, so that the people who tend to have the most fragile health benefit from it. During the same period, the number of retirees covered increased from 3.69 million to about 50 million, accounting for more than 80 per cent of retirees, proportionally much higher than the coverage of younger, active employees.

Figure 5: The Coverage of Basic Medical Insurance Schemes for Urban Residents (Millions)

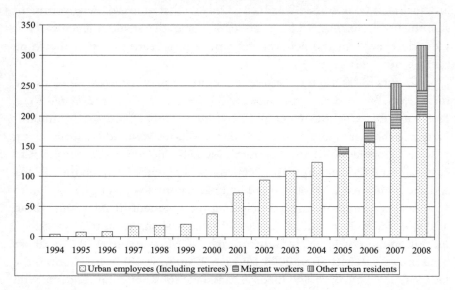

Starting around 2005 some cities began experimentally to provide medical care to other non-working urban residents. Approximately 10 million more people joined such medical care insurance schemes by the end of 2006. Finally, to achieve 'seamless' coverage for all urban residents, the State Council decided at its executive meeting in April 2007 to pilot a Basic Medical Insurance for Urban Residents in 88 cities. This new system aimed at covering all those who were not eligible for the Basic Medical Insurance for Urban Employees, such as children, students, the elderly, and other non-employed urban residents. Then, in February 2008, the central government decided to expand the experiment to a half of all Chinese cities. By the end of 2008, an additional 74.01 million urban residents had joined the scheme. This medical insurance scheme is expected to become fully established in all cities in China by 2010.[45]

Medical insurance for migrant workers is more complicated because they tend to be unwilling to participate in insurance due to their young age and high mobility, and because their employers are reluctant to pay for their insurance. In the late 2002 and early 2003, Shanghai and Chengdu began to pilot a system designed to provide migrant workers with comprehensive insurance. In 2003 and 2004 the Ministry of Labour and Social Security stepped in, requiring local governments to cover all migrant workers who had formed stable working relationships with their employers.

A turning-point came in March 2006, when the State Council issued

Opinions on Solving Migrant Worker Problems, stressing 'the top urgency of solving medical care problems for migrant workers on serious diseases' and placing migrant worker medical insurance issues in a prominent position on the agenda. The Ministry of Labour and Social Security subsequently set an objective of 'striving to increase the number of migrant workers participating in medical insurance to 20 million by the end of 2006 ... striving to cover all migrant workers (who have entered into long-term working relationship with urban employers) with medical insurance by the end of 2008'. This signals entry of migrant worker medical care into a new 'push' stage. Each locality responded swiftly with 'opinions', 'regulations' and 'measures' to solve migrant workers' medical care problems.[46] The number of migrant workers participating in medical insurance reached 23.67 million by the end of 2006, and rose to 42.49 million by the end of 2008 (Figure 5).[47]

Finally, on April 6, 2009, after three years of preparation, including months of public consultation, China announced the outlines of a comprehensive reform of its healthcare system that pledged to extend some form of basic health insurance to 90 per cent of the population by the end of 2011, and to provide 'safe, effective, convenient and affordable' basic health services to all citizens by 2020. With five medical care schemes (that is, Basic Medical Insurance for Urban Employees, Basic Medical Insurance for Urban Residents, Basic Medical Insurance for Migrant Workers, the New Rural Cooperative Medical Scheme, and Medical Assistance to Rural and Urban Residents) already in place, and covering 1.17 billion of the country's 1.32 billion people by the end of 2008, China should have little difficulty in achieving these goals.

Good health is both intrinsic to human wellbeing and instrumental to a whole range of human functioning.[48] The absence of good health can deprive people of their right to exercise choices, pursue social opportunities and plan for their future. Moreover, cross-national comparisons have established that a healthy population can help alleviate poverty, reduce wider social inequality, and enhance economic growth.[49] For both ethical and practical reasons, therefore, ensuring the health of every citizen must be an important goal for policymakers of any country, but particularly China, a country that still professes to uphold the socialist principle of equity. In Mao's era the health of the population was one of the country's proudest boasts. But the market-oriented reforms of the 1980s and 1990s gradually shattered the country's social safety nets, including its once famous healthcare system, making it difficult for many rural and urban residents to afford treatment. In reaction to this, a burgeoning protective counter-movement emerged in recent years. A growing number of people, including government decision-makers, have come to realize not only that relying primarily on the free market to finance and provide health care would inevitably lead to reduced access to health services for the poor and the vulnerable, but that since health is so important to everyone's wellbeing, it should never be allowed to flounder at the mercy of the market. The Chinese government has now committed itself to restoring an affordable and equitable healthcare system. With both political will and fiscal capacity on the part of the government in place, China should be able to universalize access to basic healthcare again, as it did thirty years ago.

NOTES

1   Karl Polanyi, *The Great Transformation: The Political and Economic Origins of Our Time,* Boston: Beacon Press, 2001, p. 3.
2   Ibid., p. 77.
3   Ka-Che Yip, 'Health and nationalist reconstruction: rural health in nationalist China, 1928-1937', *Modern Asian Studies*, Vol. 26, No. 2, 1992, p. 396.
4   Harry E. Seifert, 'Life tables for Chinese farmers', *The Milbank Memorial Fund Quarterly*, Vol. 13, No. 3, 1935, pp. 223-36.
5   Xu Jie, 'Dui woguo weisheng jingji zhengce de lishi huigu he sikao' (A historical review and thought of China's health economic policy), *Zhongguo weisheng jingji* (China Health Economics), No. 10, 1997, pp. 7-8.
6   Yao Li, 'Nongcun hezuo yiliao jinyan yu fansi' (Rural CMS: experience and introspection), available at http://iccs.cass.cn/detail_cg.aspx?sid=267.
7   Gail Henderson, Jin Shuigao, John Akin, Li Zhiming, Wang Jianmin, Ma Haijiang, He Yunan, Zhang Xiping, Chang Ying and Ge Keyou, 'Distribution of medical insurance in China', *Social Science and Medicine*, Vol. 41, No. 8, 1995, pp. 1119–30.
8   Project Team of DRC, 'An evaluation and recommendations on the reforms of the health system in China', *China Development Review (Supplement)*, Vol. 7, No. 1, 2005, pp. 109-12.
9   Yuanli Liu, 'Development of the rural health insurance system in China', *Health Policy and Planning*, Vol. 19, No. 3, 2004, pp. 159-65.
10   Liu Xingzhu and Cao Huaijie, 'China's cooperative medical system: its historical transformations and the trend of development', *Journal of Public Health Policy*, Vol. 13, No. 4, 1992, pp. 501-11
11   The areas not covered by the CMS were mainly border areas, minority nationality regions, alpine areas, old revolution base areas, fish farming areas and pastoral areas.
12   Unless indicated otherwise, all data presented in this paper comes from the author's databank.
13   World Bank, *Financing Health Care: Issues and Options for China*, Washington DC: The World Bank, 1997.
14   David Blumenthal and William Hsiao, 'Privatization and its discontents: the evolving Chinese health care system', *The New England Journal of Medicine*, Vol.

353, No. 11, 15 September 2005, pp. 1165-70.

15   Kenneth W. Newell, *Health By The People*, Geneva: World Health Organization, 1975; World Health Organization and United Nation Children's Fund, *Meeting Basic Health Needs in Developing Countries: Alternative Approaches*, Geneva: World Health Organization, 1975; World Health Organization, *Primary Health Care: Report of the International Conference on Primary Health Care*, Geneva: World Health Organization, 1978; Matthias Stiefel and W.F. Wertheim, *Production, Equity and Participation in Rural China*, London: Zed Press for the United Nations Research Institute for Social Development, 1983; Dean T. Jamison, et al., *China, the Health Sector*, Washington, D.C.: World Bank, 1984; World Bank, *World Development Report 1993: Investing in Health*, Washington, DC: World Bank, 1993, p. 111; BMJ Editorial Board, 'Primary health care led NHS: learning from developing countries,' *BMJ (British Medical Journal)*, 311, 1995, available from http://bmj.bmjjournals.com; Therese Hesketh and Wei Xing Zhu, 'Health in China: From Mao to Market Reform', *BMJ*, 314, 1997.

16   Jean Dreze and Amartya Sen, *Hunger and Public Action*, Oxford: Clarendon Press, 1987, p. 205.

17   Wang Shaoguang, 'China's health system: from crisis to opportunity', *Yale-China Health Journal*, Vol. 3, Autumn 2004, pp. 5-49.

18   Project Team of DRC, 'An evaluation and recommendations', pp. 39 and 195.

19   G.B. Rodgers, 'Income and inequality as determinants of mortality: an international cross-sectional analysis', *Population Studies*, Vol. 33, No. 2, 1979, pp. 343-51; R.G. Wilkinson, 'Income and mortality,' in R.G. Wilkinson ed. *Class and Health: Research and Longitudinal Data*, London: Tavistock, 1986; J. LeGrand, 'Inequalities in health: some international comparisons', *European Economic Review*, 31, 1987, pp. 182-91; R.G. Wilkinson, 'Income distribution and life expectancy', *BMJ*, 304, 1992, pp. 165-68; R.G Wilkinson, *Unhealthy Societies. The Afflictions of Inequality*, London: Routledge, 1996; B.P. Kennedy, I. Kawachi and D. Prothrow-Stith, 'Income distribution and mortality: cross sectional ecological study of the Robin Hood Index in the United States', *BMJ*, 312, 1996, pp. 1004-7; Johan P Mackenbach, Adriënne EJM Cavelaars, and Anton E Kunst, 'Socioeconomic inequalities in morbidity and mortality in Western Europe', *Lancet*, 349, 1997, pp.1655-9; A. Wagstaff and E. van Doorslaer, 'Income inequality and health: what does the literature tell us?', *Annual Review of Public Health*, 21, 2000, pp. 543–67.

20   Guan Xinping, 'China's social policy in the context of globalization', paper presented at International Conference on 'Repositioning the State: Challenges and Experiences', Hong Kong Polytechnic University, April 25-26, 2000; Linda Wong, 'Individualization of social rights in China', in Sally Sargeson, ed., *Collective Goods, Collective Futures in Asia*, London: Routledge, 2002, pp. 162-78.

21   Wu Lixing and Zhang Yanwu 'Nongmin jianfu jixianfeng' (Pioneer in reducing farmer's burden), *Nongmin ribao* (Farmers' Daily), 27 May 2006.

22   Zhang Zikuan, 'Nongcun hezuo yiliao yinggai kending yinggai tichang

yinggai fazhan' (The rural CMS should be affirmed, promoted and developed), *Zhongguo nongcun weisheng shiye guanli* (China Rural Healthcare Management), No. 2, 1982, pp. 31-33.

23   Fujian Health Administration, 'Jianding buyi di banhao nongcun hezuo yiliao' (Unswervingly promote rural CMS). *Fujian yiyao zhazhi* (Fujian Medical Journal), No. 6, 1979, pp. 1-2.

24   Fang Jian, 'Wei nongcun hezuo yiliao dashengjihu' (Strongly appeal for rural CMS). *Zhongyuan yikan* (Central China Medical Journal), No. 2, 1980, p. 2.

25   This judgment was based on the articles published by such Chinese journals as *Health Economics*, *Journal of Shanghai Medical University* and *China Rural Health Care Management*.

26   Rural Economy Team of China Health Economics Association, 'Nongcun de yiliao baojian xuqiu yu duice disanchi quanguo nongcun weisheng jingji xueshu taolunhui zhongshu' (Rural healthcare demand and strategy: a summary of the Third National Rural Health Economics Seminar), *Zhongguo weisheng jingji* (China Health Economics), No. 1, 1986, pp. 31-5.

27   Chen Fei, Zhang Zikuan and Chang Hongen, 'Chijiao yisheng lailongqumai' (The pedigree of barefoot doctors), *Jiankangbao* (Health News), 9 November 2007.

28   Li Decheng, 'Zhongguo nongcun chuantong hezuo yiliao zhidu yanjiu zhongshu' (An overview of China's rural CMS), *Huadong ligong daxue xuebao* (Journal of East China University of Science and Technology), No. 1, 2007, pp. 19-24.

29   Zhang Zikuan, 'Zai hezuo yiliao wenti shang ying chengqing sixiang tongyi renshi' (Clarify thoughts and unify understanding with regard to CMS), *Zhongguo nongcun weisheng shiye guanli* (China Rural Healthcare Management), No. 6, 1992, pp. 8-10.

30   Shaoguang Wang and Hu Angang, *The Political Economy of Uneven Development: The Case of China*, Armonk, NY: M.E. Sharpe, 1999.

31   Shaoguang Wang and Hu Angang, *The Chinese Economy in Crisis: State Capacity and Tax Reform*, Armonk, NY: M.E. Sharpe, 2001.

32   Wang Shaoguang, 'China's health system: from crisis to opportunity', *Yale-China Health Journal*, Vol. 3, Autumn 2004, pp. 14-15.

33   Wang Shaoguang, 'State extractive capacity, policy orientation, and inequity in the financing and delivery of health care in Urban China', *Social Sciences in China*, Vol. 29, No. 1, 2008, pp. 66-87.

34   Yuanli Liu, Keqin Rao, Jing Wu, and Emmanuela Gakidou, 'China's health system performance', *The Lancet*, Vol. 372, No. 9653, 2008, pp. 1920-21.

35   For statistical purposes the Chinese government often divides rural communities into four categories, ranging from the richest Rural I to the poorest Rural IV. While Rural I villages concentrate along the east coast, Rural IV villages cluster in mountainous areas in the west.

36   Statistical Information Centre of the Ministry of Health, *Disanci guojia weisheng fuwu diaocha fenxibaogao* (The Analytical Report on the 3rd National Health Service Survey), Beijing: Union Medical College Press, 2004, p. 15.

37   Gøsta Esping-Andersen, *The Three Worlds of Welfare Capitalism*, Princeton,

N.J.: Princeton University Press, 1990, pp. 21–2.
38 Joseph E. Stiglitz, 'Second-generation strategies for reform for China', an address given at Beijing University, Beijing, China, 20 July 1998.
39 Ministry of Health, 'Guyu woguo nongcun shixian 2000 nian renren xiangyou weisheng baojian de guihua mubiao' (The planned goal of the medical care coverage of everyone in the countryside in 2000), 15 March 1990, available from http://www.chinaeh.com.
40 Zhang Wenkang, Zhai zhuangxin zhanlue luntan shang di jiangyan (Lecture delivered at the strategic renovation forum), China Academy of Science, 31 January 2002, available from http://www.cas.ac.cn.
41 CPC Central Committee and State Council, 'Guanyu jinyibu jiaqiang nongcun weisheng gongzuo de jueding' (The decision on further boosting rural healthcare endeavor), 19 October 2002, available from http://www1.china.com.cn.
42 The Chinese Government announced in January 2009 that government subsidy for each NCMS participant would increase to RMB 120 by 2011. Xinhua Net, 21 January 21 2009, available from http://news.xinhuanet.com.
43 CPC Central Committee & State Council, 2002. By the end of 2008, 27.8 million rural residents and 5.13 million urban residents were covered by medical assistance schemes.
44 Xinhua New Agency, 'Xinnonghe, nongmin jiankang de baohushan' (New cooperative medical system: a safety net of farmers' health), 17 March 2009, available from http://news.xinhuanet.com.
45 Meng Xiang, 'Disanzhangwang: quanguo chengzhen jumin yibao shidian jijiang qitong' (The third net: the experiment on the nation-wide medical insurance of urban residents will be launched.), Ershiyi shiji jingji baodao (The economic report of the 21 century), 1 July 2007, available from http://finance.sina.com.cn.
46 Bai Tianliang, 'Chengzhen jumin yibao shidian jiang quanmian qitong, feicongye jumin ke canjia' (The experiment of the urban resident medical insurance will be launched in a full scale, non-employee residents will be covered), Xinhua Net, 27 April 2007, available from http://news.xinhuanet.com.
47 Ibid.
48 Amartya Sen, Development as Freedom, New York: Alfred A. Knope, 1999.
49 J. Drèze and Amartya Sen, India, Development and Participation, Delhi: Oxford University Press, 2002; A. Deaton, 'Health, inequality and economic development', Journal of Economic Literature, XLI, 2003, pp. 113-58 and 'Health in an age of globalization', National Bureau of Economic Research Working Paper, 10669, August 2004.

'HEALTH FOR ALL'
AND NEOLIBERAL GLOBALISATION:
AN INDIAN ROPE TRICK

MOHAN RAO

At the end of the Second World War, as post-colonial nations rushed to their trysts with destiny, seeking liberation from direct colonial rule, they attempted with limited success, but success nevertheless, to make a break with the historical structures of global inequity that underlay their underdevelopment. As a result of such policies as self-reliant import-substituting growth, some measure of land reform, and attempts at establishing industries, there was a reduction in the flow of resources from the countries of the Third World to those of the First. In short, there was a decline in the rate of exploitation of the former, as they sought to protect themselves and recover from the ravages of globalisation, militarily imposed, that they had been victims of for centuries. This was in most cases partial, and half-hearted, but nevertheless real. There was thus a reversal of secular trends in food availability, in value added in production, in per capita incomes, and so on. At the same time, there were efforts to provide a modicum of health, nutrition and education. Reflecting all these changes, there were improvements in health indices as life expectations increased, morbidity and mortality rates declined, and birth rates increased.

The nature and pattern of development in the health sector was, however, marked by a singular feature: the overwhelming hubris of science and technology in relation to the social problem of maldistribution of wealth and resources. While largely ignoring the broader determinants of health, urban hospital-based services were developed, which also had the consequence of countries like India opening up their markets for medical technologies and products. This was accompanied by the launch of technology-centred 'vertical' programmes, the most spectacular being those for malaria and family planning. In 1960, for instance, the WHO's budget for malaria eradication was greater than the rest of its budget put together.[1] In India, the family planning programme, for its part, lurched from one approach to another – from extension education, to the intra-uterine device, to the vasectomy camp, to forcible male sterilisation, and finally to female sterilisation – increasingly sucking in funds and thus determining the contours of health sector development.[2] Both programmes were premised on a 'magic bullet' belief that there were technological solutions to complex epidemiological problems.

The vertical programmes, midwifed by international agencies, had certain unique characteristics. Planning these programmes was not always guided by epidemiological considerations. They were often initiated without an understanding of the nature of the disease, its distribution, its underlying causes and inter-linkages, its behaviour over time and, indeed, often even its scale. Focusing on these programmes meant that general services that could provide health care to the population were not developed. By the early seventies it was increasingly being realised that this model of health sector development had led down a blind alley. Both the malaria eradication programme and the family planning programme were now acknowledged to be failures.[3] It was obvious that without universal and comprehensive health care, and without linking health to overall development, health improvement was bound to be chimerical.

Widespread international disillusionment with vertical programmes, the recognition of the need to provide sufficient coverage to rural populations, and the faltering integration of preventative and promotional programmes, together contributed to the WHO-UNICEF initiative that led to the declaration of the goal of 'Health for All' through primary health care at Alma Ata in 1978. At this point, the WHO saw a 'major crisis on the point of developing' in both the developed and the developing world as a result of the 'wide and deep-seated error in the way health services are provided'.[4] This coincided with the growing awareness among international agencies of the failure of the family planning approach to the problem of poverty. They accepted the need for integrated programmes and the satisfaction of the minimum needs of the population in order to meet demographic goals. The World Bank and the Population Council both endorsed this 'developmentalist' perspective.[5] The sense of hope and optimism among those rallying for 'Health for All' was connected to the strength of the call for a 'new international economic order' that was adopted by the UN General Assembly in 1974.

The 1970s, then, were exciting times in health sector development, when everything appeared possible. With China's entry into the WHO in 1973 (made possible by 'ping- pong diplomacy'), it was impossible to ignore alternative models of health care.[6] Between the late 1950s and early 1970s, life expectancy in China more than doubled. Despite famine deaths, life expectation increased from around 22 years to 46, a feat that had taken the Western world more than a century to achieve. With no assistance from the WHO or any other international agency, an 'underdeveloped' country with a fifth of the world's population had created an extraordinary system of basic health care for its vast rural population. The problems of hunger and infection, and thus the diseases of poverty, had been fought not with magic wands, nor by doctors trained on western lines, but with food and employment.[7]

New winds seemed to blow across continents. The West was plunged in students' struggles for democratisation, the civil rights movement surged in the USA, and second-wave feminism took on the health establishment. The decade began with the growing successes of the liberation struggles against Portuguese colonial rule in Africa, and ended with the Iranian revolution. And with the defeat of the US in Vietnam giving a piquant new twist to Cold War politics, the Soviet Union attempted to take a new leadership role, not least by pushing the WHO towards Alma Ata. The USSR, long critical of vertical programmes in general and the malaria programme in particular, argued that they hampered health sector development.[8] The Soviet delegate at the WHO stated that 'the Soviet Union was prepared to show participants what had been done over the last 50 years'.[9] The Alma Ata declaration, promising something revolutionary for health in Third World countries (since it was evident that the goal of 'Health for All' could only be achieved through broad and equitable development), thus had a complex political heritage.

But this period of optimism proved to be extremely short-lived. The primary reason for this was of course the new wave of globalisation. The 1980s saw the Keynesian world increasingly under attack from neoliberalism, and by the end 'actually-existing socialism' also had been overthrown. In these circumstances, the goals of Alma Ata became impossible to achieve. 'Health for All' was soon replaced by the oxymoron of 'Selective Primary Health Care', and both UNICEF and the WHO beat a retreat from Alma Ata.[10] A secondary reason was the widespread misconception that primary health care was something that concerned only poor countries, and that it only had to do with the provision of the most essential health care. What was, above all, forgotten was that health is only partly an outcome of health interventions. But with neoliberal globalisation even those interventions were now to be increasingly based on market principles. As the prospects for health for all receded, the magic bullet approach to health policy reappeared, accompanying what Renaud cuttingly but aptly described as eliminating society from disease.[11]

All this was epitomised by the World Bank, whose rejection of the ideas of Alma Ata was unequivocal. In its influential 1987 document *Financing Health Services in Developing Countries: An Agenda for Reform*, the World Bank stated, 'the approach to health care in developing countries has been to treat it as a right of citizenry and to attempt to provide free services for everyone. This approach does not work'.[12] The role of the state, then, was to be confined to regulation – and hence the salience of the word 'governance' – while the private sector was to be encouraged, often through state subsidy, to take on the provision of health services, with the exception of a minimum clinical package, that ironically included family planning. The role of the World Bank in health sector development increased enormously, while that of the WHO shrivelled; indeed World Bank loans for one programme, malaria, exceeded the entire budget of the WHO.[13] By the end of the century, the Bank had become 'the largest single source of healthcare finance in developing countries with an unparalleled degree of policy-making authority'.[14] New players, international NGOs, were now doing to public health what had been earlier done with population control – divorcing it from its determinants and building a market for technologies. At the same time, the health sector in developing countries emerged as a leading source of multi-national profits as it was prised open for investment in a range of areas, from high-level technologies to insurance, and indeed also in routine technologies such as immunisation.

THE CONTEXT OF GLOBALISATION

Neoliberal globalisation is the product of economic policies that reflect an ideological commitment to unbridled market principles. One of the significant lessons of post-war economic growth had been the singular role that the capitalist state could play, and indeed needed to play, to avoid recurrent periods of crisis due to falling demand. For instance, state involvement in public health had been considered critical, not simply because health is a merit good, but also because state provision of such goods was at the heart of the strategy to stabilise the economy and to increase productivity. In the new environment of the 1980s, these Keynesian policies increasingly came under fierce attack. The new neoliberal consensus involved a profoundly cynical view of the state, especially in relation to developing countries, although neoliberal free-market rhetoric often contrasted sharply with the actual practices of the Reagan and Thatcher governments in their own countries where the state was increasingly subsidising the rich.[15] Indeed, neoliberal globalisation has been described as a global project to restore upper-class privileges to the levels that prevailed early in the twentieth century, in a profound *trickle up* of wealth and resources.[16] Reducing the role of the state and increasing that of the market, irrespective of the social and indeed long-term economic costs, was thus at the centre of this model of capitalist therapy.

Deflation, liberalisation and privatisation were applied broadly across Latin America and Africa in the 1980s – what Patnaik described as imperialist globalisation.[17] In the agricultural sector, where the majority of the population of the world still worked, this led to the reinforcement of colonial patterns of agricultural production, stimulating the growth of export-oriented crops at the cost of food crops. The problem at the heart of this pattern of production is that it was implemented at a time when the prices of primary commodities were the lowest in history. Indeed by 1989, prices for agricultural products were only 60 per cent of their 1970 levels. Thus the more successful these countries were in increasing the volume of exports (in competition with other Third World countries exporting similar products), the less successful they were in raising foreign exchange to finance their imports. It is not surprising that many countries shifted back in time to being exporters of unprocessed raw materials and importers of manufactured goods, albeit with a sharp deterioration in the terms of trade against developing countries in general and agriculture in particular, plunging the peasantry into crisis.[18]

These policies increased the indebtedness of Third World countries, shifted wealth from productive to speculative sectors, raised levels of exploitation of wage-workers across the globe, and led to the growth of casual, poorly paid and insecure forms of employment. Funding cuts in education and health also meant that already weak and under-funded systems of health, education and food security collapsed. It is not accidental that these policies increased levels of poverty in already poor countries, even as a section of the population became richer. They obtained access to consumer goods hitherto available only in the rich countries, and with the vociferous support of the electronic media called for further globalization. In India, while this portion of the middle and upper classes has been described as having seceded from the nation, some sections, largely upper caste, supported the growth of the rightwing crypto-fascist party, the BJP.[19] Having benefited in the past from state intervention, they now forgot India's anti-imperialist history, abandoning ideas of democracy and secularism, and were impatient to integrate into the global economy, albeit as a junior partner of the US. Supporting them financially with dollars, and with laughable intellectual capital, were large segments of an extremely successful body of diasporic

Indians, in the USA in particular, dying to say with pride, we are Hindus.[20]

A major consequence of economic globalisation has been commonly described as the 'feminisation of poverty', as women increasingly strive to hold families together in face of increasing economic insecurity. In many countries, more women entered the labour force but typically at lower wages and with working conditions inferior to those of men; in others, women lost jobs as levels of unemployment increased markedly. In India, the extent of unpaid labour in households, performed largely by women, increased as public provision of basic goods and services declined. Young children, especially girls, were sometimes withdrawn from school to join the vast and grossly underpaid informal labour market or to assist in running the household. Rising food prices, along with cuts in subsidies for the poor, meant that an increasing proportion of families with precarious resources were pushed under the poverty line. This had a disproportionate effect on women and girls. It also meant that more young women were driven into the sex industry.

It is not surprising that under these conditions hunger and morbidity levels rose, even as poor people were increasingly unable to access health institutions, which under structural adjustment 'reforms' typically introduced the requirement for patients to pay fees for health services. Given the rising levels of under-nutrition, rates of infant and child mortality, which had hitherto shown a secular decline, either stagnated, as in India, or in the case of some countries actually increased. So unambiguous and deleterious were these changes, and so extensively documented, that even UNICEF issued calls for structural adjustment programmes to be given 'a human face'.[21] Increasing inequalities in income and in health were also apparent in other countries that had followed similar economic trajectories. In a number of the developed industrial countries, mortality differentials rose sharply in parallel with widening disparities in socio-economic status.[22]

HEALTH AND HEALTH POLICY IN INDIA
UNDER NEOLIBERALISM

Shortly after Alma Ata, the Indian government made a commitment to provide health care for all by 2000.[23] Towards this end, during the 1980s efforts were made to strengthen rural infrastructure while the government itself spoke of the failures of vertical programmes and the need to provide integrated services.[24] The decade thus saw some investment in rural infrastructure and social support programmes such as nutrition programmes, including the creation of a network of publicly-funded healthcare institutions – subcentres, primary health centres and district hospitals all over the country. These were largely used for family planning, and were by and large avoided by those who could afford to do so. In any case, the bulk of the funding, meager as it was, went to urban institutions, medical colleges and the new vertical programmes. Over the same period, there was also increasing attention paid to the private and NGO sectors. In effect, the dual structure of Indian health services reappeared in a reinforced form: a public one – derelict, short of staff, funds and infrastructure – for the poor who also lacked access to the determinants of health; and a private system for those who could afford to pay. Given the increasing weakness of the public system, more and more people opted for the hugely exploitative private system.

The distance between the two systems particularly grew through the 1990s. In early 1991 India's foreign exchange reserves – helped by capital flight – fell to the value of two weeks of imports. India came close to defaulting on her commercial debt. The IMF hurriedly approved a $1.8 billion loan for India, staving off the impending default, followed later in the year by another $2.3 billion loan, which committed India to negotiate a further structural adjustment loan of $5 billion.[25] One of the IMF's conditions for this loan was that state expenditures, including for health and education, were to be sharply reduced, and in fact public health spending declined from 1.4 per cent of GDP in the mid–eighties to 0.9 per cent in 2002. The universal public distribution of food – which provided a certain amount of subsidised food – was sharply curtailed. Other policies affecting the agrarian sector – such as reduced spending for irrigation, infrastructure and rural credit – meant that the per capita availability of food has shown an alarming decrease. As Patnaik has forcefully pointed out, per capita annual food grain consumption declined from 178 kilograms in 1991 to 154 in 2004, even as India exported food grain for animal feed in the West. Utilising the accepted daily required calorie norm of 2,400 calories, 75 per cent of the rural population could be classified as poor in 1999-2000 (instead of the figure of 27 per cent which the Planning Commission obtains by arbitrarily reducing the calorie norm to 1900 per day).[26]

The full effect of these policies in terms of preventable and communicable diseases remains to be seen. In the 1990s, although life expectancy had increased and infant and child mortality rates had declined, these positive changes were relatively modest, and infant and child mortality still took an unconscionable toll of the lives of 2.2 million children every year. Despite the 1983 National Health Policy target of reducing the Infant Mortality Rate (IMR) to less than 60 per 1000 live births in all the states of the country, the rate of decline in the IMR decelerated from 27 per cent over the decade of 1980s to only 10 per cent over the 1990s. The same is true for the rate of decline in the mortality rate of children under five, from 35 per cent in the 1980s to 15 per cent in the 1990s.[27] Today, it is clear that India will not reach the Millenium Development Goals for reducing infant and under-five mortality. The 1983 National Health Policy target was also to reduce the Maternal Mortality Rate to less than 200 per 100,000 live births by 2000. In fact, between 115,000 and 170,000 women died in childbirth in 2000, accounting for about one-quarter of all maternal deaths worldwide.[28] Far from declining over the 1990s, maternal and neo-natal morbidity and mortality rates in India at best plateaued, or even increased.[29] High and unconscionable as these levels of maternal mortality are, it is nevertheless critical to bear in mind that they represent just a fraction of the morbidity and mortality load borne by women in India. Communicable diseases take a much higher toll.[30]

Thus, instead of an expansion of the state's commitment to public health as promised in the early 1980s, over the two decades since India embarked upon structural adjustment we have witnessed a decline from already low levels. The 2002 National Health Policy admitted that India's public expenditure on health was the fifth lowest in the world as a percentage of GDP.[31] In 2006 general government spending on health was less than 20 per cent of all health expenditure.[32] The decline in public investment in health was matched by growing subsidies to the private healthcare sector, the largest and one of the least regulated in the world. [33] Evidence from across the country indicates that access to health care has declined sharply over this period. The policy of levying user fees has had a negative impact on access to public health facilities, especially for poor and marginalised communities, and for women more generally.[34] As the 2002 National Health Policy also acknowledged, medical expenditure had by then already emerged as one of the leading causes of personal indebtedness. Equally significant have been other changes. Inter-regional, rural-urban, gender and economic class differentials in access to health care in India were already well-documented before the 1990s. But since the onset of the liberalisation policies, these differentials have considerably widened.[35]

State support for private health care grew with the initiation of various kinds of private-public partnerships.[36] This was given an international imprimatur, particularly specifically for HIV/AIDs, tuberculosis and malaria, through an alliance between a tired, financially emasculated and visionless WHO and ruthlessly energetic new international NGOs.[37] These provided a new impetus to vertical programmes, but with a difference: private funds also made their entry through these partnerships. For instance, under the aegis of Global Alliance for Vaccines and Immunisation (GAVI) and the

WHO, plans are underway in the Indian Ministry of Health and Family Welfare to introduce a range of epidemiologically unnecessary, and expensive, vaccines.[38] It is remarkable that GAVI conditions for support include a guarantee for 'reasonable prices', support for sustainable markets (in vaccines), and prohibitions on compulsory licensing that would enable their manufacture in the country. India has accepted the support of GAVI for the introduction of hepatitis B vaccine in selected pilot projects. Thus, the creation of new markets was combined with the neglect of the determinants of diseases.[39] This effectively undermines comprehensive public health care: in several of India's states routine immunisation rates have declined.

A range of incentives has also been offered to the private health sector. These include the provision of land at throw-away prices, customs duty exemptions for importing sophisticated medical technology, and loans from financial institutions at low interest rates. The period thus witnessed the emergence of a corporate health sector, increasingly influential in policy-making. The institutions involved have not always provided free services to the poor as they were expected to under the terms of their contracts.[40] A committee set up by the Government of Delhi found gross violations on every commitment made.[41] The report of course gathers dust.

The incentives offered to the private health industry have led to the burgeoning of high-technology diagnostic centres in urban areas, with excess capacity.[42] But government employees can now obtain reimbursement for medical expenditure at these institutions, creating effective demand for high cost medical care. In India's private health sector, supply creates demand. Over the same period there has been a burgeoning of medical colleges in the private sector, charging exorbitant fees for admission.[43] Given the urban concentration among doctors, it is not surprising to find small-scale studies providing evidence of severe competition leading to unethical medical practices.[44] By offering higher pay the private sector also sucks out personnel from the public health system. The incentives given to the private sector have led to India's emergence as a major destination for health tourists, including as a centre for reproductive health.[45] Thus while India produces more than enough doctors – but not enough nurses – for her public health system, she is facing an acute crisis in human health resources for the public health system.[46]

India has also emerged as a major exporter of human health resources.[47] The emigration of skilled workers does bring some benefits to the migrants and their families, with further benefits to the state in terms of foreign exchange flows, but it comes at a heavy price for the country. It was already estimated in the 1990s, for instance, that 4,000 to 5,000 doctors, trained at public expense, emigrated every year at an estimated annual cost of US$160 million to the Indian exchequer.[48] A more recent study carried out at India's premier public medical institution, the All India Institute of Medical Sciences (AIIMS) in New Delhi, estimated that 50 per cent of doctors trained in India migrated overseas or internally to the private sector between 1989 and 2000, with those from the privileged upper-castes especially tending to migrate abroad.[49] This makes the reservation of places in medical schools for the less-privileged castes all the more important, not just for affirmative action but also for public health.[50]

At the same time there were far-reaching changes in drug policies. India used to be known for its relatively low costs of drugs and pharmaceuticals and for its significant indigenous production of drugs. With her accession to the WTO, India has witnessed a greater concentration of drug production, a larger role for multinationals, a higher proportion of imported drugs and a dramatic increase in the cost of drugs.[51] This too has contributed to the steep rise of medical care costs.

All these policies have combined to bring about marked shifts in healthcare utilisation. It was already the case in the mid-1990s that among people who sought out-patient services more than 80 per cent did so in the private sector, and this was visible even in the poorer states of the country.[52] The same was true of in-patient care: in 1995-96, 55 per cent of patients in rural areas and 57 per cent urban areas were treated in private hospitals, compared to 40 per cent in both rural and urban areas in 1986-87. By the mid-point of the current decade things had worsened. A further 4 per cent in rural areas and 5 per cent in urban areas had shifted to private services by 2004. In short, more people were turning away from the collapsing public system, a collapse that was an outcome of public policy. An increasing proportion of people borrowed or sold assets in order to access medical care in the private sector.[53]

Class inequality in the use of health facilities has also increased. In rural areas class differences in the in-patient use of public hospitals, insignificant in the mid-1980s, turned statistically significant in the mid-1990s. In urban areas, inequality in the use of public facilities did not worsen significantly, but inequality in use of private facilities did. The steep fall in rural hospitalisation rates, along with increasing use of hospitals by the better-off, indicates that the poor are now being squeezed out. User fees are one important reason for this. In other words, the type of market-oriented policies on health famously advanced by the World Bank in its 1993 *World Development Report* succeeded in doing exactly the opposite of what was ostensibly their *raison d'être*: to reduce the utilisation of public services by the better-off in order to increase access for the poor.[54]

What people need to pay for both out-patient and in-patient care increased sharply in both rural and urban areas of India after the mid-1980s. In rural areas, private out-patient costs increased by 142 per cent as against 77 per cent in the public sector. In urban areas, private out-patient costs increased by 150 per cent compared to 124 per cent in the public sector. The increase in what people had to pay for in-patient care is even more striking: average charges rose by 436 per cent in rural areas and 320 per cent in urban areas.[55] The counterpart to poor public financing is that India has one of the highest levels of private medical expenditures in the world: out-of-pocket personal expenditure accounts for 83 per cent of the total health expenditure. At the same time, the proportion of people not getting *any type* of medical care due to financial reasons had already increased between 1986-87 and 1995-96: from 10 to 21 per cent in urban areas, and from 15 to 24 per cent in rural areas.[56] Since then, even the middle classes are finding it increasingly difficult to meet medical care costs.[57]

As economic inequalities have increased,[58] so have health inequalities: between the states, between rural and urban areas and between different social groups.[59] Such was the evident mismatch between the country's economic growth and her stagnation in health that the government initiated a series of moves to improve health infrastructure. The results of the National Rural Health Mission, initiated in 2005, partly as a consequence of the influence of the Left political parties on the government at the time, are yet to unfold.

One important feature accompanying health sector reforms has been its NGO-isation.[60] Some NGOs have been doing excellent work in health and family planning; some have served as models. A range of NGOs is involved on issues of primary health care with no assistance from either state or foreign donors. It is nevertheless important to question the current policy romanticisation of NGOs, and their increasing utilisation, often at public cost, to implement health and family planning schemes. NGOs comprise a broad and heterogeneous category in terms of ideology, activities, funding, outreach and effectiveness, and any generalisation about them would be extremely weak, if not foolish. But they are not necessarily either more effective or efficient than publicly-funded institutions and cannot be used as a substitute for them, for a variety of reasons. First, by definition, NGO activities are discretionary and not mandatory: they are not legally obliged to serve all people, as public institutions are. Thus they can be socially exclusive, and indeed the fear that NGO-isation may be against the interests of dalits has been frequently voiced by dalit activists and scholars.[61] Second, they are not necessarily accountable. Thus, while a politician has the (admittedly infrequent) chance of being voted out for incompetence or corruption by his constituents, NGOs do not. Third, the whole issue of monitoring and regulation of the private and NGO sectors is a vexed question, but we have only to remember that the scandal of quinacrine sterilisations in the country was largely carried out by NGOs.[62]

Notably, a study in Delhi revealed that 'people repose little hope in civil society agents to negotiate their problems: 94 per cent of the respondents held the government responsible for providing medical care to the people, while a negligible percentage (1 per cent) felt that it is the job of NGOs'.[63] But the myth that NGOs are somehow more 'representative' than political bodies has been so assiduously created in the age of neo-liberalism that this fundamental point has often been ignored. So has the problematic fact that the space afforded 'civil society organisations' in policy-making bodies rigorously includes NGOs while excluding other more representative organisations such as trade unions.

IN CONCLUSION

Health sector developments in India, then, did not meet the goals set out at Alma Ata. India has always had a dual system of health care, and public health, for the haves and have-nots. What the last many years have done is to widen this chasm. They have reinforced state policy tendencies towards a selective and targeted approach; declining public investments, especially in primary care; increasing use of private sector facilities for both in-patient and out-patient care; falling levels of efficiency and effectiveness in the public sector; and even a further squeezing-out of the poor from access to publicly-funded health care. At the same time, the private sector has grown, with active support from the state.

The characteristic feature of the approach to health that international institutions such as the World Bank have fostered – and not just in India – is the tendency to deal with disease and health merely at the individual level, and to conceive of populations merely as aggregates of individuals, disregarding the social and economic context of diseases.[64] Central to this approach was the ideology of introducing market principles into hitherto sacrosanct areas of public goods, converting health care into a market-driven, profit-maximising enterprise. To do so required a philosophical commitment to methodological individualism in public health, an oxymoron, but nevertheless achieved globally not only through the World Bank but also the WHO and its Commissions on Macroeconomics and Health. Their focus on proximate causes led to what has been described as individualising and psychologising health.[65] This reflects the dominance of the behavioural approach to public health, which has always characterised the major schools of public health in the US: this is not only hubris but also profoundly cynical, given the US's own dysfunctional healthcare system.

The three most influential people in India's financial policies today are all former World Bank employees. The Prime Minister, Dr. Manmohan Singh is one of them, as is the Governor of the Reserve Bank of India and the head of the Planning Commission. The political class in India does not now even require the imprimatur of the West and its institutions: they are confident that they have arrived at a muscular new India on the global stage. The yearning to be part of the global US project, the aching for a nuclear India accepted globally, leads to a search for a mantra that would do away with India as it really is – an Indian rope trick. If the film Slumdog Millionaire can do it, why can't public policy?

The sabotage of Alma Ata was neither accidental nor innocent. It emerged out of a new political economy both globally and within India. The consequences for health are profound.

NOTES

I am grateful to Achin Vanaik, Betsy Hartmann, Githa Hariharan, Matt Anderson and Ramila Bisht for their comments. Oommen C. Kurian was, as always, of extraordinary help in many ways. My many salaams to all of them.

1   Sung Lee, 'WHO and the developing world: the contest for ideology' in Andrew Cunningham and Bridie Andrews, eds., *Western Medicine as Contested Knowledge*, Manchester: Manchester University Press, 1997, p. 29.
2   Mohan Rao, *From Population Control to Reproductive Health: Malthusian Arithmetic*, New Delhi: Sage, 2004.
3   K.W. Newell, 'Selective primary health care: the counter revolution', *Social Science and Medicine*, Vol 26, No. 3, 1978. pp. 903-906.
4   Ibid.
5   D. Hodgson, 'Orthodoxy and revisionism in American demography', *Population and Development Review*, Vol XIV, No. 1, 1988. pp. 541-569.
6   Marcos Cueto, 'The origins of primary health care and selective primary health care', *American Journal of Public Health*, Vo.94, No.11, 2004. pp. 1864-1874.
7   Jean Dreze and Amartya Sen, *Hunger and Public Action*, New Delhi: Oxford University Press, 2004.
8   Socrates Litsios, 'The long and difficult road to Alma Ata: a personal reflection', *International Journal of Health Services*, Vol.32, No.4, 2002, pp. 709-732.
9   Sung Lee, 'WHO and the developing world', p. 42.
10   David Sanders, David Werner, Jason Weston, Steve Babb, and Bill Rodriguez, *Questioning the Solution: The Politics of Primary Health Care and Child Survival*, Palo Alto: Healthwrights, 1997.

11   M. Renaud, 'On the structural constraints to state intervention in health', *International Journal of Health Services*, Vol. 5, No. 4, 1975, pp. 625-42.

12   Quoted in John Gershman and Alec Irwin, 'Getting a grip on the global economy' in Jim Yong Kim, Joyce V. Millen, Alec Irwin and John German, eds., *Dying for Growth: Global Inequality and the Health of the Poor*, Maine: Common Courage Press, 2000, p. 30.

13   M. Rao and R. Lowenson, 'The political economy of the assault on health', Discussion papers prepared by the Peoples' Health Assembly's Drafting Group, Savar, Bangladesh, Gonoshasthaya Kendra, 2000.

14   Kim et al., *Dying for* Growth, p. 143.

15   Gershman and Irwin, 'Getting a grip'.

16   David Harvey, *A Brief History of Neoliberalism*, New York: Oxford University Press, 2005.

17   Prabhat Patnaik, 'The political economy of structural adjustment: a note', in Rao Mohan, ed., *Disinvesting in Health: The World Bank's Prescriptions for Health*, New Delhi: Sage, 1999.

18   Utsa Patnaik, *The Republic of Hunger and Other Essays,* Gurgaon: Three Essays Collective, 2007.

19   Anurag Pandey, 'Communalism and separatism in India: an analysis', *Journal of Asian and African Studies*, Vol. 42, No. 6, 2007, pp. 533-49.

20   '*Garv se kaho hum Hindu hai*' (Say with pride that we are Hindus) was the war cry of the 'Hindu' fascists as they destroyed the historic Babri mosque in 1992, plunging the nation into a communal cauldron, but, sadly, reaping rich electoral dividends.

21   G.A. Cornia, R. Jolly and F. Stewart, eds., *Adjustment with a Human Face: Country Case Studies*, Oxford: Clarendon Press, 1988.

22   G. Davey-Smith and M.M. Egger, 'Socio-economic differentials in wealth and health', *British Medical Journal*, 307, 30 October 1993, pp. 1085-86.

23   Government of India, *Health For All by 2000 AD*, New Delhi: Ministry of Health and Family Welfare, 1980.

24   Government of India, *Sixth Five Year Plan*, New Delhi: Planning Commission, 1980.

25   Achin Vanaik, ed., *Globalisation and South Asia: Multidimensional Perspectives*, New Delhi: Manohar Publications, 2004.

26   Utsa Patnaik, *The Republic of Hunger and Other Essays,* Gurgaon: Three Essays Collective, 2007.

27   Rajiv Misra, Rachel Chatterjee and Sujatha Rao, *India Health Report*, New Delhi: Oxford University Press, 2003.

28   L. Freedman, M. Wirth, R. Waldman, M. Chowdhury and A. Rosenfield., *Interim Report of Millennium Project Taskforce 4 on Child Health and Maternal Health*, New York: UNDP, 2004.

29   R.R. Ved and A.S. Dua, 'Review of women and children's health in India: focus on safe motherhood', in S. Rao (ed.) *Burden of Disease in India: National Commission on Macroeconomics and Health Background Papers,* Delhi: Ministry of Health and Family Welfare, 2005, pp. 103-69.

30 Imrana Qadeer, 'Reproductive health: a public health perspective', *Economic and Political Weekly*, Vol.33, No.41, 1998, pp. 2671-85.

31 Government of India, *National Health Policy*, New Delhi: Ministry of Health and Family Welfare, 2002.

32 WHO Statistical Information System (WHOSIS), 2009, http://www.who.int/whosis/en.

33 Rama Baru, *Private Health in India: Social Characteristics and Trends*, New Delhi: Sage, 1998.

34 Government of India, *Report of the Commission on Macroeconomics and Health*, New Delhi: Ministry of Health and Family Welfare, 2005.

35 Rama Baru, K. Nagaraj, Acharya Arnab and Sanghamitra Acharya, 'Inequalities in utilisation of health services', *Lancet*, (forthcoming).

36 Two states, leading in PPPs, Andhra Pradesh and Gujarat, have entered into PPPs in the health sector with Satyam computers, at considerable cost to the state exchequer. Satyam has recently been revealed to be India's biggest corporate fraud, its CEO the Bernard Madoff of India. The PPPs however continue.

37 Eduardo von Missoni, 'A long way back towards Alma Ata', *Bulletin von Medicus Mundi Scheiwz,* No.111, February, 2009. pp. 10-20.

38 Indira Chakravarthy, 'Role of the World Health Organisation', *Economic and Political Weekly*, Vol.43, No.47, 2008, pp. 41-46.

39 J.M Puliyel and Y. Madhavi, 'Vaccines: policy for public good or private profit?', *Indian Journal of Medical Research*, January, 2008, pp. 1-3.

40 R. Bhat, 'Private health care sector in India: issues arising out of its growth and the role of the state in strengthening public-private interaction', Unpublished Paper, Ahmedabad, Indian Institute of Management, 1998.

41 Government of Delhi, 'High Level Committee for Hospitals in Delhi: Enquiry Report', Justice A.S. Qureshi Committee, New Delhi, 2001.

42 S. Nandraj, V.R. Muraleedharan, Rama V. Baru, I. Qadeer and R. Priya, *Private Health Sector in India: Review and Annotated Bibliography*, Mumbai: Cehat, 2001. See also the earlier A. Jesani and S. Anantharam, *Private Sector and Privatisation in Health Care Services*, Mumbai: FRCH, 1993.

43 There was uproar in Parliament on 8 June 2009 regarding what was described as the 'auctioning' of seats in private medical colleges, said to be charging 10-20 million rupees for a post-graduate seat. See 'Govt under fire over capitation fee scam in both houses', *Times of India*, 9 June 2009.

44 S. Nandraj, 'Beyond the law and the lord: quality of private health care', *Economic and Political Weekly*, Vol.29, No.27, 1994, pp. 1680-85.

45 There is a flourishing trade, a black market of body parts, in the private sector in India, including reproductive ones. Newspapers frequently report kidney removal scandals. There is also a burgeoning industry in assisted reproduction, including commercial surrogacy.

46 Mohan Rao, A.K. Shiva Kumar, Mirai Chatterjee, K. Sundararaman and Krishna D. Rao, 'India's health resource crises: too many and yet too few', *Lancet,* (forthcoming).

47   There is indeed a great deal of anecdotal evidence about unemployment among doctors in India, concentrated in urban areas, and fiercely competing for practice with little attention to medical norms or rational prescription practices. Reflecting this, it appears that doctors are the second largest category of applicants to the Indian Administrative Services exams. But, of course, we have no firm data. However unreliable government data in India are, the private sector is even averse to academic enquiries.

48   Voluntary Health Association of India, *Report of the Independent Commission on Health in India*, New Delhi, 1997.

49   Manas Kaushik, Abhishek Jaiswal, Naseem Shah and Ajay Mahal, 'High-end physician migration from India', *Bulletin of the World Health Organization*, Volume 86, No 1, 2008, pp. 40-45.

50   The question of reservations, or affirmative action, for the backward castes in India is a hugely divisive political issue playing out on familiar tropes from racist debates in the West, with of course peculiarly Indian complexities. Doctors, largely upper caste, and the dominant section in the media, also largely upper caste, have opposed reservations on the grounds of merit, on the grounds of maintaining standards and so on. Indeed, they implicitly argue that characteristics such as intelligence, merit and efficiency have a genetic basis and in their protests, medical students have swept streets and polished shoes, considered quintessentially lower caste occupations. See Abhay Mishra, 'Anti-quota protests: complaints against students', *Indian Express*, 8 May 2006.

51   Amit Sengupta, 'Economic reforms, health and pharmaceuticals', *Economic and Political Weekly*, Vol. 31, No 48, 1996, pp. 3155-59.

52   Gita Sen, Aditi Iyer and Asha George, 'Class, gender and health equity: lessons from liberalising India', in Gita Sen, Asha George and Piroska Ostlin, eds., *Engendering International Health*, Massachusetts: MIT Press, 2002.

53   Baru et al., 'Inequalities in utilisation of health services'.

54   World Bank *World Development Report 1993: Investing in Health*, Washington: World Bank, 1993.

55   Sen et al., 'Class, gender and health equity'.

56   Government of India, Ministry of Statistics and Programme Implementation, 'Note on morbidity and treatment of ailments: NSS 52nd Round (July 1995-June 1996)', *Sarvekshana*, Vol.23, No.3, Jan-March, 2002.

57   Baru et al., 'Inequalities in utilisation of health services'.

58   Abhijit Sen and Himanshu, 'Poverty and inequality in India I' and 'Poverty and inequality in India II' in *Economic and Political Weekly*, Vol. 39, No.38, 2004 and Vol. 39, No. 39, 2004.

59   Joe Williams, U.S. Mishra and K. Navaneetham, 'Health inequality in India: evidence from NFHS 3', *Economic and Political Weekly*, Vol. 43, No. 25, 2008, pp. 41-49.

60   Hartmann perceptively noted in the early 1990s that 'In India, the government's recent capitulation to the IMF and consequent intensification of population control efforts are being accompanied by what activists call a "buying-up" of NGOs by USAID. In the state of Uttar Pradesh alone, USAID is planning to spend 325 million dollars to reduce population growth in a scheme which

includes the involvement of over a hundred NGOs'. Betsy Hartmann, 'Old maps and new terrain: the politics of women, population and the environment in the 1990s', Paper presented at the International Conference on Reproductive Rights, WGNRR, Madras, 1993. p. 18.

61   Sukhdeo Thorat, 'Strategy of disincentives and targeting for population control: implications for Dalits and Tribals', Paper presented at the National Colloquium on Population Policies, Center of Social Medicine and Community Health and the Singamma Sreenivasan Foundation, New Delhi, 2001.

62   Mohan Rao, 'The rhetoric of reproductive rights: Quinacrine sterilisation in India', in Imrana Qadeer, Kasturi Sen, and K.R. Nayar, eds., *Public Health and the Poverty of Reforms*, New Delhi: Sage, 2001.

63   Neera Chandhoke, '"Seeing" the state in India', *Economic and Political Weekly*, Vol. 40, No. 11, 2005, p. 1035.

64   This provoked a rich and heated debate. See Neil Pearce, 'Traditional epidemiology, modern epidemiology and public health', *The American Journal of Public Health*, Vol. 86, No. 5, 1996, pp. 678-83; Ann V. Diez Roux, 'Bringing context back into epidemiology: variables and fallacies in multilevel analysis', *American Journal of Public Health*, Vol. 88, No. 2, 1998, pp. 1027-32; M. Susser, 'Does risk factor epidemiology put epidemiology at risk?', *Journal of Epidemiology and Community Health*, 52(10), 1998, pp. 418-26; N. Kieger, 'Questioning epidemiology: objectivity, advocacy and socially responsible science', *American Journal of Epidemiology*, Vol. 89, No. 8, 1999, pp. 1151-53.

65   V.K. Yadavendu, 'Changing perspectives in public health: from population to an individual', *Economic and Political Weekly*, Vol. 36, No. 49, 2003, pp. 5180-88.

THE SHAPING OF GLOBAL HEALTH POLICY

MERI KOIVUSALO

The enjoyment of the highest standard of health is one of the fundamental rights of every human being.... Governments have a responsibility for the health of their peoples which can be fulfilled only by the provision of adequate health and social measures.

WHO constitution, 1948

The role of the World Health Organisation in the context of the United Nations system was clearly specified in Article 2 of its constitution: 'to act as the directing and co-ordinating authority on international health work'. Yet new institutions, networks and operators are increasingly active at the global policy level, often with substantial funding and increasingly limited respect for traditional United Nations operators such as the WHO. One aspect of this is the way commercial interests operating at the international level seek to define global and national health standards and the focus of health policy at both global and national levels. It is also becoming important to consider the institutional background and legitimacy of global organisations, as well as the ways in which global agendas and actors are influenced and shaped by commercialisation and commercial policy priorities set in other sectors, such as trade or industry, outside the remit of ministries of health. This often undermines the remit of the WHO, the normative agency for global health policy.

There are three different ways of understanding what agencies involved in global health policy actually do: first, establishing global regulatory measures and standards; second, setting broader global policy agendas for common global action (e.g. 'health for all' primary health care; HIV/AIDS) and third, determining how global policies for health either enhance or limit the scope for national health policies and the global distribution of health resources. The institutions traditionally involved in making global health policy, in particular the WHO, have shared a common conceptual framework and language derived from medical and public health knowledge and language, and shared priorities. While the 'medicalisation' of policy can be a problem, the shared discourse of medicine and public health does permit evidence-based analysis and the assessment of problems across countries. By contrast, when the emphasis in global policy efforts is focused overtly on trade and economic policy, the institutions involved, such as the World Bank, the World Trade Organisation (WTO) and the OECD, become the first and main reference point, with different discourses, priorities and assumptions. These emphases have often dominated policies also within development policy and the so-called development community.

SETTING HEALTH STANDARDS

The role of the WHO in a global standard-setting agenda is crucial. Where global standard-setting for health interferes with key commercial interests, struggles take place aimed at limiting the WHO's regulatory activities, shifting responsibility for setting standards to other intergovernmental organisations or coalitions ('forum-shopping'), or directly influencing the standard-setting process and its outcomes. One telling example was the global Framework Convention on Tobacco Control. In spite of the overwhelming evidence on the health impact of smoking tobacco, corporate lobbyists used their power to sidetrack the WHO from, for example, initiating and negotiating the tobacco framework agreement. The argument used to limit the regulatory activities of the WHO or other United Nations agencies is usually that there is no need for global regulatory guidance, or that the organisation in question is inappropriately changing its focus. As Zeltner reported:

> The Tobacco companies' own documents show that they viewed WHO, an international public health agency, as one of their foremost enemies. The documents show further that the tobacco companies instigated global strategies to discredit and impede WHO's ability to carry out its mission. The tobacco companies' campaign against WHO was rarely directed at the merits of the public health issues raised by tobacco use. Instead, the documents show that tobacco companies sought to divert attention from the public health issues, to reduce budgets for the scientific and policy activities carried out by WHO, to pit other UN agencies against WHO, to convince developing countries that WHO's tobacco control program was a 'First World' agenda carried out at the expense of the developing world, to distort the results of

important scientific studies of tobacco, and to discredit WHO as an institution.[1]

Corporate interests in pharmaceuticals, nutrition, alcohol, infant foods, etc. have also made considerable efforts to limit, influence or undermine the role of the WHO. Forum-shopping has been one key way of limiting the scope of global health policies. One example of this is the transfer of pharmaceutical and research-related regulatory issues from the WHO to the International Conference on Harmonisation,[2] an organisation with an office in the headquarters of the International Federation of Pharmaceutical Manufacturers and Associations (IFPMA) in Geneva. This represents a move by the USA, Japan and the European Union to shift decision making from the WHO towards a more corporate-led forum. Another example of shifting issues from one forum to another can be seen in the broadening of the scope of the work of the International Standards Organisation (ISO), which is more directly linked with the corporate world. However, not only strong global corporate actors, but also governments, or coalitions of governments, likewise influence regulatory measures and priorities. One of the most recent instances of this was the Bush administration's engagement in a broad variety of global regulatory efforts, e.g. its opposition, alongside the sugar industry, to the WHO's proposed global strategy on nutrition.[3]

Another strategy is to claim that the standards are too strict, and are in effect protectionist measures. While 'too strict' health standards can be used to protect particular corporate or industry interests, this strategy has also been used in some of the most prominent WTO cases involving the adjudication of disputes between advanced capitalist countries in areas concerning asbestos regulation and the use of hormones in cattle raising. Trade-related interests and concerns can be used to undermine legitimate health-related regulatory efforts. In the field of services the role of the WTO and the promotion of the liberalisation of services through the General Agreement on Trade in Services (GATS) is especially problematic for health systems, insofar as it locks in commitments to the liberalisation of health services while diminishing the scope for national regulatory policies. While governments have the option of not making such commitments, and can change them provided that they compensate for doing so through making other commitments, the danger is that, whether deliberately or just through approaching negotiations with insufficient care, governments can make too far-reaching commitments which tie the hands of future governments if they seek to further regulate, or back off from, market-driven healthcare systems.[4]

Another dimension of standard-setting is the commercialisation of national health systems, making health services much more subject to WTO provisions. Publicly-funded but outsourced health services can become subject to trade regulations.[5] The WTO's focus on trade in health services is, however, likely to have more relevance for richer countries with better funded healthcare markets. It is less likely that a multinational corporation will seek to utilise WTO provisions so as to take over governmental health responsibilities in very poor countries with inadequate funding in the health sector. Their interest in using the WTO is more likely to focus on countries where money can be made. For their part, developing country governments are likely to be more eager to seek trade liberalisation in order to secure the expansion of health tourism and greater mobility for health professionals, however problematic this is for their national health systems.

Intellectual property rights and related measures have also become an increasingly important part of global trade policy, especially with respect to the interests of the global research-based pharmaceutical industry. While the 2001 Doha declaration is often seen as an example of the successful articulation of health concerns in the context of global trade policies, any real movement in terms of trade policies was limited. Instead, as a result of efforts in support of access to medicines and R&D, global health policy-making in this area has been restructured into a field of myriad coalitions, initiatives and measures, with a lack of coordination or a clear focus on how these relate to global or national health policy priorities. The tensions are particularly strong in relation to trade in generic medicines and the extent to which competition can be maintained in this area, so as to reduce prices. The upward-ratcheting movement of global standards for intellectual property rights,[6] which benefit global corporations, is much stronger than for global labour, health and safety or other standards which have more problematic implications for global corporations.

GLOBAL HEALTH GOVERNANCE

The WHO's global role in both the regulatory and the development context has always been shared with other United Nations agencies, such as the International Labour Organisation, the FAO, and United Nations funds such as UNICEF and the UN Population Fund. But since the 1980s the OECD and the World Bank have also become involved with health and public sector reform policies which have been more in line with neoliberal policies and priorities. The institutional basis and context of policy discussion in both OECD and World Bank has been more conducive to a focus on economics and on the financing and organisation of health care. The 1980s and 1990s can be seen as a time when epistemic communities with competing agendas for global health policy engaged in institution–shopping. In health systems, this was reflected in the healthcare reforms promoted through research networks working alongside the OECD and the World Bank.[7]

While the 1978 Alma Ata declaration was based on a joint UNICEF/WHO initiative, these two organisations' different approaches to global health largely defined their response to neoliberalism in the 1980s.[8] The competing frameworks of more selective health care promoted by UNICEF, and more comprehensive health care promoted by the WHO, were both effectively undermined by structural adjustment programmes and the decline in health financing, as well as by the increasing involvement of the World Bank. Yet while the UNICEF's focus on selective health care fitted better with the neoliberal economic policies and health reform agenda, it was UNICEF, rather than the WHO, which more vocally took up the issue of structural adjustment policies and their implications for health.[9]

The WHO's capacity to undertake research, analysis and action in relation to health systems has been limited, and the organisation has also been struggling with the prominence of 'vertical programmes' (programmes targeted at specific diseases or actions).[10] When the OECD began working on healthcare reform issues and public sector reform in the 1980s, as well as on compiling data on health systems, it was filling a gap. The WHO's lack of a focus on data collection and its limited capacity for global oversight provided scope for OECD and World Bank entry into the area. The World Bank had previously contributed to the establishment of the 'selective healthcare' agenda and along with the OECD had more control over the agendas and priorities of development aid agencies.[11] Thus the declining support for health systems development and 'health for all' policies within the WHO cannot be accounted for only in terms of a failure to support the idealism embedded in the 'health for all' strategy, but was also a result of the politics of development funding and policy amongst key countries active on global health. The lack of funding for health as result of structural adjustment programmes in the 1980s was a key concern, as was the use of loan conditionality, which imposed user charges to generate resources for health care. The greater World Bank involvement in global health policy during the 1990s was also related to the way development funds were allocated through national development agencies, while the WHO remained primarily a terrain of ministries of health. Channelling technical assistance for health through other international agencies with different policy priorities compromised the WHO's role as the global normative agency.

The World Bank's focus on healthcare reforms was important, but the policies prescribed under these reforms have attracted widespread criticism.[12]

The Bank's engagement with health reforms had broader relevance, first of all, in relation to global guidance on policy matters within the development policy community (reflecting to a large extent policies set for developed countries in the context of the OECD); and secondly, in relation to the allocation of global health financing. While much of the Bank's thinking on healthcare reform was based on work done within the OECD and related epistemic networks, the Bank's engagement with public sector and healthcare reforms gained substantial attention not only due to the magnitude of the funding involved, but also by virtue of the initiative it took in redrawing the global health policy agenda in its flagship 1993 World Development report *Investing in Health*.[13] Global actors without formal normative powers, such as the OECD or the World Bank, have to a large extent become in practice norm-setting institutions through their role in providing guidance and assessment. A less high-profile but often equally effective part of this normative engagement can be seen in the World Bank's involvement in various types of policy guidelines and toolboxes for public policy, as well as through the teaching provided by the World Bank Institute.

It was in this way that global health policy in the 1990s was driven by World Bank priorities. If the 1980s was the decade of structural adjustment and lack of concern for health on the part of international agencies, the 1990s were an era of expansion and restructuring of the global policy agenda to fit the implementation of more neoliberal and market oriented policies *within* the health sector. Meanwhile, the WHO remained weak on health systems research, lacking the capacity to effectively address the issues that were raised with respect to healthcare reforms, even though some efforts were made in the late 1990s to enhance the influence of the WHO through, for example, an ad hoc working group of the WHO's Executive Board. This lack of capacity in the WHO was accompanied by a move away from the 'health for all' strategy. The WHO's controversial World Health Report 2000 on health systems was in effect largely based on World Bank expertise. While the Director General of the WHO, Gro Harlem Brundtland, formally still endorsed the values of 'health for all' policies, the report distanced itself from the strategy, explicitly emphasising that the WHO would need to base its recommendations on evidence rather than ideology.[14]

The early 2000s, however, saw a rehabilitation of the primary healthcare approach within the organisation, an approach which continued to be supported by a large proportion of the WHO's Member States. The most recent World Health Report on primary health care takes the WHO more explicitly back in support of the 'health for all' approach, with further support from the report of its Commission on the Social Determinants of Health, which addressed issues of equity and a focus on inter-sectoral action.[15] This shift has also been reflected in World Health Assembly resolutions in support of further WHO engagement in the area.[16]

Global health policies are, however, also affected by global policy priorities, such as the Millennium Development Goals (MDGs). The MDGs emerged in practice out of seven OECD development goals adopted by the World Bank and the IMF.[17] These goals are now used to define much of the work that all the United Nations agencies, including the WHO, are supposed to focus on. While there is some merit in highlighting the general aims embodied in the MDGs, as a guiding target they are problematic for global health policy and grossly inadequate to provide any general framework for WHO action.

On the other hand the human rights aspect of health, including the right of everyone to the enjoyment of the highest attainable standard of physical and mental health, has once again slowly acquired a higher policy profile. A particular aspect of this relates to issues concerning potential conflicts with intellectual property rights. For example, in his address to the UN's General Assembly, the UN special rapporteur on the right to health, Anand Grover, has taken a strong line concerning the way intellectual property laws affect access to medicines: 'Developing countries and LDCs should not introduce TRIPS-plus standards in their national laws. Developed countries should not encourage developing countries and LDCs to enter into TRIPS-plus FTAs and should be mindful of actions which may infringe upon the right to health'.[18]

THE FOCUS OF GLOBAL HEALTH POLICY: SPECIFIC DISEASES OR HEALTH SYSTEMS

One critical dilemma at the core of global health policy is that between more disease-based 'vertical' initiatives and more health systems-based 'horizontal' measures. The WHO as an institution is often still considered to be too 'medically dominated' and committed to vertical programmes, which reflect recent practice rather than the original (and only recently re-articulated) aims of the organisation. While the HIV/AIDS epidemic and growing concerns over malaria and new, more resistant strains of tuberculosis contributed to a focus on these three diseases, the vertical approach was further enhanced by the focus of the WHO's Macroeconomic Commission on communicable diseases alone.[19] The WHO's role and focus has also become further complicated since the establishment of the Global Fund to Fight HIV/AIDS, Tuberculosis and Malaria. The expansion of funding for health personnel and health systems components within vertical programmes does not resolve the more fundamental problems of health system financing. Furthermore, proponents of action in relation to non-communicable diseases have called for a similar financing mechanism, and one has already been suggested for maternal and child health.[20]

The problem is that while HIV/AIDS resources in particular have grown, and have drawn more global attention to the need for finance, there has been criticism with respect to the balance of focus, as 'the tide has not lifted all boats'.[21] In some countries HIV/AIDS funding already exceeds other funding on health.[22] A new balance in health policy is being sought, for example, through an emphasis on 'diagonal financing' for health care – i.e. using funding that is available for specific diseases to leverage funding for more comprehensive health care – and proposals have been made to change the role of the Global Fund to provide financing for comprehensive countrywide health programmes, so as to create 'islands of sufficiency in a swamp of insufficiency'.[23] However, while efforts to ensure a sufficient basis for primary healthcare and health systems is crucial to the longer-term success of more vertical programmes, in 'diagonal funding' the focus on health systems is still wrapped more around vertical programmes than the other way round. The global focus on communicable diseases can also be seen as part of a more 'security-oriented' and neoliberal policy position, in which epidemics are perceived as a security threat. It is also compatible with the key corporate concern to divert attention away from *non*-communicable diseases linked to tobacco, alcohol and food, and from pharmaceutical products for the treatment of non-communicable diseases.

WHO GETS TO MAKE GLOBAL HEALTH POLICY?

The continuity of financing for international agencies such as the WHO is in principle tackled through membership contributions, but as these have remained stagnant the role of other sources of funds has become increasingly important. This is likely to affect the WHO's global capacity to implement global normative policies, while also giving a disproportionate profile and role to the additional 'extra-budgetary' funding the WHO has increasingly come to rely on. While the World Health Assembly may decide on policy priorities, their realisation depends on the organisation's resources and capacities. In this respect the continuous limitation of the WHO's core budget has also undermined the accountability of the organisation to its Member States.

Public policies in most countries are increasingly complemented by nongovernmental and charitable work. The growing role of NGOs as delivery agents for aid and development policies has been accompanied by an emphasis on their role in global governance. In global health policy-making circles, the concept of civil society has always been understood as also including corporate interest organisations such as the International Federation of Pharmaceutical Manufacturers and Associations. The distinction between civil society and business is thus becoming increasingly blurred, not only in the context of the current emphasis on global public–private partnerships, but also where civil-society campaigns have been conducted by front organisations for commercial interests ('astro-turf' rather than 'grass roots').[24]

In the 1990s the focus of global development efforts was strongly oriented to the role of nongovernmental organisations in social and economic development. This was complemented by the global focus on philanthropic actors, and has become especially marked by the entrance of new actors with substantial resources, such as the Bill and Melinda Gates Foundation (Gates Foundation). One aspect of this change has been the emphasis on 'global partnerships', which have been especially significant in the field of health. The focus on nongovernmental actors and networks was also reflected in the establishment of the Global Fund, which gave direct representation to industry and nongovernmental organisations, and was deliberately placed outside the formal remit of the United Nations.[25] However, this has resulted in a situation where international public bodies, such as the WHO, have been underrepresented in the governance of these global health partnerships, while the corporate sector has been overrepresented.[27] In spite of high expectations, corporate funding still accounts for only around 3 per cent of financial contributions to the Global Fund.[27]

The engagement of the Gates foundation in global health policy matters has been of particular importance not only by virtue of the magnitude of the resources involved, but also due to its active approach in not only funding, but also seeking influence over organisations and policies.[28] Edwards defines 'philanthrocapitalism' in terms of three distinguishing features:[29] 1) the deployment of substantial resources earned by small number of individuals in the IT and finance sectors; 2) a belief that methods drawn from business can solve social problems, and are superior to the other methods in use in the public sector and in civil society; and 3) a claim that these methods can achieve transformation of society, rather than just increased access to socially-beneficial goods and services. Reconciling the social and financial aims of 'philanthrocapitalists' with the aims of the member states of the WHO is thus not an easy matter, and systemic change involves social movements, politics and the state, which are often ignored by 'philanthrocapitalists'.[30] The tensions between different priorities have been reflected, for example, in criticism by a high-level WHO official of the nature and dominating role of the Gates Foundation in relation to the global governance of malaria research.[31] Questions have also been raised about the Foundation's focus on technological solutions and particular diseases, as well as its emphasis on private the sector in the context of its support for the International Finance Corporation (IFC).[32]

Other new institutions and mechanisms, from the Global Fund and UNITAID, the international drug purchasing facility, to GAVI (the Global Alliance for Vaccines and Immunization), have been especially prominent in networks and partnerships in the area of access to medicines and support for research and development. The Global Fund has utilised the 'debt2health' concept to forego the payment of part of a country's debt in exchange for commitments of support for health programmes.[33] It is also engaging more with the private sector to increase its share of support, and plans to issue products called Exchange Traded Funds to tap into the wealth of the global hedge fund industry.[34] Another current trend is the promotion of AMCs ('Advance Market Commitments') which are favourable to corporate interests and needs and thus have gained substantial corporate support; the World Bank is set to take further responsibilities in relation to the pilot AMC schemes.[35] In terms of global health policies, the first pilot project on pneumococcal vaccines is estimated to cost $1.5 billion. These arrangements have been criticised on the grounds that they offer support for corporate research but are likely to be an ineffective use of public funds.[36]

While some of these arrangements may attract further funds from the corporate sector, they also give further support to the commercialisation of research and development activities as a starting point. In the light of the meagre resources that exist for many health systems and the lack of funding at the national level, there is a danger that the new initiatives become more profitable for the global commercial and consultancy sector than for health. The proliferation of these new initiatives for R&D and the financing of particular products can also be seen as a counterweight to proposals for alternative approaches, such as the R&D Treaty or Prizes.[37] Alternatives include an emphasis on public financing and co-operation, non-profit research trusts, the enhancement of open-source-based licensing requirements and policies for tying pricing to the additional clinical benefits of a new product.[38] However, these alternative mechanisms threaten the current domination of commercial interests in shaping the R&D environment which supports public-private partnerships and stakeholder coalitions, overall policies of tighter intellectual property rights and the extension of monopolies through longer data exclusivity and public subsidies for R&D. It is thus important to question whether some policy options and choices continue to be ignored and undermined in favour of more commercially-driven choices.

The role of private foundations and partnerships alongside the increasing role of the G8 – or G20 – in global health policy-making also raises concerns in terms of legitimacy and accountability. The rise of health issues onto the G8 agenda, which represents a response to the anti-globalisation movement's protests at G8 summits, may not be totally unlike what happened with the World Bank's embracing of health after criticism of structural adjustment policies. The G8's health agenda has been narrow, as reflected in particular in its concentration on initiatives related to infectious and neglected diseases. The G8 has also been explicit and strong in emphasis on the protection of intellectual property rights.[39]

The role of funding, and in particular the funding role of the Gates Foundation, needs to be understood in the context of the magnitude of its contribution to the overall financing of global health, estimated as almost US$9 billion between 1998-2007.[40] WHO extra-budgetary financing has increased substantially: the voluntary share of the WHO's budget for the years 2010-2011 was estimated at $4.5 billion, while the estimated core budget share from Member State dues was just under $1 billion.[41] In other words, more than 80 per cent of the WHO's funding is dependent on voluntary or so called extra-budgetary resources. But private global financiers have their own agendas. The Gates foundation has come under increasing criticism for being focussed on specific technological solutions, and on the allocation of financing to research in the North.[42] New initiatives on financing have also been used predominantly to enhance access to medicines and vaccines: UNITAID utilises air taxes in support of access to treatment for HIV/AIDS, malaria and tuberculosis, and the International Financing Facility for Immunisation raises funds through issuing bonds in capital markets in support of GAVI. The promotion of public funds and new incentives in support of corporate sector research for specific diseases is, however, problematic. A new initiative such as the recent US fast-track voucher can be criticised for essentially providing public subsidies to the global pharmaceutical industry,[43] while being represented as a great and innovative measure for the benefit of the poorest in the developing world. Some of these tensions are reflected explicitly in James Love's critical commentary on 'orphan drugs' legislation:

> The Orphan Drug Act is used to privatize something that is in the public domain, such as an invention paid for by tax dollars, or a patent that has expired. It is particularly important to a company

when they have done the least to deserve the benefit. Companies use the Orphan Drug Act to stop other companies from investing in clinical research, or from bringing new innovative products to market. Orphan Drug exclusivity is broader than patent protection, for a given indication… Lobbying on Orphan Drug Legislation is funded by the pharmaceutical and biotech industry, with significant and often enthusiastic assistance from patients groups, many of which receive a wide variety of financial benefits from industry groups, and which typically represent consumers whose expenses are paid for by third parties, such as taxpayers or employers who pay insurance premiums. The results are legislative programs that make sense only if money isn't scarce. What is needed are more targeted incentives to conduct essential medical research, with greater public accountability.[44]

RECLAIMING GLOBAL HEALTH POLICIES

International agencies and their legitimacy and accountability remain important for global health policies. However, we need to ask what kind of global policies we wish to have in the field of health, as well as what kind of organisations at both global and national levels are likely to be best equipped to realise these aims.

While the United Nations system of one-country-one vote can be criticised, it still remains the most representative global forum for global policy-making, and the most legitimate one because of both its mission and its membership basis of work. The shift to other types of partnerships and coalitions in global health governance has taken place without sufficient attention being paid to how they are formed and operate, blurring accountability and often giving these institutions, coalitions or networks substantial policy influence merely on the basis of their funding and ability to operate at the global level. While recognising the importance of transparency and the role of civil society we also need to be more explicit and clear about the policy aims, priorities and background of those representing civil society and making claims on behalf of it.

Defining the priorities of global health policy has never been an easy task. There is a need for global health policies to go beyond a mere focus on funding and technical guidance for developing countries. There are global common interests in health and health policies, but at the moment these are being undermined by the role of substantial commercial interests in key areas. The re-emergence of the WHO's emphasis on 'health for all', primary health care and social determinants of health, is important, but is unlikely to have broader relevance so long as the WHO continues to be starved of resources and unable to develop the capacity to further these policy aims. Furthermore, so long as global funding continues to be primarily allocated to vertical or disease-based programmes and institutions both within and outside the WHO, substantial moves towards more comprehensive policy approaches at the national level will be unlikely. Moreover, the emphasis on partnerships and corporate philanthropy in global health will continue to blur the boundaries of public and private decision–making, raising further problems of legitimacy and accountability.

NOTES

1   T. Zeltner, D.A. Kessler, A. Martiny and F. Randera, 'Tobacco company strategies to undermine tobacco control activities at the World Health Organisation', Report of the Committee of Experts on Tobacco Industry Document, July 2000, p. iii.

2   J. Braithwaite and P. Drahos, *Global Business Regulation*, Cambridge: Cambridge University Press, 2000, pp. 39–87.

3   G. Cannon, 'Why the Bush administration and the global sugar industry are determined to demolish the 2004 WHO global strategy on diet, physical activity and health', *Public Health and Nutrition*, 7(3), 2004, pp. 369–380; S. Boseley, 'WHO "infiltrated by food industry"', *Guardian*, 9 January 2003; M. Koivusalo and E. Ollila, 'Global health policy', in N. Yeates, ed., *Understanding Global Social Policy*, Bristol: Policy Press, 2008.

4   D. Luff, 'Regulation of health services and international trade law', in A. Mattoo and P. Sauve, eds., *Domestic Regulation and Service Trade Liberalisation*, New York: Oxford University Press, 2003; M. Koivusalo, T. Schrecker and R. Labonte, 'Globalisation and policy space for health and social determinants for health', Institute of Population Health, Globalization And Health Knowledge Network: Research Papers, Globalization and Health Equity, University of Ottawa, 2009; Koivusalo et al., 'Globalisation and policy space'; N. Skala, 'The potential impact of the World Trade Organisation's general agreement on trade in services on health system reform and regulation in the United States', *International Journal of Health Services*, 39(2), 2009.

5   M. Krajewski, 'Public services and trade liberalisation. Mapping the legal framework', *Journal of International Economic Law*, 6(2), 2003, pp. 341–367; D. Fidler, 'Legal review of the General Agreement on Trade in Services (GATS) from a health policy perspective', Globalisation, Trade and Health Working Paper Series, World Health Organisation, Geneva, 2003.

6   S. Sell, 'The global IP upward ratchet, anti–counterfeiting and piracy enforcement efforts: the state of play', 2008, available from: http://www. twnside.org.sg; S. Sell, 'From Forum-shifters to Shape-shifters: Rulemaking and Enforcement in Intellectual Property', Paper prepared for International Studies Association Convention, New York, 15-19 February 2009.

7   K. Lee and H. Goodman, 'Global Policy Networks: The propagation of health

care financing reform since the 1980's', in K. Lee, K. Buse and S. Fustukian, eds., *Health Policy in a Globalising World*, Cambridge: Cambridge University Press, 2002.

8   J.A. Walsh and K.S. Warren, 'Selective primary health care. An interim strategy for diseases control in developing countries', *New England Journal of Medicine*, 301(18), 1979; J-P. Unger and J.R. Killingsworth, 'Selective primary health care: a critical review of methods and results', *Social Science and Medicine*, 22(10), 1986.

9   G.A. Cornia, R. Jolly and F. Stewart, *Adjustment With a Human Face: Protecting the Vulnerable and Promoting Growth. A Study by UNICEF*, Oxford University Press: Oxford, 1987.

10   M. Koivusalo and E. Ollila, *Making a Healthy World. Agencies, Actors and Policies in International Health*, London: Zed Books, 1997.

11   T. Brown, M. Cueto and E. Fee, 'The World Health Organisation and the transition from International to Global Public health', *American Journal of Public Health*, 96(1), 2006; Koivusalo and Ollila, *Making a Healthy World*.

12   Koivusalo and Ollila, *Making a Healthy World*; J. Lister, *Health Policy Reform: Driving the Wrong Way. A Critical Guide to the Health Reform Industry*, Enfield: Middlesex University Press, 2005.

13   World Bank, *World Development Report. Investing in Health*, Washington: World Bank, 1993.

14   WHO, *World Health Report. Health Systems: Improving Performance*, Geneva: WHO, 2000.

15   CSDH, *Closing the gap in a generation: health equity through action on the social determinants of health. Final report of the Commission on social determinants of health*, Geneva: WHO, 2008.

16   WHA, 'Reducing health inequities through action on the social determinants of health' (WHA 62.14) and 'Primary Health care, including health system strengthening' (WHA 62.12) from WHA, 22 May 2009, Geneva, WHO, 2009.

17   S. Gupta, B. Hammond and E. Swanson, 'Setting the seven development goals', *OECD Observer*, 23, 2000, available from http://www.oecdobserver.org.

18   A. Grover, 'Report of the Special Rapporteur on the right of everyone to the enjoyment of the highest attainable standard of physical and mental health', United Nations, General Assembly, A/HRC/11/12, 31 March 2009.

19   E. Ollila, 'Global health priorities – priorities of the wealthy?', *Globalisation and Health*, 1(6), 2005, available from http://www.globalizationandhealth.com.

20   A. Costello and D. Osrin, 'The case for a new Global Fund for maternal, neonatal and child survival', *Lancet*, 366(9485), 13-19 Aug 2005; Leading NGOs, 'Leading NGOs call for international action to combat epidemic non-communicable diseases', Press Release, 19 May 2009, available from http://www.world-heart-federation.org.

21   L. Garret, 'The challenge of global health', *Foreign Affairs*, January/February, 2007.

22   M. Lewis, 'Addressing the challenge of HIV/AIDS: macroeconomic, fiscal and

institutional issues', Working paper no. 58, Center for Global Development, 2005.

23   G. Ooms, V. van Damme, B. Baker, P. Zeitz and T. Schrecker, 'The "diagonal" approach to Global Fund financing: a cure for the broader malaise of health systems?', *Globalization and Health*, 4(6), 2008.

24   M. Koivusalo and M. Mackintosh, 'Global public action in health and pharmaceutical policies: politics and policy priorities', IKD (Innovative Knowledge Development) Working Paper 45, 2009, available from http://www.open.ac.uk.

25   E. Ollila, 'Health-related public-private partnerships and the United Nations', in B. Deacon, E. Ollila, M. Koivusalo and P. Stubbs, eds., *Global Social Governance. Themes and Prospects*, Helsinki: Ministry for Foreign Affairs, 2004; E. Ollila, 'Restructuring global health policy-making: the role of global public-private partnerships', in M. Mackintosh and M. Koivusalo, eds., *Commercialisation of Health Care. Global and Local Dynamics and Policy Responses*, Basingstoke: Palgrave-Macmillan, 2005.

26   A. Harmer and K. Buse, 'Seven habits of highly effective global public-private partnerships: practice and potential', *Social Science and Medicine*, 64(2), 2007; K. Buse and A. Harmer, 'Power to the partners? The politics of public-private partnerships', *Development*, 47(2), 2004.

27   T. Anderson, 'Global Fund looks to boost private sector contributions', *Lancet*, 373(9675), 9 May 2009.

28   D. McCoy, G. Kembhavi, J. Patel and A. Luintel, 'The Bill and Melinda Gates Foundation's grant-making programme for global health', *Lancet*, 373(9675), 9 May 2009; A-E. Birn, 'Gate's grandest challenge: transcending technology as public health ideology', *Lancet*, 366(9484), 6-12 August 2005.

29   M. Edwards, *Just Another Emperor? The Myths and Realities of Philanthrocapitalism*, New York: Demos and the Young Foundation, 2008.

30   M. Edwards, 'Philanthrocapitalism: After the goldrush', 20 March 2008, p. 32, available from http://www.opendemocracy.com.

31   D.G. McNeil, 'Gates Foundation's influence criticized', *New York Times,* 16 February 2008.

32   McCoy et al., 'The Bill and Melinda Gates Foundation's grant-making programme'.

33   AusAID and Global Fund, 'Australia converts commercial debts to Indonesia into health programmes', Press Release, 28 May 2009, available from: http://www.theglobalfund.org.

34   T. Anderson, 'Global Fund looks to boost private sector contributions', *Lancet*, 373(1594), 2009.

35   World Bank, 'Funding New Vaccines To Save Millions Of Lives. World Bank to Provide Financial Platform for Pilot Vaccine Program', Press Release No. 2009/296/CFP, 3 April 2009.

36   D. Light, 'Making practical markets for vaccines. Why I decided that the Center for Global Development Report, Making markets for vaccines, offers poor advice to government and foundation leaders', *PLoS Med*, 2(10), 2005; A.K. Farlow, D.W. Light, R.T. Mahoney, and R. Widdus, 'Concerns regarding

the Center for Global Development Report "Making markets for vaccines"', Submission to Commission on intellectual property rights, innovation and public health, WHO, 29 April 2005; L. Gadot, 'Advance market commitments: Are they worth the hype?', May 2008, available from http://www.accessmed-msf.org.

37   T. Hubbard and J. Love, 'A new trade framework for global healthcare R&D', *PLoS Biol*, 2(2), 2004; N. Dentico and N. Ford, 'The courage to change the rules: a proposal for an essential health R&D treaty', *PLoS Med*, 2(2), 2005; J. Love and T. Hubbard, 'The big idea: prizes to stimulate R&D for new medicines', *Chicago Kent Law Review*, 82(3), 2007.

38   D. Baker, 'The benefits and savings of publicly-funded clinical trials of prescription drugs', Center for Economic Policy and Research, March, 2008; D. Baker, 'A free market solution to prescription drug crises', *International Journal of Health Services*, 34(3), 2003; A. Jayadev and J. Stiglitz, 'Two ideas to increase innovation and reduce pharmaceutical costs and prices', *Health Affairs*, 28(1), 2009; S.M. Maurer, A. Rai and A. Sali, 'Finding cures for tropical diseases: is open source the answer?', *PLoS Med*, 1(3), 2004.

39   G8, 'Growth and responsibility in the world economy. Summit declaration', G8 Agenda for Global Growth and Stability, Heiligendamm, 7 June 2007, available from http://www.g-8.de

40   McCoy et al., 'The Bill and Melinda Gates Foundation's grant-making programme'.

41   WHO, *Proposed Programme Budget 2010-2011*, Geneva: WHO, 2009, available from: http://www.who.int.

42   McCoy et al., 'The Bill and Melinda Gates Foundation's grant-making programme'; Birn, 'Gate's grandest challenge'.

43   T. Anderson, 'Novartis under fire for accepting new reward for old drug', *Lancet*, 373(9673), 25 April 2009; FDA, 'Guidance for Industry Tropical Diseases Industry Priority Review Vouchers. Draft Guidance', October 2008, available from: http://www.fda.gov.

44   J. Love, 'Brief note on the abuse of Orphan Drug programs in creating monopolies', 5 January 1999, available from http://www.cptech.org.

BUILDING A COMPREHENSIVE PUBLIC HEALTH MOVEMENT: LEARNING FROM THE HIV/AIDS MOBILISATION

SANJAY BASU

In 1978, world leaders assembled in Almaty (formerly Alma Ata) in Kazakhstan to sign an international declaration highlighting the importance of primary healthcare services around the world. The result was a landmark document in the history of public health: the 'Alma Ata Declaration' – an agreement of WHO member states to implement 'health for all' by the year 2000.

Many have regarded the Alma Ata Declaration as the most important public health document to be agreed upon in the last century. The Declaration not only indicated states' commitment to health access in a global context, but also used the broad World Health Organization definition of health, as 'a state of complete physical, mental and social well-being and not merely the absence of disease or infirmity'.[1] The definition affirmed health as a human right, including socioeconomic well-being as part of health, and stated that health equality was a major goal of member states, identifying governments as responsible for protecting their citizens' health with the support of the international community.

The Alma Ata Declaration defined 'primary care' comprehensively, stating that its purpose was to address 'the main health problems in the community, providing promotive, preventive, curative and rehabilitative services accordingly,' based on 'the application of the relevant results of social, biomedical and health services research and public health experience'. Primary care included 'education concerning prevailing health problems and the methods of preventing and controlling them; promotion of food supply and proper nutrition; an adequate supply of safe water and basic sanitation; maternal and child health care, including family planning; immunisation against the major infectious diseases; prevention and control of locally endemic diseases; appropriate treatment of common diseases and injuries; and provision of essential drugs'. Primary health care 'should be sustained by integrated, functional and mutually supportive referral systems, leading to the progressive improvement of comprehensive health care for all, and giving priority to those most in need'.[2]

While this landmark document set out a bold vision for the future, it was unfortunately followed by decades of disappointment. In spite of the progressive agenda outlined in the Declaration, it was later revealed that representatives from five wealthy nations, including the United States, had met secretly during the conference to define a 'real' agenda, consisting of the promotion of maternal and child health at the expense of comprehensive care.[3] This was thought more realistic and would avoid excessive commitments of funds from donor to recipient countries. In line with this narrower focus, over the next few years the comprehensive definition of primary care adopted in the Alma Ata Declaration evolved into a 'minimum package' of 'essential' services and goods.[4] The list of essentials was codified in World Health Organization documents, reducing broad arrays of services, pharmaceuticals, and patient support systems to much shorter lists of very basic, cheap and often sub-standard medications and medical protocols, excluding numerous common diseases, conditions and public health needs.

The quest to build new primary care infrastructure after Alma Ata was therefore largely unsuccessful. As part of the initiatives created after Alma Ata, numerous 'health posts' appeared in poor countries, typically single-room shacks staffed by untrained members of the community conscripted as health assistants. Limited coverage of local diseases, and limited or improper treatment of patients, produced few significant benefits in terms of morbidity or mortality. Many posts lasted for short periods of time; others were related to worsening health outcomes as untrained providers misused medications or even turned public facilities into private clinics. Some countries did, thankfully, experience reductions in crude death rates and improvements in life expectancy over the past few decades since Alma-Ata; however, this appears more related to general improvements in living conditions and income among the populations, rather than enhancements in actual primary healthcare delivery systems.[5]

An undemocratic framework

In the years following Alma Ata, limited investment in primary care was accompanied by the public health community's creation of aggregate measures of disability and disease (disability-adjusted life years and quality-adjusted life years). These measures of public health programme efficacy were used to assess the health or economic returns to be expected from investments in various health programmes.[6] However, such analyses often resulted in limited investments in comprehensive primary care health services. As a result of their focus on immediate benefits and costs, cost-effectiveness analyses failed to account for the down-stream consequences of disease, or of the failure to make needed public health investments – consequences in the shape of the transmission of diseases to others (for communicable diseases) or in terms of the social and economic consequences of leaving diseases untreated until a public health problem became more severe (and potentially more costly).[7] Critical assessments of the new field of cost-effectiveness analysis in public health also revealed that the aggregate measures used in these analyses, subject to numerous assumptions and subjective judgments, were difficult to calculate with reasonable reproducibility by different analysts, and usually had weak statistical validity.[8] Nevertheless, these 'metrics' became the basis for an industry of theses by international development banks, academic groups and government agencies, giving aggregate measures of health system impact greater political weight than direct measures of population health and health system efficacy (such as waiting times for essential treatments, the availability of qualified doctors in rural populations, or the number of households with access to clean water).[9]

Assessments using aggregate indicators and cost-effectiveness measures meant that communities were often unable to engage with the evaluation of their own health systems. The assessment of health system quality was conducted through convoluted but not validated models produced primarily by American market analysts whose previous experience was in designing privatised health systems.[10] Aggregate indicators often produced nonsensical results, such as a WHO health system ranking method that rated China's as equivalent to Haiti's, or that gave high ratings to systems in which health outcomes and patient evaluations indicated very poor access and service quality.[11]

Key discussions in public health became divorced from community concerns. Rather than discussing the serious failure to implement the Alma Ata mandate, debates were focused on such things as whether donor funding would generate inflation, though there was no economic evidence to support the inflationary targets adopted, and public health spending was often decreasing or stagnant, rather than increasing.[12] Much of the concern was about providing 'returns on investment' for rich-country donors, often by accelerating mineral extraction or labour supply from poorer countries.[13]

The emergence of HIV

While these discussions preoccupied the public health community, governments failed to react urgently to what was to become the greatest public health catastrophe of our time, the AIDS pandemic, and the resurgence of tuberculosis that has followed in its wake in many parts of the world.[14] By the early 1980s it had become clear that a new public health challenge had emerged, targeting those most socially marginalised. Gay men had been reported to have 'Gay-Related Immune Deficiency' (GRID), later renamed 'Acquired Immune Deficiency Syndrome' (AIDS) as Haitians and injection drug users were added to the cluster of the feared and ostracised members of society who were thought to be vectors of this pathology.[15] Gay men, already mobilised from earlier fights for civil rights, and with relatively more social and economic capital than other affected groups, created new activist organisations to advocate for health care, argue against stigmatising and pathologising rhetoric that surrounded their association with this disease, and influence the course of medication development to treat it. They protested until they were accepted into the US Food and Drug Administration's committees, creating a new mechanism to allow experimental drug access for dying patients.[16] They also joined forces with anti-apartheid activists as it became evident that migrants and women in many regions of sub-Saharan Africa were heavily affected.[17]

While some in Hollywood would characterise AIDS as a disease that could 'strike anyone', the reality was that the human immunodeficiency virus (HIV) causing AIDS targeted those who were poorest, and who led the least socially stable lives. Academics struggled to find biological explanations for this highly skewed distribution of disease, finding that those with poor treatment for prior sexually-transmitted infections were at high risk, and attributing differences in HIV risk to differences in a variety of nutritional, sexual, regional or other factors.[18] But these proximal explanations failed to explain the full extent of variation in the disease's incidence; the focus on 'behaviour' neglected the economic and social determinants of infection.

In reality, the top epidemiological predictor for HIV infection around the world was low income. This meant that those most vulnerable to HIV infection did not significantly benefit from a model focused exclusively on education,[19] which assumed people living in poverty were sufficiently able to control the circumstances of their lives to avoid infection. Numerous surveys have established that those most at risk for HIV often do know how the virus is transmitted, and even the highest prevalence areas have sexual partnership rates lower than in many regions of the US and UK.[20] Sex was not as much the issue as the context in which sex occurred. In the South African mining sector, for example, a group of psychologists recently declared that the norm of 'masculinity' (expressed through soliciting prostitutes) in South African 'culture' increased the risk of HIV transmission among miners.[21] But to identify 'culture' as the problem would ignore the perspective of the miners themselves. In the context of a 42 per cent injury rate, it would be natural to think that catching a disease that could kill a person ten years in the future would be less pressing than trying to gain some control over life – or perhaps just enjoying life in some minor way (e.g. through alcohol or sex) before getting crushed by falling rock. But the scientists labelled miners as 'in denial', asserting that miners' 'low self-esteem' could be responsible for their increased risk of HIV infection. A similar survey among prostitutes labelled them 'liars' (in 'denial' of their agency) when they attributed their prostitution to lack of education and job opportunities, and to coercion.[22]

The error involved in seeing the issue as 'cultural' soon became clear from the failure of 'educational' solutions. Even after messages were adapted to 'local norms', 'providing information about health risks changes the behaviour of, at most, one in four people – generally those who are more affluent and better educated' according to a systematic review of evidence in the *British Medical Journal* (*BMJ*).[23] Even if the best-performing education initiatives had covered the entire globe by 2005, such programmes would still have left a rate of transmission equivalent to 1.5 million new cases a year, according to the public health community's most advanced models.[24]

What the public health community ignored is that the background of increasing HIV transmission was one of neo-liberalism – a context where short-term financial gains through deregulated trade agreements were privileged over long-term investment and the ability of most people to secure a decent livelihood. The increased rates of HIV transmission across southern Africa, East Asia, Eastern Europe and Latin America were strongly correlated with increases in forced migration, which most often occurred when rural agricultural sectors were destroyed following the liberalisation of markets and the subsequent drop in primary commodity prices, leading (mostly male) labourers to find work in urban centres and leave their families behind.[25] In sectors of southern Africa, miners housed in all-male barracks for months at a time worked six days a week, were given alcohol to 'keep them happy' (or keep them from rebelling) on the seventh – when intoxication and depression lead to the solicitation of prostitutes.[26] When sick with AIDS-related infections, the men were sent home to die, and found that either their wives had left them to find a better source of income and support, had entered prostitution or other risky professions to generate income, or were waiting for their husbands to return home (and infect them with HIV). The 'rural women's epidemic' of HIV – that is the sub-epidemic of women in rural zones who were infected by their migrant male husbands – is not so surprising in this context, even though it was considered a public health puzzle for years.

Today, HIV remains a disease of the least powerful. We often describe it as focused on Africa, but it is not all Africans who are at risk, or all non-Africans who are not at risk. Indeed, nearly one in twenty citizens of Washington D.C. have HIV, and the concentration of HIV among and within African states varies widely, primarily according to income level.[27] The dramatic reduction in mortality resulting from HIV in the US and Europe has been due to the rapid expansion of antiretroviral drug access since the late 1990s, and the integration of these highly effective medicines into primary care systems; the rate of new HIV infections remained stable while mortality from HIV plummeted in the late 1990s, while it was rising exponentially in other nations.[28]

Civil society movements

Although the WHO and other international agencies, as well as domestic ones in the US and elsewhere, were resistant to responding to the epidemic, ordinary men and women in South Africa, Thailand, Brazil, the US and Europe did react, creating a community-based movement that forced a major shift in public health funding, health system infrastructure, and notions of accountability in public health. Facilitated in part by improved Internet access and related communications resources, a massive movement of 'AIDS activists' was formed, primarily advocating that HIV-infected people themselves should have a say in how they are treated by their communities and the public health system. While this was initially a push for AIDS services, the populations hardest hit by the disease were often also ill-served by health systems because of who they were: drug users; men who have sex with men; racial minorities; women without social, educational or employment opportunities; and the poor. AIDS activists began a large movement to call for the expansion of health services in general, focused on those most marginalised, and for health systems to meet the specific needs of the communities who used them. The idea was that HIV was not a special disease, but a symbol of neglect and inequality – the most recent, and worst, manifestation of undemocratic decision-making about who should have access to health services and what it means to have a right to health.[29]

With a focus on human rights, and with a large public movement embarrassing public officials at meetings, international economic conferences, and presidential election campaign stops,[30] the institutional global health

agenda shifted from a 'minimum package' of health services to determining
how best to use a public health approach to scale-up services and meet the
grave need for care that was highlighted by the millions of HIV-related
deaths between the late 1980s and the turn of the century. In the past
10 years, the most representative instance of this shift was the debate on
antiretroviral access in poor countries. AIDS activists returned to the Alma
Ata definition of primary care, indicating that the control of locally endemic
or epidemic diseases was part of primary care. Given the astoundingly high
prevalence of HIV in many communities (over 1 in 5 adults in much of
South Africa),[31] this would assuredly include HIV treatment. But the calls
for wider availability of AIDS treatment encountered the same reaction from
those who favoured 'selective primary care' in the years after Alma Ata.

A number of arguments were advanced to indicate that antiretrovirals
should be available only to the wealthy. The first was that prevention
approaches would be more cost-effective than treatment, and a dichotomy
was established between the two.[32] But it soon became evident that prevention
initiatives were of limited benefit in many regions, as people perceived the
disease as a death sentence, and had little motivation to present themselves
to health centres that would not help them but simply provide patronising
safe sex messages, often too late to change health outcomes.[33] Furthermore,
the interventions often assumed that people lived in circumstances in which
'behaviour change' was a simple matter of education, rather than a complex
set of constraints involving gender, race and class inequality, including
migrant labour, sex work, and other conditions of survival that limited
people's priorities and control.[34]

A second argument was that the pharmaceutical industry could not reduce
drug prices, as this would discourage research and development.[35] Yet the
activist movement revealed that the prices of pharmaceuticals were several
times larger than their production cost, and that much of the research was
taxpayer-funded. The industry was spending 27 per cent of its profits on
marketing and 11 per cent on research and development, even as it ranked
highest in the world in terms of profits as a percentage of revenue (three
times the Fortune 500 average).[36]

A final argument was that poor countries had such limited infrastructure, or
the intellectual capacities of their citizens was too low, to permit the successful
implementation of medication. In 2001 the director of the US Agency
for International Development, Andrew Natsios, said that antiretroviral
medicines were inappropriate in Africa because Africans 'don't know what
Western time is… Many people in Africa have never seen a clock or a
watch their entire lives. And if you say, one o'clock in the afternoon, they

do not know what you are talking about.'[37] Pilot programmes, spearheaded most prominently by the non-governmental organisations Partners in Health and Doctors Without Borders, soon contradicted these ignorant and racist assumptions. People living with HIV in the poorest settings were able to adhere to medications at rates far better than most patients in the US or Europe, had sustained success in their treatment, and could be treated through public health approaches such as the delivery and monitoring of care by community healthcare workers, which also enhanced overall primary care delivery, besides HIV care.[38]

Because AIDS activists pushed themselves into government meetings, international development conferences, and medical research boards, a shift occurred in what was considered prudent and possible. The resulting '3-by-5 Initiative', a WHO programme to initiate antiretroviral treatment of 3 million people living with HIV by 2005, galvanised this shift. What was remarkable about the 3-by-5 initiative was its support for expanding beyond a 'minimum package' to programmes that would support the expansion of healthcare facilities and greater access to Alma Ata-like primary care in resource-denied settings. The 3-by-5 programme focused on concrete operational guidelines and high-quality management, transparency and accountability to the community, which not only meant that attention to a disease-specific problem was realized in effective protocols and care, but that this initiative would lead to broader improvements to the general health system. This involved building medical schools in poor countries, developing new hospitals, training providers in general primary care, and ensuring strong systems for manufacturing and delivering medications. The move brought previously defunct health centres back into reliable service.[39] The Global Fund for AIDS, Tuberculosis, and Malaria and similar initiatives galvanised by AIDS activists harnessed the attention brought by HIV/AIDS to expand the type of primary care called for at Alma Ata.[40]

Furthermore, a system was established whereby civil society could actively monitor progress or corruption, often by creating large email listservs from which community members could report to distant activists about problems in their local healthcare system. When health delivery systems failed, advocates were able to address the issues immediately and get the attention of the highest levels of administration to rectify failing systems and protect human rights. The recent failure to deliver medications to rural clinics in Africa, for example, was reported to listservs in the US and UK, resulting in an overnight massive lobbying effort in Washington DC; this resulted in improvements in the design of a pharmaceutical distribution programme that affected not only HIV drugs, but all general clinic medications, which had been previously mismanaged for years.[41] A comparable level of transparency and accountability, resulting from public scrutiny, has not been seen elsewhere in public health.

Conflict over control – the creation of an AIDS backlash

The galvanising power of 3-by-5 and related initiatives has been unwelcome to those keen on returning to the 'minimum package' approach. Focusing on HIV/AIDS, and in particular on HIV treatment, has been declared unwise and unsustainable. The argument has been that HIV 'competes with' other public health priorities, taking funding away from other health problems. This is said to funnel investments into a 'bottomless pit' of HIV treatment, when greater funding for HIV prevention would be a more cost-effective and strategic choice. The fact that HIV funding commitments are extensive, and have increased rapidly in recent years (including but not limited to support for anti-retroviral therapy), is used as a basis for these arguments.[42]

Empirical data analyses, however, have found the opposite—that HIV has brought in new funding, rather than diverting resources from other diseases; that the increase in funding for HIV corresponds to the burden of disease in an appropriate manner that is highly consistent and actually conservative with respect to other conditions in terms of morbidity and mortality per capita; that much funding has been displaced *from* HIV/AIDS to other causes (indeed, HIV-related fundraising nearly tripled overall health system funding, which was previously stagnant); and that improvements to health systems have often occurred through the comprehensive approaches of HIV programmes.[43]

Many critics of AIDS programming and funding refuse to acknowledge the dire state of public health in aid-recipient countries before this wave of public scrutiny,[44] when services were not transparent, frequently inefficient, and sometimes outright corrupt (with only $0.37 of every donated $1.00 going into actual healthcare delivery among African countries, on average).[45] While AIDS programmes suffer from deficiencies as well, the heightened role and capacity of civil society in providing oversight and scrutiny of the HIV/AIDS field has cast a bright light on many of these problems as they occur. Recent detailed reports, including both a systematic study of funding streams and case studies from Argentina, Brazil, Dominican Republic, Uganda, Zambia and Zimbabwe, have found that HIV initiatives have successfully expanded systems of reliable health supplies, trained and retained skilled workers for general public health benefit, and improved infrastructure as well as governance.[46] Improvements in HIV programmes have corresponded to declines in out-of-pocket expenditures for patients and a rise in per capita health funds for general health around the world. Each 1 per cent increase in funding to the US President's Emergency Plan for AIDS Relief corresponds to a 10.1 per cent increase in the rate at which out-of-pocket health expenditures have declined in affected countries, after correcting for changes in per capita income. Each 1 per cent increase in Global Fund funding has also corresponded to a 7.9 per cent increase in the rate at which out-of-pocket health expenditures are declining and a 16.5 per cent rise in the rate at which per capita funds for general health are increasing after correcting for changes in per capita income, suggesting a magnified impact of HIV funds in terms of general system benefits.[47]

Many HIV programmes have often also offered transparent, accountable, and measurable results, with community-based structures for needs assessment and resource delivery, whereas many other areas of health and development have been plagued by a dearth of clear plans, accountability structures, and measurable targets, and have a history of poor management and weak support for infrastructure development. In terms of the relative balance of funding within AIDS, HIV prevention has had far more funding since the beginning of the epidemic; the World Bank has invested nearly twice as much in prevention as in care and treatment.[48] Yet antiretroviral therapy has shown more dramatic effects on national mortality levels in the countries hardest hit by the epidemic.[49] Furthermore, in the absence of a safe and effective vaccine or microbicide, AIDS treatment has itself been modelled as an HIV prevention intervention, because it can suppress viral load, which effectively curtails transmission,[50] disrupting the false dichotomy between treatment and prevention that has been the hallmark of current debates. Data indicate that where AIDS treatment has been introduced, more people have come forward to learn about their serostatus and about personal protective measures, and that HIV funding has been effectively used to build the first medical schools and health centres in regions previously devoid of trained local providers and services.[51]

It is understandable, however, that the attention received by HIV has been met with resentment, and the concern that health programmes have become, or will become, excessively focused on HIV. This has led to a call to move to 'SWAps', or 'sector-wide approaches' to public health. The acronym refers to the idea that it is best for donors to support the 'general public health system', and should in theory be a more comprehensive approach to advancing primary care as conceived in Alma Ata. This call appeals to people with positive and progressive agendas. But the term has been manipulated to support a political agenda that can often actually undermine public health programmes, reducing donor commitments over time and returning to an era of economic development theory that compromises public health. The reality is that comprehensive care, driven by community needs, has been a priority for HIV/AIDS advocates, as for global health advocates generally, from early calls in the 1980s and 1990s for a national healthcare system in the US to current demands from leading advocates in the field to renew the global call for 'health for all'.[52] SWAps, by contrast, have been programmes devised and supported by international development banks, directing funds from donors directly to ministries of health. This approach sounds more targeted to population needs, and is intended to address issues of fragmented aid and avoid favouring issues that happen to be popular with donors by giving more power to aid recipients. In reality, however, such shifts in power have not been found to occur in practice. The national plans are actually constructed largely by donors, with a focus on the management of health ministries, not the health burdens experienced by communities.[53] The plans often involve initiatives to privatise or limit health programmes. Ministries of Health continue to be divided from the communities who receive their medical and public health services, often as a result of class divides between elite government ministers and poorer community members. The actual content and results of SWAps have not been transparent and have excluded civil society participation.[54] These factors have resulted in significant diversions of funds away from service provision to vague administrative activities, resulting in troubling medical system failures.[55]

This data indicate that extreme 'horizontal' projects (programmes for the 'general health system', or a 'basic minimum package') can be just as ineffective as extreme 'vertical' (disease-specific) initiatives. SWAps unfortunately have yet to set clearly transparent targets that can be monitored and critiqued by outsiders, and there are no data on their effectiveness, while we do have data on the risk they pose to actual on-the-ground medical services when they divert funds from tangible existing medical care programmes.[56] Many funds claimed to be for 'health system' uses are diverted into ineffective, inefficient funding streams, which are often misused for poor educational initiatives, bureaucratic events, and salaries for those who operate development consulting programmes, rather than for training local healthcare workers, building infrastructure, and providing needed community-based services.[57]

Those advocating a retreat from the HIV-style of programme construction and calling for general health system development are also often concerned about 'sustainability'. Arguments about the sustainability of healthcare financing have not been met, as they well might, with the rebuttal that the living standards of rich countries would often be 'unsustainable' without the labour and resources of the poorest nations.[58] The reality is that poor health systems will not be 'sustainable' at any level until we address critical issues of health worker training and retention, comprehensive public health and medical services, and reliable and affordable supplies and pharmaceuticals.[59] We are in truth faced with the choice of expanding the HIV effort to continue developing comprehensive care systems, or regressing to an era in which the idea of 'sustainability' is used to justify minimal or no services. It is not 'sustainable' for societies to avoid treating major diseases that can lead to social collapse and result in turmoil and ruin.

The sterile dichotomy that pits HIV/AIDS policies against general health systems development fails to realise that all health systems need both focus and breadth. Without continued and sustained focus on disease-specific standards of care and treatment, many millions of the poorest and most marginalised will die due to substandard medical management, inadequate measures to meet resource allocation needs, training demands, and detailed assessments to evaluate the critical bottlenecks and failures in health systems. This has already occurred with the transfer of funds from tuberculosis programmes to SWAps in Zambia, for example, resulting in grave health outcomes for the population. [60] It is also manifest in the significant epidemics of drug-resistant tuberculosis resulting from medical mismanagement and inadequate resource allocation to achieve sufficiently high standards of medical practice in many poor communities.[61] The need is for both vertical protocols and stronger primary care across the board. We will miss a historic opportunity to build functioning health systems in some of the poorest countries in the world if HIV is not recognised as a social indicator to redistribute capital and healthcare decision-making power to those actually affected by the greatest burden of disease.

Plans for the Future

A critical lesson from HIV/AIDS has been that community mobilisation and attention to global health is capable of dramatically expanding the availability of funds and their appropriate use, as well as what is considered 'possible' in resource-denied settings in terms of public health and medical delivery programmes. This can move us from an era in which disease advocates compete for the scraps that are left after development consultants and ministries have filtered away the majority of funds, to an era in which advocates can jointly demand that funds, and the strategies for using them, meet actual patients needs. We have learned from many programmes that disease-specific protocols are necessary from a medical perspective, to ensure proper training of healthcare workers and monitoring of performance, to produce efficient budgets and supply chains, and to keep track of outcomes, all while improving fundamental services such as nutritional support, medical education, and physical infrastructure.[62] We have also learned that the 'minimum package' approach has marginalised large numbers of sick people, favouring the lives of groups considered, by religious or moralistic standards, as 'more worthy' of care (particularly young children) and removing care for those who are socially marginalised and at most risk of disability and death.[63] Finally, we have learned that common conceptions of health promotion and prevention are often based on assumptions made too quickly: in particular, the idea that education alone is sufficient when people have little real ability to act on the sources of risk in their lives;[64] and the idea that prevention rather than treatment saves healthcare dollars. In reality, prevention generally can reduce suffering, but by extending life does not save money; there is the false belief that somehow diseases and risks will be prevented and people will live long lives, but their bodies will magically fall apart at an old age without getting ill and costing health systems money. The reality is that deaths averted from infectious diseases or heart conditions in working-age adults result in costlier deaths from cancer or neurological diseases in old age.

Our goal is not simply to avert death, nor to save money for its own sake – it is to reduce human suffering. Hence, we should orient medical care to reduce suffering (sometimes saving costs by focusing on palliation rather than chemotherapy in old age, for example), and improve living conditions to minimise the likelihood of suffering and allow for enjoyable lives to be lived for reasonable durations. Such a goal would return to the original Alma Ata definition of health. To achieve a reduction in suffering and determine what patient priorities are for reducing suffering, and how to redistribute funds from rich areas with a plethora of options to avoid suffering to people with few options, we should ask the affected persons themselves what their priorities are. This has been among the most valuable lessons of the HIV activism movement: that those most likely to suffer should be intimately involved in determining how public health systems should reduce their suffering.

The recent call for the withdrawal or redeployment of AIDS funds essentially repeats the mistakes of history, proposing to retrace the path of Alma Ata's failure rather than taking the opportunity to achieve Alma Ata's mandate. The call to limit and shift funding would in reality allow governments to renege on their prior commitments to global public health.[65] Recent analyses have shown that in difficult financial times, public health funding for major epidemic diseases must be maintained to avoid disastrous resurgence.[66] In the current financial crisis, the temptation will be strong for governments and funding agencies to simply raid AIDS funding to sustain initiatives that appear more general but may have questionable population impact; the goal should be sustaining and increasing resources for community-based health programmes overall and community-based decision-making in particular. Even if no monies are diverted from AIDS, donors are already cutting back on promised resources to public health programmes, while increasing evidence indicates that deficit spending on health in times of economic downturn actually produces greater social protections and less economic destabilisation than cutting budgets for short-term savings.[67]

It is often said that the health of the global economy is dependent on the health of its people, and no one can expect strong economies without healthy workers and with an avoidance of the rising tertiary health costs resulting from poor primary care access and excessive services for the elderly, or when diseases have been allowed to progress to expensive end-stages requiring hospitalisation.[68] This is true, but the other question is what we want our society to look like: is having a good economy the end result, or is this part of a larger effort to make life more enjoyable? If the latter, then good health must be seen as its own end, and it should be seen as perverse that we must appeal to financial gain as a reason to fund health.

The time is now for a 'new deal' on global health, which builds upon the successes in AIDS to revive the movement for comprehensive primary care focused on patient decision-making. We have the basis for civil society participation to achieve a form of direct democracy in bringing patient communities into planning and debates about what health services should look like. Realigning our focus around an agenda to prioritize health and allow it to be patient-based, rather than based on development theories that have demonstrably failed the poorest and least powerful, should be our mandate.

In looking at concrete examples of how HIV programmes have been successful at achieving this goal, we can see common trends in the design and implementation of successful programmes. First, the most successful HIV programmes have critically involved community decision-making (not just 'participation'), particularly the involvement of affected patients in constructing programme logistics.[69] Analogously, the programmes that have been least oriented towards community voices and priorities seem to be ineffective. For example, a recent World Bank funding offer called for programmes to reduce HIV-related stigma in western Nepal. Community groups were excluded from the meeting, but a coalition of public health workers and NGOs discussed the proposal and observed that many patients in the region did not agree with the central premise that stigma-reduction programmes should be the point of focus of new healthcare programmes.

Rather, they argued in a series of community meetings that HIV stigma-reduction programmes, rather than focusing on renovating a local hospital to care for both HIV and non-HIV-infected patients, were actually pathologising HIV and focusing so much on HIV patients that the public had the misperception that only HIV patients could receive care at local clinics. Furthermore, the stigma-focused programmes were making it harder for HIV-infected persons to receive treatment, as the publicity around HIV on billboards and radio stations made it ironically more embarrassing and shameful to enter testing centres. While the World Bank ignored this information and proceeded with their programme, a group of local healthcare providers and members of the public have worked to renovate the local hospital and to 'mainstream' HIV as one of many diagnoses that are treated as a primary care condition in general health clinics.

Similarly, programmes in Haiti which have involved community healthcare workers, or lay members of the public trained to provide services to those who are distant from central clinics and hospitals, have allowed for a greater patient voice in priority-setting. The HIV programmes in the central plateau of Haiti have thus been able to expand into programmes that address fundamental systemic causes of HIV infection − particularly women's lack of access to credit for their own businesses, which resulted in dependency on men to provide them with basic income, sometimes in exchange for sex. Creating a local 'pro-poor' bank has helped reduce the risk of HIV among women by facilitating their access to credit. Programmes in nutrition, reducing indoor air pollution and respiratory diseases from wood-burning stoves, and providing local jobs to avoid migrancy, have similarly resulted from community-based HIV initiatives in other settings.[70]

The common principle is to remove power from those who have traditionally harboured it in ministries and institutions far from actual health problems, and allow patients to identify the greatest risks in their daily lives and conceptualise their own health system approaches. Sometimes this will involve extensive HIV programmes, sometimes not; communities must be allowed to decide what their local problems are, receive the technical assistance they need to execute improvement programmes, and create systems to protect the most marginalised of community members. The process of building a civil society that protects the most marginalised members of a community often results in ideas that are not focused on traditional public health methods of simply expanding particular education or discipline-specific programmes (e.g., 'maternal child health' or 'infectious disease'), but address daily household risks and problems of access to health services, from road conditions to clinic locations and costs of care that are specific to the poor.

Moreover, the practical implementation of this approach involves measures that do not require extensive financing: community meetings, focus groups with patients, training local providers as mobile roving community health workers, and improved access to reporting and feedback avenues among those most affected by public health programmes.[71]

In addition, successful HIV programmes appear to have set clear targets that have population benefits which can be monitored. The programmes declare which people they will reach, how they will do so, and what intended outcomes are sought over what time-scales. Such an approach relies on data that are straightforward to collect (percentage of people reached, waiting times, etc.), rather than requiring economic modelling by outside consultants to produce metrics highly subject to manipulation (such as quality-adjusted life-years). It also permits the public to identify weaknesses in the programme. Some of the weaknesses in HIV treatment programmes that are not very successful appear to be due to an excessively narrow focus on medications alone, rather than support for adherence to the medications (general public training and community coordination on issues of side-effects and family support), nutrition (malnutrition programmes including access to therapeutic foods), transportation support (coordinating with ministries responsible for road development and public transport), and programmes to directly address poverty (job training and credit).[72] The current sector-wide approaches to public health that are being presented as alternatives to HIV programmes have lacked definitive targets; even if targets cannot be quantified because they are inherently qualitative (such as the improvement in organising skills of local health ministers), the health system improvement process should involve priority-setting with community members, and the results should be reported to the public, such that the class (and often gender and racial) divide between the elite ministers of health and the poorest of patients can be breached. HIV programmes in Latin America, East Asia, and elsewhere have been notable for their 'open source' approach to tracking and publishing the actual expenditures and outcomes of public health programmes, often via posting all of their development materials, epidemiological statistics, and logistical manuals on the Internet – a practice that was previously unheard of in public health.[73]

As we expand the field of 'global health', we must recognize that the debates we construct and respond to are intimately tied to our power to define what is relevant and not, what is appropriate and not, what is sustainable and not, and what is worthy and not. The HIV activism movement has taught us about democratising this process, such that who makes these declarations is as important as the declarations themselves; we risk losing the power of this lesson if we attempt to return public health to an activity that is focused on elite economic theories devised in distant centres (however sensible they may seem rhetorically), rather than community-based programmes decided by patients. Elites everywhere will often assume that particular initiatives are 'impossible', too involved, not basic enough, and not sustainable; in reality, this reflects their failure to appreciate that resource-denied locales are also denied resources by this very language, and that they will never gain more resources or health improvements unless we move beyond the idea that certain places will always be poor and undeserving of more than 'basic' needs. If we always focus on the most minimum care, the most basic and cheapest services, then the poor will always remain so; the fundamental principles of redistribution require that we abandon this rhetoric, which is devised to preserve current inequalities, and instead create both the language and systems to redistribute the power of decision-making from traditional public health decision-makers to patients.

NOTES

1   World Health Organization, *Declaration of Alma-Ata*, Alma Ata: International Conference on Primary Health Care, 1978.
2   Ibid.
3   Naomi Rogers, 'A History of the World Health Organization', New Haven: Yale University Global Health Course, 2008.
4   Marcos Cueto, 'The origins of primary health care and selective primary health care', *American Journal of Public Health*, 94(11), 2004, pp. 1864–74.
5   Michael Marmot and Richard Wilkinson, *Social Determinants of Health*, Oxford: Oxford University Press, 2005. Vicente Navarro, *The Political and Social Contexts of Health*, Amityville: Baywood Publishing, 2004.
6   Christopher Murray and Julio Frenk, 'World Health Report 2000: A step towards evidence-based health policy', *Lancet*, 357(9269), 2001, pp. 1698-700.
7   A. David Paltiel, et al., 'Expanded screening for HIV in the United States – an analysis of cost-effectiveness', *The New England Journal of Medicine*, 352(6), 2005, pp. 586-95.
8   Gerald Duru, et al., 'Limitations of the methods used for calculating quality-adjusted life-year values', *Pharmacoeconomics*, 20(7) 2002, pp. 463-73. Erik Nord, *Cost-Value Analysis in Health Care: Making Sense out of QALYs*, Cambridge: Cambridge University Press, 1999.
9   Vicente Navarro, 'World Health Report 2000: Responses to Murray and Frenk', *Lancet*, 357(9269), 2001, pp. 1701-2.
10 Ibid.
11 Vicente Navarro, 'Assessment of the World Health Report 2000', *Lancet*, 356(9241), 2000, pp. 1598-601.
12 Eleonora Cavagnero, et al., 'Development assistance for health: should policy-

makers worry about its macroeconomic impact?', *Bulletin of the World Health Organization*, 86(11), 2008, pp. 864-70.

13   David Stuckler, et al., 'International Monetary Fund programs and tuberculosis outcomes in post-Communist countries', *PLoS Medicine*, 5(7), 2008, p. 143. Walden Bello, et al., *A Siamese Tragedy: Development and Disintegration in Modern Thailand*, Bangkok: Food First, 1999. Jim Yong Kim, et al., *Dying for Growth: Global Inequality and the Health of the Poor*, Monroe: Common Courage Press, 2002.

14   Barton Gelman, 'A turning point that left millions behind', *The Washington Post*, 28 December 2000.

15   Steven Epstein, *Impure Science: AIDS, Activism, and the Politics of Knowledge*, Berkeley: University of California Press, 1996.

16   Ibid.

17   Samantha Power, 'The AIDS rebel', *The New Yorker*, May 2003.

18   Salim Karim and Quarraisha Karim, *HIV/AIDS in South Africa*, Cambridge: Cambridge University Press, 2006.

19   Tony Barnett and Alan Whiteside, *AIDS in the 21st Century: Disease and Globalization*, Basingstoke: Palgrave, 2002.

20   Ibid. David Schmitt, 'Sociosexuality from Argentina to Zimbabwe: A 48-nation study of sex, culture, and strategies of human mating', *Behavioral and Brain Sciences*, 28(1), 2005, pp. 247-311.

21   Catherine Campbell, 'Migrancy, masculine identities and AIDS: the psychosocial context of HIV transmission on the South African gold mines', *Social Science and Medicine*, 45(2), 1997, pp. 273-81.

22   Janet Wojcicki and Josephine Malala, 'Condom use, power and HIV/AIDS risk: sex-workers bargain for survival in Hillbrow/Joubert Park/Berea, Johannesburg', *Social Science and Medicine*, 53(1), 2001, pp. 99-121.

23   Catherine Campbell and Yodwa Mzaidume, 'How can HIV be prevented in South Africa? A social perspective', *BMJ*, 324(7331), 2002, pp. 229-32.

24   John Stover, 'Can we reverse the HIV/AIDS pandemic with an expanded response?', *Lancet*, 360(9326), 2002, pp. 73-7.

25   Bello, *Siamese Tragedy*.

26   Barnett and Whiteside, *AIDS in the 21st Century*.

27   Michelle Martin, 'D.C. HIV/AIDS rate higher than West Africa', *National Public Radio*, 18 March 2009. World Health Organization, *HIV/AIDS epidemiological surveillance report for the WHO African Region*, Geneva: WHO, 2009.

28   Faculty of Harvard University, *Consensus Statement on Antiretroviral Treatment for AIDS in Poor Countries*, Cambridge: Harvard University, 2001.

29   Epstein, *Impure Science*. Gregg Gonsalves, *The HIV/AIDS Response and Health Systems: Building on success to achieve health care for all*, New Haven: International Treatment Preparedness Coalition, 2008.

30   Epstein, *Impure Science*.

31   WHO, *HIV/AIDS epidemiological surveillance report*.

32   Elliot Marselle, et al., 'HIV prevention before HAART in Sub-Saharan Africa', *Lancet*, 369(9320), 2002, pp. 1851-56.

33   Justin Parkhurst, '"What worked?": the evidence challenges in determining the causes of HIV prevalence decline', *AIDS Education and Prevention*, 20(3), 2008,

pp. 275-83. Paul Farmer, et al., *Women, Poverty and AIDS*. Boston: Common Courage Press, 1998.

34   Ibid.

35   Gellman, 'A Turning Point'.

36   Families USA, *Off The Charts: Pay, Profits, and Spending by Drug Companies*, Washington DC: FUSA, 2001.

37   Andrew Natsios, *USAID Administrator Natsios Press Remarks on HIV/AIDS in Africa*, Washington D.C.: U.S. Agency for International Development, 2001.

38   David Walton, et al., 'Integrated HIV prevention and care strengthens primary health care: lessons from rural Haiti', *Journal of Public Health Policy*, 25(2), 2004, pp. 137-58. David Coetzee, et al., 'Integrating tuberculosis and HIV care in the primary care setting in South Africa', *Tropical Medicine and International Health*, 9(6), 2004, pp. A11-5.

39   World Health Organization, *The 3-by-5 Initiative*, Geneva: WHO, 2003.

40   Gorik Ooms, 'Shifting paradigms: how the fight for "universal access to AIDS treatment and prevention" supports achieving "comprehensive primary health care for all"', *Global Health*, 4(8), 2008, p. 411. Dongbau Yu, et al., 'Investment in HIV/AIDS programs: does it help strengthen health systems in developing countries?', *Global Health*, 4(8), 2008, p. 48.

41   Gonsalves, *HIV/AIDS Response and Health Systems*.

42   Roger England, 'Are we spending too much on HIV?', *BMJ* 334(7589), 2007. Laurie Garrett, 'The challenge of global health', *Foreign Affairs*, (January/February) 2007. Malcolm Potts, et. al., 'Reassessing HIV prevention', *Science*, 320(5877) 2008, pp. 749-50. Helen Epstein, *The Invisible Cure: Africa, the West, and the Fight Against AIDS*, New York: Farrar, 2007. William Easterly, *The White Man's Burden*, New York: Penguin, 2006.

43   Ooms, 'Shifting paradigms'. Yu, et al., 'Investment in HIV/AIDS'. David Stuckler, et al., 'WHO's budgetary allocations and burden of disease', *The Lancet* 372(9649) 2008, pp. 1563-9. Gonsalves, *HIV/AIDS Response and Health Systems*.

44   Garrett, 'The challenge of global health'. England, 'Are we spending too much?', p. 344.

45   USAID, *Health Systems 20/20: Data Analysis*, Washington D.C.: USAID, 2008.

46   Gonsalves, *HIV/AIDS Response and Health Systems*. Ooms, 'Shifting paradigms'.

47   All of these findings are significant at the $p<0.05$ confidence level, after regression upon the USAID *Health Systems 20/20* dataset.

48   Jon Cohen, 'The great funding surge', *Science* 321(5888) 2008, pp. 512-9.

49   Jose Zuniga, et al., *A Decade of HAART: The Development and Global Impact of Highly Active Antiretroviral Therapy*, Oxford: Oxford University Press, 2008.

50   Kevin DeCock, et al., 'Can antiretroviral therapy eliminate HIV transmission?', *The Lancet* 373(9657) 2009, pp. 7-9.

51   University of Pennsylvania, *Botswana UPenn Partnership*, Philadelphia: University of Pennsylvania, 2008.

52   Epstein, *Impure Science*.

53   Jesper Sundewalla and Kerstin Sahlin-Andersson, 'Translations of health sector SWAps – a comparative study of health sector development cooperation in Uganda, Zambia and Bangladesh', *Health Policy*, 76(3) 2006, pp. 277-87.

54   Guy Hutton and Marcel Tanner, 'The sector-wide approach: a blessing for public health?', *Bulletin of the World Health Organization*, 82(12) 2004, pp. 891-970. Anders Jeppsson, 'SWAp dynamics in a decentralized context: experiences from Uganda', *Social Science and Medicine*, 55(11) 2002, pp. 2053-60.

55   Marlein Bosman, 'Health sector reform and tuberculosis control: the case of Zambia', *International Journal of Tuberculosis and Lung Disease*, 4(7) 2000, pp. 606-14.

56   Ibid.

57   Firdu Zawide, *Victims of Ineptitude: An Insider's Account of Injustice within the World Health Organization*, Bloomington: AuthorHouse, 2007. John Farley, *Brock Chisholm, The World Health Organization, and the Cold War*, Vancouver: UBC Press, 2008. Dorothy Porter, ed. *The History of Public Health and the Modern State*, Amsterdam: Rodopi, 1994.

58   Gorik Ooms, 'Health development versus medical relief: the illusion versus the irrelevance of sustainability', *PLoS Medicine*, 3(8), 2006, p. 345. Anup Shah, 'Effects of over-consumption and increasing populations', *Global Issues*, 26 September 2001.

59   Ooms, 'Health development versus medical relief'.

60   Bosman, 'Health sector reform and tuberculosis control'.

61   Sanjay Basu and Alison Galvani, 'Extensively drug-resistant tuberculosis in South Africa', *Lancet*, 369(9558), 2007, pp. 272-3.

62   Gorik Ooms, et al., 'The 'diagonal' approach to Global Fund financing: a cure for the broader malaise of health systems?', *Globalization and Health*, 4(1), 2008, p. 6.

63   Cueto, 'The origins of primary care'.

64   Sanjay Basu, 'AIDS, empire and public health behaviorism', *International Journal of Health Services,* 34(1), 2004, pp. 155-67.

65   Cohen, 'The great funding surge'.

66   Stuckler, 'International Monetary Fund programs and tuberculosis outcomes'.

67   David Stuckler, et al., 'Bracing for the challenges of recession: how have previous economic recessions in Europe affected health?', *The Lancet* 2009, in press.

68   WHO Commission on Social Determinants of Health, *Closing the Gap in a Generation. Final Report of the Commission on Social Determinants of Health*, Geneva: World Health Organization, 2008.

69   Paul Farmer, *Pathologies of Power*, Berkeley: University of California Press, 2003.

70   Ibid. Nyaya Health, *Annual Report 2008*, New Haven: NHN, 2009. Gonsalves, *HIV/AIDS Response and Health Systems*.

71   Farmer, *Pathologies of Power*.

72   Partners in Health, *Global Health Delivery*, Boston: PIH, 2009.

73   Gonsalves, *HIV/AIDS Response and Health Systems*. Nyaya Health, *Annual Report 2008*.

MENTAL HEALTH IN A SICK SOCIETY: WHAT ARE PEOPLE FOR?

JULIAN TUDOR HART

All wealth originates from work. Now that work with our hands has been replaced, in the industrialised world, either by machines, or by cheaper labour in less developed economies, the capacity to work depends increasingly on mental health. The conventional illusion that capacity to work can be assessed while ignoring our specifically human qualities, measuring only the strengths we share with draught animals, can at last be dismissed. Wealth depends on a healthy workforce, in whom mental health is more important than any other variable.

In the industrialised world, each year roughly one third of all adults meet consensus criteria for mental illness.[1] In Wales, where I worked in primary care for forty years between 1952 and 1992, about 75 per cent consult their NHS (National Health Service) family doctor each year. Of these, about 44 per cent are recognised to have a mental health problem; and of those thus recognised, about 25 per cent are then referred to hospital-based psychiatrists.[2]

The division between the one-third of adults recognised to have a mental health problem and the two thirds who don't is as arbitrary as the division between people who are happy or unhappy. Everybody knows the difference between a happy person and a miserable one, but where best to place a useful division between them, or to define emotional health, depends entirely on what actions, if any, are justified by evidence that they make people healthier. The same reservation applies to most deviations from any aspect of health, only a few of which ever end up as medically recognised diseases, defined and named.

Fewer than 3 per cent of all adults have a clearly defined psychotic illness (schizophrenia, bipolar disorder, or several other rare disorders of brain function) at any time in their lives.[3] These are what we used to call mad people, who perceive and react to the world so differently from the rest of us that we can hardly communicate with them. So of the one third of Welsh adults who admit they have ever been mentally ill, 10 per cent at most have had a psychotic disorder.

In my work I became very interested in helping my patients with mental illness, particularly this small number with psychotic illness, who are still mostly regarded as a responsibility for hospital-based specialists. The NHS provides some access to psychiatric care for our whole population, mostly by family doctors.[4] As family doctors, to me they still seem best placed to respond, at least initially, to any medical problem, whatever its nature. Above all, they seem best placed to anticipate, and often to prevent, crises and emergencies. In my experience they can certainly do this, if they take the trouble to know their patients and organise continuing care around continuity and respect for patients' stories, rather than merely respond to each problem as an isolated episode.

This has become increasingly difficult, as successive governments have sought to remodel all health care on the same patterns of management and employee incentives as industrial commodity production for profit. Under the name of managed care, this process was first imported from the United States, with the health economist Alain Enthoven as its European ambassador.[5] It has been adopted by the central leaders of conservative, liberal and nominally socialist parties with equal enthusiasm, though it has recently been rejected outright by elected regional governments in Wales, Scotland and Northern Ireland, all of which are now doing their best to restore a non-profit, public service tradition. A major effect of managed care has been fragmentation of care and delegation of tasks to less expensive staff. Knowing patients' life stories seems never to be included even as a necessary function, let alone one central to all the others. Really knowing patients is becoming a skill delegated by default to nurse-practitioners, nurses, or even to healthcare assistants, but it still in fact remains an essential element in effective care.

In my working lifetime from 1952 to 1992, all referrals to specialists for mental illness were strictly zoned. Each district had its own psychiatrist. We had no choice. The consultant psychiatrist for our locality happened to be alcohol-dependent. He clung to 19th century views, recognising only two kinds of mental illness: patients were either mad, bad, or weak. It took seven years for the NHS machine to offer him early retirement. In that time I learned that for a family doctor living within his working-class community and trying to make friends with his patients, management of psychotic illness was usually much easier than managing so-called neuroses. I certainly needed specialist help from time to time, but for most patients, the specialised knowledge required was mostly local and personal, not clinical. I also barred the door to all sales representatives from pharmaceutical companies, depending only on peer-reviewed medical journals for information about claimed advances in treatment.

Ninety per cent of my psychiatric workload was composed of so-called neurotic illness. This included the most time-consuming, recurrent, challenging and exasperating parts of primary care. It is concentrated disproportionately in our most deprived communities (as are also psychotic illness, and almost all other sorts of illness).[6] So-called neuroses are the heaviest burden for family doctors, but they are also most easily dismissed as being outside our responsibilities. But if patients who can't make sense of their world get no help from their doctors, eventually they no longer ask for it. A large part of this mental ill-health presents as physically inexplicable incapacity to work. Of all clinical problems, this is the most complex and difficult, demanding all the skills of an experienced practitioner. Ignoring this, we hear confident assertions, over and over again, that the problem would soon be solved if we took certification of illness away from personal doctors and created an independent medical police force to act boldly and with common sense.[7] Holland took that path more than a century ago.[8] By 1990, Dutch sickness absence was 7.1 per cent, compared with 5 per cent in Germany and 2.6 per cent in UK, a stable ranking through many years.[9] The difficult, delicate, complicated work being done by Mansel Aylward at the Wales Institute for Health is far more likely to reduce sickness absence than any police measures.[10] The less doctors act as critical advocates for their patients, the more they appear to their patients as uncritical advocates for employers.[11]

Even today, when NHS GPs are paid on fixed tariffs rewarding specific interventions, but ignoring much that is hard to measure or define, most UK family doctors accept responsibility for frontline psychiatry. The biopsychosocial model of disease has been nominally accepted in the UK since the early 1970s.[12] However, research shows that GPs still rate their responsibility for care of acute physical problems about twice as high as for chronic physical problems, and more than three times higher than for psychological problems.[13] They know that consultations for psychological problems take much more time than physical disorders. Time rather than skill is their perceived limiting factor,[14] but they often underestimate the urgency of mental illness. It seems that only those who have suffered it know that suicidal depression can be more painful than any other disease, and often more dangerous.[15]

How people think largely determines *what* they think, and what they want to know. Most doctors, and most patients, seem to believe that no sickness is real unless it can be named as a disease, qualitatively different from health, with a label recognised by an insurance company. In a civilised society, sick people have a right to sick roles, and thus to support from other people through services paid from taxation. In a civilised society, we recognise that sickness of all kinds is a misfortune to which everybody is liable, so the cheapest, most efficient and effective insurance system must be to pool risks and share costs: we all pay for care we hope we may never need. One price we must apparently pay for this is medically certified possession of a named disease, however irrational that naming may be.

This apparently inevitable but essentially irrational reification of illness is only part of a much larger, dominant global tendency to push everything we think, do or create into clearly defined categories, each with its own place in the market inventory. It is powerfully reinforced by product and process promotion. Drugs have certainly made psychotic illness more manageable. So the idea that the other 90 per cent of mental sickness might somehow resemble psychosis, but in attenuated form, could potentially increase the drug market tenfold. Can we really believe that every sort of dysfunctional thought and behaviour is classifiable as some kind of disease, that this truly reflects human biology, and therefore justifies tinkering with the brain chemistry of unhappiness and fear in ways similar to treatment of psychosis, albeit with smaller doses of less potent agents?

However irrational, this idea has a powerful appeal to both clinicians and the general public. Mental illness of any kind presents complex and difficult problems, often apparently insuperable. Who would not welcome so simple a solution as swallowing a pill? It takes much less time to write a prescription than to explore disordered thought or behaviour, let alone change a world that seems to make so many people miserable. The pharmaceutical industry employs an army of friendly, flattering, and in their own way sincere brainwashers to promote chemical solutions for social problems. The European Union is even now pressing for prescription drugs to be freely advertised directly to the public, as they already are in USA, so that pharmaceutical companies can bypass the growing proportion of doctors who reject their brainwashing, and reach consumers with all grades of mental distress directly.[16]

As each tranquillising or antidepressant drug has come into fashion, it has become so widely prescribed that we might as well have it in the tap water. Eventually all these panaceas turn out to be no more effective, and to create just as much dependence and as many harmful side-effects (including suicides) as their predecessors. Over the centuries we have seen these come and go:

gin, opium, cocaine, bromides, barbiturates, benzodiazepines, serotonin uptake inhibitors – on and on and all to nowhere except colossal profits, and damage to our most obvious means for recovery, the brain itself.[17]

In USA in the 1990s, they began herding unreasonable children into the same market, labelling just under 8 per cent as having Attention Deficit Hyperactivity Disorder,[18] and sweeping many others into treatments doubtfully validated even for adults.[19] Where the US market leads, the UK market follows, albeit more sceptically.[20] Writing in 1991, George Dunea suggested an excellent collective brand name for all these simple answers to complex problems – *Nonsenserine*.[21]

How will we ever learn? Even to start, we need to look in an entirely different direction – to causes within the structure of our economy. If we understand them, we can change them, so understanding itself can become the first step toward restored mental health.

That doesn't mean that primary care should wash its hands of people with serious organic brain disorders, or attribute all these to damaging formative experiences of a personal or social kind. Psychotic illness is real, and most if not all its diseases probably do start from disturbed brain chemistry, which may be at least partly reversible by biochemical means. But in population terms, psychotic illness is a small and more or less constant problem, similar in all economies.[22] If every practice accepted responsibility for primary care of its average dozen or so people with psychotic illness,[23] referring to specialist psychiatrists only when generalists couldn't cope, and with continuing support from psychiatric nurses based in communities rather than in hospitals, we could achieve a great deal more than we do now, though primary care would need more staff and more in-service training. Compared with the cost of occupying Iraq and Afghanistan, recently running at £3.3 bn a year,[24] or the £15-20 bn replacement cost of Trident nuclear missiles,[25] costs for such services would be trivial.

Psychosis is a far more manageable problem than the other 90 per cent of recognised mental illness, linked with the apparent failure of unhappiness and dysfunctional behaviour of entire societies to diminish, even when average incomes and measures of physical health have substantially improved.[26] We should stop looking for biochemical mechanisms and start looking at social causes, and what we can do to reduce and oppose them.

What do most of these unhappy, fearful, or unreasonable people have in common, who have no disease but are certainly ill? They can find no secure or satisfying place in this world, or belief in any alternative. Their views are not so much irrational, as dysfunctional responses to an irrational society. Since the 1970s a social earthquake has occurred, that has almost destroyed the robust industrial working-class culture which took us about 200 years to build. By 2005, the UK economy was losing about £67 bn a year in the exchange of real things – the consequence of destroying most of our manufacturing industry in the 1980s, and shifting to a paper economy. This accelerated a process that started before the First World War. Our masters demoted manufacture and promoted financial services whenever the country was at peace. Big investments in new manufacture, research and technology development were prompted chiefly by wars or preparation for wars. In the intervals, investors returned to what gave them the highest profit, paper transactions in the City of London, Wall Street, and other finance casinos.

How does this connect with mental health or mental wealth? Our manufacturing sector has been in free fall since government allowed our machine tool industry, the foundation of our industrial independence, virtually to disappear in the 1980s.[27] I have a photograph of six Glyncorrwg boys, schoolmates of my own three children, taken around 1980. All were unemployed for most of the next 10 years, and one was murdered by his young wife.

Their fathers, miners and steelworkers, were profitable to their employers and therefore accepted as useful to society. These boys were no longer profitable, so they no longer seemed useful. Over the whole of the next decade, youth unemployment (ages 16 to 24) in my practice never fell below 60 per cent. We had to survive a tidal wave of drug and alcohol dependence and demoralised behaviour not seen even during years of hunger and cold in the 1930s, whose long-term effects were only recently receding. When I emigrated from London to Wales in 1961, our nearby steelworks at Port Talbot employed about 15,000 workers in a nationalised industry. Today it employs fewer than 3,000 to produce three times as much steel, and is now owned by Tata Steel of Mumbai. Tata dates from 1904, with a good record as enlightened employers: the company introduced an 8-hour day for its Indian workers in 1912, when UK steelworkers still had to work 12 hours. However, an Indian steelworker today earns 88 per cent less than a UK steelworker. Port Talbot lives in dread of the day when the owners decide to produce even more with even fewer workers at far lower cost and higher profit, leaving our steelworks and all its supporting local industries to rot as a giant carcase – not their responsibility.

By those who live from what they own and control, including our media of mass communication which define the agenda for public discussion, people are valued by their usefulness not to themselves and their communities, but to a handful of remote billionaires who own and control most of the world we live in. People are there to be used, a flexible labour force to do anything or nothing whenever they're needed or discarded by players at the casino. People are losing their value and dignity as producers, and are expected to accept valuation by what they consume. Regardless of their skills, nobody can be sure that in ten years time they will still be needed. Stripped of their dignity, is it any wonder that people once strong enough to face any eventuality now fall victim to weaknesses they never thought they had?

In the 1990s Richard Inglehart organised sociologists all over the world to study the relation of material wealth to happiness.[28] Predictably, the most miserable countries were found lying in the wreckage of failed socialist societies, both poor and demoralised – Moldova, Belarus, Ukraine, Russia. Most of the happiest countries had average incomes per head of over $15,000; they had capitalist economies but with varying degrees of state intervention. Above that $15,000 threshold, however, there was no clear association between wealth and happiness, nor did there seem to be any obvious difference according to existing individualist or collectivist cultures, so far as these can be perceived. The same study showed that in the USA, over the years from 1946 to 1996, increasing average wealth ceased to promote happiness around 1956. Thereafter happiness slowly diminished, as inequality grew.

According to the United Nations Human Development Report, by 1996 there were 358 US$ billionaires. Their total wealth equalled the combined national incomes of the countries with the poorest 45 per cent of the world population, 2.3 bn people.[29] Classical economists, and the UK's Labour government and the official Conservative opposition, justify this by utilitarian arguments. They believe that an economy fuelled by greed leads paradoxically to the greatest good for the greatest number; that an irrational distribution of wealth and investment nevertheless creates the happiest societies the world has so far achieved. Beyond this, they suggest it may be neither prudent nor possible to go; we should accept the residue of unhappiness we still have as more or less inevitable, and concentrate on getting more psychiatric help for people apparently unfitted for our competitive society. Professor Lord Richard Layard, a Labour peer, has called for 250 new centres in the UK to provide cognitive psychotherapy to do just this.[30] Cognitive therapy is no panacea, but it works as least as well as any medication, and usually better.[31]

But what is cognitive therapy? It treats mental illness by helping people to understand their own lives, and how these relate to the world they live in – to make sense of the world. Surely that should include understanding why whole communities suddenly find themselves redundant to the larger society within which they live, why 358 billionaires came to command as much personal wealth as whole countries containing 2.3 bn poor people and now have greater power than any elected government to decide how global wealth is made or spent? They need to rediscover the political literacy gained for us by our ancestors. They fought for it and won, we have stopped fighting for it and have lost. John Hutton, Business and Enterprise Minister in the UK New Labour government, proclaimed in 2008:

> Rather than questioning whether huge salaries are morally justified, we should celebrate the fact that people can be enormously successful in this country. Rather than placing a cap on that success, we should be questioning why it is not available to more people. Our overarching goal that no one should get left behind must not become translated into a stultifying sense that no one should be allowed to get ahead.[32]

If we believe that an entire society can ever consist entirely of billionaires, we really will be insane. Happiness, contentment, mental health, or whatever we choose to call it, depends on creative work and good company; on respect and affection from others, which we can ourselves return. People need to believe that they serve and share some socially useful and respected purpose, that they are of value to others and therefore valued in return, and that at the end of their lives, they have achieved something. It is capitalism, an economic system that hands all moral responsibility to market decisions, and threatens even that slender thread of human responsibility still embodied in ancient cultures and religions, which drives people with normal brains into fear, confusion, desperation and destructive behaviour.

It is true that the world's first clumsy attempts to construct a socialist society in impossible circumstances, and without the economic and social development that we can now see as preconditions for success, more or less completely failed – not only because rich countries did (and still do) their best to ensure that failure, but chiefly because of fundamental faults inherent in the original social development of those new states, which had not yet created the super-productivity necessary for the next step toward a new sharing society. We now have that potential super-productivity. If we continue to allow this to be used chiefly to make more weapons and more billionaires, we shall earn only the contempt of posterity.

In previous economic systems and previous cultures, to produce more wealth always required more people. Capitalism began, for the first time on a mass scale, to produce more with fewer people. We are nearing the end of that process. In all advanced economies, most of their manual workforce is now approaching redundancy for commodity production. What's left of their jobs is being transferred to less developed economies with larger and cheaper reserves of labour, more recently driven from the land. We now have over 6.7 bn people in the world, most of whom will eventually enter this relentless progress toward redundancy.

At this final stage people still have some value, but as consumers. In the age of commodity production, we were told that to save the nation our duty was to work harder, spend less, and save more. With the demise of manufacture, our duty changed: to save the nation, we were required to work harder, but only until our jobs could be done more cheaply somewhere else. From then on, our duty was to spend – to buy the goods now produced by poor people abroad. How could we pay for them? By borrowing, promoting a deregulated industry of moneylenders and City of London speculators, who somehow create wealth out of paper. As a result, average household debt came to be 20 per cent higher than disposable income in USA, and 40 per cent higher in UK.[33] Now banks have failed, more will fail, and the Wall Street and City casinos are in a crisis even deeper than the last time big business was allowed to operate without social control. That was in 1929, when people faced having no value at all, either as consumers or as producers, and the world entered a nightmare.

This puts a preposterous question on the agenda: "What are people for?" It is capitalist society's failure to provide any consistent answer to this question which drives most of our unhappiness and some of our madness. It is dangerous to generalise about mental illness, but for the 90 per cent of mentally sick people who have no chemical disturbance of brain function, what they need is not more biochemical tinkering, but greater understanding of our world and their own relation to it, so that they can begin to take an effective share in making a better future for us all. Some, indeed any, participation in struggle against what is irrational in our lives must be our principal means of escape. Not to any immediately different society, because that is not an option for the people we now have, but participation in struggle toward such a society for our children and our children's children, learning as we go with sceptical humility.

That requires that we dare to emerge from about thirty years of political illiteracy to rediscover the idea of true participatory democracy, rebuilding on deeper and wider social and material foundations than were ever possible before. What right do we have to be happy in a world of such growing extremes both of unhappiness, and of material capacity to relieve it, unless we play some part in ending this absurd situation? Only by doing this can we, as an entire society, begin to recover our mental health – not just for those identified as having a mental illness, but for the much larger number of people who don't yet admit their sickness or understand its cause.

Whatever else we may do, these should be our first steps toward the mental health we need to operate a knowledge-based and evidence-based economy with a rationally balanced product. True wealth will follow.

NOTES

This essay is based on the keynote speech to the Conference on Mental Health in NHS Wales Primary Care, 29 April 2008, in Cardiff City Hall.

1   T.B. Üstün and N. Sartorius, eds., *Mental illness in general health care: an international study*, New York: John Wiley/WHO, 1995.

2   Figures from the Needs Assessment, Client Groups, Mental Health page of http://www.merthyr.gov.uk.

3   K.S. Kendler, T.J. Gallagher, J.M. Abelson and R.C. Kessler, 'Lifetime prevalence, demographic risk factors, and diagnostic validity of nonaffective psychosis as assessed in a US community sample: the National Comorbidity Survey'. *Archives of General Psychiatry*, 1996: 53:1022-31; M.G. Carta and J. Angst, 'Epidemiology and clinical aspects of bipolar disorders: controversies or a common need to redefine the aims and methodological aspects of surveys', *Clinical Practice & Epidemiology in Mental Health,* 2005: 1:1-4.

4   M. Shepherd, 'The prevalence and distribution of psychological illness in general practice'. In, 'The medical use of psychotropic drugs'. *Journal of the Royal College of General Practitioners*, 1973: 23 suppl.2:16-9.

5   A. Enthoven, 'Reflections on the management of the National Health Service: an American looks at incentives to efficiency in health services management in the UK', Occasional Papers no. 5, London: Nuffield Provincial Hospitals Trust, 1985.

6   A.M. Stirling, P. Wilson and A. McConnachie, 'Deprivation, psychological distress, and consultation length in general practice', *British Journal of General Practice,* 2001: 51:456-60.

7   M.J. Stanger, 'Incapacity, work and benefits', *BMJ (British Medical Journal)*, 2008: 336:735.

8   J.P. Van der Brugh, 'The law of sickness insurance in Holland', *BMJ,* 1914: i:1130-4.

9   P. Beljaars and R. Prins, 'Combatting a Dutch disease: recent reforms in sickness and disability arrangements in the Netherlands', ABP World (Dutch Public Sector Pension Fund publication), 1997.

10   C.J. Phillips, C.J. Main, R. Buck, L. Button, A. Farr, L. Havard and G. Brown, *Profiling the Community in Merthyr Tydfil: Problems, Challenges and Opportunities.* Cardiff: Wellbeing in Work Final Report, Wales Centre for Health, 2006.

11   P. Buijs, R. van Amstel and F. van Dijk, 'Dutch occupational physicians and general practitioners wish to improve co-operation'. *Occupational & Environmental Medicine,* 1999: 56:709-13.

12   Working Party, *The Future General Practitioner: learning and teaching*, London: Royal College of General Practitioners, 1972.

13   C. Dowrick, C. May, M. Richardson and P. Bundred, 'The biopsychosocial model of general practice: rhetoric or reality?' *British Journal of General Practice*, 1996: 46:105-7.

14   A. Howe, ' "I know what to do, but it's not possible to do it": general practitioners' perceptions of their ability to detect psychological distress', *Family Practice*, 1996: 13:1227-32.

15   J. Horder, Personal communication, 2000.

16   Editorial, 'The direct to consumer advertising genie', *Lancet*, 2007: 369:1.

17   C. Medawar, *Power and Dependence: Social Audit on the Safety of Medicines*, London: Social Audit, 1992.

18   L. Eisenberg, 'Commentary with a historical perspective by a child psychiatrist: when "ADHD" was the "Brain-Damaged Child"', *Journal of Child & Adolescent Psychopharmacology*, 2007: 17:279-83.

19   S. Timimi, 'Antidepressants in childhood are neither effective nor safe', *BMJ*, 2007: 335:751.

20   D.C. Naylor, 'Grey zones of clinical practice: some limits to evidence-based medicine'. *Lancet* 1995: 345:840-2; S. Rose, 'Neurogenetic determinism and the new euphenics', *BMJ*, 1998: 317:1707-8.

21   G. Dunea, 'Nonsenserine', *BMJ*, 1991: 303:253.

22   J.J. Schwab and M.E. Schwab, *Sociocultural Roots of Mental Illness – An Epidemiologic Survey*, New York: Springer, 1978.

23   M. King and I. Nazareth, 'Care of patients with schizophrenia: the role of the primary health care team', *British Journal of General Practice*, 1996: 46:231-7.

24   H. Siddique, 'Cost of Afghanistan and Iraq operations soars', *Guardian*, 10 March 2008.

25   http://ww.quaker.org.uk.

26   R. Layard, 'Happiness: has social science a clue?', Lionel Robbins Memorial Lectures, 2002/3, London School of Economics.

27   R. Lloyd-Jones and M.J. Lewis, *Alfred Herbert Ltd and the British Machine Tool Industry, 1887-1983*, London: Ashgate, 2006.

28   R. Inglehart and H-D Klingemann, 'Genes, Culture, Democracy and Happiness', In E. Diener and E.M. Suh, eds., *Culture and Subjective Well-being*, Cambridge Mass.: MIT Press, 2000.

29   Mahbub ul Haq and Richard Jolly, eds., *Human Development Report 1996*, United Nations Development Programme, New York: Oxford University Press, 1996.

30   R. Layard, 'Mental illness is now our biggest social problem', *Guardian*, 14 September 2005.

31   J. Holmes, 'All you need is cognitive behaviour therapy?' *BMJ*, 2002: 324:288-90; N. Tarrier, 'Commentary: yes, cognitive behaviour therapy may well be all you need', *BMJ*, 2002: 324:291-2; N. Bolsover, 'Commentary: the "evidence" is weaker than claimed', *BMJ* 2002: 324:292-3.

32   P. Wintour, 'Celebrate huge salaries, minister tells Labour', *Guardian*, 10 March 2008.

33   F. Lordon, 'The market in worse futures', *Le Monde Diplomatique*, March 2008: 2-3.

Socialist Register is now available online

Individual subscribers:

Options:

Permanent online access to the current volume, plus access to all previous volumes for the period of the subscription.
or
as above plus the paperback printed copy.

Details at www.merlinpress.co.uk

Institutional subscribers:

Options:

A. To buy current volume only:
1. Permanent online resource ISBN 978 085036 701 0
2. Permanent online access plus hardback printed copy. Mixed Media ISBN. 978 085036 702 7

B. For ongoing subscriptions: ISSN 0081-0606
3. Ongoing online access with permanent access to the current volume a access to previous volumes for the period of the subscription.
4. As 3 plus hardback printed copy.

Prices and other information available at www.merlinpress.co.uk (or order through a subscription agent)

Socialist Register – Published Annually Since 1964

Leo Panitch and Colin Leys – Editors
2009: VIOLENCE TODAY: Actually existing barbarism

Is this the new age of barbarism? The scale and pervasiveness of violence today calls urgently for serious analysis.

Contents: Henry Bernstein, Colin Leys, Leo Panitch: Reflections on Violence Today; Vivek Chibber: American Militarism and the US Political Establishment - the Real Lessons of the Invasion of Iraq; Philip Green: On-screen Barbarism - Violence in US Visual Culture; Ruth Wilson Gilmore: Race, Prisons and War: Scenes from the History of US Violence; Joe Sim & Steve Tombs: State talk, state silence - work and 'violence' in the UK; Lynne Segal: Violence's Victims - the Gender Landscape; Barbara Harriss-White: Girls as Disposable Commodities in India; Achin Vanaik: India's Paradigmatic Communal Violence; Tania Murray Li: Reflections on Indonesian Violence - Two Tales and Three Silences; Ulrich Oslender: Colombia - Old and New Patterns of Violence; Sofiri Joab-Peterside & Anna Zalik: The Commodification of Violence in the Niger Delta; Dennis Rodgers & Steffen Jensen: Revolutionaries, Barbarians or War Machines? Gangs in Nicaragua and South Africa; Michael Brie: Emancipation and the Left - the Issue of Violence; Samir Amin: Tehe defence of humanity requires the radicalisation of popular struggles; John Berger: Human Shield.

286 pp. 234 x 156 mm.

9780850366075 hbk £40.00   9780850366082 pbk £15.95
Canada: Fernwood Publishing; USA: Monthly Review Press; UK and Rest of World: Merlin Press

Leo Panitch and Colin Leys – Editors
2008: GLOBAL FLASHPOINTS: Reactions to imperialism and neoliberalism

New forces of resistance have emerged to both American imperialism and neoliberalism. But how far do these forces represent a progressive alternative? This volume surveys the key flashpoints of resistance today.

Contents: Aijaz Ahmad: Islam, Islamisms and the West; Asef Bayat: Islamism and Empire - The Incongruous Nature of Islamist Anti-Imperialism; Gilbert Achcar: Religion and Politics Today from a Marxian Perspective; Sabah Alnasseri: Understanding Iraq; Bashir Abu-Manneh: Israel's Colonial Siege and the Palestinians; Yildiz Atasoy: The Islamic Ethic and the Spirit of Turkish Capitalism Today; William I. Robinson: Transformative Possibilities in Latin America; Margarita López Maya: Venezuela Today - A 'Participative and Protagonistic' Democracy?; Marta Harnecker: Blows and Counterblows in Venezuela; João Pedro Stédile: The Class Struggles in Brazil - the Perspectives of the MST; Wes

Enzinna: All We Want Is the Earth - Agrarian Reform in Bolivia; Ana Esther Ceceña: On the Forms of Resistance in Latin America - Its 'Native' Moment; Richard Roman & Edur Velasco Arregui: Mexico's Oaxaca Commune; Emilia Castorina: The Contradictions of 'Democratic' Neoliberalism in Argentina - A New Politics from 'Below'?; G.M. Tamás: Counter-Revolution against a Counter-Revolution: Eastern Europe Today; Raghu Krishnan & Adrien Thomas: Resistance to Neoliberalism in France; Kim Moody: Harvest of Empire - Immigrant Workers' Struggles in the USA; Alfredo Saad-Filho, Elmar Altvater & Gregory Albo: Neoliberalism and the Left - A Symposium.

362 pp. 234 x 156 mm.

9780850365863 hbk £35.00   9780850365870 pbk £14.95
Canada: Fernwood Publishing; USA: Monthly Review Press; UK and Rest of World: Merlin Press

Leo Panitch and Colin Leys – Editors
with Barbara Harriss-White, Elmar Altvater and Grego Albo
2007: COMING TO TERMS WITH NATURE

Can capitalism come to terms with the environment? Can market forces and technology overcome the 'limits to growth' and yet preserve the biosphere? What is the nature of oil politics today? Can capitalism do without nuclear power, or make it safe? What is the significance of the impasse over the Kyoto protocol?

Contents: Brenda Longfellow: Weather Report - Images from the Climate Crisis; Neil Smith: Nature as Accumulation Strategy; Elmar Altvater: The Social and Natural Environment of Fossil Capitalism; Daniel Buck: The Ecological Question - Can Capitalism Prevail?; Barbara Harriss-White & Elinor Harriss: Unsustainable Capitalism - the Politics of Renewable Energy in the UK; Jamie Peck: Neoliberal Hurricane - who framed New Orleans?; Minqi Li & Dale Wen: China - Hyper-development and Environmental Crisis; Henry Bernstein & Philip Woodhouse: Africa - Eco-populist Utopias and (micro-) capitalist realities; Philip McMichael: Feeding the World - Agriculture, Development and Ecology; Erik Swyngedouw: Water, Money and Power; Achim Brunnengraber: The Political Economy of the Kyoto Protocol; Heather Rogers: Garbage Capitalism's Green Commerce; Costas Panayotakis: Working More, Selling More, Consuming More - capitalism's 'third contradiction'; Joan Martinez-Alier: Social Metabolism and Environmental Conflicts; Michael Lowy: Eco-socialism and Democratic Planning; Frieder Otto Wolf: Party-building for Eco-Socialists - Lessons from the failed project of the German greens; Greg Albo: The Limits of Eco-localism - Scale, Strategy, Socialism.

384 pp. 234 x 156 mm.

0850365775 hbk £35.00   0850365783 pbk £14.95
Canada: Fernwood Publishing; USA: Monthly Review Press; UK and Rest of World: Merlin Press

Leo Panitch and Colin Leys – Editors
2006: TELLING THE TRUTH

How does power shape ideas and ideologies today? Who controls the information on which public discussion rests? How is power used to exclude critical thought in politics, the media, universities, state policy-making? Has neo-liberal globalisation introduced a new era of state duplicity, corporate manipulation of truth and intellectual conformity? Are we entering a new age of unreason?

Contents: Colin Leys: The cynical state; Atilio Boron: The truth about capitalist democracy; Doug Henwood: The 'business community'; Frances Fox Piven & Barbara Ehrenreich: The truth about welfare reform; Loic Wacquant: The 'scholarly myths' of the new law and order doxa; Robert W. McChesney: Telling the truth at a moment of truth: US news media and the invasion and occupation of Iraq; David Miller: Propaganda-managed democracy: the UK and the lessons of Iraq; Ben Fine & Elisa van Waeyenberge: Correcting Stiglitz - From information to power in the world of development; Sanjay Reddy: Counting the poor: the truth about world poverty statistics; Michael Kustow: Playing with the Truth: the politics of theatre; John Sambonmatsu: Postmodernism and the corruption of the academic intelligentsia; G.M. Tamás: Telling the truth about the working class; Terry Eagleton: Telling the truth.

304 pp. 234 x 156 mm.

0850365597 hbk £35.00   **0850365600 pbk £14.95**

Canada: Fernwood Publishing; USA: Monthly Review Press; UK and Rest of World: Merlin Press

All Merlin Press titles can be ordered via our web site:
www.merlinpress.co.uk

In case of difficulty obtaining Merlin Press titles outside the UK, please contact
the following:

Australia:
Merlin Press Agent and stockholder:
Eleanor Brasch Enterprises. PO Box 586, Artamon NSW 2064
Email: brasch2@aol.com

Canada:
Publisher:
Fernwood Publishing, 32 Oceanvista Lane, Site 2A, Box 5, Black Point,
NS B0J 1B0
Tel: +1 902 857 1388: Fax: +1 902 857 1328 Email: errol@fernpub.ca

South Africa:
Merlin Press Agent:
Blue Weaver Marketing
PO Box 30370, Tokai, Cape Town 7966, South Africa
Tel. 21 701-4477 Fax. 21 701-7302 Email: orders@blueweaver.co.za

USA:
Merlin Press Agent and stockholder: Independent Publishers Group, 814 North
Franklin Street, Chicago, IL 60610.
Tel: +1 312 337 0747   Fax: +1 312 337 5985 frontdesk@ipgbook.com

Publisher:
Monthly Review Press, 122 West 27th Street, New York, NY 10001
Tel: +1 212 691 2555 promo@monthlyreview.org